HISTORY
OF RUSSIA

Sergei Mikhailovich Soloviev

The Academic International Press Edition of Sergei M. Soloviev's History of Russia From Earliest Times. *Peter von Wahlde, General Editor.*

Contributing Editors:

HUGH F. GRAHAM

JOHN D. WINDHAUSEN

ALEXANDER V. MULLER

K. A. PAPMEHL

RICHARD HANTULA

WALTER J. GLEASON, JR.

WILLIAM H. HILL

G. EDWARD ORCHARD

LINDSEY A.J. HUGHES

SERGEI M. SOLOVIEV

History of Russia

Volume 15

The Time of Troubles

Tsar Vasily Shuisky and the Interregnum
1606–1613

Edited, Translated and With an

Introduction by

G. Edward Orchard

Academic International Press

1989

The
Editor and Translator
Dedicates this Volume
to the Memory of

Milos Mladenovic
1903-1984

The Academic International Press Edition of S.M. Soloviev's
History of Russia from Earliest Times in fifty volumes.

Volume 15. *The Time of Troubles. Tsar Vasily Shuisky and the
Interregnum*. Unabridged translation of the text of Volume 8, Chapters 4–8, of S.M. Soloviev's *Istoriia Rossii s drevneishikh vremen*
as found in Volume IV of this work published in Moscow in 1963,
with added annotation by G. Edward Orchard.

Library of Congress Card Number: 75–11085
ISBN: 0-87569-111-0

Composition by Barbara Knoelke

Printed in the United States of America

A list of Academic International Press publications is found at the
end of this volume.

ACADEMIC INTERNATIONAL PRESS
Box 1111 Gulf Breeze FL 32562

CONTENTS

Maps

Illustrations

WEIGHTS AND MEASURES

Linear Measure

Verst: 500 sazhen, 1166 yards and 2 feet, .663 miles, 1.0668 km.
Sazhen: 3 arshins, 7 feet, 2.133 m
Arshin: 16 vershoks, 28in. (diuims) 72.12 cm
Chetvert: 1/4 arshin
Fut: 12 diuims, 1 foot, 30.48 cm
Vershok: 1.75 in., 4.445 cm, 1/16 arshin
Diuim: 1 inch, 2.54 cm
Desiatina: 2400 square sazhens, 2.7 acres, 1.0925 hectare
Chetvert (quarter): 1/2 desiatine, 1.35 acre (sometimes 1.5 desiatinas or ca. 4.1 acres)

Liquid Measure

Stof: Kruzhka (cup), 1/10 vedro, ca. 1.3 quarts, 1.23 liters
Kufa: 30 stofy
Vedro (paid): 3.25 gallons, 12.3 liters, 10 stofy
Bochka (barrel): 40 vedros, 121 gallons, 492 liters
Chetvert (quarter): 1.4 bochka, 32.5 gallons

Weights

Berkovets: 361 olbs., 10 puds
Pud: 40 funts, 36,113 lbs. (US), 40 lbs. (Russian), 16.38 kg
Funt: 96 zolotniks, .903 lb., 14.4 ozs., 408.24 grams
Grivenka: 205 grams
Korob (basket): 7 puds, 252 lbs.
Rad: 14 puds, 505.58 lbs
Chetvert (grain measure): 1/4 rad, 3.5 puds, 126.39 lbs., ca. 8 bushels
Chetverik (grain measure dating from 16th century): 1/8 chetvert, 15.8 lbs.
Zolotnik: 1/96 lb., 4.26 grams

Money

Chervonets (chervonny): A gold coin minted in the first half of the 18th century worth
  about 3 rubles
Muscovite Denga: 200 equals 1 ruble
Novgorod Denga: 100 equals 1 ruble
Ruble: 100 copecks, 200 dengas
Altyn: 6 Muscovite dengas, 3 copecks
Grivna: 20 Muscovite dengas, 100 grivnas equals 1 ruble, 10 copecks
Poltina (Poltinnik): 50 copecks, 100 dengas
Polupoltina (-nik): 25 copecks, 50 dengas
Poltora: 1 1/2 rubles
Peniaz: 10 equals one grosh (Lithuania)
Kopa grosh: 60 groshas, one Muscovite poltina
Chetvertak: silver coin equal to 25 copecks or 1/4 rubles (18-19th centuries)
Copeck: two Muscovite dengas
Foreign Denominations: 1 efimok or 1 thaler (Joachimsthaler)-about 1 ruble, 1 chervonets
  or chervonnyi—a ducat, about 3 rubles
Levok—Dutch silver lion dollar

Note: Weights and measures often changed values over time and sometimes held more than
  one value at the same time. For details consult Sergei G. Pushkarev, *Dictionary of
  Russian Historical Terms from the Eleventh Century to 1917* (Yale, 1970).

PREFACE

This book is an unabridged translation of Volume 8, Chapters 4-8, which are pp. 459-690 in Volume IV of the multi-volume edition of Soloviev's *Istoriia Rossii s drevneishikh vremen* (History of Russia From Earliest Times, 29 vols., St. Petersburg, 1851-1879) published from 1959 through 1966 in Moscow.

The present translation endeavors to render the text and Soloviev's thought as accurately as possible. No attempt has been made to reproduce his style and text word for word for this would have yielded a bizarre Russianized text. The main consideration has been to make his history as readable as possible consistent with accuracy, while retaining at least something of the flavor of the language of the era. An effort has been made to find English-language equivalents for all technical terms Soloviev employs (ranks, offices, titles, legal, administrative and so forth) in the belief that English is no less rich in such terms than other languages. This is intended to smooth the flow of the narrative for the reader and to avoid marring the pages with annoying untranslated words. The exception involves Russian words which have become common in English—boyar, tsar, cossack, and others. In all of this the translator remains painfully aware of the inevitable shortcomings that may remain.

Soloviev's pages are featureless and interminable, one long and complex sentence marching after the last. To make the text easier to follow for today's readers, long paragraphs and sentences have been broken into shorter ones. Most of the subtitles are based on the descriptive topic headings clustered at the beginnings of the chapters in the Russian edition. These headings have been moved into the body of the text as subtitles to mark and ease for the reader the transition from one subject to another. In some cases, to even the frequency of breaks in the text or to show topics not listed by Soloviev at the beginning of chapters, new subtitles have been added. Soloviev's arrangement of the material has been followed strictly.

Brief explanatory or interpretive materials have been inserted into the text enclosed in brackets, or added as footnotes to each chapter at the end of the book. All material enclosed in brackets has been added by the present editor and all materials in parenthesis is the author's. Emphasized words or phrases in italics are the author's.

The general policy followed in annotating has been to identify prominent personalities at first mention, and to give explanation and elucidations of less common or obscure terms and passages, assuming the typical reader to have relatively little familiarity with Russian history. If brief, these have been included in the text in brackets; otherwise they appear as numbered footnotes at the back of the book by chapters. Most of the author's own notes are not included because of their highly specialized archival, documentary and bibliographic nature is of value solely to specialists who, in any case, will prefer to consult the original Russian text. In addition, most of the notes added by the editors of the edition published in the Soviet Union which also are technical in nature—fuller bibliographic citations than those in Soloviev's notes—have not been included. When the author's notes and those of the Soviet editors are included, they are so designated. All other notes are those of the present editor.

Russian personal names are preserved in their Russian form except for Alexander, Alexis, Michael, Nicholas, Catherine and Peter, which English usage has made familiar with respect to Russian historical figures, and important ecclesiastics whose names have been recast into Latin or Greek equivalents, especially for the earlier period of Russian history. This applies to prominent individuals; Russian forms usually are used for the less prominent. Certain other names and terms have been anglicized for the sake of clarity and because they are used widely—Casimir, Sophia, Danzig, boyar, rubles, versts, Dnieper river, and others.

The editors of the edition published in the USSR frequently have added patronymics and other names, and these have been retained without brackets; patronymics appearing in the original edition have also been included. Plural forms for names and terms which might be confusing have been anglicized—Vologdians rather than Vologzhane, Voguls and not Vogulichi, the Dolgorukys not Dolgorukie, and so forth. Even so, in a few cases the Russian plural form is used when this form is common. Most Slavic surnames show gender, and this has been preserved. Since an "a" at the word end usually signifies a female, Golovkin would have a wife or daughter Golovkina. The final "iia" in feminine personal names has been shortened to "ia"—"Maria" and "Evdokia" instead of "Mariia" and "Evdokiia".

Non-Russian names, locations, terms, ranks and so on are spelled according to the language native to the person or particular to the city, region or culture when this can be determined. Confusion arises at times because the text is not clear about nationalities. An excruciating example is Lithuania where at least three languages intermingle. In such cases the context is the guide used and as a last resort the Russian spelling in the text is accepted. Individuals whose names were once non-Russian but had been in Russian service for generations are named by the original spelling of the family name. Turkish, Tatar, Persian and other names and terms are spelled in the original according to accepted forms in scholarly books. In some instances, if not otherwise ascertainable they are translated from the Russian as given by Soloviev. The names of geographical locations conform to commonly accepted English usage—Podolia, Moscow, Copenhagen, Saxony and so forth.

Finally, with respect to transliteration, this translation follows a modified Library of Congress system omitting diacritical marks and ligatures, and rendering the initial "ia" and "iu" as "ya" and "yu" ("Yasnaia" and "Yury"), the suffixes "ii", "skii", "skaia" and "skoe" are rendered as "Dmitry Poliansky" (instead of "Dmitrii Polianskii"), "Polianskaia", "Polianskoe", and the form "oi" has been replaced by "oy" ("Donskoy" not "Donskoi"). In some cases "i" has been inserted in place of hard and soft signs, or apostrophes indicating these signs. Hence Soloviev, not Solov'ev. The soft sign is not indicated by an apostrophe, as in some transliteration systems, but is dropped completely.

All dates, as in the original, except where otherwise specified, are according to the Julian calendar ("Old Style"); that is, for the sixteenth and seventeenth centuries, ten days behind the Gregorian calendar used in the West. A table of weights and measures is included at the front of this volume for the convenience of the reader.

The task of text editing and preparing the manuscript was expedited greatly by the Computer Services of the University of Lethbridge. I would like to express appreciation to the School of Slavonic and East European Studies, University of London, which was my host institution during a period of study leave in the academic session of 1984-1985, and also the Russian and East European Center, University of Illinois, where the final stages of the project were completed. I would like to express my appreciation to Diane Bland for her help in preparing the manuscript, and to Lindsey Hughes of the School of Slavonic and East European Studies for her careful copy editing and helpful advice. Above all I am grateful for the overall direction of Peter von Wahlde, general editor of this series.

G. Edward Orchard

INTRODUCTION

As the action left off at the end of Volume 14 of this edition of Soloviev's *History*, Russia was in a state of great confusion. Tsar Dmitry, who barely eleven months before had been hailed as Moscow's rising sun and savior, was now deposed and murdered, while the new tsar, Vasily Ivanovich Shuisky, affirmed that Dmitry was an impostor who designed to betray Moscow into the hands of King Sigismund of Poland and overturn the holy Orthodox faith of Russia in favor of the hated Latin heresy.

On the face of it, the new tsar's credentials were impeccable. The late ruler was clearly exposed as an impostor, and the old ruling line was extinct. Everybody in the genealogy-conscious Muscovite ruling circles knew that the Shuisky family was descended from the great Russian hero Alexander Nevsky and, moreover, from a senior brother to Daniel, the progenitor of the house of Moscow. The Shuisky family had a formidable power base, not only in their ancestral land of Suzdalia, but also in the northwest. Vasily's uncle Ivan Petrovich had distinguished himself in defending Pskov against the Polish king, Stefan Bathory. Added to this, Vasily himself had put his life on the line in defense of Russia and Orthodoxy when, soon after the pretender's entry into the capital, he had denounced the new tsar as a brigand and heretic. It is true that he was spared by Dmitry's injudicious act of clemency, but he was soon at it again, and it was he who led the conspiracy which finally rid Muscovy of Grishka Otrepiev.

What then was wrong with him? He is somewhat reminiscent of those politicians in modern times who win elections by a landslide, but for whom subsequently nobody will admit to having voted. With one notable exception, the *So-called Other Tale*, all contemporary sources, Russian and foreign, are hostile to him. His legislative acts and grants were recognized as legitimate by his Romanov successors, he was technically a lawful tsar, yet historians customarily refer to him as Vasily Shuisky, or simply Shuisky, almost never according him the courtesy of an ordinal as Vasily IV. Neither in historical literature, nor in the consciousness of the Russian people did Vasily Ivanovich fully attain legitimation.

According to Soloviev's verdict, with which it is difficult to disagree, Shuisky's failure was a moral one. This is consonant with a theme which runs through Soloviev's narrative like a scarlet thread. The Time of Troubles was basically the result of moral failure, not only of rulers, but also of the Russian people as a whole. Only when they made a conscious effort to overcome these moral failings, as they do towards the end of this volume, can they turn things around and reconstitute the shattered body politic. Soloviev, for example, in his treatment of Boris Godunov, is not primarily concerned with whether or not he murdered Tsarevich Dmitry, but points rather to his deep-seated moral failings, which rendered him unequal to the dignity of the tsardom.

Shuisky similarly had grave moral failings. First, he was a notorious liar. He had been a leading member of the commission sent to investigate the death of Tsarevich Dmitry in 1591. He personally vouched for the fact that the child had died accidentally, and had been buried in the cathedral church at Uglich. Then, as the pretender advanced upon Moscow, he changed his tune in order to get rid of his Godunov rivals, only a few weeks later to revert to his original story, denouncing the new tsar as the renegade monk Grishka Otrepiev. Then, after seizing the throne following the murder of the tsar who so graciously had delivered him from the executioner's block, he countenanced the story that the real tsarevich had been murdered at the instigation of Tsar Boris, not killed accidentally, as Shuisky himself solemnly had sworn in 1591.

His perfidy was demonstrated further after his seizure of the throne, when he had sworn not to execute or persecute anyone without due process of law. Perhaps this was a reckless promise to have made, and one which certainly was untenable as soon as the second False Dmitry had a well-established fifth column within Moscow. Yet all sources speak of his suspiciousness and willingness to listen to denunciations and, as Soloviev cites in many examples, the innocent frequently suffered along with the guilty. There was also his homosexuality, at which most chroniclers hint, and of which Ivan Timofeev accuses him outright.

There is also another factor which militated against both Boris Godunov and Vasily Shuisky. Edward L. Keenan and Nancy Shields Kollmann have likened the Muscovite political system to a series of concentric circles around the person of the tsar. Closest to the sovereign was the extremely charmed circle of boyars, to which access was granted by an unwritten and unspoken, but clearly understood set of rules, which even the theoretically autocratic sovereign did not transgress; the one attempt to do so, Ivan IV's creation of a realm consisting of crown estates (oprichnina), had to be abandoned. In theory boyardom was granted by the sovereign's will; in practice there was a sacrosanct pecking order. Those admitted to the boyar circle had paid their dues by long and meritorious service, and display a remarkably uniform age and career profile. The boyars also tended to be drawn from a discernible pool of aristocratic families, among whom some kind of balance generally was maintained, but aristocratic birth was not in itself a guarantee of a seat on the boyar council. Membership of this council also was granted from the mid-sixteenth century to non-boyars; lords-in-waiting (okolnichie) were, so to speak, candidate members of the council (duma), some awaiting promotion to boyar, others permanently in the lesser rank. Leading bureaucrats increasingly were co-opted as conciliar secretaries (dumnye diaki), and some representatives of the rank-and-file gentry were admitted as conciliar nobles (dumnye dvoriane).

Both Boris and Vasily had displayed ability and leadership while members of the ruling elite, yet when they stepped out of the inner circle into the epicentre they failed. They were acutely sensitive to any aspersions on the legitimacy of their rulership, since they themselves were aware that they had transgressed the most basic precept of the unwritten and unspoken code. A boyar was a boyar, and could never be a tsar.

Theoretically the autocratic tsar was all-powerful, but in practice he did the bidding of the ruling elite. The Prussian nobility in the eighteenth century had a saying: "Let the king reign absolute, so long as he does what we want." The Russian boyars of the early seventeenth century would have responded positively to this sentiment. To use an anachronistic metaphor, the tsar was a rubber stamp. A tsar with initiative and ability, a former boyar, did not fit into the role. Ivan IV's crown estates may be seen at least partly as an attempt to break free of the constraints of boyar rule with his own handpicked entourage of class renegades, low-born favorites and foreign adventurers, according to some modern historians a recurring phenomenon in Russian history whenever an innovative ruler came to power. Grishka Otrepiev was groomed for the role of Dmitry by boyars in opposition to Boris, but when he displayed initiatives of his own he was dumped unceremoniously by his erstwhile backers. The retarded Fedor Ivanovich and the dim-witted Michael Romanov were, from the point of view of the boyars, ideal autocrats, presiding vacantly at court and religious functions while in reality the boyars ran the show. Also like Michael the alternative candidates for the throne in 1610-1613 were young and impressionable. Wladyslaw or Karl Philipp would have filled the bill admirably, had the boyars been able to obtain firm guarantees against undue interference by their Polish or Swedish kinsmen.

Yet if Shuisky appears unattractive as ruler, what of the alternatives which presented themselves? Even though his body was burned and his ashes fired from a cannon to the west, whence he had come, the spectre of Dmitry was not so easily exorcized. Former supporters of the Pretender immediately spread rumors that he had escaped to Poland; yet it was to be a while before anyone could be found to play the part. Meanwhile his forerunner, Bolotnikov, and his putative nephew Tsarevich Peter, alias Ileika Muromets, had conjured up afresh the threat of popular rebellion on behalf of the "just tsar," which drove many of the dissident gentry elements back into the arms of Shuisky. The Liapunovs, Sunbulov and Istoma Pashkov were jealous of continued boyar dominance under a boyar tsar, but their ambitions were for the moment overweighed by fear of social revolution. The second False Dmitry, when at last he appeared, too late to help the besieged in Tula, was very different from the first. Grishka Otrepiev did have attractive qualities, stood at least for something, had some kind of program and ideas, and was very much his own man. Whoever the second pretender was, and this has never been determined for sure, he was a drunkard and degenerate, entirely lacking in any positive qualities, "unworthy to bear the name even of a false tsar."

And what of his adherents? Marina, wife to all the pretenders, had enjoyed a few weeks of splendor as consort of the Muscovite ruler. It was an experience she never forgot, and which she spent the rest of her short life trying to recapture. While charitably it may be assumed that her original marriage to Dmitry was motivated by concern for church and country, her willingness to acknowledge the Tushino brigand as her husband can be seen only as blind ambition. Though her eventual fate must evoke pity, it is difficult to extend her any sympathy. Hers was the fate, not of the tragic heroine, but of the unsuccessful gamester. The brigand's forerunner Bolotnikov, originally praised in Soviet historiography by I. I. Smirnov as leader of the first major peasant uprising, since has been demythologized by D. P. Makovsky as a déclassé noble and run-of-the-mill soldier of fortune. Dmitry's backers, Miechowicki and his supplanter

Rozynski, were seedy Polish-Ukrainian adventurers. Jan-Piotr Sapieha and Lisowski were archetypal condottieri, like so many freebooters marching and countermarching in various liveries all over early seventeenth-century Europe, while Dmitry's Russian supporters at Tushino may have obtained pardon for their treason, but not the respect of posterity. As for the cossacks, the constant extras to this historical drama, Soloviev presents them in a very deromanticized light. The antisocial nature of cossackdom is a theme to which he frequently returns, both in the preceding and in this volume. Cossackdom was a repudiation of social ties, a parasitical growth living at the expense of the productive members of society. Yet even Soloviev is bound to admit that the cossacks under Trubetskoy and Zarutsky held the line against the Poles, while later Avraamy Palitsyn brought them onside in the final struggle for the liberation of Moscow.

The final two chapters of this volume present what is perhaps the most perplexing epoch in the turbulent history of Russia. During the latter half of 1610 the two main antagonists of the foregoing years, Shuisky and False Dmitry II, were eliminated from the contest, one by deposition and the other by murder. The elements engaged in the conflict scattered like a cluster of iron filings when a magnetic force is removed. The deposition of Shuisky had deprived the Swedes of their paymaster, so they were transformed from allies into another set of interventionists. Anglo-Saxon, particularly American, colleagues are wont to take me to task for using this anglicized form of the Russian word *interventy*, sometimes characterized as "unlovely." This may be so, but it describes an unlovely phenomenon, from which the Russians in particular have suffered so much.

The ruling boyars of Moscow, fearful of False Dmitry II at Kaluga and unrest within the city, opted for Wladyslaw and admitted Zolkiewski's Poles into the Kremlin. Zolkiewski concluded with the Muscovites what was thought to be a mutually beneficial deal, only to have it repudiated by King Sigismund, who plainly was negotiating in bad faith outside Smolensk with the embassy led by Filaret and Golitsyn. With the murder of the pretender in December 1610 the elements which supported him dispersed throughout the country, subsisting as best they could, usually to the detriment of the local population. By process of elimination, Wladyslaw was now the sole contender in the running, and given certain conditions was generally acceptable. But now King Sigismund, who never learned that politics was the art of the possible, had an active fifth column within the city. The leading boyar, Fedor Ivanovich Mstislavsky, offered no leadership or initiative, and the king's men, Saltykov and Andronov, in conjunction with the Polish commander Gasiewski, had things very much their own way. Patriarch Hermogen caught the popular mood when he repudiated the collaborationist regime and closely identified Russian nationhood with Orthodoxy, for which he died a martyr's death. The provinces, deprived of leadership from the center, seized the initiative, first making their own arrangements for mutual defense against marauding Poles and cossacks, and then coalescing into the national army defense force, or militia (*narodnoe opolchenie*) movement. Their agenda was to get rid of the foreigners, and then see about electing a tsar. The first national army, led by Prokopy Liapunov, foundered upon the mutual jealousies of gentry and cossacks, but the second, led by the eponymous heroes Minin and Pozharsky who filled the void left by the absence, collaboration or lack of leadership of the boyars, liberated Moscow and cleared the way for the convocation of the Assembly of the Land (*zemskii sobor*) and the election of Michael Romanov.

Despite this, the Troubles were far from over, and the liquidation of the problems inherited by the new tsar will form the subject of much of the succeeding volume. It was to take another six years before the foreigners finally quit Russian soil, and the reconstruction of the country after the devastations of many years of warfare took much longer.

Soloviev's account of the Time of Troubles is certainly the first to be so richly documented. In fact, he has the habit of incorporating large segments of primary source material into his text, rather than, as a modern author would do, paraphrasing them or relegating them to the notes. From the standpoint of the modern scholar, his annotation techniques leave much to be desired. For instance, for the whole of Chapter V of this volume there is in the text a single marker for a note which lists all the source material he chooses to cite for the entire chapter, without any indication of what belongs where. I have tried to unscramble the omelette as best I could and given fuller annotation than in the preceding chapters in the hope that this might benefit the specialist as well as the general reader. Soloviev similarly has the annoying habit of referring to "the chronicler," without specifying *which* chronicler. After more than two decades' study of the Time of Troubles, I know my way fairly well around the sources, but occasionally I have had to admit defeat in my attempts to identify the nameless chronicler.

The eighth volume of Soloviev's original history, from which the chapters in Volumes 14 and 15 of this series were drawn, went into three editions during the author's lifetime. The volume in question first appeared in 1858, and subsequently with revisions in 1866 and 1873, with numerous revisions in each case. All the while he was engaged in the staggering task of bringing out an average volume a year over the period of twenty-eight years. His feat is all the more amazing when we consider that the source material was not so readily accessible as in our own day.

Several major collections of official acts and government documents had found their way into print by this time, notably the *Acts Collected in the Libraries and Archives of the Russian Empire by the Imperial Archeographical Commission* (Volume 2, St. Petersburg, 1836), the *Collection of State Documents and Treaties* (Volume 2, St. Petersburg, 1819) and *Historial Acts Collected and Edited by the Archeographic Commission* (Volume 2, St. Petersburg, 1841). With regard to Russian narrative sources, Soloviev was less fortunate, since the magnificent compilation by S. F. Platonov of chronicle material relating to the Time of Troubles did not appear until 1891, nor did the definitive edition of the *New Chronicler*, the official court chronicle of the Romanovs compiled about 1630 and an invaluable source, appear until 1910. For many narrative sources Soloviev had to make do with defective or not readily available material.

Considering these factors and the speed with which he worked, Soloviev's achievement is truly amazing, and his text a mine of information, providing intimate contact with primary sources rare indeed in general histories. He is sometimes rather cavalier in his attribution, his quotations sometimes inaccurate, and sometimes he will quote some documentary source at great length and then pass on without comment, leaving the reader shrugging his shoulders in resignation. It is not, however, the task of the translator-editor to second-guess the author's intentions.

The early seventeenth century was a period of burgeoning literacy, when almost every foreign traveller and soldier of fortune seemingly fancied himself a memoirist. Some of these foreign accounts have found their way into English translation, notably those of Isaac Massa, a teenage Dutch merchant apprentice who lived in Moscow from 1600 to 1609 and whose work was rediscovered in 1866 (English translation: *A Short*

History of the Muscovite Wars, Toronto, 1982); Stanislaw Zolkiewski, the Polish hetman who occupied Moscow in 1610 (English translation: *Expedition to Moscow*, London, 1959) a modern scholarly Polish edition, by Jarema Maciszewski, was published in Warsaw in 1966, and an English translation of the chronicle of Konrad Bussow is shortly to appear. A Russian translation of this chronicle appeared in 1831 in N. G. Ustrialov's collection *Tales of Contemporaries Concerning Dmitry the Pretender* (second edition, 1859), but was attributed to Bussow's son-in-law, the Lutheran pastor Martin Beer. Fortunately, by the time Soloviev was writing the scholarship of Ya. K. Grot and A. A. Kunik had re-established Bussow's authorship, and it was under his name that the first German text was printed in 1851 in the first volume of *Rerum Rossicarum Scriptores Exteri*. The definitive edition, upon which my own translation is based, is by I. I. Smirnov (Konrad Bussov, *Moskovskaia Khronika 1584-1613*, Moscow, 1961). Much of Bussow's chronicle was pirated by the Swedish soldier and diplomat Peer Peerson de Erlesunda, who under the pen-name Petreius published his Moscow narration in Swedish in 1615 and a more popular German edition in 1620, although his history also contains original material which occasionally serves as a corrective to Bussow.

Other foreign sources contained in the Ustrialov anthology used by Soloviev were those of Georg Peyerle, Jacques Margeret and Samuel Maskiewicz. The memoirs of the French Huguenot soldier of fortune are available in English translation by Chester Dunning, but unfortunately relate only to Margeret's first sojourn in Muscovy, and stop short in 1606, which is a pity since, as will be seen in this volume, he experienced more colorful adventures later on.

On the Polish side, apart from the Zolkiewski memoir already mentioned, which to Soloviev was most readily available in the Russian translation by P. A. Mukhanov (1835), there is Mikolaj Marchocki's *History of the Muscovite War*, available in a printed edition published at Poznan in 1841. This is an account of an active participant, who appears more than once in Soloviev's narrative. Two significant anthologies of Polish sources upon which Soloviev was not able to draw are contained in the first volume of the *Russian Historical Library* (St. Petersburg, 1872) and Aleksandr Hirschberg's *Poland and Moscow in the First Half of the Seventeenth Century* (Lwów, 1901), which among many other valuable items contains the diaries of Jan-Piotr Sapieha and Marina's chamberlain Waclaw Dyamentowski.

Turning to Russian narrative sources, there are as yet no English translations available, though it is hoped that this situation soon will be remedied, since the Time of Troubles called forth a new genre of Russian historical literature which deserves an international readership. Almost for the first time, authors were not content merely to record events, but also to explain and draw some lesson from them.

The most important "family" of chronicles is that of the so-called *New Chronicler*, the official court annalist of the Romanovs, who compiled his definitive version around 1630. The standard printed version is that edited by Platonov, which appeared in the fourteenth volume of the *Complete Collection of Russian Chronicles* in 1910. A new edition is believed in preparation, taking into account many variants which have come to light since Platonov's day. The version which Soloviev preferred was the *Chronicle of Many Rebellions*, a recension of the *New Chronicler* compiled at the court of Patriarch Nikon in the mid-seventeenth century, and edited and published by N. I. Novikov in 1771. Soloviev also had at his disposal a printed version, published in 1853, of a codex belonging to Prince M. Obolensky. Of the other chronicles on which Soloviev draws extensively, the *Pskov Chronicles*, on which he relies heavily for his account of the turbulent events within that city, are now conveniently available in two volumes (Moscow, 1941-1955). The Novgorod Fourth Chronicle is reprinted in Volume 3 of the *Complete Collection of Russian Chronicles* (St. Petersburg, 1841).

Another important genre containing much valuable information about the Time of Troubles is the *Chronograph*. This is a Byzantine form of historical writing, a type of universal history, but containing fairly detailed entries on Russian and Slavic matters. These were extracted and put together by Andrei Popov in his *Selection of Slavic and Russian Works and Entries Introduced into the Chronographs of the Russian Edition* (Moscow, 1869). Platonov in his second (1909) edition of the thirteenth volume of the *Russian Historical Library* (RIB 13), included *Entries on the Troubles Extracted from the 1617 Chronograph*, also published as a separate fascicle in the same year.

The rich lode of publicist literature is gathered conveniently in RIB 13, two of the most important accounts in which have appeared in annotated scholarly editions in Soviet times. These are the chronicles of Avraamy Palitsyn (1955) and Ivan Timofeev (1951). Palitsyn, cellarer of the Trinity monastery, was not only an astute observer, but also an active participant in the events described in this volume. His account was circulated widely, but was so tendentious that at least one reader felt impelled to compose a rebuttal, the *So-called Other Tale*, which is the only chronicle to present Shuisky in a positive light. Ivan Timofeev, the paranoid Novgorod bureaucrat wrote, so to speak, for the desk drawer. He was terrified lest any of his writings be discovered and read, so he kept them hidden in various caches. His language is tortuous and periphrastic, even at times reverting to cipher, making it the only Russian source of the period to which the Soviet editor felt it necessary to append a modern Russian translation. Yet for this very reason we have a unique insight into the private thoughts of a Russian who experienced the Troubles at close quarters.

Another fascinating source is the so-called *Book of Annals*, which originally Platonov attributed to Prince Ivan Mikhailovich Katyrev-Rostovsky, though even at the time he was rather dubious, and modern scholarship seems to indicate Prince Semeon Ivanovich Shakhovskoy as the author. RIB 13 also includes an account which actually bears Shakhovskoy's name, but this is probably a gloss on the *Book of Annals*. There are altogether sixteen chronicle sources in the first edition of this volume, and several more were added in the subsequent editions which appeared in 1909 and 1925.

The classic historian of the Time of Troubles is Sergei Fedorovich Platonov, whose *Notes on the History of the Troubles in the Muscovite Realm in the Sixteenth and Seventeenth Centuries*, originally published in 1899, has gone through four editions, the most recent in 1937. His popular version of the same work, *The Time of Troubles*, originally published in 1924, has been translated ably into English by J. T. Alexander. The first edition of this translation was published by the University of Kansas Press in 1970, and contained a bibliography of materials on the Time of Troubles published since Platonov's day. The second edition (1985) contains a very useful "Bibliographical Update." More recently Academic International Press has published the first major study of the Time of Troubles since Platonov in any language. The author is the Leningrad scholar Ruslan Grigorievich Skrynnikov, who prepared the manuscript specifically for first publication by Academic International Press, and it is an essential companion volume for readers of the present work. It is ably translated by Hugh F. Graham, a trailblazer in the present Soloviev series.

Skrynnikov's reassessment is valuable, not only for its own considerable intrinsic merit, but also because of the fact that, partly owing to the promptings of official Soviet ideology, much work has been done on certain aspects of the question. On the Bolotnikov rebellion there is the work of I. I. Smirnov and D. P. Makovsky already mentioned. (English readers may want to consult Paul Avrich, *Russian Rebels*, New York, 1972). There is also Vadim Koretsky's vast archival research on the enserfment of the peasantry, V. N. Floria's work on Russo-Polish relations, I. S. Shepelev's *Liberation War and Class Struggle 1608-1610* (Piatigorsk, 1957), I. P. Shaskolsky's work on Russo-Swedish relations and the multifarious labors of the great Soviet medievalist L. V. Cherepnin, to mention only a few.

This is not to say that Soloviev's account is superseded; far from it. In reading through its pages, we have a feeling of immediacy. We are being led through the most labyrinthine epoch of Russian history by a guide who knows all the twists and turns, and can point out many features we otherwise might have missed.

History of Russia

Volume 15

The Time of Troubles

Tsar Vasily Shuisky and the Interregnum

1606–1613

I

TSAR VASILY SHUISKY
1606–1608

THE NEW TSAR PROCLAIMS HIS ELECTION

In fulfillment of the promise given to his fellow-conspirators, Shuisky announced his election in this manner: "By the grace of God we, the great sovereign, Tsar and Grand Prince Vasily Ivanovich of All Russia, through the generosity and loving kindness of our praiseworthy God, and in answer to the request of the Holy Synod[1] and the petitions and pleas of all Orthodox Christendom, have assumed the patrimony of our forefathers, and have become tsar and grand prince of the Russian realm. God gave this dominion to our ancestor Rurik, who was descended from the Roman caesar, and then, after the passing of many years, it was inherited by our direct ancestor Grand Prince Alexander Yaroslavich Nevsky,[2] and my ancestors ruled over this Russian realm; but then they were relegated to the Suzdal principality, not by confiscation or compulsion, but because of family precedence, since it was the custom for elder brothers to rule in the larger centers.[3]

"And now we, the great sovereign, seated upon the throne of the Russian tsardom, wish Orthodox Christianity to be our safeguarding principle in quiet, in peace and benevolence. And I, the tsar and grand prince of All Russia, have seen fit to kiss the cross to this; that I, the great sovereign, will not condemn any man to death, or take away the patrimony, dwelling or goods from his brothers, wife or children, if they were not associated in his guilt, without true judgement in consultation with my boyars. Also if merchants and trading people are brought to me for judgement or investigation, even for a capital offense, I will not thereafter take houses, shops or goods away from their wives or children if they were not associated in their guilt. And also I, the great sovereign, will not heed any false witness, and I will investigate strenuously all matters, and will hold confrontation with witnesses, so that thereby Orthodox Christians will not perish innocently.

"And whosoever shall be found to have borne false witness against anybody shall be executed, considering the evil which wrongfully he wrought. To this, and to everything which is in this rescript I, Tsar and Grand Prince Vasily Ivanovich of All Russia, kiss the cross before all Orthodox Christendom that I, taking pity upon them, will judge righteously and with just judgement, and will not lay my disfavor upon anyone who is innocent, neither will I hand anyone over to their adversaries, and I will preserve them from all violence."

LIMITATION OF THE TSAR'S AUTHORITY

The chronicler relates that as soon as Shuisky was proclaimed tsar he went to the Dormition cathedral,[4] and began to speak in terms which had not been heard from time immemorial in the Muscovite state. "I will kiss the cross that I will do no harm to anyone without consulting the Assembly, and if the father is guilty, I will do nothing against the son, and if the son is guilty, I will do no harm to the father; and whosoever insulted me during the reign of Tsar Boris, to him I shall bear no malice." The boyars and all the people, continues the chronicler, said to him that he should not kiss the cross because in the Muscovite realm this had not been necessary. But he did not heed anyone, and kissed the cross.[5]

It is interesting, if the chronicler was not mistaken, to note that initially Shuisky also undertook not to pronounce death sentences without the resolution of the Assembly, as False Dmitry had done in the case of Shuisky himself, and then, in the actual document, in place of the word "assembly" there is written "not without taking counsel with his boyars," which was more in accordance with his previous promise at the time of the organization of the conspiracy, "to rule the Russian realm by general counsel." Furthermore, here also the term "general counsel" was a sufficiently imprecise expression, since the boyars were persuaded that this "general counsel" could relate to themselves, which was most likely, but could also signify an Assembly of the Land.[6] As far as the promise not to punish innocent relatives along with the guilty is concerned, this, in all probability, was an idea concerning the justice of legislation, brought by False Dmitry and his companions from Poland, where for a long time, as a consequence of the much earlier weakening of clan relations, the relatives of a criminal did not suffer along with him. Thus Mniszech[7] promised the boyars an enlargement of their rights under False Dmitry.

CHARTERS TO THE PROVINCES

Another document also was sent around the provinces in the name of the boyars, lords-in-waiting, gentry and all the Muscovite people, with news of the death of False Dmitry and the accession of Shuisky to the throne.

"We have found it true that he really was the brigand Grishka Otrepiev,[8] and also that the mother of Tsarevich Dmitry, the tsaritsa and nun Martha,[9] and her brother Mikhail Nagoy and another brother, solemnly told the people of the Muscovite realm that her son, Tsarevich Dmitry, truly had died and was buried at Uglich, and that this brigand called himself Tsarevich Dmitry falsely. And when they caught him, he himself said that he was Grishka Otrepiev, and that he had obtained the government of the realm with the aid of the Devil, and had tempted all the people by necromancy.[10] And this Grishka, for his evil deeds, received his reward from God, and ended his life by an evil death.

"After this, begging pardon from God, the metropolitans, archbishops, bishops and all the Holy Synod, and also we, the boyars, lords-in-waiting, gentry, junior boyars and all the people of the Muscovite realm, chose for all the Muscovite realm him whom God wished to be sovereign of the entire Muscovite realm. And Almighty God, glorified in the Trinity, showed his mercy upon us and upon you, and proclaimed sovereign over all the Muscovite realm the great sovereign Tsar and Grand Prince Vasily Ivanovich, autocrat of All Russia, a pious sovereign, a champion of God's church and Orthodox Christianity, from the stem of the great sovereigns of Russia, descended from the great sovereign Prince Alexander Yaroslavich Nevsky. He suffered many mortal persecutions for the Orthodox faith together with his brother for many years, and more than anyone else suffered deadly torments at the hands of that brigand, apostate and heretic."[11]

Immediately following that document the new tsar sent around another in his own name, in which he again announced the fall of False Dmitry with a more precise explanation of the causes, specifically revealing the contents of the papers found in the pretender's apartments. "There were taken from his chambers many items of criminal correspondence with Poland and Lithuania, concerning the ruin of the Muscovite realm." But Shuisky did not go into any details concerning the contents of these criminal letters, even though immediately afterwards he gave details concerning the contents of letters from the pope of Rome. Next Shuisky wrote of the testimony of the Buczynski brothers,[12] that the tsar had intended to slay all the boyars in the course of military maneuvers, and then, after giving all principal government posts to the Poles, to introduce Catholicism. In actual fact this testimony was extant, but its veracity has been disproven.[13]

Shuisky further introduced in evidence notes actually given to Mniszech and the king in Poland concerning the cession of Russian territories, and concluded: "Hearing and seeing this, we render thanks to Almighty God that He has delivered us from such evil deeds." Finally, a circular letter in the name of Tsaritsa Martha was sent around, in which she renounced False Dmitry. Martha said: "By means of sorcery and necromancy he called himself the son of Tsar Ivan Vasilievich; by the dark deeds of the Devil he tempted many people in Poland and Lithuania, and threatened us, ourselves, and our relatives, with death. Before now I warned the boyars, gentry and all the people of this secretly, and now I tell them openly, that he was not our son, Tsarevich Dmitry, but a brigand, an apostate and a heretic. And after he, by means of his witchcraft and sorcery, came from Putivl to Moscow, he, being conscious of his brigandage, did not send for us for a long time, but sent his advisers to us, and told them to guard us strictly, so that nobody might come and talk to us of him. And when he ordered us to be brought to Moscow, and met with us alone, he did not allow the boyars or any other people to come with him, and spoke to us in great privacy, so that I might not accuse him. He threatened to murder us and all our family, admonishing me not to bring down evil death upon myself and my family. He placed me in a convent, and ordered his advisers to guard me and to keep a strict watch, so that his brigandage should not be unmasked. Because of his threats I did not dare denounce his brigandage openly among the people."

Martha said, or it was said on her behalf, that False Dmitry sent his advisers for her, but there is no word as to who exactly these advisers were. This raises an even more important question: who were False Dmitry's advisers, who knew of his imposture and who, despite this, were still acting on his behalf? Either these advisers did not exist at all, or if they did exist, now they were so powerful that their names could not be made public. But it is known that Dmitry sent Prince Mikhail Vasilievich Skopin-Shuisky[14] to fetch Martha. Consequently Skopin was the chief of these advisers of False Dmitry, who were ordered to keep a strict guard upon her, so that nobody should approach her and speak with her concerning the tsar.

It easily can be imagined what an impression these declarations by Shuisky, Tsaritsa Martha and the boyars made upon many of the inhabitants of Moscow itself, let alone the inhabitants of the provinces! Surely there were many to whom it must have appeared strange how the brigand

Tsar Vasily Ivanovich Shuisky
Sixteenth-century Dutch Lithograph

Grishka Otrepiev by his sorcery and necromancy could have tempted all the Muscovite rulers! Not long ago they had announced to all the people that the new tsar was the true Dmitry; now they asserted the contrary, maintaining that Dmitry had threatened the ruin of the Orthodox faith, wished to divide the Russian lands with Poland, and declared that this had been the cause of his ruin. But how did he fall? This remained obscure. They announced that a new tsar had been elected, but how, and by whom? This was not specified.

None of the inhabitants of the provinces had attended the assembly. All this had been done without the knowledge of the Russian land. Counsellors had not been sent to Moscow who, returning thence, could satisfy the curiosity of their fellow citizens, relate to them the circumstances of the matter and resolve their doubts. The strangeness and darkness of the events related inevitably gave rise to perplexity, doubt and distrust, especially since the new tsar had ascended the throne in secret from the Russian land, in violation of the forms already hallowed by ancient usage. Hitherto the provinces had trusted Moscow, had acknowledged every word coming to them from Moscow as genuine; but now Moscow clearly acknowledged that a sorcerer had tempted it by diabolical arts.

Inevitably the question arose—could not the Muscovites also have been bewitched by Shuisky? Hitherto Moscow had been the epicentre around which the provinces had revolved. The link between Moscow and the provinces was trust in the power vested in the capital city. Now that this confidence was shaken, and the link weakened, the realm began to sicken. Faith, once shaken, inevitably was transformed into suspicion. Having lost political faith in Moscow, Russians began to believe everything and everyone, especially when people came into the provinces who were unhappy with the revolution and the man who had brought it about, and who said that things had happened differently from the way it had been set forth in Shuisky's documents. And so there began a time of diabolical gloom for the entire realm, a gloom brought about by the spirit of falsehood, by a dark and unclean deed, carried out furtively, out of the sight of the Russian land.

CORONATION AND PATRIARCH

On the first day of June of 1606 Shuisky was crowned tsar. The new tsar was a small old man, in his fifties,[15] very unprepossessing, with poor eyesight, well read, very clever and very miserly. He loved only those who whispered denunciations in his ear, and he was a firm believer in magic.

Next to the tsar there appeared also the second person to him in the realm, namely the patriarch. This was Hermogen, former metropolitan of Kazan, known for his opposition to the un-Orthodox actions of False Dmitry. This opposition certainly showed Hermogen to be a man of strong character, ready to suffer for his convictions, for truth and for the inviolability of what had been entrusted to him. In this manner the new patriarch was by nature equal to his high position in the stormy Time of Troubles. But contemporaries complained that this strength was allied with a vindictive spirit, an unattractiveness in speech, and an immoderate severity. They also complained that he was eager to listen to gossip, could ill distinguish between truth and falsehood, and believed everybody. Shuisky's enemies took advantage of this weakness. They told tales against the tsar to the patriarch, and succeeded in embroiling the two. Because of his hardness of heart, the patriarch did not conceal his discontent, and was very unfriendly in his relations with the tsar, even though at the same time, because of his basic convictions, he was still prepared to defend Shuisky, as the crowned tsar, against scandalmongers.

THE SECOND PRETENDER

It is also easy to understand how harmful for Shuisky were such relations with the patriarch, when even without this he did not enjoy great trust and confidence among his subjects. As a result of the oath given them at his accession they began to regard him differently from the manner in which they had regarded previous sovereigns. The restriction of the tsar's power with regard to punishment, its limitation by the boyars in relation to a tsar whose position was weak, promised impunity for lawless acts and treason. A supporter of Golitsyn[16] or any other mighty boyar might dare anything at the instigation of his patron, knowing that the latter could protect him. Contemporaries say outright that from the accession of Shuisky the boyars began to have more power than the tsar himself. Several of the boyars plotted against the tsar with the aim of usurping his place; others did not wish to see him as tsar, because of previous dealings with him.

Not all boyars had been party to the conspiracy with Shuisky against False Dmitry. Several, among them some of the most able, for example Mikhail Glebovich Saltykov,[17] Prince Rubets-Mosalsky[18] and others, remained faithful to False Dmitry and consequently were hostile to the new government, which also did not hesitate to place them in disfavor. Prince Rubets-Mosalsky was sent as governor to Korela, Afanasy Vlasiev[19] to Ufa, Saltykov to Ivangorod, Bogdan Belsky to Kazan.[20] Other table attendants and gentry similarly were sent to the various towns, and some were deprived of their estates and patrimonies.

In this manner, to the more distant provinces, and even in the capacity of governors, embittered people were sent, those very people who would be reliable agitators, or who at least would be prepared to take a very active role in any agitation leading to the overthrow of a government hostile to them. They also quickly noticed that in general the new tsar had broken his promise, in that he was persecuting people who previously had been his opponents. The head of the conspiracy, the guilty party in the rising, namely Shuisky, had been proclaimed tsar by the participants in the conspiracy, in the uprising, by the most restless people, by a claque in the square, and by agitators who three times had shown their power in the overthrow and elevation of tsars. They put their leader Shuisky forward in the hope of rich rewards from him, but from the miserly old man they could not expect anything. Thereafter they became a ready instrument in the hands of Shuisky's enemies.

But all these people—mighty boyars who had their eyes upon the throne, secondary figures hostile to Shuisky either for personal or family reasons, or because of their devotion to his predecessor or, finally, agitators from people of all classes, to whom it was advantageous to bring about change—none of them would have dared risk a direct attempt to overthrow Shuisky. Golitsyn had not sufficient rights or power to put himself directly forward as a rival to the new tsar, and to act openly against him. Which of his rights could Golitsyn put forward, which could be greater than Shuisky's? He could hope to receive the throne only after Shuisky had been overthrown by somebody else, and not in his own name. Consequently he could only plot against him, not act openly.

The same could be said for all the others, those who for whatever reason might have been discontented with Shuisky and were wishing for a change. In whose name could they act, whom could they propose in place of Shuisky? They all needed a pretext for the rising; they needed someone in whose name they could act, a man powerful enough to overthrow Shuisky, yet at the same time so insignificant that he could not be an obstacle to the fulfilment of their known aims.

In a word, they needed a pretender. Shuisky could be overthrown only in the same manner as the Godunovs. This was the reason for the appearance of a second pretender and his successes within the realm. As far as the cossacks were concerned, a pretender was indispensible to them.

Even during the lifetime of the first, they had put forward a second pretender.[21] As for a peaceful, well-ordered state the sovereign, the government, cannot die—the king is dead, long live the king!—so for the Russian society of those days, shaken to its foundations, the pretender could not die. And so, even as the bloody corpse of the first False Dmitry lay upon Red Square, word was spreading about a second.

MOLCHANOV

On May 17, while the conspirators were busy with the destruction of the pretender and the Poles, Mikhail Molchanov,[22] one of the murderers of Fedor Godunov,[23] succeeded in slipping out of the palace and out of Moscow. Accompanied by two Poles, Molchanov made his way across the Lithuanian frontier, spreading everywhere along the way the rumor that he was Tsar Dmitry, who had fled from Moscow, and in place of whom the Muscovites mistakenly had killed another person. This rumor quickly reached Moscow and spread among its inhabitants. This phenomenon, strange at first glance, is not surprising if it is remembered that not all Muscovites had taken part in the murder of False Dmitry, that many of them had come into the Kremlin with the aim of rescuing the tsar from the hands of the Poles, and suddenly had thrust before them the disfigured corpse of False Dmitry, on which it was difficult to distinguish its previous features.

People believe what they want to believe. As is usually the case in such instances, each tried to put forward his own opinion of the mysterious, secret events, his own guess, his own interpretation. Thus it appeared to a certain French merchant that upon the corpse of False Dmitry there had been clear traces of a thick beard, which had been torn out, whereas the living tsar had not had any beard. The same Frenchman thought that the hair on the corpse was much longer than it had been on the living tsar the day before. The valet of the slain Dmitry, the Pole Chwalibog, swore that the body exhibited on Red Square did not in any way resemble that of his former master. There lay there, he said, some small fat man, with a shaven brow and a hairy chest, whereas Dmitry was thin, groomed himself with small curls on each side in the fashion of a student, and there was no hair on his chest because of his tender years. The mask placed upon the face of False Dmitry also gave rise to rumors that a substitute had been concealed there, and so the rumor gained momentum.[24]

But if some inhabitants of Moscow believed in the escape of False Dmitry, how much greater must have been the belief of the inhabitants of the provinces? Even Shuisky saw that he could not suppress rumors among the people concerning a second False Dmitry, and that he would be much better advised to arm himself against the rights of the first, so that even if, in the opinion of some, the pretender in fact had escaped from his murderers, he remained all the same an impostor. Therefore Shuisky immediately ordered the body of Tsarevich Dmitry be brought with great ceremony from Uglich to Moscow, after which documents were distributed with news of this event, together with a repetition of the evil deeds of False Dmitry, to which were appended the depositions of the Buczynski brothers, the documents issued by the pretender to the governor of Sandomir and his correspondence with the pope, together also with news of Tsaritsa Martha's change of mind. But at the same time as in Uglich and in Moscow the sanctity of the child who had fallen under the knives of the murderers was being praised, on the throne sat a man who during the lifetime of Fedor solemnly had sworn that the tsarevich had killed himself during the course of an epileptic fit! Shuisky even decided himself to carry the tsarevich's body through all Moscow to the Archangel cathedral.[25]

STIRRINGS IN THE BORDERLANDS

Shuisky's documents did not help. While Molchanov, at the very instant of False Dmitry's murder, was designing his resurrection, Prince Grigory Petrovich Shakhovskoy thought of the same plan, and during the commotion at the palace carried off the royal seal as an indispensible tool for the fulfilment of his plans.[26] The new tsar could not have aided him better in this design, as he sent him to be governor of Putivl to punish him for his devotion to False Dmitry. Shakhovskoy, on his arrival at Putivl, gathered together the inhabitants, declaring to them that Tsar Dmitry was still alive, and was hiding from his enemies. The inhabitants of Putivl immediately rose up against Shuisky, and their example was followed by the other towns of Severia. In Chernigov the rising was led by the same boyar, Prince Andrei Teliatevsky, who previously had not wished to take part in the desertion of the whole army to the side of the first False Dmitry, but now declared himself to be on the side of the second. Nobody knew anything about the circumstances of this event.[27]

UNREST IN MOSCOW

Signs of unrest began to appear in Moscow. Here the conspirators did not yet dare to pronounce the name of Dmitry out loud, and therefore tried to attract the people to the movement by other means. On the houses of foreigners and boyars they wrote that the tsar would give the houses of these traitors to the people to be plundered. Crowds began to gather, but on this occasion were dispersed. Some time later, on a certain Sunday, when the tsar was going to mass, he saw a crowd before the palace. Shuisky halted and, weeping with frustration, spoke to the boyars surrounding him, saying that they did not need to seek underhand means if they wanted to get rid of him. Since they had chosen him as tsar, they also could depose him if he did not suit them, and he would quit the throne without any resistance. Then, handing them the tsar's staff and cap, he continued: "If this is so, choose whomsoever you wish."

Seeing that nobody stirred, and that there was no opposition from any quarter, Shuisky thought he had intimidated the conspirators, and that the majority was in his favor. Taking back the staff, he said: "I am quite weary of these intrigues. Some want to kill me, others want to kill the boyars and foreigners, or at least want to plunder them. If you recognize me as tsar, then I demand the execution of the guilty." On this occasion everyone hastened to assure him of their devotion, and begged him to punish the agitators. They seized five persons from the crowd, lashed them with the knout, and sent them into exile.

Shuisky wished to take advantage of this devotion in order to unmask the plot hatched in the name of Prince Mstislavsky,[28] but in the course of the investigation they found that this boyar was in no way implicated, even though his relatives, among whom Peter Nikitich Sheremetev[29] was the most deeply involved, were acting in his name. Sheremetev was sent to Pskov as governor.

BOLOTNIKOV

Meanwhile Shakhovskoy, for the success of the uprising which he had stirred up, needed a pretender, no matter from where. Knowing that Molchanov at first had given himself out to be Dmitry, he summoned him from Putivl to Sambor, where he had, with the agreement of Marina's mother, spread rumors concerning the tsar's escape. But Molchanov did not wish to play the role of the pretender, neither could he find anyone who could agree or would be suitable to take it on, even though there was no time to be lost. It was necessary to strengthen the uprising by giving it a brave leader; such a leader appeared to be Bolotnikov.

Bolotnikov had been a bondsman of Prince Teliatevsky. It is said that in his youth he had been taken prisoner by the Turks, and that for some years he had been a galley slave. Having somehow gained his freedom, he was cast up by fate in Venice whence, at the time in question, he had reached his homeland by way of Poland. In Poland he had heard of the events which had stirred up Russia. As a Russian, Bolotnikov had been arrested and brought before Molchanov, who saw in him a man useful for his cause. He gave him gifts, and sent him with a letter to Putivl, to Prince Shakhovskoy, who received him as a delegate of the tsar, and gave him command of a detachment of troops.[30]

The bondsman Bolotnikov immediately found the means to enlarge his entourage, and to strengthen the cause of the pretender in the "pre-Ruin Ukraine,"[31] promising the people freedom, riches and honors under the banner of Dmitry,. Now, under these banners of Dmitry there began to flock brigands, thieves who had found refuge in the Ukraine, fugitive slaves, peasants and cossacks. He was also joined by townsmen and musketeers. In the towns they seized the governors and cast them into prison. Peasants and slaves attacked the houses of their lords and plundered them. They looted, killed the men and compelled the wives and daughters to marry them. On the streets of Moscow secret missives circulated in which Muscovites were reproached for their malevolence towards Dmitry, who had saved himself from their blows, and threatened them with his return to punish the capital not later than September 1, which at that time was New Year's Day.

DEFEAT OF THE TSAR'S FORCES

The tsar summoned the crown secretaries and compared their handwriting with the handwriting of these missives, but no resemblance could be found. The documents apparently came from the Ukraine, where it was necessary to direct his arms. But before the commencement of military actions the tsar wished to attempt to calm the rising by religious means. To this end, he sent clergymen with promises to the Severian land.[32] The boyar Mikhail Nagoy[33] was sent to Elets[34] with a document of his sister, Tsaritsa Martha, including a picture of Tsarevich Dmitry. But these measures were to no avail.

The boyar Prince Ivan Mikhailovich Vorotynsky[35] then besieged Elets. The table attendant, Prince Yury Trubetskoy,[36] besieged Kromy, but Bolotnikov came to relieve it. With thirteen hundred men he attacked five thousand of the tsar's army, completely routing Trubetskoy. The victorious cossacks mocked the vanquished, calling their tsar, Shuisky, the "furrier."[37] The Muscovite army, even without this reverse, was not very fond of Shuisky. Consequently the army's morale was already weakened, and Bolotnikov's victory had undermined what remained of it. Servitors seeing the common disorder and general vacillation, no longer wished to fight for Shuisky and dispersed to their homes.

The commanders Vorotynsky and Trubetskoy, weakened by this desertion, could not undertake any decisive action, and retreated. Considering the state of mind which prevailed at that time in the Muscovite realm, the general unsteadiness, lack of confidence, the absence of any focus, it was no wonder that the first success, on whichever side it occurred, created important momentum, since it attracted the uncommitted masses, who were eager to get involved and to support one side or the other, even if only to resolve their own indecision, which for every man, and also for society in general, is a difficult and intolerable state of mind. As soon as it was heard that the tsar's army had retreated, the rising in the south became general. The junior boyar and lieutenant, Istoma Pashkov, incited Tula, Venev and Kashira.[38] At the same time the ancient principality of Riazan also rose up against Shuisky. There, at the head of the rising was the governor, Grigory Sunbulov[39] and the nobleman Prokopy Liapunov.[40]

THE LIAPUNOVS

Foreign writers praised the bravery of the ancient population of Riazan. The Muscovite chroniclers are surprised by its impertinence and haughty speech. The Riazan followers of Liapunov justified both descriptions. At the time of the popular uprising at the death of Ivan the Terrible, the Liapunovs and the Kikins of Riazan were in the forefront. Zakhar Liapunov, the brother of Prokopy, daring both in word and deed, the first to act in any affair where only a very few were capable of acting decisively, appears for the first time when he refused to be one of the cossack captains, together with Kikin, and excused himself from service at Elets. In 1603 further information about him is forthcoming. Tsar Boris ordered the junior boyars of Riazan to be interrogated as to who had sent the atamans and cossacks on the Don quantities of wine, powder, sulphur, saltpetre, lead, firearms, armor, helmets and various of munitions, which were contraband materials. They answered that it was rumored that Zakhar Liapunov had sent wine to the Don Cossacks, and had sold armor and steel helmets to them. For this Zakhar was beaten with the knout.[41] His brother Prokopy, a handsome, wise, brave man, who was skilled also in military matters, as contemporaries have described him, possessed amazing energy, which did not give him any rest, compelled him always to push his way into the foremost ranks and deprived him of the ability to await the outcome of events. Such men normally become popular leaders in troubled times. The people, tired and oppressed by indecision, awaits the first firm word, the first movement, and the first who pronounces the momentous word, who is the first to move, becomes the leader of the popular movement.

Liapunov was for Dmitry and against Shuisky. There is no justification for asserting that Liapunov was convinced of the imposture of the man who called himself Dmitry, of the falsity of rumors concerning his escape. In all probability he, like the majority if not all inhabitants of Riazan, and like the majority, if not all inhabitants of all Muscovite provinces, held no strong convictions about this, but acted on hearing news of the uprising, obeying his energetic nature, unlike others unable to tolerate indecision and delay. Furthermore a rising under the banners of Dmitry against Shuisky—against government by the boyars, who upheld ancient custom, and refused to admit new members to their ranks—attracted men such as Liapunov, Sunbulov and Pashkov, men who felt the urge to leadership but whose ancestry hindered them.

Apart from Riazan, twenty towns in the present governments [provinces][42] of Orel, Kaluga and Smolensk rose up in favor of False Dmitry. In the Eastern Ukraine, in the Volga basin, even as in the Severian Ukraine, slaves and peasants rose up. They were joined by non-Russians who only recently, after lengthy resistance, had been compelled to submit to the Russian crown, and who now were glad of the opportunity to cast off this subjection. Mordvins,[43] slaves and peasants besieged Nizhny Novgorod under the leadership of two Mordvins, Moskov and Vokorlin, and the rising spread to the regions of Viatka and Perm. Differences arose among the inhabitants of Perm, who had been summoned to the army on the tsar's behalf. They fought among themselves, and almost killed the tsar's agent who had been sent to recruit them, and in the end they fled from him on the march. In the land of Viatka the Muscovite official sent to raise levies was met with loud mockery of Shuisky. They said that Dmitry had taken

Moscow already, and they proposed toasts to him. But in Astrakhan it was not the common people who rose in favor of Dmitry. Here Shuisky was betrayed by the governor, Prince Khvorostinin.[44] And here, on the contrary, the town secretary Afanasy Karpov and the lesser people were beaten and mocked.

BOLOTNIKOV BEFORE MOSCOW

Bolotnikov, having joined up with Pashkov and the levies of Riazan, crossed the Oka, capturing and plundering Kolomna. The detachment of the tsar's army under the leadership of Prince Mikhail Vasilievich Skopin-Shuisky gained the victory in a skirmish on the banks of the Pakhra river, but the main force under the command of Prince Mstislavsky and other boyars of ancient lineage was defeated seventy versts[45] from Moscow near the village of Troitskoe. Bolotnikov, pursuing the defeated, reached Moscow and halted in the village of Kolomenskoe.[46] The reign of Shuisky, it appeared, was coming to an end. With the disaffection of many towards him, he had little means for defense. There was little hope to be placed in the remnants of the regiments beaten by Bolotnikov, while the surrounding provinces, from the south to the southeast and the west had recognized False Dmitry. Bread prices were rising in Moscow, and who was willing to suffer hunger on account of Shuisky?

THE GENTRY DESERT BOLOTNIKOV

But in the regiments which had come to besiege Shuisky there was division, which this time saved him. Arriving before Moscow, Bolotnikov immediately revealed the character of the uprising. In the capital there appeared letters from him, appealing to the lowest stratum of the population. They ordered the boyars' slaves to smite their boyars, promising them their wives, their patrimonies and estates. Beggars and thieving paupers were ordered to strike the leading merchants and all the trading people, to plunder their goods. They summoned these brigands, wishing to give them boyardom, governorships and offices as lords-in-waiting and crown secretaries.[47] The gentry and junior boyars of Riazan and Tula, the entourages of Liapunov and Sunbulov who had joined with Bolotnikov, seeing with whom they were dealing, decided to choose what in their opinion was the lesser of the two evils, that is, to serve Shuisky once again. They came to Moscow bearing their submission to Tsar Vasily, without doubt being assured beforehand of pardon and favor, since to punish the first of the repentant traitors would mean to compel all others to fight desperately and wage internecine struggle. Liapunov and Sunbulov were the first to appear, and Liapunov received the rank of conciliar noble.

SHUISKY'S OFFENSIVE

At the same time another turn of events favorable to Shuisky occurred in the northwest. If in the south, influenced by the example of energetic men such as Liapunov, Sunbulov and Pashkov, the inhabitants had rushed to the side of the pretender, in Tver, on the other hand, things had gone very differently. There the archbishop at that time was Feoktist, a man apparently of strong spirit, capable of assuming the leadership of the population. When a crowd of supporters of the Pretender appeared in the Tver province, Feoktist called together the clergy, the officials, his own junior boyars, the tradesmen and townsmen, and so urged them to be loyal to Shuisky that the supporters of False Dmitry were met with arms in hand, and were defeated. Other towns of Tver province which had sworn allegiance to the pretender, observing this turn of affairs, forthwith followed the example of Tver, and the servitors set off to help Shuisky around Moscow.

The inhabitants of Smolensk also showed strong devotion to Shuisky. According to contemporaries, they were hostile to the Poles and Lithuanians, who were their enemies from time immemorial. They lived close by, and battles with them were frequent; therefore the inhabitants of Smolensk could not expect anything good to come of a tsar who was a friend of the Poles, and who in exchange for the help given him could be expected to cede Smolensk to Poland. As soon as it was known in Smolensk that a tsar was about to arrive from Poland (no matter whether a false or true tsar, new or old, this was of no consequence, because nobody knew anything for sure), the servicemen immediately gathered and advanced on Moscow, choosing as their leader Grigory Poltev, and on the way they cleared Dorogobuzh and Viazma of the supporters of False Dmitry. The servicemen of Dorogobuzh, Viazma and Serpeisk joined with those of Smolensk, and together arrived at Mozhaisk on November 15, where they were also joined by Kolychev, the commander who successfully had cleared Volokolamsk of brigands.

Shuisky took heart. He sent to Bolotnikov to persuade him to desert the pretender, but Bolotnikov's army favored not so much the Pretender as of the opportunity to live at the expense of the realm, and could expect no advantage from any reconciliation with the crown. Bolotnikov was not tempted by the tsar's promise to grant him noble rank, and replied: "I gave my soul to Dmitry, and I will keep my oath. I will be in Moscow, not as a traitor, but as a victor."

The matter had to be decided by force of arms. The young commander Skopin-Shuisky led his regiments to the neighborhood of the Danilov monastery,[48] and on December 1, having awaited the arrival of the levies from Smolensk, approached Kolomenskoe. Bolotnikov met him head on, and they fought by the hamlet of Kotly. The slaves and cossacks fought desperately but Istoma Pashkov, with the gentry and junior boyars, deserted to the side of the tsar. The reason for Pashkov's desertion is said to have been that Bolotnikov refused to defer to him, and that Pashkov refused subordination to a bondsman.

Bolotnikov, having suffered a defeat, regrouped his forces in the fortified encampment of Kolomenskoe. For three days the commanders bombarded the encampment with cannon, but could not destroy it. Finally they used red hot cannon balls and set fire to the encampment. Then Bolotnikov fled towards Serpukhov, called together a council, and asked whether they had enough provisions to feed themselves and the army for a whole year. If they answered yes he would remain with them and await Tsar Dmitry. If not, he would go away. The inhabitants of Serpukhov answered that they did not have enough even to feed themselves for a year, let alone the army. Then Bolotnikov marched further, and set up his headquarters at Kaluga, whose inhabitants declared that they could support his army for a year.

A number of his cossacks encamped in the village of Zaborie, but were compelled to surrender to the tsar's commanders. Shuisky ordered them to be taken to Moscow, to be billetted in the houses, that they should be fed, and that they should be untouched. But those captured in battle were ordered to be drowned. If in this figure those who were captured at Kotly were to be included, they were numerous since the chronicler[49] records that there was not enough room for them in all the Moscow prisons.

Shuisky soon moved over to the offensive. Five commanders moved southwards to besiege the towns loyal to the pretender. The tsar's brother, Prince Ivan Ivanovich Shuisky,[50] besieged Kaluga. Several times he advanced to the assault, but did not achieve anything. The tsar sent to Kaluga his last army under the command of Prince Mstislavsky, the most senior boyar, together with Skopin-Shuisky and Prince Tatev,[51] but

Bolotnikov beat off the approach of these commanders also. The attempts on Venev and Tula were also unsuccessful. But Boyar Ivan Nikitich Romanov[52] and Prince Mezetsky defeated Prince Vasily Rubets-Mosalsky, who had approached Kaluga in order to relieve Bolotnikov. The commander, Prince Mosalsky, was killed, and his soldiers placed themselves on top of powder barrels and blew themselves up. Shuisky also found the news from the east encouraging. There Arzamas was captured, the siege of Nizhny Novgorod was relieved, and Metropolitan Ephraim of Kazan[53] had placed an interdict upon the inhabitants of Sviyazhsk, who had sworn allegiance to Dmitry, but who later conveyed their submission to Shuisky.

So began the year 1607. Despite successes in various places the cause of Shuisky was far from being in a favorable position, since the south held out strongly for the pretender. Material means did not help, so it was decided to resort to spiritual weapons. Even in 1606, being compelled to struggle with the phantom of False Dmitry, Shuisky had considered it necessary to rehabilitate Tsar Boris and his family, who had fallen victim to the pretender. With this aim, he ordered the coffins of the Godunovs to be taken from the Barsonophius monastery. Xenia (Olga) Borisovna[54] accompanied the coffins of her family and, according to custom, loudly bewailed her misfortunes.

DISPENSATION BY PATRIARCHS JOB AND HERMOGEN

At the beginning of the year 1607 another ceremony was devised, designed to create the strongest impression. On February 3 the great sovereign ordered Patriarch Hermogen, together with the senior clergy, to call upon him to consult on affairs of the realm and matters dealing with the land, and resolved to send to Staritsa for former Patriarch Job, that he might come to Moscow and to forgive absolve all Orthodox Christians from their perfidy.[55] Metropolitan Paphnutius of Krutitsa[56] was sent to Staritsa with the summons, and brought Job the letter from Hermogen.

"To our lord and father, our most holy Patriarch Job. Your son and pilgrim, Hermogen, patriarch of Moscow and All Russia, prays to God and bows before you. The noble, faithful, pious and Christ-loving great sovereign, Tsar and Grand Prince Vasily Ivanovich, autocrat of All Russia, has taken counsel with me and all the Holy Synod, with his boyars, lords-in-waiting, gentry, chancellery officials, and with all his crown councillors, with the merchants, tradesmen and all Orthodox Christians of your flock. They have sent to beg your blessing, that you will make the effort and come to the capital city of Moscow, to consult on the affairs of the realm and matters pertaining to the land. Also we heartily pray your holiness, and bend our knees before you, that it may be granted to us to see your fair countenance, and to hear your most sweet voice."

On February 14 Job arrived at Moscow in the tsar's carriage, lined with sables, and he was lodged in the Trinity hospice.[57] On the 16th the two patriarchs, with the archbishops, compiled the following document: "Tsar Ivan Vasilievich ordered his son Fedor Ivanovich to reign over the Russian realm, and his second son, Tsarevich Dmitry Ivanovich, was given the town of Uglich as his appanage, and Tsarevich Dmitry died at Uglich. He was done to death innocently at the hands of those who betrayed him.[58] When Tsar Fedor Ivanovich went to God, we and all the people of all the Muscovite realm kissed the cross to Tsar Boris Fedorovich. During his reign, the fire-breathing Devil, the cunning serpent and poisoner of human spirits sent us the monk Grishka Otrepiev. When Tsar Boris Fedorovich died, all Orthodox Christians kissed the cross to his son, Fedor Borisovich, but because of our sins the renegade monk tempted all the people of God in the name of Tsarevich Dmitry Ivanovich. Orthodox Christians, not knowing the truth of the matter, accepted this brigand as lord of the Russian realm. They consigned Tsaritsa Maria and Tsarevich Fedor to an evil death.[59]

"Then the multitude of the people burst into the cathedral church with arms and cudgels during the chanting of the Divine Service and, not allowing the Liturgy to be completed, went up to the altar and took me, Patriarch Job and, dragging me through the church and the square, heaped many reproaches upon me, and in the tsar's palace they defiled the images of Christ's body, the Virgin and the Archangels, which had been prepared for the Holy Shroud. They impaled them upon their spears and lances, and carried them about the town, forgetting the fear of God.

"Then this enemy, the renegade monk, arrived at Moscow with the Lutherans, Jews, Lithuanians and Romans, and with other unclean races, and, calling himself tsar, reigned for almost a year. What evil diabolical injuries he inflicted, and what violence he saw fit to offer, it is not befitting to write. He defiled the Christian churches with Lutherans and Jews and, not being satiated by such diabolical poison, summoned from the Lithuanian land his wife, a daughter of the Lutheran faith.[60] He led her into the cathedral church, crowned her with the crown of tsars, and within the Holy Doors anointed her with the holy oil.

"Seeing his inheritance in such ruin, God sent to it an avenger, our great sovereign, the truly holy and just Tsar Vasily Ivanovich. By his deeds the enemy was finally crushed, and Vasily Ivanovich was chosen sovereign over the Russian realm, because he was from the stem of previous sovereigns, from the pious Grand Prince Alexander Yaroslavich Nevsky. Our holy faith has returned to its former fair tranquility, and has begun to shine as a sun in the heavenly firmament. The holy churches have been cleansed from defilement, and all we Orthodox Christians, as though awakening from sleep, instead of turbulence have received healing and wisdom.

"But Satan in his arrogance has sown the tares of evil, seeking to stifle the nourishing grain. In the pre-ruin Severian Ukraine there have gathered together Severians and others from the towns of Riazan and the Ukraine, musketeers and cossacks, robbers, brigands and fugitive slaves. They have tempted the Severian Ukraine, which once before was darkened by madness, and from that same Ukraine many other towns also have been tempted, spilling the blood of Orthodox Christians like water. They say that the dead malefactor and renegade monk is alive, even though his death is truly known to us and to all Orthodox Christians.

"So now I, the humble Hermogen, patriarch, and I, humble Job, former patriarch, and all the Holy Synod, do pray with grieving hearts to our Most Merciful God to have mercy upon us all. Also our humble and noble princes, boyars, lords-in-waiting, gentry, officials, crown secretaries, servicemen, merchants, traders and all Orthodox Christians pray to Thee. Let us strive with our good works, our fasting and prayers, and with purity of heart and body and other spiritual good works; let us pray together with all our devotion to God and the Immaculate Virgin, all the miracle-workers of Moscow—Peter, Alexis, Jonas and the newly-appeared martyr for Christ, Tsarevich Dmitry—and all the saints, that by their prayers God may grant all of us peace, love and joy, and that the Russian realm may be delivered from all this needless division to its former harmony and peaceable unity.

"And since you kissed the cross to Tsar Boris and then to Tsarevich Fedor, and then betrayed your oath, I, Hermogen, and I, humble Job, by the grace of God given to us, pardon and absolve you from all former and present oaths. And you, for God's sake, also will forgive us in our exhortation to you, if we have shown any malice towards any of you."

On February 19, by the sovereign's decree, Patriarch Hermogen sent out an order to Land Chancelleries[61] to send out missives. They were to send to all the hundreds,[62] to the elders and hundredmen, that from the hundreds and all urban settlements master craftsmen and all persons of the male gender should be in the Dormition church on the next day, February 20. When, on the appointed day, all the multitude was gathered together in the cathedral, and some who could not find room were standing outside the church, Patriarch Hermogen recited a litany, after which the merchants, traders and the commons began to beg pardon from Patriarch Job with great sighing and inconsolable tears.

"O most gracious pastor, forgive us, your disciples and sheep of your former flock. You always wished that we should graze in the sweet pastures of your words of wisdom, and should drink of the sweet springs of your learned, divine teaching. You firmly protected us against the temptations of the crafty serpent and ravenous wolf. But we, the accursed, fled from you, our most holy pastor, and lost our way in the maze of sin, giving ourselves for food to the evil and cruel beast, who is ever ready to destroy our souls. Deliver us, O God-given judge. Give us your blessing, and deliver us from these constricting bonds."

After this speech, the merchants and traders handed Job a petition, written in these pretentious terms: "The Christian people turned away from your salutary teaching, and turned toward the tempting wiles of the crafty viper. But God, by your prayers, most gloriously has liberated us from the hands of the malevolent wolf. In place of dishonor, He has given us piety. Instead of crafty temptation, He has given us His beauteous truth, and instead of a beast of prey, a kind benefactor, the sovereign Tsar Vasily Ivanovich. The clan which from its roots has put forth so fair a flower such as you, sovereign and father, you yourself well know, as it is written in the genealogical records. But you should know that from that day until this we have sat in darkness, and nothing to our advantage could be expected. We have understood that in everything we have sinned before God; we have not heeded you, our father, and we have broken our oaths. And now I, Lord Tsar and Grand Prince Vasily Ivanovich, pray to you concerning the sins of the whole world, the breaking of the oath, and beg forgiveness and absolution."[63]

When they handed this petition to him, Hermogen ordered the archdeacon of the church of the Dormition to ascend the pulpit and read it aloud, and after that the patriarch ordered the same archdeacon to read the act of absolution. The people rejoiced, falling at the feet of Patriarch Job, saying: "We are guilty in all things, honorable Father. Forgive,

forgive us, and give us your blessing, and we will receive this great joy into our hearts."

As the affair is described in the official account, the same spirit is here evident as that which influenced the composition of documents concerning the election of Tsar Boris. Many of those present in the Assembly naturally might consider it strange how this same Vasily Ivanovich Shuisky had testified solemnly that Tsarevich Dmitry had killed himself in an epileptic fit, and this same Patriarch Job had declared that his testimony had been true, and now both were saying that Tsarevich Dmitry had been killed by those who had betrayed him! It is interesting that in this which affair of the solemn absolution, only the merchants and traders were active; they begged for forgivenness by word of mouth, and they handed over the petition.

But if, as the account says, the people rejoiced that they had received absolution from the patriarch, this joy was short lived. Several days later the rumor spread through the city that the sentry who had been posted at night at the entrance to the Archangel cathedral had heard voices, conversations and laughter within the church, and then weeping. The church became illuminated, and one powerful voice had drowned out all the others, incessantly asking to be left in peace.[64]

Even as he wished to act in order to quieten the people, to raise their morale by spiritual and religious means, Shuisky wished at the same time to curtail opposition by other methods. He accepted the proposal of the German, Fiedler, to poison Bolotnikov at Kaluga. Fiedler swore this oath: "In the name of the Most Holy and Most Glorious Trinity, I give my oath that I will destroy Ivan Bolotnikov by poison. If I betray my sovereign, then may the Lord deprive me forever of participation in celestial bliss. May Jesus Christ renounce me for ever, and may the blessing of the Holy Ghost not strengthen my soul, and may all the angels abandon me, and may the Devil have power over my body and soul. I will hold to my word and by this poison I will destroy Ivan Bolotnikov, relying on the aid of God and of the Holy Gospel." The tsar gave Fiedler a horse and a hundred rubles, promising that in the event of a successful conclusion to the undertaking he would receive a hundred peasant souls and three hundred rubles annual salary. But Fiedler, when he came to Kaluga, revealed everything to Bolotnikov, and even handed the poison over to him.[65]

BOLOTNIKOV AND PRETENDER PETER IN TULA

The position of Bolotnikov and his companions was very awkward. The long absence of the proclaimed Dmitry sapped the spirit out of his supporters and well-wishers. Shakhovskoy insistently begged Molchanov to appear at Putivl under the name of Dmitry, but Molchanov refused. In this extremity Shakhovskoy summoned Peter, the cossack pretender who, learning of the fall of the first False Dmitry, had returned to the steppe.

Tsarevich Peter answered the call. Having tortured several governors who still remained loyal to Shuisky, also having dishonored the daughter of Prince Bakhterianov, whom he had killed, and receiving reinforcements from the Zaporozhian Cossacks,[66] he advanced on Tula, together with Shakhovskoy. Hearing of this movement, and the arrival of reinforcements from one of the detachments sent by the pretender, Teliatevsky advanced from Tula to Kaluga to help Bolotnikov, and on the Pchelna he routed a royal force which had been sent against him by Mstislavsky from outside Kaluga. News of this encounter caused alarm in Mstislavsky's army, which quickly retreated from Kaluga, while fifteen thousand men deserted to the side of Bolotnikov. The latter, taking advantage of this, left Kaluga and joined False Peter in Tula, in order from there to act with united forces.

VICTORY OF THE TSAR'S FORCES

Then Shuisky took decisive measures. Stern orders were sent to gather servicemen from everywhere, monastic and ecclesiastical estates also were to provide armed men, and in this manner were gathered up to a hundred thousand, whom the tsar decided to lead in person. On May 21, 1607 Shuisky engaged upon the great affair of the realm and of the land (as it is expressed in the patriarch's letters) and called for prayers for the success of the campaign. Soon other letters were received from the patriarch in which he now called for prayers of thanksgiving for the victory of the tsarist forces over the rebels at the Vosma river. All day there was bitter fighting, the tsar's regiments were wavering, when the commanders, Prince Andrei Golitsyn and Prince Boris Lykov, going around the regiments, said with tears to the soldiers: "Whither shall we flee? Better to die here, at one mind with each other." The soldiers answered: "You set the example, and we shall die for you!"

The tsar's army gained the victory. Prince Teliatevsky, the leader of False Dmitry's forces, fled with a few people. But, according to other accounts, Prince Teliatevsky, during the battle, deserted with four thousand men to the side of Shuisky, and thereby won the day for the latter.

SHUISKY BESIEGES TULA

Shuisky wished to take advantage of the victory and end the entire episode. He personally besieged Tula, where Shakhovksoy (Teliatevsky),[67] Bolotnikov and False Peter were sheltered. The besieged twice sent a messenger to Poland, to the friends of the Mniszechs, immediately to try and send some False Dmitry or other. In desperation they wrote to them: "From the borderlands to Moscow all the territory is ours. Come and possess it; only deliver us from Shuisky!"

APPEARANCE OF THE SECOND PRETENDER

Finally the pretender was dispatched. What sort of man he was, nobody could say for sure. Various rumors were current. Some said that he was the son of a priest, Matvei Verevkin, whose family was from the Severian land. Others said that he was a priest's son, Dmitry, from Moscow, from the church of the Sign on the Arbat, which Prince Vasily Mosalsky had built. Others spread the rumor that he was a son of Prince Kurbsky,[68] others that he was a secretary of the tsar, others that he was a schoolmaster by the name of Ivan from the town of Sokol, others said that he was a Jew, others that he was a serviceman from Starodub.

More detailed than other sources is a Belorussian chronicle[69] which speaks of him thus: "In the same year 1607, in the month of May, on the seventh day, there came from Shklov,[70] from Mogilev to Popova Gora, a certain Dmitry Ivanovich, who claimed to be the Muscovite tsar. This man Dmitry Nagy was at first in the household of the parish priest of Shklov, in the capacity of a teacher of grammar to the children. He ran the school, and also taught the children in the household of the priest Fedor Sezonovich Nikolsky, in the village, and this same Dmitry Nagy lodged at Mogilev with Tereshka, who was sacristan of the church of St. Nicholas, and he visited Tereshek on many occasions, dropping in to see everybody and doing odd jobs for them. He had upon him a worn sheepskin, and he went about dressed in this, even in summer."

The only thing which seems certain is that this second False Dmitry in no way resembled the first in appearance, and that he was a literate man, who was well versed in sacred writings.[71] This last circumstance also leads us to guess that he was from the clergy, since the chronicle says: "All the brigands who called themselves by the name of the tsar were known to many of the people from whom they were sprung. But this brigand, who called himself by the name of the unfrocked monk, was not known to anyone. It was not known whence he came. Many guessed that he was not from the servicemen. They thought that he was either a priest's son, or an ecclesiastical subdeacon, because he knew all the ecclesiastical cycle."

As far as his moral character is concerned, the sort of man he was, one who consciously assumed the role of a pretender, may be surmised. Therefore we have no right to dismiss as exaggerated those accounts of foreign origin, which are therefore impartial, which call him a godless, crude, cruel, perfidious, degenerate man, guilty of all manner of crimes, unworthy to bear the name even of a false sovereign. It merely must be pointed out that it is evident from his actions that he was a man who knew how to fit in with his position and take advantage of circumstances.

The man known in our history under the name of the brigand of Tushino, or simply as the brigand (brigand by preference), appears first in the little Belorussian settlement of Propoisk, where he was arrested as a spy, and was thrown into prison. There he identified himself as Andrei Andreevich Nagoy, a relative of the Tsar Dmitry who had been killed in Moscow. He was hiding from Shuisky, and begged to be sent to Starodub. Ragoza, elder of Chechersk, with the assent of his lord, Zenovich, the prefect of Chechersk, sent him to Popova Gora, whence he reached Starodub.

Having spent some time at Starodub, the alleged Nagoy sent his companion, known as the Muscovite clerk Rukin, around the towns of Severia to announce that Tsar Dmitry was alive, and was to be found at Starodub. At Putivl the inhabitants heeded Rukin's words, and sent several junior boyars with him to Starodub so that he might show them Tsar Dmitry, and then threatened him with torture if he was lying. Rukin referred to Nagoy. This, for a start, indicates that he knew nothing about Tsar Dmitry, but when the inhabitants of Starodub threatened him with torture, and were on the point of arresting him, he seized his staff, crying out: "Ah, you are still children, you still do not recognize me! I am your sovereign." The inhabitants of Starodub fell at his feet, and cried out: "We are guilty, sovereign, before you."

The inhabitants of Starodub gave their sovereign money and sent around to the other towns letters calling upon them to dispatch their soldiers to help the tsar. As in other towns, so also in Starodub the inhabitants now obeyed one man, a certain Gavrilo Verevkin, who succeeded in harnessing the people's will. There was to be found among the inhabitants of Starodub a junior boyar who decided to go to the siege of Tula into the tsar's encampment and ask Tsar Vasily himself why he sought to take the tsardom away from the rightful sovereign. The martyr of deceit died heroically, having been grilled upon a slow fire, repeating the same words, that Shuisky was seeking to deprive the rightful sovereign.

This "rightful sovereign" in the meantime was sending documents requesting help around the Lithuanian border towns. "Once before," he wrote, "I took Moscow with the help of the Lithuanians; now I hope to go to Moscow with the same people." On the same matter the lord lieutenant and governor of Roslavl, Prince Dmitry Mosalsky, wrote to Pats, prefect of Mstislavsk "In order that you might serve rightly our lawful sovereigns, Dmitry and Peter, you should send servicemen against the traitors to the crown, and there they will be much rewarded. If the lord tsar and the lord tsarevich come to their ancestral throne, they will reward you, all his servicemen, with great generosity, more than you can imagine."

THE TSAR CAPTURES TULA

Around the pretender there gathered a retinue, over which he placed as commander the Pole, Mikolaj Miechowicki.[72] At the end of October Lord Budzilo, standardbearer of Mozyr,[73] came to him from Lithuania. But with the lack of numbers in his retinue False Dmitry could not proceed to the relief of Tula, and its fate was sealed.

The Murom junior boyar Krovkov, or Kravkov, proposed to the tsar that they flood Tula by damming the Upa river. At first the tsar and the boyars laughed at this proposal, but then they let Krovkov have his way. He ordered each of the military men to bring a basketful of earth, and they began to dam the river. The water surrounded the town, flowed within it, cut off the inhabitants' communications with the surrounding district and caused famine, while Bolotnikov and False Peter, it is said, entered into negotiations with the tsar, promising to give up the town if Vasily would promise them pardon. If not, they threatened that they would sooner devour each other than willingly submit to execution. Shuisky, who already had the second False Dmitry on his heels, naturally wished to deliver himself from False Peter and Bolotnikov as soon as possible, and therefore he promised pardon.

On October 10 Tula surrendered. Bolotnikov came into the tsar's encampment, approached Vasily, fell to his knees before him, and, placing his sword upon his shoulder, said: "I have fulfilled my promise, I have truly served him who called himself Dmitry in Poland. Whether truly or not, I do not know, since I had never seen the tsar before. I have not broken my oath, but he has betrayed me. Now I am in your power. If you wish to have my head, then order it to be cut off with this sword. But if you grant me life, I will serve you as truly as him who did not support me."[74]

In the fearful Time of Troubles and universal wavering a man such as Bolotnikov, who had no way of finding out the truth of events, at the same time could think that he had fulfilled his duty if he had served truly to the last extremity him whom he had once served. But not everyone thought the same way as Bolotnikov. Others, not knowing who was the lawful tsar, Shuisky or the so-called Dmitry, thought themselves justified in leaving one of them the moment the fortunes of war turned against him. Others, considering both Shuisky and False Dmitry equally unlawful, consequently placed both rivals on the same level of illegitimacy, and considered their relations with both equally, thinking themselves justified in going from one to the other. There were many in both categories.

Bolotnikov was sent to Kargopol, and there he was drowned. Shakhovskoy, the "organizer of all the bloodshed," according to the expression of the chronicler,[75] was sent to the Kubensk island, in the wilderness. False Peter was hanged. Concerning the fate of Teliatevsky, little is known.[76]

Shuisky returned to Moscow in triumph, as though he had conquered a kingdom. Properly speaking, Shuisky's campaign was more important than the conquest of many kingdoms, because the defeat of Bolotnikov's bands was the defeat of an anti-social principle. But the victory was not complete, so the celebration was inappropriate. Shuisky should not have returned to Moscow. He should have followed up his success, moved against the pretender, and by destroying him establish himself upon the throne. But we must take into account the current state of the army, which did not allow him to remain for a long time in the field, and especially at this particular time of year, in the depths of autumn. The landowners had to disperse to their homes by the "winter road."[77] It seemed that there was no hurry.

FALSE DMITRY II'S FORCES

The pretender was at first in a very awkward predicament. Having recruited one to three thousand troops, False Dmitry had come to the outskirts of Kozelsk, and there, suddenly attacking, defeated a detachment of the tsar's forces. But when, from there, they returned to Karachev, the Lithuanians wanted to go off in search of the plunder taken outside Kozelsk, and mutinied. The pretender was alarmed, and withdrew from them with a small detachment of people on whom he especially relied, and set up his headquarters in Orel. But even there he took fright, especially after an attempt to kill him one night. Miechowicki did not know at first where the tsar had hidden and then, when he heard that he was at Orel, he sent to him, asking him to return, because only his presence could hold the army together.

False Dmitry returned, but seeing that the army did not cease to agitate, once again took the road to Putivl by stealth. There he met Walawski, who had come to him from the Kievan Ukraine from Prince Roman Rozynski,[78] with one thousand men. Then he met Tyszkiewicz[79] with one thousand Poles, Prince Adam Wisniowiecki,[80] the famous Lisowski,[81] and others. Following Lisowski's advice, False Dmitry proceeded to the siege of Briansk, to the help of which the commanders Prince Kurakin and Litvin Mosalsky hastened. The latter arrived on December 15 at the Desna, which separated him from the town. Despite the lateness of the season the river had not yet frozen over, and ice was floating along it in large floes. The inhabitants of Briansk, seeing that the soldiers were being held up behind the ice, cried out to them: "Help us! We are perishing." The soldiers, hearing this, said: "It is better that we all die than see our brothers' utter ruin. If we die on behalf of the Orthodox faith, then we shall receive from Christ the martyr's crown." Bidding each other farewell, they jumped into the river, and swam over. Neither ice, nor the fire from the opposite shore where the besiegers stood could hinder them, and they successfully reached the town. Not one man, nor a single horse perished. Following Mosalsky there also came Prince Kurakin. Not thinking that he could disengage from False Dmitry, he retreated, having provided Briansk with provisions, and he set up his headquarters at Karachev. False Dmitry, who did not hope to capture this town, established his winter quarters at Orel.

ROZYNSKI AND ZARUTSKY

When news of the appearance of the pretender spread through Poland all those who hoped to live at the expense of Moscow began to gather from all sides under the banner of Dmitry, which had been raised by Prince Rozynski. When almost four thousand troops had assembled, Rozynski opened his campaign, and halted at Kromy. From there he sent his emissaries to False Dmitry at Orel, to declare to him concerning his arrival, to propose conditions of service, and also to demand money. The pretender met the emissaries ungraciously. To their proposals he replied in the Muscovite idiom: "I was glad when I heard that Rozynski was coming to me, but I was given to understand that he wishes to betray me. Let him deal more favorably with me. God placed me in my capital once before without the help of Rozynski, and now He is placing me there again. You are already demanding money, but I have here with me many Poles who are no worse than you, yet I have not given them anything. I fled from Moscow, from my dear wife, from my dear friends, and could not get hold of anything. When you held your meeting outside Novgorod, did you try to ascertain whether Tsar Dmitry was genuine or not?"

The emissaries answered him with passion: "We now see that you are not the true Tsar Dmitry, because he knew the true worth of cavalrymen, and received them into his service, but you do not know how to do so. We shall tell our brothers who sent us of your ungraciousness, and they will know what to do."

With these words the emissaries went away. False Dmitry then sent to ask them to dine, begging them not to be angry at his words. It happened that the pretender met them rudely at the behest of Miechowicki, who anticipated that he would have to yield his power to Rozynski. When the emissaries returned to Kromy, and told their comrades of the reception the tsar had given them, the Poles then decided to go home. But those Poles who were in Orel with False Dmitry detained them, letting them know that everything would proceed otherwise when Prince Rozynski himself came.

Rozynski arrived in Orel with a detachment of his army, and spent the night in the town. The next day he received an invitation to an audience with the tsar, but when he made ready and set off, a herald came and turned him back. The tsar was still in his bath. The pretender took a bath every day, saying that he relaxed from his labors there. But Rozynski did not turn back and entered the house where False Dmitry was lodged. There ensued a quarrel between his companions and the household servants. The latter demanded that the Poles leave the hut, allow the tsar time to come and sit in his place, and when he was ready the Poles might come when invited to do so. But Rozynski did not agree to this either, so the pretender made his way between the Poles. On his way out he turned his face away from the side where Rozynski stood; when he was seated upon his throne the prince approached him, began his speech, and kissed his hand. After this there was a dinner. Rozynski sat with the tsar at one table, the rest of the Poles at another.

At dinner and after the meal there were many and varied discussions. The pretender asked about the serious uprising, the *rokosz* (rebellion) then going on against the king in Poland,[82] and among other things said that he would not like to be king in Poland. A Muscovite monarch was not born to be ruled by some archbishop or other. The next day Rozynski demanded that he be allowed to speak alone with the tsar. This dragged on from one day to the next. Rozynski was angry was making ready to leave when suddenly there came to him captains and simple Poles who had been with False Dmitry. They begged him and his companions to wait until the next day. "We have taken counsel together, and have decided that if the tsar will not change his mind we will side with you. We will overthrow Miechowicki and will proclaim you, Prince Rozynski, as hetman." Rozynski left the town for the suburb, and there he resolved to wait until the morrow.

On the next day, in fact, the Poles gathered together in council on horseback. They invited Rozynski and his companions. There they pronounced that Miechowicki was deprived of his hetmanship, and was cashiered from the army, together with several others, and if they dared stay with the army, everyone would be free to kill them. They acclaimed Rozynski as hetman and sent an embassy to the tsar, that he might name those who had accused Rozynski of treason in his presence. The latter refused to say anything about this through the emissaries, but promised that he would attend the council personally, and in fact he arrived upon a richly caparisoned horse, in garments of cloth of gold, accompanied by several boyars and some infantry.

Entering the council and hearing the noise, False Dmitry cried out with unbecoming abuse. When everything had quieted one of the members repeated in the name of the council of war the request to name those who had called Rozynski a traitor. At first the pretender ordered one of his Russians to reply, but he did not reply properly, and the pretender said: "Be quiet, you do not know how to speak concerning this matter. I shall speak for myself."

Then he began: "You sent to me to hand over to you my faithful servants, who have protected me from harm. Such a request was never made of any Muscovite sovereign, that they should abandon their faithful servants, nor shall I do this, neither for you, nor even if God should come from the heavens and order me to do so."

They answered him: "What do you want? Do you want to remain only with those who serve you merely by whispering in corners, or with an army which has arrived in good order, and will serve you with the sword?"

"Do whatever you want, only go away!" answered the pretender. Then there arose a fearful clamor. They cried out: "Kill the scoundrel! Cut him down!" Others shouted: "Let us seize him, the rogue! He brought us here, now how are we going to feed ourselves?" The pretender was not intimidated, but calmly entered the town and went to his lodging where Rozynski's Poles placed a guard upon him so that he could not take flight. Thereupon he was reduced to despair and, still sober, drank a great quantity of spirits, thinking thereby to kill himself. Despite this, he remained alive. Meanwhile, throughout the rest of the day and all through the night his attendants, Walawski his chancellor, Czarlinski his marshal, Prince Adam Wisniowiecki and his groom, scampered between him and the army, trying to bring about a truce. Finally they were reconciled. The pretender once again attended the council, apologized, and Rozynski quietly proceeded to his encampment near Kromy. At that time other allies came to False Dmitry. Three thousand Zaporozhian Cossacks came as well as five thousand Don Cossacks under the command of Zarutsky.[83]

This Zarutsky came from a Tarnopol family. While still a child he had been taken prisoner by the Tatars. When he grew up he joined the Don Cossacks, distinguished himself among them, and now came to serve False Dmitry as an officer. He was in fact famous among his comrades for his good looks, his slimness and his bravery. The Don Cossacks brought to False Dmitry, in place of False Peter who had been executed at Moscow, another relative, also a son of Tsar Fedor. The "uncle" ordered him executed.

NEW PRETENDERS

The cossacks were very fond of pretenders. In Astrakhan there appeared a certain Tsarevich Augustus, and then a Prince Ivan, who was said to be a son of Ivan the Terrible by Princess Koltovskaia.[84] There also appeared in Astrakhan a third tsarevich, Lavrenty, said to have been a grandson of Ivan the Terrible, from Tsarevich Ivan. In the steppe yurts[85] there appeared tsareviches by the names of Fedor, Klimenty, Savely, Simeon, Vasily, Yeroshka, Gavrilka and Martynka, all sons of Tsar Fedor Ivanovich. Throughout the south appeared clear signs suggesting that the grievous sickness of the body politic would long endure. Moscow continued to be shaken by fearful rumors.

UNREST IN MOSCOW

At the very moment of the capture of Tula, even before the tsar had returned to the capital, Moscow was terrified by a vision. Some holy man in his sleep had seen Christ appearing in the Dormition church, threatening fearful punishment against the Muscovite people, this New Israel, which was mocking Him with its treacherous deeds, its luxurious ways and its profane language. Muscovy had accepted corrupt customs, had shaved beards, committed sodomy and rendered unjust judgements. Muscovites did violence to the just, plundered other people's possessions, and truth lacked in the tsar and patriarch, and among the clergy and the populace in general.

The man witnessing this vision related it to Archpriest Terenty of the Annunciation church, who scribed word for word, and gave a copy to the patriarch. It was given to the tsar, but the name of the man receiving this vision was kept secret for Terenty had sworn in the name of God not to reveal his identity. This vision was read to the people in the Dormition church and a fast was proclaimed, from October 14 to October 19.[86]

Despite these evil prophesies Shuisky hastened to take advantage of the peaceful winter season and on January 17, 1608, he celebrated his marriage to Princess Maria Petrovna Buinosova-Rostovskaia, to whom he had become engaged during the reign of Dmitry.[87]

FALSE DMITRY HASTENS TOWARDS MOSCOW

In the spring of 1608 the pretender and Hetman Rozynski moved towards Bolkhov, and there, in a two-day battle on May 10-11, routed the tsar's army, which was under the command of Prince Dmitry Shuisky and Prince Vasily Golitsyn, who was the first to be thrown into confusion and turn his back on the enemy. Bolkhov surrendered to the victors who, confident that soon they would place their tsar upon the Muscovite throne, summoned an assembly and demanded from the pretender a promise that the moment he was in Moscow he would pay their salary in full, and send them home without delay. False Dmitry gave his word that he would pay their salary, but implored them not to leave him. "Without you," he said, "I cannot be lord in Moscow. I would like the Poles always to be with me, so that a Pole holds one town and a Muscovite another. I wish that all gold and silver be yours, and I would be content with the glory alone. But if you really want to go home immediately, do not leave me in this state. Wait until I can summon others from Poland to take your places."

Fugitives from the battle at Bolkhov, whether truly defeated by fear or in self-justification, spread the rumor in Moscow that the pretender had innumerable forces, that they had fought only with the vanguard of the Poles whereas the rearguard was as far distant as Putivl. Wishing to take advantage of victory and the fear instilled into the adherents of Shuisky, the pretender hurried towards Moscow, covering seven or eight miles a day. But five thousand soldiers who had surrendered at Bolkhov, and who had sworn allegiance to Dmitry, now betrayed him. They were the first to cross the Ugra and under cover of night they distanced themselves from the Poles and, fleeing to Moscow, declared to the tsar and the people that there was nothing to fear for the pretender had very few troops.

But the pretender hastened to increase his army. To swell the number of his supporters he ordered declared in all towns that the peasants whose lords served Shuisky take the estates and patrimonies for themselves, and marry their lords' daughters. In this manner, says one contemporary, many servants made themselves masters whilst their lords in Moscow were made to suffer hunger in remaining with Shuisky.

The pretender proceeded to Moscow by way of Kozelsk, Kaluga, Mozhaisk and Zvenigorod, nowhere encountering any resistance. On the other hand in Zvenigorod he encountered Peter Borskowski, who had been sent from Moscow by the royal Polish ambassadors. The ambassadors ordered the Poles accompanying Dmitry to quit Muscovite territory and not break the peace which they, the ambassadors, were attempting to conclude between Muscovy and the Polish crown.

PEACE WITH POLAND

We left Marina, her father Mniszech and his companions, and the Polish ambassadors in the fearful moment of False Dmitry's destruction. We saw that Shuisky immediately took measures to safeguard the lives of prominent Poles. Marina was sent to her father, to whom questions were addressed concerning the appearance of the pretender in Poland, and of his dealings with him, the governor.[88] Concerning the appearance of the pretender in Moscow, Mniszech answered what was well known to everybody. Concerning his own connections with him, he said that he had recognized him as the true Tsarevich Dmitry. He had accompanied him and helped him because the entire Muscovite realm had recognized him as such. All the Russian people had greeted him and had assisted him in his bid for the throne.

After this interrogation the common Polish soldiers who still remained alive were permitted to leave the country, taking with them only their arms and horses. But the prominent Poles, as well as the king's ambassadors, remained in Moscow as important hostages, to serve as bargaining counters to extort peace from Poland, since this peace was very badly needed. The ambassadors Olesnicki and Gasiewski[89] were summoned to the palace where the boyars, in a long speech, attempted to make excuses for the murder of the Poles, shifting all blame upon them. Gasiewski, as Mniszech before him, could easily counter this accusation. He showed that the king at no time had thought of taking up arms on Dmitry's behalf, but had left everything to the will of God. If the border towns had not recognized Dmitry as the son of Ivan IV, the Poles would never have thought of accompanying him further. So when Dmitry first encountered resistance at Novgorod Seversk, and when at the same time Boris wrote to the king concerning the imposture of Otrepiev, reminding him of the peace treaty recently concluded between Moscow and Poland, immediately the king had recalled all the Poles from Dmitry.

At the time of Tsar Boris's death the king had expected that the Muscovites, taking advantage of their freedom, would provide him by their decisions a reliable proof of the truth; thus the army and all the best commanders had submitted to Dmitry. The boyars who had remained in Moscow, Mstislavsky and Shuisky, came out to meet him thirty miles from the capital. These Muscovite ambassadors and boyars incessantly asserted that it was not the Poles who had seated Dmitry upon the throne, for the Russians themselves had accepted him willingly, and thereafter no one said to the Poles that Dmitry was not the true tsarevich.

Gasiewski concluded his speech thus: "Now, having killed Dmitry, suddenly, despite your words and oaths, you contradict yourselves, and unjustly accuse the king. The responsibility remains entirely yours. We will not argue about the slaying of Dmitry, because we have no regrets for him. You yourselves saw how he received me, how he made outrageous demands of me, how he insulted the king. In that connection we cannot fail to be surprised how you, the boyars and members of the council, whom we suppose to be intelligent men, allow yourselves such contradictions, and vainly accuse the king, not taking into account that the man who called himself Dmitry was a native-born Muscovite, and it was not our people who vouched for him, but your own Muscovites, who met him on the frontier with bread and salt.[90] Moscow surrendered towns, Moscow led him to the capital, swore allegiance to him, became subject to him and crowned him. In one word, Moscow began and ended this affair, and you are laying unjustly the responsibility for this on others.

"We merely complain that so many of the king's eminent subjects were slain, who had no quarrel with you concerning this man, were not protecting his life, did not know about the assassination, and were remaining peacefully within their lodgings, under the protection of treaties."

Gasiewski advised the boyars, for their own good and in the interest of peace, to release Mniszech and the other Poles with him, as well as the ambassadors, and let them go home to their own country, promising in that case to strive for the prolongation of the peace. Gasiewski's words troubled the boyars. They were silent, they glanced at each other, but among them there was Lord-in-waiting Tatishchev,[91] who rose to answer Gasiewski. Repeating the previous accusations, Tatishchev added that Poland was now in the most perilous position, threatened by the Tatars, Swedes and turbulent Diet (sejm).[92] Tatishchev was speaking the truth because in fact at that time, as a consequence of a fearful uprising there had arisen some doubt as to whether Sigismund would remain upon the Polish throne. Gasiewski stated that everything Tatishchev had said was pure fabrication, that the enemy never had penetrated so deeply into Polish territory as they, the Poles, had penetrated into Muscovite territory, and that the Russians were in no position to intimidate the Poles. Finally, the boyars agreed that in the matter of False Dmitry, nobody was to blame. "All this came about on account of our sins. This brigand deceived both you and us."

After that the ambassadors thought they would soon be dispatched back to Poland, but they were deceived in this hope. In vain Gasiewski wrote to the boyars that they request the tsar to release them immediately, otherwise the king and the Commonwealth would assume that the ambassadors had been murdered, and accordingly would open hostilities. In vain he threatened that were the tsar to send his own ambassadors to Poland without them, they would not be held responsible for their safety, for the brothers of the Poles killed in Moscow would take their revenge. The same Tatishchev came with the response to these representations. He repeated his earlier speeches and showed, as a new accusation, the rescript of the pretender to Marina and the letter of the king in which he boasted that through his Poles he had placed Dmitry upon the throne. He also brought up the letters of the papal legate and Cardinal Malagrida concerning the introduction of Latinism into Muscovy. In addition Tatishchev declared that, after discovering such designs, the ambassadors and other Poles could not be permitted to depart until such time as the Muscovite ambassadors returned from Poland with satisfactory explanations.

Gasiewski directly answered the first charge concerning the rescript to Marina, saying that the governor, convinced by the testimony of the entire Muscovite realm, had decided to give his daughter to Dmitry. In agreeing to this marriage he naturally wished to secure the most favorable prospects for his daughter; therefore it was certainly no surprise that he demanded from the tsarevich such terms, the fulfilment of which, however, depended upon the Muscovites. When the governor had visited Moscow the late tsar had taken counsel with the boyars as to Marina's provision in the event of her widowhood. The boyars themselves had given her more than Novgorod and Pskov, since they had agreed to recognize her as the hereditary sovereign lady, and even before the coronation they had sworn to be faithful to her.

But it was difficult for Gasiewski to answer the accusation concerning the attempts of the Roman clergy to spread Latinism in Muscovy. In an unskillful and confused manner the ambassador alluded to the right of Poles and Lithuanians serving in Russia to buy possessions therein, to maintain their own churches, and to have services celebrated in them according to their own rites. This right was not referred to in the letters of the Roman clergy.

It was much easier to give a rebuttal to the accusation concerning the king's letter. "You yourselves," said Gasiewski, "through your ambassadors, ascribe this honor to the king, and you sanctioned it." Finally, it was announced categorically to the ambassadors summoned to the palace that the tsar would not dismiss them until the return of his own ambassadors from Poland. The ambassadors were desperate. Their people spoke unkind words about the new government, and therefore the tsar ordered the ambassadors' rations be halved. Because of this increased harrassment the ambassadors even contemplated fighting their way home, but of course this would not have succeeded. When an undersecretary came to reproach them for this in the name of the crown secretary of foreign affairs, they answered: "We have lived here for a long time. Many of our people have died from the pestilent air, and others lie sick on their beds, and we would rather die than live in such a manner. We will go, and we will fight against anyone who tries to oppose us. What your sovereign is inflicting upon us is very vexatious to us. He has laid his disfavor upon us. He has forbidden food be given us. We are not subjects of your sovereign, but the king's subjects. It is not befitting for your sovereign to place his disfavor upon us and restrain us. We all will die of this ill treatment and, rather than die here of hunger, it would be better for you to kill us."

The official replied: "Truly much Christian blood has been shed on your account, but even now you are embroiling us in blood again. You see yourselves how much it costs the people. Make only one move and you will soon see how the Muscovite people will set upon you on account of your many insults The boyars have cut short your rations because your people say such insulting things that it is dangerous to repeat even a word of them, and also because they beat the junior boyars." The ambassadors were detained in Moscow but Mniszech, his daughter and his relatives were transferred to Yaroslavl.

On June 13, 1606 emissaries were sent to the king—Prince Grigory Volkonsky and Crown Secretary Andrei Ivanov. Volkonsky was given three hundred rubles' allowance, but the tsar ordered it recorded in the Chancellery of Foreign Affairs that this allowance must not be regarded as a precedent since it had been granted Prince Grigory on account of his straitened circumstances. The emissaries were instructed to explain recent events to the Poles. They were to account for the success of the pretender thus: "Some of the Russian people were weakened by fear, others by temptation, and some even knew that they were being tempted falsely, but they were breathing anger against Tsar Boris because he governed severely, and not in the manner of a tsar." If the lords of the council asked in what manner the brigand and renegade monk had been killed, they were to reply: "As the gentry and the servitors reached Moscow from all the towns of the Muscovite realm, then Tsaritsa Martha, our great sovereign Vasily Ivanovich, the boyars, the gentry, all the servitors and the merchants confronted the brigand and renegade monk Grishka Otrepiev with all his evil blasphemous deeds, and he himself said before our great sovereign and before all the multitude of the people that he was truly Grishka Otrepiev, and accomplished all that he had done by devilish dreams, turning away from God, and on account of those evil blasphemous deeds of his the people of the Muscovite realm killed him in righteous judgement." If the lords of the council made reference to the testimony of Afanasy Vlasiev, formerly the ambassador in Poland, Volkonsky was to reply: "How are we to believe Afanasy Vlasiev? Afanasy, a brigand and subverter of the Christian faith, was a counsellor of that brigand. He came to your sovereign King Sigismund at his behest without the consent of the senators (boyars)."

After the emissaries had crossed the frontier the escort told them that Tsar Dmitry was alive, and was at the house of the wife of the governor of Sandomir. The ambassadors replied that it was not befitting to utter such words. Mikhalko Molchanov had fled when they had killed the brigand, and had lived in the brigand's household to practice necromancy. "If Molchanov is calling himself Dmitry, let him be shown to us. He has marks upon his back. When he was interrogated about his brigandage and sorcery he was beaten with the knout, and the scars of these strokes can be seen upon him. If another brigand is similarly calling himself Dmitry, you should not receive him or listen to him. If you are so fond of him, then place him on the throne in your own kingdom. For it is not befitting for your sovereign to send him into the Great Russian realm, and place him upon the throne, even if he were truly the rightful sovereign Tsarevich Dmitry. If we do not want him to be our ruler, it will be impossible to impose him by force upon this realm. For how are we to credit this brigand, who fled from death and calls himself the tsarevich?"

The escort replied: "The Poles and Lithuanians who arrived from Moscow say and have heard from your own people that he was killed and placed upon a fire, but they do not know for sure whether it was he who was killed, or whether someone else was killed in his place." The emissaries asked the escort: "Did they see who this brigand was? Did they see his face? Or his hair?" The escort replied that he was "of short stature, swarthy complexion, nose slightly upturned, large black eyebrows, stooped, small eyes, curly black hair on his head sweeping upwards from his forehead, black moustache and a shaven beard. On his cheek there was a mole with hair. He speaks in Polish. He can read and write in Polish, and knows how to speak Latin."

The emissaries replied to this that Molchanov was such a man, whereas the previous brigand and renegade monk had not been swarthy, and his hair was reddish. Another escort said that during the reign of Dmitry, at Sambor, Prince Mosalsky was friendly with Zabolotsky, and Dmitry had sent Zabolotsky into the Severian land to persuade the inhabitants not to submit to Shuisky, and that he, Dmitry, would come to them as soon as he had gathered his people together.

The people in Lithuania gave the Muscovite emissaries a poor reception. In the towns and on the suburbs, and in the estates of the lords they were treated with dishonor. They were abused with indecent words and called traitors. In Minsk stones and dirt were thrown at their party, and they were challenged to fisticuffs. People approached the emissaries in their lodgings, abused them and threatened to kill them. The emissaries said to the escort that such dishonor and ill use against emissaries were unheard of. The escort replied that in their country people now were lawless. They did not obey the king, neither could they be controlled. In Cracow the king did not invite the emissaries to dine and instead of feeding them sent them no rations. The emissaries submitted to the king a written declaration in which the origins of the pretender were set forth, his deeds, describing how he, with Poles and Lithuanians, arrived in Muscovy; how thereafter he invited to Moscow the governor of Sandomir with his friends, and how they desecrated the churches of God and the holy icons; how the Poles and Lithuanians committed much violence and bloodshed against the Muscovites, dishonored the wives of the magnates, seized them from their carriages, and did such violence as had never before been seen in Moscow. Then in the declaration mention was made concerning the appearance in Poland of a new pretender, who was none other than Mikhailo Molchanov, who in no way resembled the first False Dmitry. The emissaries demanded satisfaction for the bloodshed and plundering of the tsar's treasury, which had been the consequence of sending False Dmitry into Poland.

The lords of the council replied: "Our sovereign is not to blame for anything. You say that Dmitry, who was your sovereign, has been killed, and out of the Severian land there have come many people who seek this Dmitry within our kingdom. They say that he is alive, and that he managed to escape. How is our sovereign able to control your people? Moreover in the Severian land there rules some Peter or other. Surely our sovereign did not set him up there? The people of the Muscovite realm themselves are fighting one another, yet you are blaming us! If your sovereign will set free the governor of Sandomir and his companions, and all the Poles and Lithuanians in Moscow, there will be neither any Dmitry, nor any Petrushka. But if your sovereign will not set them free, then both Dmitry and Peter will become genuine, and our people will aid them for the sake of our compatriots."

The emissaries threatened the lords of the council that if the king gave no satisfaction Tsar Vasily would send Prince Gustav against Livonia.[93] But for Sigismund the Polish *rokosz* was more dangerous than any Gustav, and therefore he wished no war against the new Muscovite tsar and was pleased that the latter was also in no position to wage war, being threatened by Dmitry and Petrushka. The king could have no regrets over the fate of the first False Dmitry, and not only because the "invincible caesar" had not wished to yield anything to Poland. Rumors were spreading that some of the rebels had secret relations with False Dmitry, and that there was a move afoot among them to proclaim him as king of Poland; that Dmitry had promised to send money to some lords, among them Stadnicki, the most bitter adversary of the king.[94] This is why the king promised Volkonsky that in the near future he would send his emissaries to Moscow.

In October 1607 the king's ambassadors, Lord Witwoski and Prince Drutskoj, actually arrived in Moscow to congratulate Tsar Vasily on his accession to the throne, and to demand the release of the previous ambassadors and all other Poles. The negotiations lasted until July 25, 1608, when the ambassadors concluded a truce with the boyars for a period of three years and eleven months, on the following conditions: both realms would retain their former boundaries; Moscow and Poland must not aid each other's enemies; the tsar promised to release and send to Poland the governor of Sandomir and his daughter and son, and all Poles who had been detained; the king promised the same with regard to the Russians who had been detained in Poland; the king and the Commonwealth were to recall all Poles supporting the pretender, and henceforth they would not recognize the Pretender nor would they go to his aid; they would not recognize Jerzy Mniszech as the father-in-law of False Dmitry II, nor would Mniszech give his daughter to him, nor would Marina be called the sovereign lady of Moscow.

The emissaries promised to write to the Poles supporting False Dmitry with orders to abandon the pretender. On their journey home they would return to their country any Polish soldiers they might encounter, and would send through all the border towns declarations that no one in Muscovy might enlist with him. They promised to proceed directly to Poland, avoiding all relations and encounters with the Poles supporting False Dmitry, but they could not promise that the king might withdraw Lisowski from Muscovite territory, for Lisowski had been banished from the Polish realm and his honors stripped from him.

Even before the conclusion of the treaty, when False Dmitry was in Zvenigorod, the emissaries had sent Borskowski to his encampment with the order to Poles to quit Muscovite territory. But Rozynski and his companions answered that they had begun their enterprise; that no longer they would listen to anybody's decree, and that they wished to place him with whom they had come in his capital. Thereafter False Dmitry immediately advanced on Moscow, still without encountering any opposition.

The tsar had sent against him an army under the leadership of Prince Skopin-Shuisky and Ivan Nikitich Romanov, and these commanders were deployed along the Neznan river between Moscow and Kaluga. But a plot was discovered in the army. Princes Ivan Katyrev-Rostovsky,[95] Yury Trubetskoy and Troekurov, together with several others, had resolved to surrender to the pretender. The conspirators were arrested and interrogated. The notable offenders were sent to the provinces, where they were imprisoned. Those of lesser birth were executed, but the tsar now forbade his army to engage the pretender, and ordered it to return to Moscow. There, among the multitudes these words were heard: "If he were not the true Dmitry, the princes and boyars who deserted to him would have returned. This means that he really is the true Dmitry. What if the princes and boyars had routed his Poles, and had chased him away? We knew nothing of this." "He is a soothsayer." said one. "He can tell at a glance who is guilty and who is not." "Woe is me!" replied another, "I can never dare look him in the face. With this very knife I slew five Poles."

FALSE DMITRY AT TUSHINO

On June 1 False Dmitry's army approached the capital and halted on the Moscow river. At first they did not know where best to take up their position. Some said that they should cross to the other side and occupy the major road to the north, along which soldiers and supplies had to come to Moscow. This counsel prevailed, and the army crossed to the village of Taininskoe. But the place they had chosen turned out to be very unsuitable, and several days later there appeared a great danger. Some of the Russians accompanying False Dmitry carried on communications with Moscow. At night they tried to flee to Moscow, but they were apprehended by the sentries and revealed their accomplices. Some of them were impaled, while others were beheaded.

Having been fortunate in escaping this danger, the pretender no longer wished to remain at Taininskoe. He thought that he would cut Moscow off from communication with the north, but meanwhile the tsar's army cut him off from the south, rounding up all the merchants and soldiers coming to him from Poland. That is why they decided to withdraw to their former positions. But Muscovite forces stood athwart the Tver road. False Dmitry, having defeated them, then crossed over to the Volokolamsk road and finally chose a suitable place for his encampment at Tushino, between two rivers, the Moscow and the Skhodna.[96] Lord Domaradzki arrived there from the king's ambassadors in Moscow, bringing Rozynski the order to quit the Muscovite lands, but he returned with the same answer. Rozynski wanted to enter the city of Moscow after a decisive battle.

The tsar's army, amounting to seventy thousand men, stood on the Khodynka river. The tsar himself, with his court and his chosen regiments, stood on the Presnia, ready to move up in support. Suddenly, at night, Rozynski attacked the tsar's army, seized the waggon train, and chased the fugitives as far as the Presnia but there, strengthened by the tsar's regiments, the fugitives made a stand and in turn pursued the Poles. They in turn took their stand behind the Khimka river, where once again they struck against the Russians. They pursued them across the Khodynka, and returned to their encampment at Tushino, very satisfied with the outcome of the encounter, for some of them had been panic-stricken at the defeat on the Presnia, and had fled into the encampment, ordering their waggons to be loaded, so that they could withdraw closer to the frontier. The Poles were exultant in that they had given the last pursuit, and that the Russians had not pursued them further than the far bank of the Khodynka. All the same, they realized that the battle had cost them dear. Fearing attack, they dug into their encampment, put a stockade around it, and built towers and gates.

WAR AGAINST SHUISKY

In mid-August Rozynski sent to the boyars a document asking for parleys. The boyars replied: "You write to us, the boyars, and to the people of the

Muscovite realm, hinting that we, the boyars, nobles and people of all ranks should send to you to speak of a fair matter. But to us you send Polish lords and Polish cavalry. You write to us in a manner which is unbefitting an intelligent people. In the Russian realm placed above us is our sovereign, Tsar and Grand Prince Vasily Ivanovich, and we are of one mind and will in holding him, as we have been with our previous great sovereigns. In all matters we are unable to hold discussions or do anything without his consent or his say. We are surprised that you call yourself a man of good family, for are you not ashamed that you, having abandoned your sovereign King Sigismund and your country, calling some unknown brigand Tsar Dmitry, have subjected yourself to him, and wish to spill innocent Christian blood? We give you this answer: that it will be a fair matter when you, Prince Roman Rozynski, with all the Lithuanians, seize this brigand and send him to our sovereign, while you immediately depart our land and go back to your own country. You know very well that our sovereign has made peace with the Lithuanian king, and that once peace reigns he will return the ambassadors with the governor of Sandomir and all his people back to Lithuania."

Meanwhile Lisowski and the cossacks acted on their own. They took Zaraisk, in order to recapture which the governor, Zakhar Liapunov, hastened from Riazan, but he was defeated soundly by Lisowski. Thereupon Lisowski marched on Kolomna, took it by assault and sacked it, but on the road to Moscow he was defeated by Princes Kurakin and Lykov, allowing Kolomna once more to be occupied by Shuisky's forces.

Thus the war raged on with changing fortunes. But for Shuisky the future held no consolation. The pretender had established himself outside Moscow. In violation of the treaty concluded with the king's ambassadors, not one Pole departed the encampment at Tushino. On the contrary, one detachment after another arrived. First of all came Bobrowski with his regiment of hussars; after him Andrzej Mlocki with two regiments, hussar and cossack, and then Aleksandr Zborowski. Wilamowski brought one thousand excellent infantrymen. Finally, around autumn time, there came Jan Sapieha whose name, together with that of Lisowski, was to be such a sinister byword in our history.[97]

Sapieha came in defiance of the letters the king had sent to all the border towns, and to him in particular. Andrzej Sapieha, governor of Mstislavsk, directly admitted to Shein, governor of Smolensk,[98] that the Polish crown was powerless to restrain its subjects from crossing the frontier. "I am

writing to you frankly and honestly that all this is happening against the
will and command of his royal grace. For the sins of the people such
lawlessness has arisen in all the world, that it is difficult to write it all down.
I will not conceal from you also that many people, subjects of the king's
grace, have rebelled against the sovereign himself, and stubbornly have
dared to oppose him. But God's mercy has enabled our sovereign to resist
them, and they, fleeing the king's army, stream on their own to other
countries, against the express command of his royal grace."

In this manner Sigismund's victory over the rebels provided False
Dmitry with new allies. Learning of Sapieha's campaign, Dmitry sent him
a letter in which he begged Sapieha not to plunder in passage inhabitants
who had sworn allegiance to him. The letter concludes with these words:
"When you come before Us, and enter into Our presence, We will reward
you to a greater extent than you can imagine."

MARINA AND HER FATHER AT TUSHINO

But more essential for the pretender than all these reinforcements was the
presence of Marina within his encampment. Learning that, in fulfilment
of the treaty, Mniszech and his daughter had been released from Yaroslavl
in order to proceed to Poland, and were travelling towards the frontier
under the protection of an escort numbering one thousand, the pretender
sent into the border towns which had sworn allegiance to him the following order: "You will intercept the Lithuanian ambassadors and their followers, and not allow them to reach Lithuania, and wherever you man-
age to get hold of them, build a prison for them and place them within
it."

Not content with this command, he also sent Walawski with his
regiment to intercept them. Yet the Poles who had been in Dmitry's service for some time did not, for some reason, want Marina within their encampment, most likely because, being convinced of the imposture of their
tsar, they did not wish to compel Mniszech, and especially his daughter,
to recognize the brigand as being truly the late Dmitry, and they also
feared dire consequences for themselves from such violence. They could
not have been aware that the Mniszechs were willing to sacrifice everything to their ambition. Whatever the case may have been Walawski, according to the testimony of one of his companions, deliberately failed to
catch up with Mniszech. Then the pretender sent Zborowski who, recently
arrived, wished to ingratiate himself with Dmitry. He moved very quickly,

caught up with Mniszech near Belaia, routed the Muscovite detachment escorting them, and turned back Mniszech and his family, together with the ambassador, Olesnicki.

Gasiewski, who was several days' journey ahead of them, crossed the border by another route. But now the complicating factor was that Marina

Marina Mniszech

and her father did not wish to proceed directly to the pretender at Tushino. They did not want to adopt him unconditionally. First they went to Sapieha's quarters in the encampment, and only when they had gone that far did they conduct negotiations with False Dmitry. It is said that Mniszech and the ambassadors previously had agreed that they would be rescued from Tushino, and for that purpose they remained for two days in one place, doubtless inviting pursuit. According to another account Marina, having caught sight of the Tushino brigand, and having realized that there was no resemblance between him and her late husband, under no circumstances wished to acknowledge him. In order to convince her, both time and lengthy negotiations were needed.

These two versions are compatible. Marina could have known ahead of time that the emissaries from Tushino were deceiving them, and she could have been quite agreeable, since she better than anyone alive knew the truth concerning her husband's survival. At the very least she may have wanted to believe that her husband was still alive, but being faced with evidence to the contrary, at first refused to recognize the impersonator as her husband.

It is said that on her approach to Tushino she was exceptionally cheerful, laughing and singing. But as she reached the eighteenth mile from the encampment a young Polish squire approached her carriage, saying to her: "Marina Yurievna! You are happy and singing. You should indeed be happy if you could expect to find your real husband in Tushino, but in reality you will find someone completely different." Marina's face fell on hearing these fearful words, and her singing gave way to sighs.[99] This reluctance on the part of Marina to travel directly to Tushino, and the long negotiations with her husband, were very harmful to False Dmitry, as was recognized by the Poles serving her, and so the subsequent agreement by Marina to recognize him as the same person as the first Dmitry came too late to dispel the first harmful impression created by their hesitancy, even though the pretender urged that this be glossed over. Thus, in one letter to Marina he says that she, after she had reached Zvenigorod, should stay at the local convent at the time of the solemn deposition of the relics. "This action," wrote False Dmitry, "will create greater respect for us in Moscow, since you know that the contrary conduct caused us to be hated by the people, and cost us our throne."

Only when the second pretender had given him a rescript stating that as soon as he occupied Moscow he would give him thirty thousand rubles, and grant him full sovereignty of Severia, with fourteen towns, did Mniszech acknowledge him as his son-in-law. Olesnicki also received a grant of the town of Belaia. On September 5, in Sapieha's encampment, there took place a secret marriage between Marina and the pretender, solemnized by her confessor, a Jesuit, who of course convinced her that all things were permissible to further the cause of the Roman church.

In Rome hopes for the resurrection of Dmitry had not yet been abandoned, as can be seen from the letters of Cardinal Borghese to the papal nuncio in Poland.[100] At first he wrote: "It seems to me impossible that Dmitry could be alive, or could have saved himself by flight from his realm, for in that case he would not have taken so long to appear at Sambor, where he is said to be now." Later he wrote that "If only he were alive it still would be possible to arrange everything. We will send letters, and we will do everything possible to reconcile him with the Polish king." Later it was written: "We now believe that Dmitry is alive, but since he is surrounded by heretics there is no hope that he will persevere in his original intention. The Polish king very wisely thinks that we cannot rely upon him for a second time. His misfortunes should have prompted him to show signs of his good intentions; but friendship with heretics shows that this feeling is not within him."

In the instructions written by Cardinal Borghese to the new nuncio, Simonetta, there are the following words: "Concerning Muscovite affairs, we cannot now say anything because hope of turning this realm towards the Apostolic See has vanished with the death of Dmitry, even though now it is rumored that he is alive. Thus it merely remains for me to say to you that when the reform is introduced into the monastic order of St. Basil[101] among the Greeks it will be possible, in time, to nourish many fair seeds which, by means of their relationship, may communicate the true light to its people."

Despite all this, Rome continued to waver between hope and despair, and continued to intervene in the affairs of the pretender. Thus, at the beginning of the year 1607 Borghese wrote that if Peter Ivanovich were recognized as the lawful successor, Dmitry would have no hope of carrying his cause through to a successful conclusion. In November 1607 hopes were raised. Borghese wrote: "The sons of the governor of Sandomir, who are now in Rome, have given his holiness reliable information that Dmitry is alive, and that their mother would be writing to him about the matter. We ardently desire to find out the truth."

Then, in August 1608, he wrote: "Dmitry is also alive here in the minds of many. Even the most incredulous do not now argue with such conviction as they did before. We greatly desire to be convinced that he is alive, and to hear of his victories." In the same month the cardinal wrote: "If news concerning Dmitry's triumph is correct, we need to be convinced that he is the true Dmitry."

POLISH CONDITIONS

In Poland a decree had been drafted for the resurrected Dmitry stating how he was to behave for his own security and to further the introduction of the Uniate religion into the Muscovite realm.[102] The compilers of the decree[103] considered it necessary to specify the causes why False Dmitry was not to demand the imperial title:[104] (a) This title did not come to him by inheritance from his predecessors; consequently he should show some new cause to justify his obtaining this title. (b) The Russians themselves were opposed to that title; what then of foreigners? (c) Not one Christian sovereign recognizes it, and in embassies and other affairs of state it is not befitting to give rise to further complications. (d) Even concerning the royal title there have been, and still are, quarrels with neighboring states; what then of the imperial title? (e) In order to assume that title a new coronation would be necessary, which the patriarch cannot perform; there were not the necessary electoral princes.

But the tsar could achieve his wishes through a union, the detailed conditions for which followed thereafter.

(1) It would be as well if offices of the realm and their perquisites were not awarded according to seniority of family. It is fitting that valor, not ancestry be rewarded. For magnates this would be an incentive to true service, and also to union. At the same time we should beware lest there arise quarrels between old and new senators. It would be as well to postpone the implementation of this provision until the union, and then give the highest offices in the form of a reward to the most devoted to it, so that the sovereign himself, in consequence of the union, will have received the imperial title, and the officers who will advise him will receive the title of senator, that is, in order that everything should stem from the pope. It is also necessary to promise other dignities in order more quickly to win people to God's cause.

(2) Permanent attendance on the tsar's person by the clergy and the boyars is a cause of treason, intrigues and danger for the sovereign. Let them remain in their own houses, and await the summons to appear. Instead of them, let his highness have as his advisors mature and valorous men, both for judicial and state affairs. Let him converse principally with those upon whom the tranquillity of the realm and the love of the people for its sovereign depends, not especially neglecting the others, but alternately having at his side sometimes some, sometimes others. For incessant entertaining of boyars and councillors and long audiences with them entail waste of time, danger and unnecessary expense, give rise to discontent, and most likely were the cause of the present tragedy. Care must also be taken that these boyars do not hatch anything dangerous far removed from the eyes of the sovereign. All gatherings must be forbidden.

The sovereign should at times eat publicly, at other times in his chambers, according to the custom of other sovereigns.

(3) Recent experience has taught that your highness needs bodyguards who, as formerly, will not allow anybody into the palace or any place where the sovereign happens to be. There must be foreigners among the bodyguards, although half should be of your own people, as much for appearances as for security. As for the servants of your chamber, you should choose with great care. For the office of bodyguards and servants of the chamber, you should choose people whose happiness and life depend upon the safety of the sovereign or, to speak plainly, true Catholics, if the union is to be consummated. From the Muscovites you should choose as bodyguards supporters of the union who, speaking and conversing with our people, would wish to see our form of worship, hear our sermons, and so forth. In this manner, from your own subjects, and not from the sovereign, there will arise conversations concerning union. The sovereign will be rather an intermediary and judge than an initiator and stimulator. This will be necessary to avert hatred, especially now, at the beginning. To this end you must choose people who are devoted to the house of his imperial majesty. You must take care, since the loyalty of people for whom it is impossible to return to their homeland is always suspect. Among many of our people here there are those who, because of their immorality and turbulence, are greatly hated by the Muscovites. You must take care that the conduct of Catholics at the court of your highness does not bring reproach upon the holy faith and upon the union.

(4) You also should not banish the Muscovites from the sovereign's court, since this is hateful and dangerous for the sovereign, and also for the foreigners. Those Muscovites close to the tsar could, by their example, stimulate others towards the union. The sovereign can remain close to his subjects in matters necessary for the state only through them. Finally, they have shown their loyalty in that, as the recent conspiracy was discovered, they exposed their lives to danger for the sake of the sovereign. Caution must be taken in order not to give rise to new conspiracies; on the other hand, foreign soldiers are always necessary, but any coercion should be of a short duration. Since it is difficult without the aid of the Russians to receive warning in the event of a mutiny, treason and so on, those entrusted with responsibilities must be known to the sovereign and proven by experience. At the same time we must not forget the state of the realm at the death of the sovereign. If everything is done by force and fear, then

unfortunately the good intentions of the sovereign regarding the transformation of the faith, the people and the realm will be in vain. Therefore we must be solicitous of his highness and of his court. It is of the utmost importance to bring about a rapprochement between our people and the Muscovites, and friendly conversations with them, especially at the sovereign's court. Let our people have servants and pages from the Muscovite people, but they must carefully watch how much, and in what matters they can trust any of them. It would not be a bad idea if the tsaritsa had at her court persons of either sex from the great Muscovite families. It would be gratifying if the Poles, if possible, would take with them to Poland the sons of noble boyars; this would serve to promote a change in manners and faith, and would guarantee the security of our people here. With the distribution of court dignities, it would be most politic to give the Poles the more intimate household offices, and the Muscovites the more nominal, in order to protect the life and security of the sovereign.

(5) A strict and secret investigation of the hidden conspirators and participants in the plot should be carried out. The attitudes of persons close to them should be ascertained, in order to find out who can be trusted with what.

(6) For the receiving of petitions, crown secretaries well known for their loyalty, able to conduct business as expeditiously as possible, should be appointed, thereby, on the one hand, to obtain the support of your subjects, and on the other hand to guarantee the security of the sovereign, since petitions can include warnings.

(7) The chancellery should use the national language rather than Latin, especially since the Latin language is considered pagan by the inhabitants. The sovereign, however, needs to have close to him people who know the Latin language, politics and theology, true Catholics who will not impede a good intention, will not bring the sovereign into the company of heretics, will not smuggle in Arian and Calvinist books, to the ruin of the realm and of souls, and will not use their power to prevent alliances with Catholic sovereigns. Such scholars are at least needful for relations with Christian sovereigns.

(8) The dowry contract given the tsaritsa must be presented for the signature of the councillors. One copy must remain here, and the other in Poland, with seals and signatures. If the opportunity should arise, it should be included in a treaty with the Polish kingdom, so that her majesty the tsaritsa might be under the protection of the kingdom of Poland if

circumstances should change. Senators and subjects throughout all the towns must give an oath of allegiance to her majesty the tsaritsa, as to their sovereign lady, swearing submission and obedience. One list of signatories should remain here, and another in Poland with the signatures of the governors and town elders. On all suitable occasions the tsaritsa should be allowed to purchase landed possessions in Poland, adjacent to districts ceded to her from the Muscovite realm.

(9) The transfer of the capital, at least temporarily, appears necessary for the following reasons. (a) It would be safer for the sovereign. (b) It would be more convenient for the recruitment of foreign troops and to receive help from a neighboring king and other Christian sovereigns. (c) If the tsar should be removed, it would be more convenient for the tsaritsa to receive help from her own people, more secure and easier to leave with her valuables and in freedom for her homeland. It is not necessary, however, to make public anything concerning the transfer of the capital, since this would not serve any useful purpose. It would be as well to live in some place other than Moscow. (d) The Muscovite community will be more peaceful. The Muscovites esteem a sovereign who is far removed from them, but are turbulent when their sovereign is present, and have little esteem for him. The customary feasting with councillors could more easily be discontinued if the sovereign is at a distance. (e) It would be more convenient for the conduct of talks concerning union. (f) It would be more convenient to seek out suitable people. (g) It would be easier to found colleges and seminaries closer to the Polish border. (h) It would be easier for young Muscovites to travel to Wilno and other places to gain learning.

(10) The advantageous consequences of the union with regard to enlightenment in Russia are enumerated.

(11) The imperial dignity scarcely can remain vested for much longer in the House of Austria and the German realm, as a consequence of the spread of Protestantism in Germany. If the heretical Electors choose a heretic, or if there occurs dissension arising out of the election, the pope may well transfer the imperial dignity to whomsoever among the sovereigns is the most ardent defender of the church. Who knows whether the time has not arrived when the imperial dignity, transferred during the reign of Charlemagne from the east to the west, might not now be transferred from the west to the north?[105]

(12) If the son of the elder brother of the tsar is alive, the throne rightfully belongs to him, in which case the union will be a safeguard for

Dmitry, since the church has power to depose infidel tsars from rulership over the faithful, and to entrust the sceptre to her true sons.

(13) The protection of his majesty the tsar from sudden death justly can be ascribed to the prayers of the church. To the power of the same prayers must be ascribed the fact that the people who rose up against the tsar with the aim of hindering the union have suffered many misfortunes, and many of them have perished at the hands of a lesser force.

Following this, there is a special exposition of the means whereby to expedite the matter of union.

(1) Heretics who are hostile to the union should be forbidden entry to the realm.

(2) Monks coming from Constantinople should be expelled.

(3) The way for intrigues to come to Russia from Poland should be blocked. Even now, by Poland's example, there has arisen bloodshed. His Majesty the Tsar barely managed to escape, and there has arisen even greater hatred towards the union than before.

(4) Choose carefully people with whom to discuss this matter, since premature proclamation, even now, would be harmful.

(5) The sovereign must keep at hand a very small number of Catholic clergy. Letters relating to this matter should be received, written or sent as cautiously as possible, especially from Rome.

(6) The sovereign should speak of this very rarely, and then with caution. On the other hand, he should take good care not to give rise to any talk concerning this.

(7) The Russians themselves should be induced to make propositions concerning some unimportant matters of faith, demanding reform, which could open the way to union. One means to this end could be a process and inquiry concerning the late conspiracy, in which the clergy also took part, the transformation of the morals and facilities for learning available to the clergy, and the banishment of ignorant priests, who themselves do not know of the faith, and do not instruct others. As a consequence of this, their parishioners do not know the creed, the Ten Commandments or the Lord's Prayer, from which arise among them perfidy, adultery, drunkenness, sorcery, deceit, brigandage, pillage and murders. There are few who consider brigandage and plunder to be sins. There are no learned sermons for the people. Priests are noted for their ignorance while preaching. The priesthood is venal. Let us pose the question concerning the relationship of the Muscovite patriarch to Byzantium. From where does he derive his

authority? Let us turn our attention to the fact that some young people do not receive education, that much of the income of the clergy is not converted into useful works. Why not introduce learning, as it was in the days of St. John Chrysostom, St. Basil, St. Nicholas and other saints, who were learned, who studied, and ordered people to study? To achieve this end, we must bring about a union with the Latin church, which produces so many learned people. Why do we not follow the example of previous holy patriarchs? Why do we not introduce a reformation in faith and morals, so that everything should be as it was before, as they lived before the schism of the churches and before the Turkish domination, since from that time everything began to decay in spiritual matters? Why should we not have seminaries and a college? If the opportunity arises, hint at the building of a Catholic church, for the sake of emulation. Promulgate a decree, so that everything might be introduced under the guise of the resolutions of synods and the Greek fathers, and entrust the fulfilment of the law to people favorable to the union. There will arise disputes. The matter will be brought to the sovereign who will, of course, summon a synod and there, with the help of God, the matter of union can be broached.

(8) Give offices to those who are favorable to the union and suggest to them what advantages will come of it. The higher clergy especially must be in favor of union. They must manipulate the people towards the proposed end; but this is in the hands of his majesty the tsar.

(9) Hint to the monastic clergy concerning tax exemptions, to the secular clergy concerning dignities, to the people concerning freedom, to all concerning the slavery of the Greeks, who can be freed only by means of union among Christian sovereigns.

(10) There should be at the sovereign's hand court chaplains of ability, able to show the true path by words and by writing.

(11) Establish seminaries in which learned people, even laymen, can be employed.

(12) Send young people to study in Wilno or, better, to where there are no schismatics, to Italy, to Rome.

(13) Allow Muscovites to be present at our services.

(14) It would be good if the Poles here would take young people and entrust them to the Jesuit fathers in Poland for instruction.

(15) It would be good if at the tsaritsa's residence, among the priests, there should be one or two Uniates, who could conduct services in the Russian rite, and could converse with Russians.

(16) For the tsaritsa and the Poles living here, a church or Catholic monastery should be founded.

This instruction was written in vain. False Dmitry did not succeed in capturing Moscow, and his companions had to think of how to spend the winter in Tushino, since the snow had begun to drift against their tents. The pretender had at this time, apart from his Russian followers, a Polish cavalry army of eighteen thousand, two thousand infantry, thirteen thousand Zaporozhian and fifteen thousand Don Cossacks. The Poles would not let many of the latter stay within the encampment, because they did not trust them. There were at one time or another about one to three thousand Polish merchants within the Tushino encampment. They stayed in a special quarter.

Some thought that the army should divide into a number of detachments and winter in the various Muscovite provinces, but the majority thought that it would be dangerous to divide the forces, and decided that all must winter at Tushino. They started to dig pit huts. For their horses they made stalls out of brushwood and straw. For their provisions they divided the conquered provinces among the detachments, and huge waggon trains rolled into Tushino as soon as the roads were open. Each troop needed a thousand or more waggon loads. "They brought us only what was needed to keep body and soul together," said one of the Tushino Poles. They tired of living in pit huts, and began to take log cabins from the nearby hamlets, and reassembled them in the encampment. Some had two or three such huts, and used the pit huts for storage cellars. In the middle of the encampment they built a villa for the tsar, and the Tushino encampment was transformed into a city.

THE TUSHINO BRIGAND
1607–1610

SWEDISH HELP FOR SHUISKY

The pretender had built himself a capital just outside Moscow itself, and Polish units arrived to assist him. The treaty concluded in Moscow by the royal emissaries clearly had been violated. Mniszech and his daughter had recognized the Tushino brigand as the true Dmitry. But if there had been such an obvious breach of the treaty on the part of the Poles, if the brigand indeed was establishing himself with Polish aid, naturally Shuisky must address a request for assistance to the enemy of Poland and its king, namely Karl of Sweden, especially since the latter for a long time had been offering him aid.

In February 1607 the governor of Vyborg had written to the governor of Korela, Prince Mosalsky, that his king was prepared to aid the tsar, and Swedish emissaries had long been standing at the ready on the frontier awaiting the arrival of the Muscovite emissaries for negotiations. But Shuisky, who had succeeded in repelling Bolotnikov from Moscow, thought that he could deal with the pre-ruined Ukraine with the forces of Northern Russia, and therefore he ordered Mosalsky to answer the letter from Vyborg in the following terms: "You have written to me that the embassy of your sovereign, Archduke Karl, has been standing vainly along the frontiers, awaiting his majesty the tsar. I am surprised at the terms of your letter, in that you write concerning questions on which we have given you an answer more than once. Once again I beg to inform you that we have no instructions concerning emissaries from the great sovereign, neither have we written to you concerning the intention of the great sovereign to send emissaries to meet with yours.

"Henceforth you will please refrain from writing to us concerning diplomatic negotiations because there never have been any diplomatic negotiations, neither have we any information concerning emissaries in Korela. In any case our sovereign would have ordered the governor of Novgorod to deal with matters pertaining to diplomatic negotiations.

"You write that the governor of your sovereign is present at Vyborg with many of his people, and that he is recruiting soldiers daily. But this merely will cause unnecessary expense for your sovereign, for his recruiting is no concern of ours. You yourselves know that our great sovereign has many of his own government troops at his disposal, who are always at the ready, and that these are neither extraordinary levies nor mercenaries. Our great sovereign has not given any orders that the previously established peace be violated in any manner. On his side there has not been any injustice or defiance.

"You also write to me to enquire who is our tsar and grand prince. Surely your sovereign is acquainted with events, and knows that our sovereign is Vasily Ivanovich, tsar of All Russia. You also in your writing allege that his subjects have risen up against him, and that therefore the couriers of your sovereign do not have any access to him. You also assure us that you have instructions to help our sovereign with soldiers against his enemies, and that your sovereign does not wish to do any harm to the Russian land. He also wishes to help the Novgorod land. But it is also well known to you that, by the grace of God, by hereditary right, at the entreaty of the Holy Synod, and in response to the petition of all the multitude of the people of the Muscovite state, Vasily Ivanovich has acceded to the great realms, and that everybody is serving him, and there is no discord whatsoever among them. It is so by the grace of God, and so it will also be in the future.

"So now you, guided by we know not what sinister intentions, write such unseemly and ill-intended words. Concerning the aid about which you write, I wish to inform you that our great sovereign requires no help whatsoever from anybody. He can withstand his enemies without your interference, and does not deign to ask aid from anyone but God. Moreover, your messengers were prevented from travelling because of an outbreak of plague in the Novgorod province."

On another occasion Karl sent his courier to Moscow while the tsar was besieging Tula. At first they tried to conceal from the courier the objective of the tsar's campaign. The official told him that Vasily was in the Ukraine standing guard against the Crimean khan. The tsar wrote to the boyars that an answer should be given Karl under every article, but they should not answer him rudely, but graciously. Despite these instructions, the boyars thought it necessary to express their indignation to the king, who had even written in the letter sent by the courier that the reason

Karl IX
King of Sweden, 1604–1612

for detaining the couriers was not the plague, but the activities of the tsar's enemies.

The boyars answered him, on behalf of the tsar: "It is customary among us, and among all other great sovereigns, that when we correspond concerning love and friendship between us, there should be no unbefitting words in our communications. You would do well to take heed of this, and henceforth not to write such impudent words to us. When the Muscovite realm killed its evil foe, the heretic apostate renegade monk Grishka Otrepiev, then some lawless cossacks and runaway slaves, counsellors of the renegade monk, anticipating punishment for their crimes, and fearing death, fled from Moscow to Ukrainian and Polish towns, and began to foment unrest. But now we have defeated these brigands, and there is no longer any unrest in our great realms. In all great realms there exist certain brigands, thieves and murderers, who flee and engage in criminal activities, evading execution. You have written to say that you wish to help us against our enemies. Our lord tsar commends you in that you wish us well and seek to earn our affection towards you, and in response to this, we extend our affection to you. As we have written to you before, so now also we declare that we have no enemy. Although a neighboring sovereign is contemplating opening hostilities against us, we are not afraid of him. We only seek help from the one Almighty God, and it is also known to you that our lord tsar has many and innumerable Russian and Tatar forces."

Soon Shuisky had to change his tune when his innumerable armies were defeated, and the pretender had built himself a capital outside Moscow. Despite the fact that he had twice rejected the aid offered him by Karl, he now considered it necessary to send his kinsman, Prince Skopin-Shuisky, to Novgorod, in order from there to conduct negotiations with the Swedish king concerning aid. In Novgorod Skopin was received with honor. The citizens of Novgorod of old were noted for their affection towards the Shuisky family. During the time of Ivan the Terrible the whole town had supported them, but in Pskov things turned out quite differently.

CIVIL STRIFE IN PSKOV

Despite the pogrom in Pskov during the reign of Grand Prince Vasily,[1] this town still preserved remnants of its former independence. As a relic of old times there remained in Pskov enmity between two factions, the so-called "better" and "lesser" people. After the final unification with Moscow this enmity was reinforced by the fact that the "better" people of Pskov were deported, and in their place others were introduced from the provinces of Muscovy proper.

Naturally in peaceful times this enmity could not be expressed sharply but now, in the Time of Troubles, it flared again. "Merchants, vainglorious men, thinking themselves great before God and the people, being puffed up with riches," as they are described by the chronicler,[2] took the opportunity to terrorize the leaders of the opposing faction, "who spoke justly against them concerning civic matters and the general state of affairs, and in defense of poor orphans."

Shuisky sent to Pskov to ask its inhabitants for monetary aid. The merchants and rich people in general collected nine hundred rubles from all of Pskov, including the better and lesser people, and even widows, and sent the chief representatives of the opposing side to take the money to Moscow, against their own wishes. These included Samson Tifints, Fedor Umoisia-Griaziu, Yeremey the tanner, Ovseiko Rzhkov and Iliushka the butcher. Concerning them, the better people wrote: "We, the merchants of Pskov, rejoice, and we send these five men to you, sovereign. They do not wish you well, neither did the lesser people give into your treasury." Then the prominent merchant, Grigory Shchukin, boasted: "These people have come with the treasure so that they may not meet with the elders of the Lifegiving Trinity, and so that they might be absent from Pskov."

Consequently, even as they reached Novgorod, by reason of the aforementioned missive to the tsar from the richer inhabitants of Pskov, four of the Pskov emissaries who had been sent with the money were put in prison, and were detained until it was quite certain that the road was clear of brigands, and it was safe to send them on to Moscow. Only Yeremey the tanner remained free, because his name was left out of the document. The governor of Pskov, Peter Sheremetev,[3] favored him, for Yeremey had rendered him many gratuitous services.

When the emissaries arrived in Moscow they were ordered to be executed in accordance with the aforesaid document. Fortunately at the time there was in Moscow a detachment of Pskov musketeers, who had been summoned by the tsar to aid him against False Dmitry. These musketeers hurried to Shuisky, petitioned for the lives of these inhabitants of their home town, and secured their release, stating: "They are not traitors towards you, O tsar, and their heads are our heads."

Meanwhile Yeremey had returned from Novogorod to Pskov and told his friends that his four companions had been sent directly on to Moscow from prison with the treasure, and that treacherous allegations had been written about them. Then the people rose up throughout Pskov against seven of the leading merchants, and petitioned the governor concerning them. Sheremetev put the merchants in prison, and took advantage of this opportunity to demand from them great sums of money. Meanwhile he sent word to Moscow that no harm should be done to the four men from Pskov, and that they should be set free immediately and sent home, since on their account there had arisen great disorder in Pskov, and the merchants were being threatened with ruin.

Shuisky was intimidated and set the men from Pskov free. From that moment there arose fearful hatred between the upper, or better, and the lesser people. "The better were against the lesser, and the lesser against the better, leading to the ruin of all." It is understandable what consequences arose from such dissension within the town when, according to the expression of the chronicler, "The Russian tsar split it in half, and there were two tsars, and two peoples at each other's throats." When Shuisky sent prisoners taken from the pretender to be interned in the towns, including Novgorod and Pskov, the citizens of Novgorod drowned these unfortunates in the Volkhov; but the inhabitants of Pskov fed them, gave them drink, clothed them, and wept while gazing upon them. This was an evil omen for Shuisky!

PSKOV SUPPORTS THE PRETENDER

In May 1607 musketeers from Pskov and the surrounding towns arrived in the Tushino encampment, and also junior boyars who had been taken prisoner by the pretender. They kissed the cross to him, and graciously were sent home. The musketeers, dispersed throughout the surrounding towns, and the junior boyars, who returned to their estates, raised up the bytowns[4] and districts, persuading them to swear allegiance to the cossack tsar Dmitry. Sheremetev, the governor of Pskov, gathered together the soldiers and sent his son Boris as their commander against the rebels, but Boris barely managed to make his escape from them and return to Pskov safe and sound.

At that time there arrived in Pskov some inhabitants of Novgorod who urged the inhabitants of Pskov to join together and combine forces against the brigands. "For the Germans (Swedes)[5] will soon come from across the sea to help Novgorod and Pskov." But this promise that foreigners would come to their aid merely served to drive the inhabitants of Pskov into the arms of False Dmitry. For several centuries Pskov continually had fought foreigners who threatened their independence and faith. There was scarcely a child in Pskov who did not remember that the most deadly foe was the German. In addition to this historical enmity there was also a new danger. The lesser people saw that foreigners, the allies of Shuisky, together with the citizens of Novgorod, were coming to reinforce the governor and the faction of the better people, who would use this force to suppress the opposing faction. The inhabitants of Pskov declared to those of Novgorod that they did not want to ally themselves with Novgorod, especially on account of the foreigners.

At that time, because of the appearance of two tsars, Pskov was divided. What was the Pskov leadership doing, namely Governor Sheremetev and Crown Secretary Gramotin, of subsequent fame?[6] They took advantage of the Troubles and used the weakening of the tsar's power for their own advantage. They took the best court villages as their residences, and to provide for their own subsistence. Then the governor appointed by Tushino, Fedor Pleshcheev,[7] came with an army recruited in the bytowns, and began to administer the oath of allegiance to the district of the Pskov province. Peasants from the countryside appeared in Pskov, appealing to the governor to protect them against Pleshcheev, but Sheremetev answered that they must kiss the cross to the cossack tsar. They, being powerless, kissed the cross, and gave Pleshcheev provisions and paid him the hearth tax.[8]

But then Sheremetev and Gramotin sent an armed detachment to plunder and arrest peasants throughout the countryside. They tortured the peasants, extorted money from them, and then sent them away, saying that they had done this because the peasants had kissed the cross to the pretender. The peasants knew very well that it was the governor himself who had ordered them to do so. The inhabitants of Pskov grew increasingly agitated, seeing the ruin of the bytowns and the peasantry, the injustices of the governor, the injuries and plundering.

Then they heard that the citizens of Novgorod were coming in the company of foreigners, so that Sheremetev would become even more powerful, and would spare nobody. One junior boyar put about a rumor that a letter had been sent to Moscow denouncing seventy of the townsmen. They fearfully pointed out to each other the massive prisons built at the order of the governor, whereas previously the prisons had been simple structures without a stockade. Sheremetev repeatedly asked the citizens of Pskov: "What are your thoughts? Tell me!" The citizens were silent; they had no thoughts. But when the governor said "The foreigners are coming to Pskov," they answered: "We do not want the foreigners, and we will die rather than let them come."

The better people also, instead of trying to pacify the people, seemed to go out of their way to antagonize them. They ceased to attend the municipal chancellery, they shunned the lesser people and mocked them. When summoned to the council they did not come, leaving everything to the lesser people, musketeers, cossacks and villagers. The musketeers praised the anti-tsar, Dmitry, for his benevolence and kindness, his skill in war and for great strength. These words filled everyone with joy. They were hoping for the truth, delivery from evil and from the acts of violence perpetrated by the authorities; for the governors, not satisfied with bribery and plunder, had shaken the community through every arbitrariness, had deprived Pskov entirely of all justice, and had undermined all good order. They had increased the number of brigands and multiplied the number of their clients, informers, spies and calumniators, leaving law-abiding people nowhere left to live in peace.

Just as the lower strata of the people thus were alienated from the governor and the better people, news came on September 1, 1608 that the foreigners were approaching. Then the people rose up, as though drunk, according to the expression of the chronicler. They opened the gates, kissed the cross to the pretender, and admitted Pleshcheev's soldiers into the city. Thus Pleshcheev assumed his position as governor in Pskov.

Ivangorod also swore allegiance to False Dmitry. At Oreshek, Skopin was not admitted by the local governor, Mikhail Glebovich Saltykov, who also had declared himself for Tushino. In Great Novgorod itself an agitation began among the common people, but Metropolitan Isidore[9] pacified them. Skopin, hearing of this uprising, left Novgorod, but returned after he had been informed that everything was back to normal, and entered into negotiation with the Swedes concerning an auxiliary army. The king's secretary, Mons Martensson, who was called by the local Russians Monch Martinich, arrived in Novgorod and agreed with Skopin that the Swedes would send five thousand men to help the tsar. The Muscovite government promised to give them four hundred thousand *efimoks* per month for their maintenance.[10] The final conclusion of the treaty was postponed until a conference in Vyborg.

SHUISKY BESIEGED IN MOSCOW

But at the very moment when the Swedes merely were promising aid the Poles in Dmitry's camp were active on behalf of their allies outside Moscow and in the north. Sapieha, who wished to act independently, approached the Trinity monastery, which controlled Moscow's communications with the northern and eastern provinces. Being informed of Sapieha's movements, Shuisky sent his brother Ivan to block his way but the Muscovite army was defeated soundly at Rakhmantsevo, and Shuisky returned to Moscow with a mere handful of followers. The rest had dispersed to their homes to await the outcome of the conflict, for they did not wish to shed their blood either for the Moscow or the Tushino tsar.

Many of the inhabitants of Moscow were of the same frame of mind. Shuisky must have known how dangerous the indifference of the citizens was after the first failure, and therefore let it be known that he intended to withstand siege within the city, but that if any one did not wish to remain with him he might leave. To agree to such a proposal would be to declare open disaffection against the tsar, or otherwise cowardice, and this would seem either shameful or dangerous. Had not Shuisky already put loyalty and devotion to the test, only later to punish cruelly those who had been disloyal or lacking in devotion?

THE TUSHINO COURT

Everyone kissed the cross to die for the church of the Immaculate Virgin but the next day, the day after, or in succeeding days went over to Tushino. These included junior boyars, high court officials, stewards, gentry, burghers, secretaries and clerks. Among the high court officials were Prince Dmitry Timofeevich Trubetskoy,[11] Prince Dmitry Mamstriukovich Cherkassky,[12] Prince Alexis Yurievich Buturlin and the two Zasekin princes.[13] We have seen that at first the people from the lowest strata of the population rallied to the banners of the pretender; we also have gathered the reason they rallied there. The peasants, for example, gave support, not entirely because they were motivated by class interest nor in order that, while remaining peasants, they might receive more extensive rights. The peasants rallied to the pretender in order no longer to be peasants, to gain a more advantageous position, and to become landlords in place of their own previous landlords. But similar movements occurred among all elements of the population. The trader came to Tushino to become an official, a secretary or clerk to become a conciliar secretary. Finally, people of noble families, princes, but of the junior line who, because of various relationships, had no hope of elevation to the ranks of the boyars in Moscow either quickly or at all, came to Tushino, where a separate court was being created, in opposition to the Muscovite court.

SIEGE OF THE TRINITY MONASTERY

Having defeated Shuisky, Sapieha, together with Lisowski, approached the Trinity monastery on September 23. The army of the besiegers amounted at the outside to 30,000 men, but since the first attempts to capture the monastery had been unsuccessful Sapieha saw the necessity of a long siege. He therefore had to see to it that supplies were gathered for the winter, and had to send detachments to other towns. Thus the number of his army frequently diminished, sometimes being reduced to as few as ten thousand men. It is difficult to estimate the number of the besieged because of lack of evidence, but there exists a contemporary list of those involved in the siege, which comprises 609 men. If we add to this number the seven hundred miscellaneous personnel over whom some of the junior boyars from the various towns were put in command, and if we also add to this the number of monks capable of bearing arms, we arrive at a figure of about fifteen hundred men, not including monastic servitors and peasants. In arriving at this estimate we must take into account also the population of the various settlements which had sought refuge within the monastery, and which also included many women and children. Large numbers of inhabitants from the surrounding countryside had poured into the monastery, and the overcrowding was fearful. The commanders of the monastery guard or garrison were the lord-in-waiting, Prince Grigory Borisovich Dolgorukov-Roshcha,[14] and the noble, Alexis Golokhvastov. The archimandrite of the monastery was at that time Joseph, about whose character it is difficult to say anything definite.[15] The figure of the cellarer of the monastery, Avraamy Palitsyn, to whom particular attention must be paid, stands out more clearly.

Avraamy Palitsyn was called in secular life Averky Ivanovich. In 1588, during the reign of Fedor, Averky Palitsyn fell into disgrace. His possessions were confiscated by the treasury, he was exiled, and became a monk, either voluntarily, or under constraint. The reason for his disgrace is unknown but the year in which it occurred, 1588, is significant. Not long before that time, namely at the end of 1587, when the Shuisky princes had fallen, their friends and supporters also had fallen into disgrace as a consequence of evil intentions against Godunov. In 1600 Tsar Boris lifted his disfavor from the monk Avraamy but the latter, during the reigns of Godunov and the pretender, remained in banishment, and only with the accession of Shuisky to the throne did Avraamy receive an important appointment. He became the cellarer of the Trinity monastery, the leading monastery in the realm, and thus the intermediary in dealings between the monastery and the sovereign.[16]

This circumstance in itself gives an indication concerning Palitsyn's previous ties with the new sovereign. In 1609 a case concerning a mortgage contract was decided in his favor, and he received his own share in a village despite the fact that he was forbidden as a monk to receive any land in pledge. Nevertheless, when the deed to the land was issued Palitsyn had to pay two rubles into the treasury. Avraamy did not wish to pay, and requested that the sovereign excuse him from paying this fee. The sovereign agreed that the fee be waived until the end of the siege.

Observing the conduct of Avraamy at this particular time, it can be concluded that he was a very skillful, businesslike, compliant and learned man and, according to the conventions of the time, eloquent. In a word, a true cellarer, since the cellarer was the monastery's representative before the secular powers, the guardian of its wealth, its proctor in legal matters. If any monastery needed an experienced and skillful cellarer, so much more did the Trinity monastery, which controlled such vast quantitites of immoveable property, had so many privileges and, in normal times, its cellarer frequently had to be absent from the monastery, living in the capital in order to present petitions concerning the affairs of the monastery. At the time of the siege Palitsyn was in Moscow at the request of the tsar, as he himself writes.

Sapieha and Lisowski thought that they would soon capture the Trinity monastery, but they encountered strong resistance. All their assaults were beaten off, and their siege works were destroyed. The monks eagerly aided the soldiers. Even as some were conducting religious services, others were working in the bakeries and breweries, preparing food and drink for the soldiers. Others remained day and night upon the ramparts, alongside the soldiers. They took part in sorties, and even commanded detachments. Many of them had probably been military servitors before they had become monks. Sapieha and Lisowski, in their report, bear personal testimony to the conduct of the Trinity monks, as they wrote to them: "You lawless men have had contempt for the generosity, kindness and gracious-ness of Tsar Ivan Vasilievich. You have forgotten his son, but are sup-porting Prince Vasily Shuisky, and are training soldiers within the fortress of the Trinity, and instructing the people to rise up against the sovereign, Tsar Dmitry Ivanovich, and say shameful and scurrilous things about him and Marina Yurievna, and also about us. And we also bear witness to you, Archimandrite Joseph, and we write with the tsar's words, that you should forbid priests and other monks to instruct the soldiers not to submit to Tsar Dmitry."

Sapieha and Lisowski also wrote to the commanders of the Trinity monastery, and to all the soldiers, promising that if they surrendered they would receive rich rewards. Otherwise they threatened them with an ig-nominious death. These promises and threats fell on deaf ears. The monks and soldiers did not see beneath the walls the man who called himself the son of Ivan Vasilievich. Rather, they saw before the walls of the sanctuary of St. Sergius[17] hordes of schismatics, Poles and Lithuanians, who had come to mock and despoil the church and sacred treasures. It was not a question of whether they should be loyal to the Tushino or the Moscow tsar, but whether they should hand over the tomb of the great miracle-worker to the mockery of the enemies of the Orthodox faith. The besieged in the Trinity monastery were not simply protecting Shuisky's throne, but also the shrine of St. Sergius, and treason could not overcome their loyal-ty. The nature of what inspired the besieged can be seen in their answer to Sapieha's missive: "Your dark dominion knows well that it is vain to tempt the flock of Christ in the fold of Orthodox Christendom. What ad-vantage is it to a man to love darkness more than light, and to the truth prefer a lie? How shall we abandon our ancient, holy, true Orthodox Christian faith of the Greek dispensation, and submit to new heretical laws, which have been accursed by the four ecumenical patriarchs? And what advantage would it be to abandon our Orthodox sovereign, the tsar, and submit to a false enemy, especially to you, a schismatic Latin, thus being like unto the Jews, or even worse than them?"

While religious inspiration predominated, treason could not overcome loyalty within the Trinity monastery, even though treason had insinuated itself there. On the one hand, within the camp of the besiegers there were cossacks who were troubled in their consciences because they had raised their hands against the shrine of St. Sergius. These deserted to the de-fenders, and informed them of the enemy's intentions. On the other hand there were deserters among the monastic servitors, and even among the junior boyars, who could not endure a siege which had become very arduous in winter time. In autumn, when it was still warm, a large number of people could still live in the open, but when the frost set in everybody crowded into the cellars. There was therefore fearful crowding, followed by epidemic disease, and compounded by lack of fuel.

In addition to these physical ills there was a moral sickness, enmity between the monks, disagreements between the commanders, and accusations of treason were voiced. On March 29, 1609 the daughter of Boris Godunov, Xenia (or Olga) wrote to one of her aunts from the Trinity monastery where she happened to be at the time of the siege, stating that "she was scarcely alive in the midst of all these woes. She and the other nuns were very sick, and not one of them had any hope of life. They were hourly expecting death because during the siege there was much wavering and great treason."[18]

The musketeers and the lesser monastic servitors were envious of the archimandrite and his brethren, or complained to the archimandrite that they were not being fed enough. The archimandrite wrote to the tsar, excusing himself on the grounds that "since we have been under siege everybody is eating the bread of the Trinity monastery, for they have very few provisions of their own. We also have given money where we have seen fit, and as soon as the money in the treasury was exhausted we collected one ruble from each of the brethren, and one and a half rubles from all the others. We have taken this money, and have given to the others according to their needs. We told the soldiers to eat what the brethren eat in the refectory. Take my archimandrite's rations, I said, and put your own before me. But they go around the cells begging food from the brethren, even though in the refectory the ration is four times what it is in the cells. Some have their wives and children in the cells, others have just their wives. What more can we do to promote harmony? On the eve of the feast of St. Philip we ate dry rusks with bread. Because of the siege we are suffering oppression and great hardship. The roofs of the cells, the back porches and the storage sheds have been used for firewood, and now we are burning our granaries."

But it was not only the soldiers who were writing complaints against the archimandrite and monastery brethren. There were also complaints from some of monks, among whom there had arisen dissension caused by the denunciation against the monastic treasurer, Joseph Devochkin.

Palitsyn writes that the deacon, Gury Shishkin, the principal chorister of the left choir, detected treason on the part of Devochkin, and denounced him to the chief commander. Dolgorukov immediately arrested the treasurer, and ordered him to be put to the torture. Such action by the commander towards one of the leading personages of the monastery caused indignation on the part of the archimandrite and the monastic brethren, who in turn caused a denunciation to be drawn up against the informer Shishkin and his friends, who, in their letter to the tsar, dated July 3, 1609, complained that, because of their denunciation against Devochkin "the archimandrite and the monastic brethren aroused great hatred against them, and were starving them to death by every deprivation, hunger and thirst, while the monastic brethren themselves ate with their fellow-conspirators, drank in their cells, as daily they had done before; for the monastic brethren had done much harm to the soldiers, gentry, junior boyars and monastic servitors." Dolgoruky wrote to Palitsyn in Moscow that "I know who among the brethren is the cause of this great dissension. Following the matter concerning Joseph, they have sowed much dissension, and have stirred up the community."

But there was a major quarrel between the commanders as well. Dolgoruky wrote to Avraamy: "About four days before the assault the monastic servitor Mikhail Pavlov came to me, and said: 'You are preparing to meet the attack of the brigands, but Alexis Golokhvastov is whispering in your ear. He is also telling Brother Malachi Rezhevitin to go to the military servitors whom he can trust, and to the peasants of Klementievo, and tell them that we all will perish at the hands of Prince Grigory, while we are maintaining the siege. Therefore we must do something about Prince Grigory. Perhaps we should take the keys away from him.' But I, Prince Grigory, hearing these words, spoke with the gentry, captains and hundredmen, the junior boyars and the soldiers, saying that, even as we were preparing to resist the assault of the enemy Alexis was saying words shameful to us in this holy place. Having heard this, Alexis made excuses, and Brother Malachi begged pardon before all the gentry, saying that he had never heard such words from Alexis. But then he sent to me, saying, 'I am guilty, Prince Grigory Borisovich, for having begged pardon in the first place. For if I had opened my mouth you would have been very troubled. But if God gives us an opportune moment I shall not make any excuses before the sovereign.' And then a second time he sent to me with these words. Before I arrested the malefactor Joseph Devochkin, Alexis, at the seventh hour of the night, called upon the monastic servitors, begging them not to deliver the treasurer to Prince Grigory. As I was going to interrogate the treasurer, Alexis ordered all the peasants be driven from the fortress. I sent my servant to find out what was going on. When he returned he said that the square was full of peasants who had come armed from the meeting hall, but I dissuaded the peasants from their mutiny and went to interrogate the treasurer. But Alexis did not take any part in the questioning, and his dissent was obvious to many of the gentry and junior boyars, as well as the soldiers, and they spoke to me of it afterwards, asking why Alexis had not co-operated with me on such an important matter." The same was reported by the brethren in the aforementioned document.

The attempt by Golokhvastov to discredit Devochkin, who had been accused of treason, and his attempt to take the fortress keys away from Dolgorukov, gave rise to the suspicion that Golokhvastov was party to the treasurer's treason, and to suspicion that the deputy commander wished to take the keys into his own hands, setting a date on which he would open the gates of the monastery to the enemy. Golokhvastov intended that when the besieged staged a sortie he would shut the gates, sacrificing those who had ventured forth to attack the Poles, and at the same time open to the enemy another entrance to the monastery.

According to Palitsyn's story, it transpires that Devochkin, confessing under torture to his own treason, implicated his fellow-conspirators, including Golokhvastov. "Unable to bear the pressure, Joseph revealed all his crafty plans, and it was strange to hear the twisted thoughts of this treacherous Judas. Not in vain did Oska Selevin cry out: 'Not only did he attempt to betray us, he also sent several ignorant peasants after me, and tempted several others to betray us to the Poles. His treachery, and that of the deputy commander, Alexis Golokhvastov, was such as I have referred to.'"

And so it went. But here it must be pointed out, first, that Palitsyn discredits his own assertion by being silent about the details, concealing the truth in a bombastic style. Dolgoruky concluded his denunciation to Palitsyn concerning the conduct of Golokhvastov with the following words: "But I will not write anything more about this to the sovereign because, for our sins, the siege is still dragging on. I am here without my family and, Avraamy Ivanovich, if the siege continues any longer you must be so good as to inform the tsar so that no further harm befalls the holy places within this monastery. Many people within the monastery are aware of Alexis's behavior, because Alexis does nothing but stir up dissension. If I were to write down everything that had happened, I would never finish this letter. So please, my lord, concern yourself with this holy place." In another letter, to the same Palitsyn, Dolgoruky wrote: "I beg of you, Averky Ivanovich, to inform the sovereign secretly that here, even while we are under siege, Alexis Golokhvastov is causing great dissension. This is in order that the sovereign may see fit, as soon as the roads are dry, to send a hundred reliable men here so that Golokhvastov may be investigated, and sent under arrest to Moscow. If the sovereign sees fit, let him write to me secretly." From these words it appears that Dolgoruky feared to act openly against Golokhvastov, who had many supporters including, at least for some time, the archimandrite and the monastic brethren. At a time when Shuisky's reputation was low, or when people always might seek refuge from his anger at Tushino, it was not sufficient to replace a commander simply by issuing a decree from Moscow. It was necessary to send a hundred reliable men, and move with great caution and secrecy.

But these documents from Dolgoruky and the brethren did not reach Moscow. Golokhvastov remained in command until the end of the siege, neither did he show any signs of treason. The hundred reliable men were not dispatched from Moscow, and the matter remained univestigated. To this day it is difficult to find any evidence against Golokhvastov, since Palitsyn's forceful accusation is weakened by the silence of Golokhvastov's enemies, and also by the very character of Palitsyn's narration, which does not give rise to much credence. It is also difficult to accuse Devochkin with any certainty, for we cannot even believe his own confession, which had been extracted by torture. The treasurer's fellow-conspirators, Grisha Briushin and Khudiak, died without saying anything. It is said that Devochkin himself declared his intentions to Gury Shishkin, but again the character of this Gury detracts from the credibility of his denunciation. It is evident that Shishkin was an agent of Palitsyn. He addresses himself thus to Palitsyn in Moscow: "Lord Cellarer, Brother Avraamy, by your great grace and favor, your pupil, the monk Brother Gury." From this same document it appears that Gury, having accused the treasurer Kochergin and the brethren of plundering the monastic treasury, was seeking the treasurer's position for himself. He hoped to obtain it through the good offices of Palitsyn and Shuisky, against the wishes of the brethren, who were hostile to him. He asked that the documents containing his appointment be addressed to Dolgoruky, and kept secret from the brethren.

More than one reference has been made to the document addressed to Shuisky by several of the Trinity brethren, with the denunciation against Golokhvastov, the archimandrite and the cathedral chapter. It was written in the name of a number of brethren; in fact it was speaking on behalf of them all. "To the tsar and sovereign, Grand Prince Vasily Ivanovich of All Russia, from your clergy, priests and brethren of the monastery of the Life-giving Trinity and St. Sergius, who pray to God and present their petition." But the document concludes with the following passage: "Furthermore there is great dissension in the monastery, caused by the queen of Livonia, the nun Martha.[19] She utters vain and reproachful words against the sovereign, and calls the brigand the true tsar and her brother. She long has been meddling in the contentious affair among the common people. For when the brigands first came to the monastery, during the first sortie the treasurer sent to the brigands the young monk Oska Selevin with treasonous letters, which conveyed the same message as those of the treasurer. She sent to the brigand, calling him her brother. She also wrote to the Lithuanian lord, Sapieha, and his companions, thanking him for having come on behalf of the Muscovite sovereign, Tsar Dmitry Ivanovich. She further wrote to the headquarters of the Polish lord, Rozynski, and his companions. She also sends Joseph Devochkin pies, pancakes and other delicacies. And, she also takes mead from the tsar's vault in the Trinity monastery cellars. The queen's servants wait on him incessantly, and heat baths for him once a week, at night. When I, your monk, remonstrated with her about the fact that she daily sends that traitor to your majesty drink and food, the queen conceived a great hatred for me, and writes to you with false accusations, saying that I insulted her. I implore you, therefore, sovereign, to send us your decree, so that this holy place will not enter danger through her folly."

It is strange how suddenly the brethren of the Trinity monastery become transformed into a single monk. Who was that monk? It is not hard to guess. At the beginning of the missive it is stated that the archimandrite and the brethren bore a grudge against them, the group of brethren, meaning against him, the solitary monk, by reason of the denunciation against Devochkin. But we know that the informant was Gury Shishkin. In this manner the accusers of Devochkin and Golokhvastov, themselves acting in such an underhanded manner, forfeit their own credibility.

TUSHINO SEIZES THE NORTHERN TOWNS

Whatever the case, whatever the feeble impulses of treason may have been, the Trinity monastery held whereas other towns of the northern sector of the Muscovite realm easily capitulated to the Tushinites. But even here the successes of the latter were of short duration. It has been seen that the struggle known as the Time of Troubles was fought, properly speaking, between anti-social and social elements; between the cossacks, those without homes, people discontented with their lot and trying to live at the expense of others, and the people of the land, the guardians of public order. In this respect, the Muscovite realm was divided into two parts—the southern and northern.

In the southern part, in the Ukraine, adjoining the steppe and the Lithuanian frontier, the cossack element predominated. Here the towns for the most part bore the character of military strongholds. To that region there streamed from all parts of the realm people unable for various reasons to remain in their places of residence. The northern regions, which for a long time were peaceful, were in a flourishing condition in comparison with the southern regions. Here peaceful trade had not been disrupted by Tatar raids. Commerce had been concentrated in the north since the opening of the White Sea trade route. In short, the northern regions were the richest, and among their population the people tilling the land predominated—people devoted to peaceful, profitable occupations, wishing to defend the fruits of their labor, desirous of order and tranquility. The anti-social element acted in the name of the Tushino tsar, but unfortunately the people cultivating the land had no leader since even in Moscow, and so much more so in the provinces, disorder, uncertainty and doubt reigned in the wake of the recent fearful and strange events. Tushino took advantage of this situation, which tied the hands of the people inhabiting the land, and seized the northern towns.

The first town to fall was Suzdal. Here the citizens wanted to defend themselves, but a certain Menshik Shilov gathered around him a number of people who proceeded to kiss the cross to Tsar Dmitry. It has been observed how during the Time of Troubles the first to set an example, the first decisive voice, acted powerfully on an indecisive crowd. The whole town followed the lead of Shilov, and even the archbishop was compelled to go along with them. Lisowski set up his headquarters in Suzdal after laying waste the surrounding countryside.

Vladimir was swayed by Ivan Ivanovich Godunov. Having held out valiantly before Kromy for his kinsman against the first False Dmitry, Godunov now was unwilling to support Shuisky. He refused to obey the tsar's decree, and did not proceed to Nizhny Novgorod. Instead he remained at Vladimir and induced its inhabitants to swear allegiance to the pretender, even though at first, like the inhabitants of Suzdal, they wished to hold out against him.

But the inhabitants of Pereiaslavl, the very moment that Sapieha's forces appeared before the town, swore allegiance to the pretender, and together with the Tushinites moved against Rostov. The inhabitants of Rostov, according to the words of a contemporary account, lived simply. They had no advice or warning. They sought to flee to towns further north but were prevented by the metropolitan, Filaret Nikitich Romanov,[20] and their governor, Tretiak Seitov, who had gathered together several thousand soldiers, and with them they attacked Sapieha's cossacks and followers from Pereiaslavl. But Seitov was beaten and fled back to Rostov, where he valiantly continued to defend himself for yet another three hours. Having finally defeated the governor, the cossacks and men from Pereiaslavl burst into the cathedral church where Filaret had sought sanctuary with a crowd of people. Despite the pleas of the metropolitan, who had come out with bread and salt, they broke down the doors, slaughtered many of the people, desecrated the sanctuary, and even the chronicler says that all this was done not by the Lithuanians but by his own people, the men of Pereiaslavl.[21]

Such an act committed by the latter is difficult to explain, except in terms of traditional enmity between Pereiaslavl and Rostov. Filaret was conveyed ignominiously to Tushino, where he was conferred an honor even more degrading than the previous abuse. The pretender, out of consideration for his kinship with his putative brother, Tsar Fedor, proclaimed him patriarch of Moscow, and Filaret was compelled to send out documents proclaiming his elevation to the patriarchate from Tushino, throughout all the territories which had recognized the pretender. In such a manner there is preserved his letter to Sapieha concerning the consecration of a church. It begins: "The blessing of the great lord, the Most Holy Filaret, metropolitan of Rostov and Yaroslavl, called patriarch of Moscow and all Russia."

The fugitives from Rostov harrassed and terrorized the inhabitants of Yaroslavl, the more substantial of whom had abandoned their homes and fled. The remainder, with their governor, Prince Fedor Boriatinsky, sent their submission to Tushino. "Have mercy, sovereign, on us, your servants, and take away our guilt, since we have resisted you, sovereign, unwittingly because of our sins. For we, your servants, were tempted by traitors to your crown, who plotted against you, and told us that you had been killed in Moscow. Thus we are guilty before you only in so far as we believed the traitors to your crown. Have mercy upon us, for we are ready to serve you, and to prepare everything in your favor, and also to die for you, our legitimate sovereign. We beg you to forgive us, so that we may have faith in the favor of your highness." Boriatinsky thereafter sent to Vologda, to the local governor Pushkin, a decree and an oath of allegiance. The latter sent the decree to Totma, the inhabitants of which "being under duress, kissed the cross with tears." In Totma even Kozma Danilovich Stroganov swore allegiance to the brigand but at the same time, under the cover of night, he gathered together the junior boyars and the better people, and read to them an admonitory epistle from the Muscovite tsar. Whom were they to believe? For whom were they to decide? Twenty-two towns had sworn allegiance to the Tushino tsar, but most of them against their will. Being taken by surprise, following the lead of others, who could be certain which side was in the right? (October 1608)

POLISH RAPACITY

But soon afterwards the people of the land, the inhabitants of the northern towns and villages, were shaken out of their uncertainty by the behavior of the Tushinites. One of the latter, describing the arrival of the Polish detachments to aid False Dmitry, said: "It was amazing how, the more people gathered together in our camp, the less we were able to achieve, because with the arrival of more people, the number of factions among us multiplied."

Sapieha and Lisowski acted independently of one another. People were found who, to spite Rozynski, and in defiance of the council's decision, wanted to bring Miechowicki back into the host. He therefore returned to Tushino. When Rozynski found out about this, he sent word that Miechowicki must leave immediately, otherwise he would give the order for him to be killed. Miechowicki hid in the tsar's house but Rozynski came there with four of his followers, personally seized

Miechowicki and ordered his companions to kill him, which they immediately did. The pretender was angry, but was silent, for Rozynski threatened him also.

But even the factions at Tushino could not harm False Dmitry as much as the conduct of his supporters, whose first thought was of money, which they demanded of the tsar. He vainly begged them to be patient. They took away his personal insignia and ordered him to write out documents addressed to the towns, assessing fresh contributions upon them. With these documents, one Pole and one Russian travelled to each town. The chief instigator of this business was Andrzej Mlocki.

At first the pretender had sent letters of commendation to towns which had submitted to him. He promised the gentry and the servicemen the tsar's bounty, money, cloth and lands, and to the clergy and the remaining inhabitants he sent charters of immunity, according to which none of the tsar's taxes would be collected from them. But suddenly, at the instigation of Mlocki and his companions, there arrived documents demanding heavy contributions. When such documents were read out in Vologda before all the people the inhabitants said nothing against them, but wept, secretly saying to one another: "Even though we have kissed the cross to him, we only wish God to avert His just anger from us, and give victory to our sovereign, Vasily Ivanovich. Thus would we be glad to serve him with our lives. If only the other towns, Ustiug, Usolie and the maritime towns would help us!"

COMMUNICATIONS AMONG THE NORTHERN TOWNS

The inhabitants of Ustiug, by reason of their remote situation, had time to gather information, and to consider and take counsel. Those who had come from Yaroslavl and Vologda told them of the hasty oath of allegiance the people had sworn to the Tushino tsar, the rapacity of the Tushinites, and the oppression those who had sworn allegiance had suffered. They said that the towns were only awaiting help before rising up against their oppressors, that the integrity of the Muscovite realm, by which order was maintained in the land, now had been violated, and that the old times of disunity had reappeared. "These towns which defend themselves, or even willingly kiss the cross, are all given to Polish lords as prizes, as patrimonies, just as formerly there were separate principalities."

The inhabitants of Yaroslavl sent to Tushino thirty thousand rubles, and promised to raise a thousand mounted men, but these sacrifices did not save them from oppression. The Poles broke into the houses of the nobles and the shops of the merchants. They took goods without payment and insulted the common people in the streets. Hearing such stories, the people of Ustiug decided not to swear allegiance to him who called himself Tsar Dmitry. They could not call him the pretender, since they did not know anything for sure. They resolved to stand firm, and assemble people from all the region of Ustiug. They immediately sent to the inhabitants of Vologda with news of their decision, urging the leading townsmen to take counsel with the Stroganovs, Maxim Yakovlevich and Nikita Grigorievich.[22] "What is their intention? Do they want to stand firm with the townsmen of Ustiug in this matter and reach a firm decision and hold fast by it?" In the event of their agreement, they requested the dispatch of five, six or ten men to act as a liaison. The inhabitants of Ustiug concluded their letter with the following words, from which it was evident that they firmly wished to resist the Tushino tsar: "For in Yaroslavl they have levied eighteen rubles from each ploughland, and have taken an inventory of all the goods of the trading people, and have sent them to the regiments."

Not receiving any reply from Vychegodsk, the inhabitants of Ustiug sent them a second letter, in which they gave news of Shuisky's success. They complained about their long silence, and concluded the letter once again with the significant words, from which the current state of mind might best be guaged: "You should also bear in mind for what reason we have entrusted our souls to Tsar Vasily Ivanovich. If we hear that God has sent His just wrath against all the Russian land, even though Tsar Vasily is far away, we shall succeed in sending our submission to him."

The inhabitants of Ustiug persuaded those of Vychegodsk not to kiss the cross to Dmitry, since if they were to kiss the cross on account of the letter from Pushkin, governor of Vologda, all honor would be ascribed to him, and not to them. The letter concludes: "We beg you, take firm counsel with the community, and do not make haste to kiss the cross. We cannot tell how things will turn out."

In the same spirit Abbot Joel wrote from Nizhny Novgorod to Abbot Jonas of the Tikhonov hermitage that he should persuade the inhabitants of Balakhna not to desert the inhabitants of Nizhny Novgorod, who had resolved to remain loyal to the tsar who reigned in Moscow. "In order that Christian blood may not be shed, let the inhabitants of Balakhna and all the people remain as before of one mind with the people of Nizhny Novgorod, and let them send some of their better men. You should speak with them concerning this matter to this effect; that whosoever is sovereign over all the Muscovite realm must be sovereign over us and over you. Until now we have not sent to you, and you have not come in arms to Nizhny Novgorod. But now the inhabitants of Balakhna should come to Nizhny Novgorod with all that they can muster, and Nizhny Novogord will rally to the support of Balakhna. Thus we will correspond on matters of common concern, but not concerning oaths of allegiance." In fact, for peaceful people the difficult question of to whom to kiss the cross was a contentious matter, breaking peace and good relations between the inhabitants of a single realm.

UPRISING AGAINST THE TUSHINITES

At the very time when several towns were in correspondence, urging each other not to swear allegiance to the Tushino tsar, the inhabitants of Ustiuzhna Zhelezolpolskaia set an example of heroic resistance.[23] On December 6, 1607 there arrived a letter from the inhabitants of Beloozero, with the advice that they should not violate the Christian faith, but be ready to lay down their lives for the house of the Blessed Virgin, for Tsar Vasily and for each other, and not surrender to the Poles and Lithuanians. The inhabitants of Ustiuzhna were encouraged by such advice, and sent the inhabitants of Beloozero a similar letter.

At that time there arrived emissaries from Tushino to collect provisions. The inhabitants of Ustiuzhna refused them, sending them on to Beloozero, while they themselves decided to hold out, even though they had neither stockade nor fortifications. They sent a summons to all boyars and gentry of the province. They kissed the cross in the cathedral church, swearing not to surrender to Lithuania. They also elected a captain, Solmen Otrepiev, and also Bogdan Persky, as well as the chancellor, Alexis Suvorov, for at the time there was no governor in Ustiuzhna. Soon afterwards Andrei Petrovich Rtishchev arrived from Moscow, and the inhabitants of Ustiuzhna accepted him as their governor. Then Foma Podshchipaev came from Beloozero, with four hundred men to assist him.

Hearing of the approach of the Poles, Cherkassians and Russian brigands, Rtishchev advanced with his army to meet them, but he did not wish to advance very far, saying that the Lithuanians and Germans were very skillful in military matters, and were advancing with a large force. "Let us go," they cried, "against the evil heretics. Let us lay down our lives for the Holy Church of God and for the Christian faith." The commander was compelled to advance and on January 5, 1608 encountered the Lithuanians near the village of Batnevka. The men of Ustiuzhna and Beloozero, having no knowledge of military matters, according to the words of a contemporary, were surrounded by the enemy and cut down like grass. Rtishchev managed to get away to Ustiuzhna, but he did not know what to do next. His men had been slaughtered. The Lithuanians were before Moscow and Novgorod, and Ustiuzhna had no fortifications.

Despite this desperate situation, the men of Ustiuzhna and Beloozero who survived the defeat gathered together and decided: "It would be better for us to die in the house of the Mother of God and for the Christian faith in Ustiuzhna." Fortunately for them, the Poles withdrew from Batnevka. The men of Ustiuzhna took advantage of this withdrawal and built a stockade, working day and night. They dug ditches and placed caltrops, they forged cannon and firearms, cannonball, shot, helmets and pikes. Skopin sent gunpowder and a hundred soldiers but, following them, came stragglers with news that the Poles under Kazakowski were approaching Ustiuzhna.

Thus on February 3 the sentries saw from their watchtowers the enemy, both Lithuanians and Cherkassians, as well as Germans and Tushino Russians. They fell like rain upon the stockade. The besieged, with the cry, "Lord have mercy!", began to open fire and effect sorties. The enemy withdrew, but at noon resumed their attack. Yet again they were forced to retreat. At the last hour of the night the Poles ordered a fresh assault, but once again the townsmen repulsed them. Then the defenders made some sorties. They captured the besiegers' cannon and pursued them some four versts from the town. On February 8, receiving reinforcements, the Poles once again assaulted Ustiuzhna on all sides, but once again were repulsed with heavy losses. After that they did not return. As is apparent from the account of the siege of Ustiuzhna, the citizens were fortified by religious inspiration. Since then, every February 10, they have commemorated the deliverance of their town from the Poles by a religious procession, in which they carry the miraculous icon of the Virgin.

Everywhere the conduct of the Tushinites increasingly restricted the choice between the Moscow and the Tushino tsar. There was no end to the contributions levied. One demand for provisions came from Tushino; then there came another from Sapieha's camp. The governors had no idea how to comply with these demands, and it was altogether impossible to keep everyone happy. The governors demanded documents with the tsar's seal, but in return they received abuse.

Sapieha was playing an important role, and the governors addressed petitions to him. For example, Prince Boriatinsky, governor of Yaroslavl, wrote to him: "You, lord, must have pity upon me, and intercede with the tsar on my behalf. I sent you a petition concerning a land grant. I asked that you obtain for me from the tsar a small estate. I am very anxious to obtain your favor, and will be glad to earn it in any way I can." But repeated monetary exactions exhausted the people's patience. The Tushinites marked their campaigns with a fearful frenzy but not the Poles, because these foreigners had entered the Muscovite realm only for the sake of booty. They were indifferent to all events going on around them; for although indifference and callousness do not lead to any good, neither do they lead to any extremity of evil. For this reason the Poles were not concerned to commit violence for its own sake within the Muscovite realm. They had come for booty, for the good life, for which they needed money and women, so their violence went no further than plunder and rape. They did not need blood. Having a good time on foreign soil, feasting at the expense of others, they could if need be return home, and that would be the end of it. The fate of their native country was not at issue, neither were their own interests.

But such was not the position of the Tushino Russians, the Russian cossacks, who had no homes. A Russian who had gone over to False Dmitry, and had thereby obtained obvious status, obvious advantages, would lose all of this, in fact would have no future at all, should Shuisky triumph. It is thus understandable how such a Russian regarded those who wished Shuisky victory, the supporters of Shuisky. He regarded them, not as compatriots, but as accursed foes capable of depriving him of all future prospects. He must consolidate the advantages of his position and free himself from fear of the future. The only way to do this was by destroying his accursed foes.

As far as the old and the new cossacks were concerned they, who for so long had been restrained by the realm, now hastened to revenge themselves upon it and live at its expense. They viewed as accursed foes not only the men who advanced against them in arms under the banners of the Muscovite tsar, but also the peaceful citizen enjoying the fruits of honorable labor, and it was upon him that they vented their fury. They needed to devastate the realm utterly, to destroy all non-cossacks, all the people of the land, in order to feel secure for the future. Therefore it is not surprising to read in contemporary accounts that they did far greater violence to their own countrymen than did the foreigners, the Poles.

When the Poles took a supporter of the Muscovites prisoner, he was treated decently and saved from death. If the same man fell into the hands of the Tushino Russians he would be put to death immediately in the most savage manner. Foreigners looked with horror upon such atrocity, and ascribed it to the innate cruelty of the nation. If Russians treat one another in this manner, they thought, how will they deal with us if we fall into their hands? But their fears were groundless. For their part, the Russians did not understand the indifference of the Poles and, seeing that they dealt decently with their prisoners, called them pusillanimous old women.

The same contemporary writer expresses amazement at how the Tushino Russians constantly served as cannon fodder for a small number of Poles, who hardly ever took part in the battles, but when it was a matter of grabbing booty the Poles were there first, and the Russians yielded the greater part of the booty to them without question. The Tushino Russians and cossacks not only looked on callously at the desecration of churches, at disregard for the sanctity of priests and monks, they also abetted the foreigners in this desecration and mockery. Human habitations were turned into cages for animals. Bears, wolves, foxes and hares freely wandered around market places, and birds wove their nests in human corpses. People replaced animals in seeking the forest as a refuge. They hid in caves, and sought darkness in impenetrable thickets. They looked forward to the onset of night, but the nights were illuminated. Instead of the moon, the glow of conflagrations lit up the fields and forests. The hunt for wild animals gave way to manhunts, for men whose tracks were pursued by hunting dogs.

The cossacks, if they could find no other way to destroy the provisions of the towns, strewed them with water and trampled them with their horses. They burned houses and frenziedly destroyed all the household goods. Where they did not burn the houses, they at least damaged them. They demolished the doors and gates in order to render the houses uninhabitable. Wild animals treated people better, says a contemporary, because a wild animal only inflicts bodily death, whereas the Tushinites and Poles brought degeneracy into society. They seized wives from their husbands, young girls from their parents. Lawlessness, inclination to vice, the easy pretext and ready justification for enslavement, the constant use of force, finally becoming accustomed to violence and degeneracy—all these things served to promote immorality. Many women escaped dishonor by killing themselves, throwing themselves into rivers from steep cliffs. Yet many who had fallen captive, and then ransomed by their relatives, once more fled to the encampment of their ravishers, unable to keep away from them, unable to turn themselves away from vice. Then there were people, even some in holy orders, who took advantage of the desolation of society to obtain personal profit, buying ecclesiastical offices from the enemies of society, with money and denunciations against people who were true to their duty. But such people did not enjoy their corrupt purchases for long for their example inspired others, who pushed up the price of this immoral auction, by means of which power changed hands. Confidence and trust in them was broken, and ecclesiastical anarchy joined hands with political anarchy.

Here is the kind of petition received by the Tushino tsar from his subjects: "To Tsar Dmitry Ivanovich, sovereign and grand prince of All the Russias. We, your orphans, your poor little peasants, plundered and burned out, bow our heads to you, and kneel before you. We have perished: we have been ruined by your soldiers. Our horses, cattle and our livestock have been taken away, and we ourselves have been burned and tortured. Our farmsteads have been burned out, and all the rye flour we had also has been burned. The remainder of the grain has been ground up by the people whom you sent, and taken away. We are now orphans, and wander from house to house begging. There is no drink or food. We and our womenfolk are all dying of hunger, yet despite this your officials come to us and demand payment of the hundred-tax, and subsistence for the Polish lords. We are tortured in the market place for our money, yet there is nowhere that we can get any."[24]

From another quarter there arrived this petition: "Lithuanian, Tatar and Russian troops have descended upon us. They beat and tortured us, and took away our livestock. Have mercy upon us, your orphans, and send your officers to keep the peace." A third letter from a peasant reads: "Your crown bailliff, Lord Mosznicki, is staying with me in the village. He forcibly abducted my little son, and took him into the encampments, and he also comes to my house every night and evicts me from my homestead. He does not give me any bread, and forcibly keeps my daughter-in-law in his bed."

Yet not a single complaint of the oppressed had any effect. The governor of Suzdal, Pleshcheev, reported to Sapieha: "In many of the towns there has occurred great unrest on account of the magnitude of the monetary contributions. The menfolk rebelled, and kissed the cross to Vasily

Shuisky. For this reason I am unable to gather the money as soon as you would wish, for among the people there is great unrest." In every one of his letters to Sapieha, Pleshcheev complains about the cossacks. Veliaminov, the governor of Vladimir, was forced to arm himself against the cossacks, or "outlaws," who laid waste the province of Vladimir. One detachment sent against them captured Nalivaiko, the leader of the plunderers.[25] According to Veliaminov, he had put many people to death, including gentry and junior boyars. He had impaled them, dishonored their wives and children, and had taken them captive. News of the crimes of Nalivaiko even reached Tushino and had moved the pretender to indignation, for he saw how the activities of the cossacks were undermining the success of his enterprise. He sent an order to Veliaminov that Nalivaiko should be executed forthwith, and addressed a reprimand to Sapieha, who had requested that Nalivaiko be released, in the following terms: "You are not acting properly when you intercede on behalf of such a brigand. For this Nalivaiko with his own hands has done to death some of our people who have served us, the great sovereign. His victims include gentry, junior boyars and all kinds of people, ninety-three men and women in all. Henceforth you should not, therefore, write to us requesting pardon from the tsar for such brigands. We have ordered that this Nalivaiko be executed for his brigandage, and that henceforth you should hunt down such brigands, in order that they may not lay waste our fatherland, or shed the blood of true Orthodox Christians."

But the pretender's commands were to no avail, and uprisings broke out in various places. The free peasantry rose up. They assembled throughout the towns and districts. In Yuriev-Polsky they gathered under their hundredman Fedor Krasny, in Reshma under the peasant Grigory Lapsha, in the region of Balakhna under the leadership of Ivan Kushinnikov, in Gorokhovets under Fedor Nagovitsyn, and on the Kholaia river the movement was led by Ilya Dengin. They gathered together and proceeded to Lukh. There they defeated the Lithuanians, and proceeded to Shuia. Lisowski sent against them the infamous governor of Suzdal, Fedor Pleshcheev, but he was defeated near the village of Danilovo, and fled back to Suzdal. The insurgents fortified themselves in a stockade within the village of Danilovo, but they could not defend it against the multitude of the enemy which came to besiege them. After many encounters the stronghold was captured, and many free peasants were slain.

But this was not the end of the uprising. Galich, Kostroma, Vologda, Beloozero, Ustiuzhna, Gorodets, Bezhetsky Verkh and Kashin all broke away from Tushino. The towns were not satisfied simply to cast off the Tushino yoke. In order that it should not fall upon them again, they hastened to equip as many soldiers as possible for the defense of Moscow, and they sent letters around to the other towns, urging them also to arm themselves and pass on the call to arms. These documents concluded thus: "If you do not attend to this great matter, you will not be looked upon favorably, either by God or by the sovereign."

The inhabitants of Vologda wrote that they had thrown False Dmitry's emissaries into prison. They had seized their letters, which allegedly concluded with the instruction to slay the inhabitants, seize their belongings, and send their wives and children captive to Lithuania. From Totma the message came that some Tushinites, who were bringing an order to free criminals from the prisons had been arrested. Under interrogation the captives answered the question about the people surrounding the Tushino tsar by naming Prince Zvenigorodsky, Prince Dmitry Timofeevich Trubetskoy and Crown Secretary Safonov. They repeated various opinions concerning the origins of the Tushino brigand. Some called him the son of Prince Andrei Kurbsky, others said that he was a priest's son from the Arbat quarter of Moscow. Others simply said that Dmitry was a brigand, not the true tsarevich, but they were ignorant of his parentage. On the other hand, some documents appeared in the northern towns, coming from the tsar in Moscow with the exhortation to preserve their unity and close their ranks. "If you do not soon stand together, but instead quarrel among yourselves, and do not stand up for each other, you will bring upon yourselves utter ruin at the hands of brigands, the devastation of your houses and the dishonoring of your wives and children. You will be traitors to yourselves, to our Christian faith and to your country."

Urging the northern population to close ranks, Shuisky himself nevertheless continued to be shut up in Moscow, with no opportunity to take command of the insurgent movement. He thus left the direction of the movement to the initiative of the towns. "If you are unable to come to us in Moscow, then proceed without delay to whatever place is best. But if, in order to gather together greater numbers, you find it better to assemble in Yaroslavl, write to us concerning this matter. If you have any news concerning our boyar and commander, Fedor Ivanovich Sheremetev[26] and his companions, by all means join up with him, and take counsel together as to what to do." In conclusion the tsar informed them that everything was in order in Moscow, that the army was eager to do battle with the brigands, and that he had information from the enemy ranks that there were many who wished to betray the Lithuanians at the opportune moment. Skopin-Shuisky, for his part, had sent letters in which he informed the towns of his imminent arrival with strong Swedish reinforcements.

The citizens of Vychegda and the four Stroganovs sent to Moscow a detachment of excellently armed troops. The insurgent towns, embittered at the Tushinites, were quick to settle the score. When Lisowski conquered Kostroma, he devastated it fearfully. Galich also was recaptured by the Tushinites. At Vologda preparations were made for a resolute defense, even though some differences had arisen between Vologda and some of the other northern towns. In Vologda the former governor, Pushkin, and Crown Secretary Voronov were still in office. These two formerly had sworn allegiance to Dmitry. The towns, therefore, did not wish to have any dealings with these men, and wrote directly to the commune. The citizens of Vologda were insulted by this show of distrust, and wrote to the people of Ustiug in the following terms: "You write that you wish to consult with us concerning military matters and the government of the land, but you do not address your letter to the governor or the crown secretary. But the governor and the crown secretary are still responsible for government and territorial matters, and consult with us, and seek our approval concerning all matters. We therefore are perturbed that you do not write to them concerning the aforementioned consultation."

The people of Totma were not satisfied, and called the governor and crown secretary traitors, but then they went further, and applied this epithet to all inhabitants of Vologda. Soldiers who had gathered in Vologda from all the various towns wrote to the inhabitants of Vychegda that the men of Vologda had kissed the cross, had sworn to stand fast with those of the other towns which had rallied, and that the representatives of the other towns had reciprocated. They had sworn to stand firm, not to betray each other, and not to leave the town without the authorization of the commune. Nevertheless there was considerable unrest among the inhabitants of Totma, who had called the governor, the crown secretary and the inhabitants of Vologda traitors, and whose letters to the governor and commune of Vologda were couched in abusive terms, for the purpose of picking a quarrel, rather than in the spirit of solidarity. They asserted that the citizens of Ustiug and Usolie were instructing them to write thus: "And you, sirs, should take counsel with the citizens of Ustiug, and should write to the citizens of Totma, that it is useless to stir dissension and hatred by writing thus to Vologda. For we who have been in Vologda have yet to notice any treason. If we do happen to notice any treason, we will observe the people concerned, and investigate them with severe torture, and will gather evidence to find out the instigators of this treason. In this we will co-operate with the inhabitants of Vologda."

Yet the inhabitants of Totma and those of the other towns still thought that they were justified in calling Pushkin a traitor. They seized one man from Tushino, who under torture declared that Nikita Pushkin from Vologda was in correspondence with the brigand's forces. He said that about a third of the inhabitants would stand firm, while another third would surrender. As soon as the enemy came, Pushkin would surrender the town.

The inhabitants of Perm did not help the common cause either. The words of the inhabitants of Ustiug plainly had an influence on them, since they had written that they would be glad to kiss the cross to him who called himself Dmitry, and they would do so when he came closer. They did not in fact kiss the cross to the Tushino tsar but, on the other hand, they did not help resist him, and waited to see which side would be victorious. The inhabitants of Vychegda wrote to them: "You write to us that you would be glad to stand together with us, as being of one mind, but you do not contribute anything. For the apostate Lithuanians and the Russian brigands who are with them are making war upon our villages and on our countryside. They dishonor the churches of God, they desecrate the icons, tear away the mountings and the metal work, trample upon the Orthodox faith, slaughter the peasants, and carry off their wives and children into Lithuanian captivity. They plunder our possessions, and boast that they wish to come to Vologda and to the places on the Sukhona in order to make war in our territories. Therefore if such ruin occurs in our lands, we shall know whom to blame, nor will it be the work of God and the tsar. Take care that you do not have any dealings with the Lithuanians, otherwise a similar fate will also overtake you."

The Time of Troubles unbound the hands of those who, with the confidence of impunity, delighted at drawing profit from the common ill. The elders of Perm and their officials, who were supposed to forward supplies of grain to the landless Siberian servicemen, purchased grain mixed with chaff at cheap prices in Verkhoturie. "And because of these defective supplies," states the tsar's document, "soldiers in the Siberian towns perished through hunger, for the inhabitants of Verkhoturie sold supplies of grain, which they mixed with stones and dust." In the Dvina land the inhabitants, now free of all government control, drowned Crown Secretary Ilya Uvarov. They also wished to kill the governor, Ivan Miliukov-Gus, accusing him of various acts of injustice, but reconsidered. They came to the prison where he was confined, and respectfully begged him come to the chancellery and govern them as before.

Yet notwithstanding the treason and quarrels among the towns, the indifference or inactivity of some regions, the cause of the people of the land in their struggle against the brigands prospered. Crowds of strangers from the Volga basin, Mordvins and Cheremiss, besieged Nizhny Novgorod, and were joined by a detachment of forces from Tushino under the command of Prince Semen Viazemsky. The people of Nizhny Novgorod affected a sortie, routed the besiegers, chased them away from their city, and also captured Prince Viazemsky. The citizens of Nizhny Novogord hanged him, without first informing Moscow.

It has been observed how the citizens of Nizhny Novgorod, through Abbot Joel, had persuaded the inhabitants of Balakhna not to enter into arguments over the rights of Dmitry or Shuisky, but to recognize as sovereign the one who was recognized by Moscow. But the inhabitants of Balakhna ignored Joel's advice, and so the citizens of Nizhny Novgorod, under the command of Governor Aliabiev,[27] captured Balakhna. There are indications that at this time the individual towns supported their own soldiers. Every serviceman sent on campaign to another town or district received from his own town a month's pay in advance and, at the expiry of this month, his home town sent him money wherever he happened to be. Skopin sent his commander, Vysheslavtsev, to take command of the troops of the northern towns, and he defeated the Tushinites, taking from them Romanov and Poshekhonie. Mologa and Rybinsk also swore allegiance to Tsar Vasily. Gathering forty thousand troops, Vysheslavtsev moved from Romanov and defeated the Tushino commander Tyszkiewicz, as a result of which Yaroslavl and Uglich were occupied. The inhabitants of Viatka wrote to Perm that in Arzamas, Murom, Vladimir and Suzdal, as well as some of the other towns, the people wished to submit to the sovereign, and to kiss the cross. They were awaiting only the arrival of the boyar and commander, Fedor Ivanovich Sheremetev, whom Tsar Vasily had ordered to leave the siege of Astrakhan and proceed northwards along the Volga, bringing into submission the towns along the way.

Sheremetev successfully fulfilled this command. In fact the inhabitants of Murom were in correspondence with Aliabiev, governor of Nizhny Novgorod, and had allowed him to enter the town. Meanwhile the inhabitants of Vladimir, as soon as they heard of the approach of the contingent from Nizhny Novgorod, immediately rose up against the Tushinites. Their governor, Veliaminov, persisted in his loyalty to False Dmitry. The inhabitants of Vladimir seized him and took him to the cathedral church in order that, having confessed and taken the sacraments, he might prepare for death. The archpriest of the cathedral, having celebrated the mysteries, brought him out before the people, saying: "Here is the enemy of the Muscovite realm!" Then the entire populace stoned Veliaminov, kissed the cross to Tsar Vasily, and took up arms against the brigands, without sparing their own lives.

In the account of this incident it is interesting to observe the solemnity with which it is related. Here we do not see a turbulent uprising of the common people, the usual consequence of which is instant violence and murder. The people restrained their passions, and gave the guilty person time to prepare for death in a Christian manner. They acted in full consciousness, not simply destroying the man because they hated him. On the contrary, they showed respect for this man, executing a governor who had been a traitor to the realm. Note also the words of the archpriest concerning Veliaminov: "Here is the enemy of the Muscovite realm!" These words show that the inhabitants of Vladimir understood the significance of Tushino and its supporters, the brigands who were threatening with equal ruin everyone who supported the realm. The archpriest did not say: "Here is the enemy of the Muscovite sovereign," for at that time, as far as the towns were concerned, the problem of the relative rights of Dmitry and Shuisky had not been decided. They generally tried to circumvent it, and for them the struggle between the two rival tsars, Dmitry and Shuisky, disappeared, leaving the struggle between the social and the anti-social principle. Besides, not all inhabitants of the northern towns acted in the same manner as those of Vladimir. In Kostroma the inhabitants tortured the pretender's governor, Prince Mosalsky, for a long time, and then, having severed his arms and legs, threw him into the river.

The chronicler was correct when he said that the citizens of Vladimir fought against the supporters of the brigands, not sparing their own lives. Their enemies say the same. The pretender's governors of Suzdal, Pleshcheev and Prosovetsky,[28] wrote to Sapieha that they had approached Vladimir together with Lisowski, and although they fought outside the town against the traitors to the sovereign, and had besieged the town, they were unable to capture it because the traitors had resisted to the death. Moreover, they had sent to all the towns of the lower Volga with treasonable messages, tempting all the people to swear allegiance to Shuisky.

In the same letter the governors of Suzdal explained the reasons which persuaded the inhabitants of Vladimir to resist to the last man during the siege. "The Lithuanian squires[29] and cossacks who remain at Suzdal commit acts of brigandage, bringing ruin and great violence to the gentry and junior boyars, the monasteries and the townsmen. They abduct their wives and daughters. They plunder and burn the sovereign's villages, and also those of gentry and junior boyars, as well as the possessions of the monasteries. We also are suffering great indignities from the Lithuanian squires and cossacks. How can we say that there is any justice in the sovereign's cause? How can we prevent the devastation of the sovereign's lands, the burning of villages and the violence and unrest in the land, while these persons insult us, the sovereign's servants? They abuse us, and seek to do violence to us."

The governors also mention acts of violence committed by Lisowski who, under the flimsiest of pretexts, was depriving people of their liberty and plundering them, even though they had committed no offense whatsoever against the sovereign. But even one of these governors of Suzdal, who was complaining so bitterly against the depredations of Lisowski, himself had a sinister reputation among the inhabitants of the northern towns. Prosovetsky, who originally had been one of the atamans of the cossack hosts, had been promoted to the rank of table attendant at Tushino. At first he had been governor of the town of Lukh, and when news came that the pretender was appointing him governor of Suzdal in place of Fedor Pleshcheev, the citizens of Suzdal wrote to Sapieha as follows: "Lord Jan-Piotr Pavlovich Sapieha, hetman to our Tsar and Grand Prince Dmitry Ivanovich of All Russia, governor of Kiev, elder of Uswiat and Kerepecki, we, your servants, the townsmen, gentry, junior boyars and all the people of Suzdal make petition. We have heard rumors that the sovereign has ordered his lord-in-waiting and governor, Fedor Pleshcheev, to rejoin him in his regiments, and we are to have as our governors Andrei Prosovetsky and Nekhoroshy Babkin, a native of Suzdal. But you, lord, should use your persuasion to intercede with our sovereign, that he should order Fedor Kirillovich to remain with us as before, so that our services to you will not become less effective. But if you do not show us mercy, and the sovereign does not grant our request, and insists on summoning Fedor Kirillovich to rejoin him in his regiments, we and all the town, including our mothers, wives and children, will petition you and the sovereign, saying we do not want Andrei Prosovetsky and Nekhoroshy Babkin for, if we do have them, our services to the realm will suffer, and we shall be utterly ruined."

The inhabitants were apparently happy that Pleshcheev remained with them as senior governor, and Prosovetsky merely was appointed deputy governor. It is also understandable why, after this, the inhabitants of Yaroslavl, like those of Vladimir, decided to resist to the last. In the spring of 1609 the Tushino forces, under the command of Naumov and Budzilo, approached Yaroslavl. For four days the townsmen of Yaroslavl blocked their river crossing on the Pakhna, about a mile from the town. Losing hope of overcoming the Yaroslavl people there, they retreated, crossed the river higher up, attacked the Yaroslavl forces in the rear, and defeated them. But when they approached the fortifications of Yaroslavl, there again they met with stiff resistance. They encountered musketeers from Archangel, numbering six hundred, and Siberians to the number of twelve hundred. The Tushinites finally succeeded in breaching the fortifications, but they could not capture the town and withdrew, fearing the arrival of Skopin, even though Yaroslavl, according to the expression of its townsmen, was for them the most coveted of prizes. Here it is worth noting that the Tushinites, having been unsuccessful in conducting the siege of towns, operated more successfully in open country against unorganized masses of the insurgent population, which had no experienced leaders. Thus the Poles, having suffered reverses at Vladimir and Yaroslavl, decisively defeated the territorial levies in various engagements.

UPRISINGS AGAINST SHUISKY IN MOSCOW

But at the moment the struggle in the north between social and anti-social elements was unfolding, while the common people were rising up in defense of the Muscovite realm, what was the condition of Moscow and its tsar, as the northern towns prepared again to rally to him? There they were playing at tsars like children, as a contemporary eyewitness commented. Demands for service and loyalty on either side, from one or other of the two bidders, inevitably raised their price, and there were many who found it convenient to satisfy the demands of both sides and receive double remuneration. Some who had kissed the cross to Shuisky in Moscow went

to Tushino, there to kiss the cross to the pretender and, having been rewarded by him, return to Moscow.

Shuisky granted them a gracious reception, for a repentant traitor was
valuable to him. His return bore witness to the others that the Tushino tsar
was false, or that there was no advantage in serving him. He who returned
received his reward, only for it to turn out that he once more deserted to
Tushino to demand new favors from False Dmitry. Friends and relatives
gathered together, dined together, and after dinner some proceeded to the
court of Tsar Vasily, while others went off to Tushino. Those who remained in Moscow felt secure. Were the Tushino tsarlet to prevail, they
thought, our brothers, relatives and friends who are with him will protect
us. If Tsar Vasily is victorious, we will do the same for them.

In houses and on public squares there was noisy discussion of events,
the Tushino tsar was proclaimed aloud, and people openly rejoiced in his
success. In Tushino many knew about these gatherings, and it was well
known that such and such persons who remained in Moscow nevertheless
favored the pretender, but made no mention of these facts to Shuisky.
Those who did report such things were called slanderers and talebearers.
Nobody dared speak ill of the mighty, since they had many supporters,
against whose will Shuisky would not dare execute them. Yet there were
incessant denunciations to the tsar against the weak, and the guilty suffered execution, and sometimes the innocent along with them. It was said
that Shuisky mistrusted those who served him personally and with their
physical strength, trusting only those who served him with their tongues.
But although Shuisky was not loved in Moscow the common people did
not wish to replace him with another boyar, still less the Tushino tsar, for
they knew very well what his triumph would mean for them. This is why
attempts to overthrow Shuisky failed.

The first attempt took place on February 17, 1609, on the Saturday
during Shrovetide. It was perpetrated by Grigory Sunbulov (whom we
have encountered before), Prince Roman Gagarin[30] and Timofey Griaznoy. There were about three hundred others involved in the plot. They first
addressed a demand to the boyars that they depose Shuisky, but the boyars
did not discuss the matter, dispersing to their homes to await the outcome
of the affair. Only one boyar, Prince Vasily Vasilievich Golitsyn, appeared
on the square. The conspirators sent to the patriarch in the Dormition
cathedral, demanding that he come to the platform on Red Square.
Hermogen did not wish to come, so they dragged him along and shoved

him from behind, blinded him with dust, while some even seized him by the chest and forcibly pulled him along. When they had set him up on the platform the conspirators shouted that Shuisky had been elected unlawfully, by his own supporters alone, without the consent of the land, that Christian blood was being shed on behalf of an unworthy man, who was in no way suitable, who was a fool, a fornicator, a drunkard and a blasphemer.

But instead of approval the conspirators heard the following words from the crowd: "He did not place himself upon the throne, but was put there by the great boyars, and by you, the gentry and servicemen. We have not heard anything about his drunkenness or any insane deeds. Even if the tsar is unpleasing to you, you cannot depose him from the tsardom without the consent of the great boyars and an assembly of all the people."

Then the conspirators exclaimed: "Shuisky secretly has slaughtered and drowned our brethren, gentry and junior boyars, women and children, and the number of those slain amounts to more than two thousand." The patriarch then asked them: "How is it that we have not heard anything about these deeds? When did all this happen? Tell us exactly who was slain." The conspirators continued to cry out: "He has had many of our brethren drowned, to this we can bear witness." The patriarch again asked: "Tell us the names of those he had drowned." They replied: "We have ordered that the lists be brought here, so that you can see for yourselves."

Then they read a manifesto addressed to the community from the Moscow regiments recruited from the Russian people. "Prince Vasily Shuisky was elected to the tsardom by Moscow alone, since the other towns do not recognize him. Prince Vasily Shuisky is not pleasing to us upon the throne, and because of him blood is being shed, and the land is not at peace. Should we not then choose another tsar in his place?" The patriarch then said: "Hitherto neither Novgorod, nor Kazan, nor Astrakhan, nor Pskov, nor any other town has commanded Moscow, but Moscow has held sway over all the other towns. Our lord Tsar and Grand Prince Vasily Ivanovich was beloved and chosen by God, by the Muscovite boyars and by you, the gentry and people of every rank, and by all Orthodox Christians. Many people were delegated from all the towns for his election as tsar, and all the land kissed the cross to the sovereign, swearing to wish him well, and not to think evil of him. But you have forgotten your solemn oath. A few of you have risen up against the tsar, and wish unjustly to cast him down from the throne. The community neither desires this end, nor recognizes the truth of your accusations, and therefore we refuse to take any further part in this assembly."

So saying, Hermogen went home. The conspirators, lacking any further support, were unable to detain him. With loud cries and abuse they rushed towards the palace, but Shuisky was not alarmed. He advanced towards them and spoke firmly. "Why do you oathbreakers come bursting into my house with such impudence? If you want to kill me, I am prepared, but you cannot depose me without the consent of the boyars and all the land." The conspirators, sensing their total failure, fled to Tushino, but Prince Golitsyn remained in Moscow in his previous status. It is nevertheless interesting that, while the Moscow populace was not willing to see Shuisky deposed, they still did not exert themselves to defend him from the conspirators.

After this the patriarch sent to Tushino two documents; one to those who had departed thence after February 17, and another to those who had gone over before that date. The first document begins: "To erstwhile Orthodox Christians of all ranks, ages and orders, though we do not know how we should address you now. Words fail me, my soul is heavy and my heart is grieved, all that is within me dissolves and all my limbs shudder, while weeping and sighing I beseech you; have mercy, have pity on your souls, and on the souls of your children. Arise, take thought, and return." The patriarch concluded his first missive by promising to obtain from the tsar forgivenness for those who repented: "The tsar is merciful, bears no malice, and knows that you are not acting thus of your own free will. Those of your brethren who rose up against him on Saturday of Shrovetide, and uttered false and uncouth words against him, and you, too, he has pardoned, and now they live here unscathed. Your wives and children are also still at liberty among us, and live in their own houses."

The second missive begins in a manner similar to the first: "To our former brethren, for now we do not know how to address you, since your deeds are incomprehensible to me, our ears before now have never heard of such things, neither have we read of such happenings in all our chronicles. Who could fail to feel amazed, who could refrain from weeping? We do not address these words to everybody, but only to those who, unmindful of the hour of their death and Christ's last judgement, and in violation of their solemn oath, have deserted, betraying the lord tsar and all the land, their kinsfolk, wives, children and all those dear to them, especially God. But as for those who have been taken captive, such as

Metropolitan Filaret, and others who are there against their own volition, who do not oppose the Christian law, nor shed Orthodox blood, these we do not denounce, but pray to God for them."

Describing the events of February 17, the patriarch concluded his letter: "These speeches were pronounced before us from the platform on Red Square on Saturday of Shrovetide. Afterwards we parted company. We went into the city, while others departed to their homes, since the enemy had no supporters, neither could they get anyone to heed their counsel. They failed to gain the support of any of the lesser people, and so their faction soon dispersed. Concerning the older people, the ancient proverb that the old people are the ornament of the city has proven false. For these older people have caused harm to the younger, for whom they will have to answer at the last judgement of Christ. We have inscribed this prodigy in the chronicles, so that the like may not be repeated. We also write to you, since the Lord has appointed us guardians over you, and has ordered us to watch over you, so that Satan cannot steal any one of you. Your fathers not only refused the foe entry into the Muscovite tsardom, but even went themselves to far-off shores, to distant places and unknown lands, even as sharp-eyed and swift-flying eagles, soaring with their wings, shielding the tsar of Moscow with their arms."

Another conspiracy was organized by Boyar Kriuk-Kolychev.[31] The plan was to assassinate Shuisky on Palm Sunday, but the conspiracy was discovered. Nobody came to Kolychev's defense, and he was tortured and executed. His fellow conspirators were imprisoned, though not all of them. The Tushino camp was well informed of all these events through the constant flow of deserters. There is an account from one of these deserters, the clerk Chubarov, explaining how he came to desert from Moscow to Tushino. "He left Moscow and joined Lord Tsar Dmitry Ivanovich on May 6, leaving by way of the Tver gates in the company of the clerk Skurygin, and went with him as far as the hamlet of Pirogovaia. From Pirogovaia he went to another hamlet, and spent the night there. The next day, in the morning, a peasant led him to the village of Cherkizovo, and from there he was sent to the village of Bratoshino, and from Bratoshino he was conducted to Tushino. His companion Skurygin left him in the first hamlet of Pirogovaia, and went through the forest, since he wished to make directly for the sovereign's encampment."

Chubarov related in Tushino that "some boyars, gentry, junior boyars and tradesmen were conspiring with Ivan Fedorovich Kolychev, and wished to kill Shuisky on Palm Sunday, but nothing happened. One of the conspirators, Ivan Fedorovich, was tortured, but he did not incriminate anybody, so they executed him, although Shuisky gave orders that none of the others should be executed. So now they are back at their old conspiracy, and wish to kill him with a musket on the feast of the Ascension." Chubarov also thought that something might happen on the feast of St. Nicholas, "for the boyars and all the common people are coming to Shuisky with cries and lamentations, saying: 'How long will this go on? Bread is dear, and there is no food we can either gather or buy'. Shuisky begs them to have patience until the feast of St. Nicholas, and places great hope in Skopin, who is coming with about seven thousand Germans. Since Skopin is coming with all this force Shuisky can gather his own force and join Skopin, and together they can attack the great rebel encampment. In Moscow the news concerning Skopin is that he has left Novgorod, but it is not known exactly where he is at present. Among those supporting the sovereign Dmitry Ivanovich are Prince Boris Lykov,[32] Prince Ivan Kurakin, Princes Vasily and Andrei Golitsyn, and Prince Ivan Dmitrievich Khvorostinin, and they are supported by gentry, junior boyars and tradesmen."

Chubarov did not mention exactly how many of them there were. All the deserters agreed that there was a scarcity of food supplies, and that there was no firewood. They were using the houses of those who had been disgraced for fuel, and the discontented were coming in a body to Shuisky, saying: "What is all this coming to? Shall we die of hunger?" It also was said that Shuisky wanted to reside in the hamlet of Ivanteevo, which belonged to the Trinity monastery. In fact, despite the victory of Prince Dmitry Mikhailovich Pozharsky[33] near the village of Vysotskoe, thirty versts from Kolomna, that town was still being besieged by a Tushino detachment under the command of Mlocki, and this caused great scarcity in Moscow. A quarter of rye cost seven rubles, and crowds of people came to Shuisky with the question—how long can we remain here suffering from hunger? Shuisky persuaded the cellarer of the Trinity monastery to release grain for sale from the monastery's rich granaries in Moscow, to be sold at the price of two rubles.

The fall in grain prices appeased the people. At the same time, on May 28, Roman Gagarin, the head of a recent conspiracy against Shuisky, arrived from Tushino and addressed the whole community, urging the people not to be tempted. The Tushino tsar was really a brigand, and the whole affair was the machination of the Lithuanian king, who was seeking to destroy the Orthodox Christian faith. It was well known in Tushino that the Germans had arrived in Novgorod and had driven the Lithuanians away. Hearing these words, the people in Moscow were encouraged, and nobody thereafter went over to Tushino.

WAR BETWEEN MOSCOW AND TUSHINO

But while Moscow had not been able to rest easy ever since the capital of another tsar had been erected near it, neither could Tushino rest easy, for the winter of 1608-1609 passed amid unrest and mutinies, which hindered the brigand from acting decisively against Moscow. In the spring the army foragers who had been sent to gather supplies mutinied, elected their own troop and regimental commanders, then went around the countryside plundering, refusing to return to their lords in Tushino. Besides this, the forces of the pretender were divided. A detachment of Zaporozhian Cossacks was sent to Great Novgorod in an attempt to sway the city to the side of the Tushino tsar. Sapieha and Lisowski were besieging the Trinity monastery, Mlocki and Bobowski were besieging Kolomna, where they were soon to do battle with Liapunov, governor of Riazan. Marchocki[34] was guarding the principal roads towards Moscow, and Zborowski was to move against Skopin as soon as information concerning his movements was received.

For the above reasons, only minor engagements were fought near Moscow, and no major ones. In one such engagement at the end of February Hetman Rozynski received a severe wound, from which he was never to recover. In the summer, on Trinity Sunday, there occurred a major engagement, which took the Tushino people by surprise. Some of them, approaching Moscow, swept aside a Muscovite detachment which had been sent against them, pursued them up to the city itself, and then withdrew, taking up position on the Khodynka river. But Tsar Vasily was informed that the Lithuanians had marched on Moscow with all their forces, and sent against his entire army against the Tushino force, with cannon and malvoisins.[35] The Poles, seeing this army, threw themselves upon it, and would have won a great victory with the capture of the malvoisins had there not occurred, in the words of the Poles, a great confusion due to an error. The Muscovites advanced and chased the enemy into the Khodynka, recovered their malvoisins, and would have broken into Tushino itself had not Zarutsky and his cossacks halted them on the

Khimka river. According to Russian accounts, the lost battle was retrieved by the arrival of fresh forces under the command of Ivan Semonovich Kurakin, Andrei Vasilievich Golitsyn and Boris Mikhailovich Lykov. The Tushinites, on their own admission, lost all their infantry. Many of them were slain, while many others were taken prisoner by the Muscovites. The Russian chronicler states that in this engagement the Muscovites showed bravery such as had not been seen even when the Muscovite realm was united.[36]

Having in his hands many captive Poles, Tsar Vasily ordered them to choose a delegate to be sent to Tushino with the proposition that he would release all prisoners if the Poles forsook the pretender and departed from the Muscovite realm. The emissary would be permitted to go on condition that if the proposal was rejected, he would return to Moscow. The choice fell upon Stanislaw Paczanowski, who proceeded to Tushino, where he received the following reply from his own people: "We sooner will die than abandon our enterprise. Our kinsmen and comrades are dear to us, but even dearer are glory and fame." Paczanowski hesitated for a long time as to whether he should remain in Tushino or return to Moscow, and finally he decided to return, for which he was greatly respected in Moscow, and was treated much better than the other prisoners. The tsar's cousin, Prince Ivan Vasilievich Shuisky, behaved particularly graciously toward the Polish prisoners. He healed the wounds of the squire, Borzecki, who had been entrusted to his care, and set him free, also giving a length of cloth to the prisoners who came out to be exchanged. Did Prince Ivan have a premonition that soon he too would have occasion to be grateful for such consideration?

TREATY WITH SWEDEN

The aforementioned battle was the last important encounter between Moscow and Tushino, since by now Skopin was not far off. We left him in Novgorod, where he had conducted his negotiations with the Swedes. At the end of February 1609 Table Attendant Golovin and Crown Secretary Sydavny Zinoviev concluded with Karl IX's plenipotentiaries a treaty with the following provisions. The king undertook to provide two thousand cavalrymen and three thousand infantry to help Shuisky. Apart from these mercenaries, he also agreed to release an unspecified number of troops as a token of friendship towards the tsar. In exchange for this aid Shuisky was to renounce for himself and for his heirs and successors all rights to Livonia. Shuisky also promised on behalf of himself and his heirs to remain in permanent alliance with the king and his heirs against Sigismund and his successors, and both sovereigns undertook not to conclude a separate peace with Sigismund. If one of them made peace with Poland, the other also must conclude peace "and conceal nothing from each other concerning the peace terms."

Shuisky agreed that, if needed, he would send to help the king as many troops, both mercenary and regular forces, as the king presently was sending him and, furthermore, payment of mercenary troops should be made equally. Shuisky undertook not to detain any Swedes sent to his aid (it is interesting that among the Swedes there are mentioned Russians in the king's service) or any couriers travelling back and forth between Russia and Sweden. If the Swedes captured any Russian traitors they must not put them to death, but give them up for ransom; but they would be free to kill or take to their own country any Lithuanian prisoners. Provisions for men and horses were to be sold to the king's troops at regular prices, and they must not be overcharged. Infantry and artillery would be transported free of charge. If a cavalryman lost his horse, or must it be killed in battle, he should receive another immediately, the loss to be charged against his pay.

The Swedish plenipotentiaries for their part undertook to forbid their soldiers, while within the Muscovite realm, to burn or plunder, to abuse icons, or kill peasants or take them prisoner. They also undertook not to make war against nor occupy those towns which remained loyal to Shuisky, or which had sent their submission, or even to occupy those towns which had either been taken by storm or which had surrendered. They were not to join with the brigands and thus betray Tsar Vasily, neither were they to commit any deceit against Prince Skopin or any others loyal to the realm, but remain in obedience to Prince Mikhail Vasilievich, heed his counsel, and refrain from lawless acts. The Swedish plenipotentiaries also obtained the concession that Swedish currency could be tendered within the Muscovite realm, and that the Russians would not refuse Swedish money, on pain of the tsar's displeasure. They also obtained free passage through Muscovite possessions for Swedish troops proceeding to Livonia.

There was yet one more codicil added to this treaty whereby Shuisky undertook, three weeks before Swedish troops were to cross the frontier, to hand under the official seal of Novgorod and the signature of Skopin the town of Korela[37] and its province, and within two months to cede the town and province of Korela under the sovereign's seal, and hand it over to the king in consideration of his love and friendship. Then, eleven weeks from the time when the Swedish forces began to serve Tsar Vasily, the Russians would evacuate the town of Korela and hand it over to the king, removing from the churches all images and all ecclesiastical vessels, and all cannon, firearms, powder and shot from the town. All Russian and Karelian[38] people who wished to go to Russia must also leave.

SKOPIN'S ADVANCE

At the beginning of January 1609 Karl IX had informed the citizens of Novgorod that, in accordance with their request, he was sending an armed force "to the relief of the ancient Greek faith." "For this reason," concludes the document, "take care, and take counsel together until help arrives for you, for you can see for yourselves that if the Poles and Lithuanians are victorious over you, they will spare neither you nor your patriarch, nor your metropolitans, nor your archbishops, nor your abbots, nor your governors, nor your crown secretaries, nor your gentry, nor your junior boyars, nor your merchants, nor your tradesmen, nor your babes in arms, nor anyone else, and so in this manner all the glorious Russian nation will perish."

There is also the letter of the Swedish governor of Kaianburg, Isaac Bem, to the abbot of the Solovetsk monastery,[39] with a plea to him not to desert Shuisky. This document is written in a broken Russian, and is noted for the naivety of its expressions. For example: "You change your grand princes so often that the Lithuanians will defeat you easily. They wish to eradicate the Greek faith, eliminate the Russian people and take all the Russian land for themselves. Are you not ashamed that you listen to any kind of raving, and accept as your ruler any worthless person whom the Lithuanians bring along?"

The Swedes fulfilled their promise. In addition to the five thousand mercenaries, they sent yet another ten thousand or so of various nationalities under the command of Jacob de la Gardie, who had learned his military skills in a good school.[40]

Skopin's first encounter was to take place with that same detachment of Zaporozhian cossacks under the command of Kernozicki that had been sent from Tushino to Novgorod, and on the way had occupied Torzhok and Tver. In order to prevent them from crossing the Msta river, Skopin wished to send a strong detachment to Bronnitsy, and Mikhail Ignatievich Tatishchev, who is well known to the reader,[41] was put in command. He has appeared several times in this history, and his character is well known. He argued vigorously with Leo Sapieha, quarrelled with the pretender over the matter of eating veal,[42] struck the first blow against Basmanov, and then exchanged insults with the Polish ambassador. It is difficult to imagine how this man, who was such a strong supporter of ancient tradition, the assassin of Basmanov, one of the most eager conspirators against the first False Dmitry, could ever wish to desert to the second. It is much more probable that Tatishchev was disliked because of his character, and people did not wish to serve under his command. Whatever the case, several men from Novgorod appeared before Skopin and reported that Tatishchev was about to betray the cause, and purposely had asked to be sent to Bronnitsy so that he might help Kernozicki conquer Novgorod. Accusation of treason was at that time an easy method of throwing suspicion on a person, or even of getting rid of him. Possibly even the accusers themselves did not mean any great harm to befall Tatishchev, but things turned out differently. Skopin, having heard the accusation, gathered together the soldiers, summoned Tatishchev, and repeated the accusation which had been brought against him. The crowds were stirred up, and without any investigation of the matter, they threw themselves upon Tatishchev and killed him.

The vanguard therefore could not be dispatched. Kernozicki approached Novgorod and set up his camp at the Khutinsk monastery. Many of the gentry had fled to the Lithuanian regiments, and Skopin was in a dreadful predicament when the men from Tikhvin arrived, with their commander Gorikhvostov and a thousand men. They were followed by Yevsevy Riazanov, with contingents assembled from the trading settlements beyond the Onega. Gorokhvostov took up position in the village of Gruzino. Several peasants were captured by Kernozicki and under interrogation stated that many soldiers had arrived in Gruzino, and that even more were to follow. Kernozicki was alarmed, and withdrew.

With the arrival of Swedish troops in the spring of 1609 Skopin opened the offensive against the Tushinites. The Swedes, led by Horn, and the Russians, commanded by Chulkov and Choglokov, expelled Kernozicki from Staraia Rusa, and won a victory at the village of Kamenki in the region of Toropets on April 25, clearing Toropets, Torzhok, Porkhov and Oreshek. The governor of the latter town, the notorious Mikhail Glebovich Saltykov, fled to Tushino.

Skopin dispatched towards Pskov a detachment under the command of Prince Meshchersky. Here the more substantial people and clergy entered into correspondence with Shuisky's forces, wishing to surrender the city to the Muscovite tsar, and thereby strengthen their own faction and overthrow their opponents. The musketeers, cossacks, lesser people and peasants came to hear of this plan, confiscated horses from the more substantial people who had left, and took an inventory of their possessions. The cossack ataman, Korsiakov, gave the alarm at Meshchersky's approach, but the more substantial people suppressed these tidings and imprisoned the messenger. The lesser people, knowing nothing about all this, went peacefully out of the city to meet the icon of the Virgin, which had been brought from the Caves monastery on May 28, when a cannon shot warned them that the enemy was upon the city. Despite the fact that a fearful conflagration laid waste the city, and that two of the walls were breached, the musketeers managed to repel the Muscovite army from their encampment, and gave the lesser people the opportunity to re-enter the city.

During this action the messenger sent by Korsiakov was released from prison, and shortly afterwards two members of the clergy, a priest and a deacon, fled through the wall towards the enemy encampment. The priest was caught and put to the torture, and implicated many others. Those implicated were interrogated, and in turn implicated many others, and the blood of many of the more substantial people flowed. The pretender's governors presided at the interrogations, but the lesser people were recalling the ancient liberties of Pskov, and paid little heed to the governors.

The tocsin, a reminder of the ancient Assembly (veche) bell,[43] summoned the people to the square. The chief among the people was the tradesman Timofey, commonly known as Kudekusha Trepets. According to the chronicler, he was the worst of all of them.[44] He told the governors what to do, insisted upon being present at the interrogations, and many similar people supported him, taking charge of the city. The malice of the lesser people towards the greater flared up increasingly. Informers captured in the course of sorties stated that the more substantial people were writing from Pskov, imploring Tsar Vasily to come to their aid. "For they have tortured many boyars, burned them and broken their ribs, and frequently the men of Novgorod have come with foreigners and cossacks, junior boyars, both from Novgorod and Pskov, Tatars and musketeers, and there has been much fighting and bloodshed, for the peasants and the bytowns have been plundered, and much harm of all kinds has been done to the citizens of Pskov."

Tsar Vasily, informing Skopin on June 2, 1609 that Zborowski and Shakhovskoy had been sent to oppose him, and telling him of the impatience with which the towns were awaiting their arrival, wrote to his kinsman: "You, my boyar, should in no wise delay your campaign, for we and all our realm require immediate aid against the brigands. Only by the mercy of God and by your enterprise shall we be relieved by our liberation from the hands of the brigands and Lithuanians. The Lithuanians are fearful of your approach and if they depart from the country, or if by the grace of God you win a victory over them, you will gain great favor from God, and honor and praise from us and from all people of our realm. You will fill the people with great joy, and the fame of your house will be remembered, both in our land, and also in neighboring countries. We are relying upon you as upon our own soul."

Skopin had moved out of Novgorod as early as May 10. Giving up hope of capturing Pskov, he recalled Meshchersky so that without wasting time they might hasten with combined forces towards Moscow. We have seen how Zborowski was dispatched from Tushino to oppose him. Zborowski had up to four thousand troops, both Poles and Russians. The latter were led by Grigory Shakhovskoy. He had managed to escape from imprisonment as the northern towns were being occupied by the forces of the pretender, and he had managed to reach Tushino.

At Torzhok[45] Zborowski met with the advance guard of Skopin's forces under the leadership of Golovin and Horn, which he defeated; but hearing from a prisoner that Skopin himself was advancing with a large army, he retreated to Tver, where he joined Kernozicki's cossacks. For his part, Skopin joined the Smolensk levies in Torzhok, and gave battle to Zborowski outside Tver. The two Polish wings crushed the Russians and their allies, but the Polish center fled. They rallied after a flight of only a few miles, and returned to their comrades, who were celebrating a victory.

But that victory was a dubious one for the Swedish infantry had not abandoned the field, and only that night, after the battle had ended, did they return to their bivouac in the rear. The Poles, even those whose action had been successful during the day, counselled immediate retreat, citing the superiority of Skopin's forces; but those who had fled, wishing to remove their ignominy, insisted that Tver not be evacuated. Zborowski insisted that the army stay together and observe great caution, but they did not listen to him. Some remained in the field while others remained in the actual suburbs, without taking any precautions.

The Russians and Swedes took advantage of this situation, struck at dawn, and inflicted a heavy defeat upon the Poles. Zborowski was compelled to withdraw from Tver, and Skopin advanced until suddenly, about a hundred and thirty versts from Moscow, he was told that the foreigners who had come on his expedition no longer would serve him, alleging that instead of four months' pay they had received only two; that the Russians had not evacuated Korela, even though the specified eleven weeks since the arrival of the Swedish troops in Russia had elapsed. Skopin, attempting to dissuade De la Gardie from leaving, himself crossed the Volga below Gorodnia in order to join up with the levies of the northern towns, and on the left bank he reached Kaliazin, where he halted.

At the same time as Zborowski, joining with Sapieha, carried out an unsuccessful assault upon the Trinity monastery, Skopin united with the levies of the northern towns and managed to persuade De la Gardie to release about a thousand foreigners who had joined under the command of Christierne Somme. Then Sapieha and Zborowski, fearing Skopin's reinforcements, advanced upon him in Kaliazin but lost the battle on the Zhabna river, and withdrew once again to the encampment outside the Trinity monastery.

Now the principal task facing Tsar Vasily and Skopin was to collect as much money as possible to pay the foreign troops. They sent one letter after another to the northern towns and monasteries, demanding money to pay the foreign troops. Tsar Vasily wrote to the Solovetsk monastery: "The Lithuanians and traitors have been occupying the Muscovite realm for a long time, and have caused great oppression. For this reason there has been much cost to our treasury in order to pay salaries to our servicemen, and money has been taken from all the monasteries in our realm, and it has been given to the servicemen. Send whatever money or valuables you may have in the Solovetsk monastery to our treasury in Moscow, and when God gives us victory over our enemies, and we settle accounts with the traitors and brigands, we will fill the monastic treasury twice over."

Skopin petitioned the crown officials in Perm in the following terms: "We have nothing to give our foreign mercenary troops, and there is little money in the crown treasury, and you yourselves know very well that the sovereign has been withstanding the siege of his enemies in Moscow for more than a year. What there was in the treasury has been given to the soldiers who remained with the sovereign in Moscow. Therefore you should tell the merchants and tradesmen, both the greater and the middling, and all the people, that for the sake of peace and Christian deliverance, and in order that the Muscovite realm be not utterly ruined for lack of money to pay the mercenaries, they should give towards the pay of these mercenaries as much money, cloth, silk and taffeta as they can. And when it pleases God that the Muscovite realm is free of brigands and Lithuanians, the sovereign will order that you be reimbursed. Also, apart from what anyone might give of his own free will, you must collect from the townspeople and from the countryside fifty rubles from each ploughland, for the sake of Christian deliverance, in order to hire foreign and Tatar mercenaries. Moreover I have from my own regiments more than once collected money, horses and cloth from the gentry and junior boyars for the benefit of the foreigners. Also in Novgorod the metropolitan, archimandrites, abbots, merchants, townsmen and peasants from the surrounding countryside have given as much money, cloth and silk as they have been able to gather."

Letters were written to the inhabitants of Perm and other towns reproaching them for their lukewarmness towards the common cause. The inhabitants of Ustiug wrote: "So far you have sent only eighty men to the tsar's service in Yaroslavl. If you do not now send money to the tsar's treasury, and do not collect any additional money, how then can you expect any favor from the tsar? For during the reign of Ivan Vasilievich you used to send a thousand men for his campaigns against the Tatars. All the Russian land is suffering along with the sovereign, and neighboring countries are fighting for our Christian faith and helping us. So you, sirs, being mindful of God, of your souls and your oath of allegiance, should finally think of the military affairs, both of the realm and of the land."

The inhabitants of Perm answered Skopin that they rejoiced in the help God had shown him, but they were quite unable to comply with his requests "because nobody is trading in cloth, silk or taffeta, and eighteen score sables already have been collected from us, and also black fox furs as a freewill offering, which we sent on without delay. Fifty rubles have been collected from each ploughland, but we cannot send the money we have collected, as the winter road is not yet open." Yet they had sent the sables and the fox furs before the winter road was open; why could they not also have sent the money?

The Solovetsk monks acted differently. Twice they sent to Moscow seventeen thousand silver rubles in present-day currency, and on one occasion they sent a silver spoon. Peter Semonovich Stroganov also acted differently, as is witnessed by a charter issued to him by Shuisky, wherein the tsar states: "Stroganov valiantly withstood the brigands and, without being asked, sent many military servitors to the tsar's service against the brigands, protected the towns from danger, and raised a loan in Moscow and the other towns to give pay to the servicemen. For such services and zeal the tsar has ordered that his name be inscribed in all the documents with the -*vich* suffix.[46] He himself, his children, relatives, servants and peasants in all places shall be exempt from the judgement of boyars, governors, crown secretaries and all chancellery officials, and must be judged only by the tsar or his designate. The fine for any offense against his honor shall be twice that of one of the best citizens of Moscow, namely a hundred rubles. He shall have as much duty-free drink as he requires, soldiers shall not be billetted in any of his premises in Moscow and other towns, neither Russians nor foreigners. He may heat huts and bathhouses on his premises in summer. In addition to all this, no road or bridge tolls or poll tax shall be collected from him, his sons, relatives, dependents or servants."

Being lukewarm in their monetary support for the tsar, the inhabitants of Perm were also half-hearted when the time came to aid their neighbors in Viatka against the brigands. The inhabitants of Viatka, Ustiug, Vychegda and the Stroganovs in vain wrote to them more than once that they call out their levies against the brigands, cossacks, musketeers and Cheremiss who were currently in Kotelnichi. The inhabitants of Perm promised to send soldiers, but did not do so. To persistent requests from Viatka they replied that their soldiers had been mustered and were ready to set out on campaign, but they were troubled by conflicting reports coming from Viatka. They had written that the traitors had evacuated Kotelnichi and had fled to Yarensk, and that the governor of Viatka, Prince Mikhail Ukhtomsky, had dismissed all the levies. For this reason the inhabitants of Perm were withholding their own soldiers. Junior Boyar Vasily Tyrkov, who had come from there, said that there were fourteen hundred traitors to the realm in Kotelnichi, while Prince Ukhtomsky had altogether twelve hundred. "With such a force," wrote the inhabitants of Perm to those of Viatka, "it should be possible to take all necessary measures against the traitors. It also appears to us that Prince Ukhtomsky purposely allowed the traitors to escape from Kotelnichi, and did not pursue them. Despite the fact that the journey from Viatka to Yarensk only takes one night, and the Karinsk Tatars, Vasily Tyrkov and the tsar's soldiers requested permission to pursue them, Prince Mikhail did not allow them to do so. And you, sirs, should pay no heed to the folly of Prince Mikhail, but should keep all the levies of Viatka under arms, in even greater strength than before, lest the traitors take you by surprise."

The irate inhabitants of Viatka replied in the following terms: "What you have just written to us shows your folly, or even drunkenness. You see us suffering great ruin from the enemy, you have soldiers under arms, yet you do not send them to Viatka, but have diverted them from the road. We will disregard your folly, but we will remind you of God, of your souls and of your oaths of allegiance. We do not have any relations with the traitors, we are opposing the brigands, and are withstanding the enemy as our merciful God gives us wisdom, and to whatever extent we are enabled to do so by the help that is forthcoming. But you have forgotten the grace of God and the Blessed Virgin, your oath of allegiance and the favor of our sovereign, for the sake of shedding Christian blood and ruin. In vain do you give the land of Viatka over to devastation by the brigands, in that you do not send soldiers to help us, and do not make common cause with us against the brigands. In this manner you will betray yourselves, and will perish because of your own folly. Previously two traitors were sent to you and you were told to execute them; but you did nothing about it. Look how the men of Ustiug and Solvychegodsk serve and support the sovereign. They sent to our defense many soldiers, and ordered them to be in Viatka before Yarensk was evacuated. As soon as you can shake off your foolishness you should send immediately and without fail many soldiers for our defense, in order that the land of Viatka may be defended and not surrendered to the brigands, and also in order that you yourselves may not suffer ruin at the hands of the enemy. You evidently believe what Tyrkov tells you, and not what we write. You seem to be as drunk as Vasily Tyrkov was in Viatka."

Even now it is difficult to find any justification for the inhabitants of Perm. It is abundantly obvious that they wished to procrastinate, to bide their time, and not burden themselves with any sacrifices. The excuse they gave for not sending help to Viatka was ludicrous. At the same time, what right did they have, in face of the rescript from the governor and the community, to credit the words of this Tyrkov, who could slander Ukhtomsky for personal motives, especially when the other towns were writing in the same vein as Viatka, and were sending soldiers to aid the cause? Even if Tyrkov's information were correct the inhabitants of Perm should have advanced immediately towards Viatka, for even if Ukhtomsky was acting badly through cowardice they would have encouraged him by their approach. If he was in league with the brigands, immediately the men of Perm ought to have hastened to Viatka to stamp out all treason there. But it was difficult to imagine any treason on the part of Ukhtomsy, since he would hardly then have been summoning from all sides soldiers loyal to the Muscovite tsar.

Finally, the evidence against the inhabitants of Perm is particularly damaging, considering their previous and subsequent inactivity. When Mansurov replaced Ukhtomsky as governor of Viatka he too wrote to the inhabitants of Perm, requesting them immediately to send soldiers and artillery; the inhabitants of Perm answered that they had many soldiers under arms but that the previous governor, Ukhtomsky, had written to tell them that the brigands had withdrawn from Kotelnichi to Yarensk, and that they should not send soldiers, since he himself had dismissed his own forces. Perm also had no artillery to spare, for they themselves needed whatever artillery there was. Despite the indifference of the inhabitants of Perm to the common cause, Shuisky gave them a charter in which he rewarded their zeal and service by exempting them from the levy of fifty rubles from each ploughland.

While matters stood thus in the northeast Prince Skopin, while he was halted at Kaliazin, was occupied with training his recruits from the north, and he was assisted eagerly by the Swede, Somme. On the other hand, active negotiations with De la Gardie regarding the return of his detachment to the tsar's service were proceeding also. Tsar Vasily was forced to hasten his compliance with the Treaty of Vyborg, and sent orders to Korela that the town be evacuated and handed over to the Swedes. Meanwhile one detachment sent by Skopin occupied Pereiaslavl Zalessky[47] while Boyar Fedor Ivanovich Sheremetev was approaching, taking Murom without resistance and Kasimov by storm. In Kasimov he was met by Prince Prozorovsky, who had come with a message from the tsar, bearing letters of commendation to those who served and supported the tsar. But Prozorovsky also had to tell Sheremetev that he was proceeding too slowly, and was not furthering the tsar's cause with sufficient vigor. Thus Sheremetev received at the same time praise and reproach for one and the same action. His colleague, Ivan Saltykov, was taken to Moscow. Evidently he was regarded as being the one principally responsible for this dilatoriness and lack of zeal. Sheremetev then moved towards Vladimir.

In this manner the north was liberated and Tsar Vasily's principal armies converged upon Moscow from east and west in order to fight the decisive battle below the walls of Moscow against the Tushino tsar, the tsar of the southern part of the realm, the "Pre-Ruined Ukraine" and the cossack steppes. Skopin's victory over Zborowski greatly alarmed Tushino. The pretender wrote to Sapieha that he abandon the siege of the Trinity monastery and hasten to the aid of Tushino. "The enemy has advanced upon Tver, and is practically upon the heels of our army. We have written to you more than once that you should not waste your time over lesser folk, who will fall into our hands easily after God crowns our enterprise with success. In view of the current change of fortune, we now ask you even more pressingly to leave everything and make all possible haste with all your forces to our headquarters, telling all the others to do the same. We beg, insist and confirm that you not do otherwise." Not being content with this, the pretender added in his own hand: "May they make all possible haste!" But another threat to Tushino was arising, from a different quarter.

III

THE FALL OF SHUISKY
1609–1610

SIGISMUND BESIEGES SMOLENSK

We have observed how, when Shuisky ascended the throne, King Sigismund, who was threatened by a fearful rebellion, was in no position to make a move against Moscow. But the rebellion ended with the triumph of the king, who now had the opportunity to concern himself with external affairs, especially since a foreign power hostile to Poland was meddling in Muscovite politics. Sigismund could await the unfolding of events with equanimity while Shuisky was locked in struggle with the pretender. But when Shuisky opened negotiations with Sweden, with Karl IX, the deadly foe of Sigismund and Poland,[1] and when a perpetual alliance against Poland was concluded between the Muscovite tsar and the Swedish king, Sigismund no longer might rest easy.

The Polish ambassadors, on the other hand, having returned from Moscow, assured the king that the boyars favored him and that he had merely to appear with his army in the borderlands of the Muscovite realm for the boyars to compel Shuisky to abdicate the throne, and proclaim Prince Wladyslaw tsar. Soon afterwards Sigismund informed the king of Spain that he had undertaken the Muscovite war first to avenge recent wrongs second to assert his hereditary right since his ancestor Jagiello was the son of a Russian princess and was married to a Russian princess,[2] and finally to recover the provinces taken from his predecessors by the Muscovite princes. The campaign had been undertaken, moreover, not only for the private advantages of the king but for the good of all Christendom as well. The king could see that the wavering principality of Muscovy was threatened from the one side by the Turks and Tatars and from the other side by heretical rulers. In Shuisky's armies there were Tatars and heretical Frenchmen, Dutchmen and Englishmen, hired by those, namely the Swedes, who wished, by concluding an alliance against Poland with the barbarians, to destroy the Catholic religion and found a heretical state with the imperial title, which the Muscovites were appropriating.

The king set off towards the Muscovite frontiers, informing the senators that he was travelling in order to observe the progress of the war against the Swedes in Livonia, as well as the course of events in Russia. He promised to keep in mind only the welfare of the Commonwealth. In Lublin he declared to the Senate deputation that he would yield his gains from the Muscovite war to the Commonwealth, and not keep anything for himself.

These obligations should be borne in mind for they establish the perspective from which the conduct of Sigismund with respect to Muscovy must be viewed. Sigismund cannot be taken to task for his shortsightedness, for his injudicious obstinacy. He desperately wanted to capture Smolensk and failed to send his son Wladyslaw forthwith to Moscow, thus antagonizing the Russians and causing an uprising which ultimately led to the expulsion of the Poles. Sigismund's position must be borne in mind, namely that he could not concern himself with his own dynastic aims, having undertaken to pursue the good of the Commonwealth. How might he then return to Poland, having expended Polish blood and treasure, simply to place his son upon the Muscovite throne unless this yielded Poland some direct benefits?

The Polish throne was elective. On Sigismund's death his son might or might not be elected king. Previous tsars of Muscovy had been candidates for the Polish throne[3] but had not been successful because of the incompatability of Polish and Muscovite interests. The situation would be the same in the case of Wladyslaw. If he, seated upon the Muscovite throne, took it into his head to be amenable to Poland, the fate of the first False Dmitry awaited him.

Another possibility was that, if Moscow were to submit to Sigismund himself, in effect bringing about a unification with Poland, this would be advantageous to the latter, and Sigismund might achieve his aim. But first he must seize some province or other for Poland in order to achieve the objective of his campaign, namely to obtain for the Polish Commonwealth something tangible, since the conquest of Moscow was the kind of enterprise whose success was very doubtful. Hetman Zolkiewski[4] wrote to the king that everyone thought the king had set out on campaign for his personal gain, not for the benefit of the Commonwealth, and therefore not only the common people, but the senators as well, were expressing reluctance concerning the enterprise. It was therefore necessary to reassure the senators that this was not the case.

Thus it was quite obvious that Sigismund quickly must provide this assurance, not by words but by actions, and hasten to make gains for the Commonwealth rather than some important advantage within the Muscovite lands. Since ancient times Smolensk had been an object of contention between Moscow and Lithuania.[5] Moscow finally had been able to conquer it; but Lithuania had been unable to forget so vital a loss since that city, the key to the Dnieper region, was considered an impregnable stronghold. Sigismund was informed that Shein, governor of Smolensk, and the inhabitants of the city, greatly desired to surrender to him. The king did not wish to let such a valuable opportunity slip, and advanced upon Smolensk against the advice of Hetman Zolkiewski, who wished to lead the army into the Severian land, where the poorly fortified little towns would not have offered very stiff resistance.

The attitude in Poland to Muscovite affairs, and to the object of Sigismund's campaign, may be judged from a letter of a certain Otojewski in Poland to a certain Waszyski in Livonia, dated December 12, 1608. Otojewski writes concerning the hiring of Swedish regiments to aid

Shuisky, and then adds: "For now we must in all things rely upon Almighty God, and place our hopes upon those who are presently in the Russian land because everything in their hands has gone happily, according to plan. The Russians in crowds betray their sovereigns to whom they have kissed the cross, and surrender their lands to our people. It is rumored widely here that our people have conquered nearly all of the Russian land, except for Moscow, Novgorod and a number of smaller towns. I declare to you that at the next Sejm this question will come up: in view of the frivolity and inconsistency of the Russian people, on whom it is impossible to rely, it will be necessary to dispossess the gentry and merchants, deport them to Podolia or some other place, and in their place settle some good people from our lands on whom we can rely in time of need. We should address ourselves to this matter without delay. Before the Swedes come we must destroy Shuisky and completely eradicate all his supporters."

From this letter it is evident that Shuisky's alliance with the Swedes aroused the Poles from their lethargy and compelled them to expedite their cause by decisive measures with regard to Moscow. On the other hand, it is also evident that as far as the Poles were concerned the object of the king's expedition was subjection of the Muscovite realm to Poland, not the imposition of the king's son upon the Muscovite throne. But if the Poles sought to take advantage of the troubled condition of the Muscovite realm in order to conquer it, this conquest would not be easy so long as the Poles were entering Muscovite provinces with an overtly hostile countenance, with the avowed aim of conquest.

Moscow was divided between two contenders for the throne. In order to make the task of conquering the Muscovite provinces easier, Poland also must put forward a candidate, namely Prince Wladyslaw, whom the boyars had cited as a likely prospect even during the lifetime of the first False Dmitry, and of whom, it was reported to Sigismund, some of them were still thinking. Thus placing Wladyslaw upon the Muscovite throne was merely the pretext for attainment of the objective, but was not the real objective of Sigismund's campaign.

The governor of Smolensk, Shein, knew all the intentions and movements of the Poles. He had sent his agents across the frontier to Lithuania. They returned news that they were hearing from informants whom they had bribed, whom they were meeting at regularly assigned locations, and who were telling their Russian contacts of all that was passing in their home territories. But Shein did not learn anything new from his peasant agents. In Poland he had bribed one Jan Woitejchow, who directly told him everything in his letters. In March 1609 Woitejchow wrote to him that at the end of the session of the Sejm the prince had wanted to go to Moscow but the governor of Sandomir had arrived, together with an ambassador from False Dmitry and emissaries from the Tushino Poles, with a request to the king and to the Polish lords that they should not send the prince to assume the Muscovite tsardom, for they had sworn to the Tushino tsar that they would sacrifice their lives, even against their brothers.

Woitejchow also relayed news from the Tushino encampment, writing that the impetuous Dmitry was thinking of abandoning Tushino and establishing himself in a new location, since the stench of the spring thaw was suffocating the army. He also wished to conquer Moscow immediately in the spring. Woitejchow wrote that the governor of Sandomir, addressing the Sejm on behalf of Dmitry, had undertaken to cede Smolensk and the Severian land to Poland, and that if at that time Mniszech had not made that promise the Poles were prepared forthwith to place the prince upon the throne of the Muscovite tsardom. Woitejchow also wrote that many Polish merchants had returned home from Tushino, saying that it appeared that False Dmitry was on the point of fleeing, since he feared Rozynski and the cossacks, and had no money to pay the Polish troops, who had apparently told him: "If the Muscovite tsar paid us, we would hand the brigands over to him and quit the Muscovite land." He also stated that it would be worth Shuisky's while to bring Zarutsky and his Don Cossacks over to his side, making it possible to burn the Tushino encampment. Concerning himself, Woitejchow wrote: "Please send me a good natural black beaver, since I mentioned to you in my last letter that I would have to show a tangible token of your esteem."

Shein also received reports of rumors going around in Lithuania concerning pretenders, and wrote that a brigand from Tushino had arrived at Velizh from Belaia, and called himself Bogdan. He had stayed at Velizh for six weeks, and had arrived at Belaia in haste at the time the renegade monk was killed. He kept saying that this man was the renegade monk's confidential secretary. He left Velizh in the company of a Lithuanian bound for Vitebsk, and from Vitebsk he went on to Poland. In Poland he began to advance his claim to be Petrushka, who had been besieged in Tula, and now was living in Lithuania. This man was the true son of Tsar Fedor, since in his place some peasant had been hanged at Moscow. Boris's son Fedor Godunov was also still alive, and was presently at the court of the Holy Roman emperor.

Meanwhile the customary disputes and border raids were taking place between the inhabitants of the borderlands of Muscovy and Lithuania. For this reason the commanders of the borderland provinces, Alexander Gasiewski, the governor of Velizh, who was recently in Moscow, and the governor of Smolensk, Shein, were obliged to enter into communication with each other. Gasiewski invited Shein to a border conference in order to resolve contentious issues. Shein, in view of the circumstances of the Time of Troubles, was fearful of assuming responsibility for such an action, especially when he had information that Gasiewski had come with the purpose of persuading the inhabitants of Smolensk to surrender to the king.

Shein reproached Gasiewski for having failed to fulfil the provisions of the treaty concluded by him and his companions in Moscow, in that the Poles had not been evacuated from Muscovite territory, and on account of this there had been fearful bloodshed. Gasiewski replied: "You demand that the Poles and Lithuanians be evacuated from Russian territory, but how do you propose we do this? By means of letters from the king? Letters were sent to them, and the king wanted to send yet one more courier, and has instructed me to discuss this matter with you, but you evade this favorable issue, holding fast to your Muscovite custom. Brothers distrust brothers, fathers distrust sons, sons distrust fathers. This habit has led the Muscovite tsardom to ruin. I know that there is no confidence among you in your rulers and in your people, as there is among our own people, nor can you even, because of the Muscovite habit, come to a meeting with me. Knowing this, I am writing to you that I have made an announcement concerning this matter to the archbishop and to the other inhabitants of Smolensk, and with their aid called a meeting. But this did not help. Calling to mind the events in Moscow, which I myself saw and heard while I was there, I am amazed to observe your present conduct. Whatever you do now seems designed to cause greater bloodshed and terror to your realm."

Gasiewski was correct in his words, but not in his deeds, since he too informed the king that the boyars wished to have Wladyslaw and more than anyone he was agitating for the surrender of Smolensk, as King Sigismund explicitly informed Zolkiewski. Consequently the news Shein received concerning Gasiewski's intentions were entirely correct, and Shein had every reason for distrusting the governor of Velizh.

It was necessary to prepare for defense, and take precautionary measures. But in the conditions of the Time of Troubles it was difficult to rely upon general enthusiasm or general obedience. The musketeer captains and the junior boyars refused to stand on guard against the Poles. Meanwhile there came across the border news concerning Sigismund's movements, each more alarming than the last. The reports of Woitejchow, that Mniszech's promises given at the session of the Sejm had restrained the Poles from war, had proven false. In May 1609 agents informed Shein that the king had strictly forbidden the governor of Sandomir in particular, and all Poles in general, to proceed towards Moscow. In July it was reported that Gasiewski was advancing upon Smolensk with artillery, and that Sigismund himself was expected there the following month. Gasiewski had administered an oath of loyalty to the king to the inhabitants of the Muscovite border regions.

These items of information were correct. At Minsk, Zolkiewski conferred with the king, and asked details of the campaign he had undertaken, demanding to know what guarantees he had of success. Those who had raised Sigismund's hopes replied that, as long as he remained at a distance, it was difficult for the Muscovite boyars to speak out in his favor and therefore, in order to force the issue and make clear his position, it was essential for the king to hasten to the border. A letter from Gasiewski arrived at Minsk, insisting that the king advance as soon as possible to the siege of Smolensk, which was undefended, for the soldiers had gone off to aid Skopin.

Sigismund left Minsk and at Orsha had an interview with the Lithuanian chancellor, Leo Sapieha, who also urged the king to make haste and set out on campaign. Sapieha went ahead to Smolensk, incessantly writing letters urging Zolkiewski to hurry. Zolkiewski disliked all this haste and, as it appeared to him, lack of planning. It seemed peculiar to this experienced military leader to suppose that such a strong fortress as Smolensk should consider capitulating to a force which consisted merely of five thousand infantrymen. Nevertheless, on September 19 the impatient Sapieha stood before Smolensk, and the king himself arrived there two days later. His total army, besides the five thousand infantrymen, consisted of twelve thousand cavalry, ten thousand Zaporozhian Cossacks and an indeterminate number of Lithuanian Tatars. The Zaporozhians were not of a constant strength, since a number of them kept going off in search of forage. Among the twelve thousand cavalrymen there was a large number of volunteers, who deserted when they had obtained sufficient booty. The number of persons conducting the defense is estimated at about seventy thousand.

Sigismund III
King of Poland, 1587–1632

Crossing the frontier, Sigismund sent a declaration to Moscow, and to Smolensk a proclamation in which it was stated that, since the death of the last descendant of Rurik, Tsar Fedor, persons not of the ruling stem had become tsars, not by the will of God, but by their own will, by force, cunning and deceit. Consequently brother had risen up against brother, friend against friend. Many of the greater, lesser and middling people of the Muscovite realm, even some in Moscow itself, seeing such ruin, had petitioned him, Sigismund, a Christian ruler and the nearest kinsmen of the Muscovite polity, to call to mind his kinship with the natural, ancient rulers of Muscovy, and take pity upon their perishing realm. Therefore he, Sigismund, was coming with a large army, not in order to shed Russian blood, but to defend the Russian people, striving above all for the preservation of the Orthodox Russian faith. Therefore the inhabitants of Smolensk should meet him with bread and salt and thereby offer an auspicious beginning to this undertaking, for otherwise the royal army would spare no one.

The inhabitants of Smolensk replied to the king that their vows had been made in the house of the Immaculate Virgin. They would sacrifice their lives for the Orthodox faith, for the holy churches, for their tsar and their oath of allegiance, and under no circumstances would bow down before the Lithuanian king and his lords. The suburbs had been burned,[6] the wives and children of the servitors sent to help Skopin had moved from the countryside into the fortress, but the peasants had not come to help with the siege nor had they sent any auxiliaries, for the king had seduced them with promises of freedom. The inhabitants of Smolensk sent petitions to Moscow, with appeals for aid, but instead of help Tsar Vasily could send only gracious letters. Nevertheless, the besieged decided to defend themselves to the last and should they enter into negotiations with the king, it would be solely to gain time.

At these parleys the inhabitants of Smolensk bluntly told the king's emissaries that they lauded Sigismund for his good intentions but they feared his subjects, whom they could not trust. Even were the king prepared to make promises under oath the Poles would not heed his words, as could be seen from the actions of those who stood outside Moscow who, claiming they were fighting on behalf of the Russians, were taking their families captive and devastating the countryside.

For these reasons, apart from some hostile exchanges across the border, which long was the custom between Lithuania and the people of

Smolensk, the latter could not surrender to Sigismund because of the weakness of royal power in Poland, and because there were insufficient guarantees that the obligations undertaken by the king would be honored by his subjects. Some of the inhabitants of Smolensk went even further, declaring that they had no wish to suffer what the inhabitants of Moscow had to suffer during the time of the first False Dmitry, and therefore they resolved to die faithful to Tsar Vasily, and sooner would kill their wives with their own hands than see them defiled by the Poles. It was difficult to place any reliance in the promises of the same Sigismund who, while assuring the inhabitants of Smolensk that he would protect their faith, at the same time had declared in Poland that he had begun the war primarily for the glory of God and for the propagation of the Catholic religion.

Among the motives for the resistance of the inhabitants of Smolensk there was the additional reason that whereas the Smolensk servicemen were in Skopin's army their families were under siege within Smolensk. Naturally these families would oppose with all their might the surrender of the city to Sigismund, since thereby they would be separated from their dear ones. On the other hand, the presence of the Smolensk servitors in Skopin's encampment inspired the besieged with hope that their country-men quickly would come to their relief, for the deliverance of their families. A final reason for resistance may be indicated here, namely the interests of the wealthiest Smolensk merchants, who had advanced Shuisky a great amount of money, which they would lose if they surrendered to Sigismund.

From the very beginning the siege went very badly. The besieged dared carry out some brave exploits. On one occasion six daredevils left the fortress, crossed the Dnieper in a boat to the enemy trenches, and in broad daylight seized a banner and brought it back across the river, returning unscathed. On October 12 the king ordered his army to make an assault. They demolished the gates with a petard and would have stormed the city had reinforcements arrived, and have were repulsed by the besieged. Polish mining operations also were unsuccessful because the besieged had secret listening posts near the walls.

DISSENSION IN TUSHINO

It was not Smolensk but Tushino that bore the whole brunt of King Sigismund's campaign. When news came of this campaign, there began a great commotion. The Poles cried out that the king had come to take the rewards they had earned, and reap the benefits they had won by their blood and toil. Hetman Rozynski was the first to speak out against the king because at Tushino he was the omnipotent lord, whereas his was not a comparable position in the royal army. He summoned a council of war and apparently convinced his comrades not to abandon a goal so nearly won, and to swear an oath to each other not to enter into negotiations, nor to abandon Dmitry but, once they had placed him upon the throne, with one voice would demand their reward from him. If the tsar procrastinated they would seize the provinces of Severia and Riazan, and live on the bounty of those provinces until they received their reward in full.

All the Poles eagerly signed the act of confederation and sent to the king outside Smolensk their emissaries, Marchocki and his companions, with the demand that he depart the Muscovite realm and not meddle in their undertaking. Rozynski also wanted Sapieha to join the confederation, and for this purpose went in person to him in his encampment outside the Trinity monastery, but Sapieha opposed a venture which would lead to an open breach with the king.

Meanwhile Skopin, joining once again with De la Gardie, moved from Kaliazin to Alexandrovskaia Sloboda,[7] whence his advance detachment, under the command of Valuev and Somme, expelled the Poles. Skopin remained in the Sloboda, awaiting Sheremetev and fresh forces from Sweden. He was hesitating, but once again Moscow was suffering from famine. A quarter of grain cost seven rubles, and the populace was restless, crying out that they had been deceived when they had been told that Prince Mikhail Vasilievich was soon to arrive. They came in a body to the Kremlin to see Tsar Vasily, caused a commotion, and once again began to think of the Tushino brigand.

In the midst of all this confusion there came a detachment from Skopin, bringing a letter to the tsar. The tsar forwarded the letter to the patriarch, and joy spread throughout Moscow, the bells pealed, and services of thanksgiving were chanted. But this joy was short lived, and the famine intensified. The peasant Salkov, with a host of Russian brigands, seized control of the Kolomna highway, by which supplies reached Moscow from Riazan, which was free of Tushinites. The tsar sent one of his commanders, but Salkov defeated him. A second commander was dispatched, but he did nothing against the brigands. Finally he sent a third commander, Prince Dmitry Mikhailovich Pozharsky, who decisively defeated Salkov on the Vladimir highway, on the Pechorka stream. On the fourth day after the battle Salkov appeared in Moscow with his submission. He had only thirty men left of his band.

In Moscow itself the cossacks were plotting treason. Hetman Gorok-hovoy, whose turn it was to defend the line at Krasnoe Selo, entered into negotiations with the Tushinites, and surrendered Krasnoe Selo to them. The Tushinites burned it down. This was not all. Led by traitors, they stole by night up to the wooden portion of the city and set fire to it. The Mus-covites chased them away and extinguished the fire, but forty *sazhens* had been burned down.

Skopin was standing by all this time at the Alexandrovskaia Sloboda. Sapieha moved there from outside the Trinity monastery, routed the de-tachment sent against him by Skopin, but could not overpower Skopin himself and, after a heated battle, retired once again to the Trinity monastery. Thereafter he urged Rozynski to cooperate with him against Skopin but Rozynski, angered by Sapieha's refusal to enter his confed-eration, refused to help him and returned to Tushino, against which the king himself shortly thereafter dealt the final blow.

PRETENDER FLEES TO KALUGA

At the very time the Tushino Poles were sending emissaries to King Sigismund outside Smolensk, the king was sending his own emissaries, the Polish lord Stanislaw Stadnicki[8] and his companions, to Tushino. They were to impress upon the Poles that it was more befitting to serve their natural lord than some foreign adventurer, and that they should think first and foremost of the welfare of Poland and Lithuania. The king promised them rewards from the Muscovite treasury should Moscow be subdued by their combined forces, and in addition promised that they would receive pay effective from the day that joined his own Polish forces. He promised the Polish leaders rich rewards, not only in the Muscovite realm, but also in Poland. Concerning the Tushino Russians, Sigismund authorized his emissaries to promise that he would respect their religious faith, customs and laws, and would give them possessions and rich rewards if they would submit to him.

On the other hand, the emissaries were to enter into direct negotiations with Shuisky and the leading people in Moscow, and deliver them letters from the king. The letter to Shuisky, dated November 12, 1609 (N. S.), begins with a reproach for wrongful acts against the Polish ambassadors at the time of the uprising against the pretender: "You concluded a truce with our ambassadors, extorting hard conditions from them, so that we might evacuate our people, who had come against our will into Muscovite territory, with some Muscovite or other who called himself Dmitry Ivanovich. You ordered our ambassadors to kiss the cross upon this, but we did not accept these conditions, nor did you send your ambassadors to us concerning the confirmation of this truce, which you yourself have violated by various actions. You did not send our people to the frontier until September 28, 1608, but detained them in Moscow and imprisoned them in various places in violation of the terms of the agreement. Others you are still detaining, and some you ordered to be killed even after the truce. You have given us no compensation for our innocent subjects who were killed, or for our plundered possessions. In addition, you have entered into relations with our enemy, Karl of Sudermania,[9] and have aided him against us with subsidies from your treasury. Nevertheless we wish to pacify the Muscovite realm, and to this end we are sending to our people who are present in their encampments before Moscow our great ambassadors, Lord Stanislaw Stadnicki and his companions. Concerning this we demand that you should order the boyars of your council to meet with our ambassadors at a safe location near Moscow and arrive at an equitable treaty, in order to bring to an end this war within the Muscovite realm."

The missives to the patriarch and the clergy included the following: "Since there has been for a long time great unrest and spilling of Christian blood in the Muscovite realm we, having pity upon you, have come in person, not because we wish there to be unrest and spilling of Christian blood in your realm, but in order that your great realm shall know peace. If you wish to win our royal favor and gratitude, and gain our protection, we assure you on our true sovereign word that we will respect your true Orthodox faith, all the ecclesiastical statutes and all your ancient customs whole and inviolate, and not only will guarantee to you your old patrimonies and grants, but will endow you, the churches of God and monasteries, with all kinds of honor and liberties, and also great rewards." The missive to the boyars and the people of Moscow was identical in content.

The ambassadors who had been sent from Tushino to the king, and the royal emissaries who had been dispatched to Tushino, met at Dorogobuzh. The king's delegates demanded to know of the Tushinites why they were travelling to Smolensk, but they gave no reply. Having arrived at Smolensk, the Tushino emissaries first sent their deputation before the king, and then before the nobility. The speech delivered before the king, while observing all formal courtesies, was most discourteous in content. The Tushinites declared that the king had no right to invade Muscovy and deprive them of the rewards they had received from Tsar Dmitry by their own toil and blood. Receiving a stern answer from the king, the Tushino emissaries immediately withdrew from Smolensk, returning to Tushino before the arrival of the royal commissioners.

Hearing their report, Rozynski and his companions began to take counsel, discussing whether or not they would receive the royal commissioners, for previously they had agreed to stand by Dmitry, and not enter into negotiations with anybody who sought to deal with them and not with the tsar. Rozynski, Zborowski and many other leaders asserted that they should honor the previous resolution, but the army did not agree. In the encampments the rumor spread that the king had plenty of money, and could pay the army if it deserted Dmitry and went over to the king's side. At the same time there appeared an emissary from Sapieha, who was besieging the Trinity monastery, demanding that the Tushinites immediately enter into negotiations with the royal commissioners, otherwise Sapieha immediately would enter the king's service. Rozynski was compelled to receive the royal commissioners. Negotiations opened, accompanied by great unrest.

What was the pretender doing in the meantime? His time had passed, and nobody any longer paid the slightest attention to him. Even worse, the leaders of the Tushino Poles turned their hearts from him the moment the king's entry into Muscovite territory placed them in an embarrassing situation. Thus Lord Tyszkiewicz[10] abused Dmitry to his face, calling him a deceiver and a swindler. False Dmitry wanted to leave the encampment with his Russian supporters, to whom this attitude towards their lawful tsar was causing alarm. Despite the fact that all his horses had been impounded by the Poles, the tsarlet was able to get away from the encampment with four hundred Don cossacks, but Rozynski pursued him and brought him back to Tushino, where he was placed under close guard.

When False Dmitry asked Rozynski on December 27 the subject of the talks going on with the royal commissioners the hetman, who appeared drunk, replied: "What business is it of yours to know why the commissioners have come to see me? The Devil knows what kind of creature you are! We have shed enough blood for you, without anything to show for it." The drunken Rozynski even threatened him with violence. Then Dmitry decided that, come what may, he must get away from Tushino.

The evening of the same day he changed into peasant clothes, climbed upon a manure sled and travelled to Kaluga, accompanied only by his jester, Koshelev.

THE THRONE OFFERED TO WLADYSLAW

After the pretender's departure Rozynski and his companions had no alternative but to seek accommodation with the king, moderating their previous injudicious demands. But there were many Russians in Tushino; what were they to do now? They could not follow the pretender, which the Poles would not allow, and it was too much to hope that the pretender would overcome his present difficulties. They could not bring themselves to ask Shuisky to change his stated position on their still uncertain fate, even assuming that he still would pardon them. Shuisky could not reward them as indulgently as those who had quit Tushino while the pretender remained in all his power. These people had not deserted the pretender now of their own free will, but had been forsaken by the pretender. The Tushino Russians, like the Poles, had only one recourse, to come to an accommodation with the king's commissioners.

The latter requested them to gather in a council of war, and so they assembled. The so-called Patriarch Filaret[11] and the clergy, Zarutsky with his soldiers, Saltykov with the council and court officials assembled, and the khan of Kasimov came with his Tatars.[12] Stadnicki delivered a speech pointing out the good intentions of the king concerning the Muscovite realm, and his readiness to take it under his protection, in order to liberate it from unjust tyrants. The speech was vague so that the consciences of many might be appeased. They listened eagerly to the ambassador's speech and the king's letter, they kissed Sigismund's signature and praised the Polish Commonwealth for its timely aid. Yet in accepting the king's protection the Russians demanded above all the inviolability of the Orthodox faith of the Greek dispensation, and the commissioners gave this guarantee. They wrote a letter in reply to the king, which clearly demonstrated their indecision and desire to gain time, and to wait and see how things turned out in Moscow and the provinces loyal to it.

"We, Patriarch Filaret of Moscow and all Russia, the archbishops, bishops and all the Holy Synod, having heard his royal highness's solicitude concerning our holy Orthodox faith, and of his valiant attempt to free Christendom, pray to God and do obeisance to him. We, the boyars, lords-in-waiting, etc., do obeisance to his royal grace, and wish to see him and his descendants as gracious rulers of our most glorious Muscovite realm. It is, however, impossible for us, people of ecclesiastical and secular rank who are here in the encampments, to resolve and establish this matter without the counsel of His Grace the Hetman and all the gentry, and without the counsel of all the Muscovite realm, comprised of men from all the towns. When we have established and resolved all these matters, we shall inform your royal grace."

The Tushino Russians conferred with the Poles, resolved not to abandon each other, and not to adhere to the fugitive tsarlet, or to Shuisky and his brothers. But, it is said, many of them sought the easiest way out of their indecision, and kissed the cross to Sigismund. It was decided also that the Tushino Russians and Poles should send delegates to the king and come to some final agreement.

On January 31, 1610 the emissaries of the Tushino Russians were presented formally to the king. Men of various ranks appeared and took it upon themselves to represent the Russian realm. Among these were Mikhail Glebovich Saltykov and his son Ivan, Prince Vasily Mikhailovich Rubets-Mosalsky, Prince Yury Khvorostinin, Leo Pleshcheev and Nikita Veliaminov. Among the crown secretaries were Ivan Gramotin, Chicherin, Solovetsky, Vitovtov, Apraxin and Yuriev. Also present were Mikhail Molchanov, Timofey Griaznoy and Fedor Andronov, the former Moscow tanner.[13] Mikhail Saltykov began a speech in which he spoke of the favorable disposition of the Muscovite people towards the king, and in the name of this people he blessed the king for his benevolence. His son, Ivan Saltykov, did obeisance to the king on behalf of Patriarch Filaret and the clergy, and blessed the king for his efforts to bring peace to the Muscovite realm. Finally Crown Secretary Gramotin, in the name of the council, the court and all the people, declared that the people of the Muscovite realm wished to have Prince Wladyslaw as their tsar, provided that the king would preserve inviolate the Greek faith, and would not infringe the ancient rights and privileges of the Muscovite nation, neither would he add any rights or freedoms unprecedented in the Muscovite realm.

CONDITIONS OF WLADYSLAW'S ELECTION

From the foregoing it is evident that the lengthy stay of the Russians and Poles in the same encampment had had its effect, and at the same time constituted the principal obstacle to the unification of the Muscovite realm with Poland. It is said that Saltykov wept as he begged the king to guarantee the preservation of the Greek faith. He could not remain indifferent to the danger that awaited Orthodoxy at the hands of Sigismund. So when negotiations opened between the senators and the ambassadors concerning conditions under which Wladyslaw might become tsar, once again the Russians demanded above all else the inviolability of the Orthodox religion.

Finally, on February 4 they agreed to set down in writing the following conditions: (1) Wladyslaw was to be crowned tsar in Moscow by the Russian patriarch, according to the ancient custom. The king added that this event must take place after the realm had been pacified completely. From this codicil it is evident that Sigismund had no intention of sending his son to Moscow but rather, on pretext of the non-pacification of the country, to seek rulership for himself. (2) In order that the holy faith of the Greek dispensation remain inviolate, teachers of Roman, Lutheran and other doctrines must not be allowed to cause a schism within the church. If people of the Roman faith wished to visit Greek churches, they must do so with respect, as becoming Orthodox Christians, and not with pride, not with their hats on, not bringing dogs into church with them, and not sitting in the churches other than at the appointed times. To this the king added that a Catholic church should be built in Moscow for the benefit of the Poles, into which Russians must enter with reverence. The king and his son promised not to convert anyone from the Greek faith, since faith is a gift of God, and it is not befitting to turn anyone from their faith by force, nor to persecute anyone on account of it. Jews were to be forbidden entry into the Muscovite realm. (3) The king and his son promised to respect the tombs and bodies of the saints, to respect the Russian clergy the same as the Catholic, and not to interfere in the affairs and judgements of the church. (4) They promised not only not to touch the possessions and rights of the clergy, but to extend them. (5) Further, the same guarantee was given to the boyars, lords-in-waiting and all conciliar, privy and chancellery officials. (6) Servicemen, gentry and junior boyars would be paid according to the rates effective during the reign of previous lawful sovereigns. (7) The same would apply to artillerymen and auxiliary soldiers. (8) Judgements were to be rendered according to ancient custom, and changes in the law would be subject to the approval of the boyars and the whole land. (9) There must be an offensive and defensive alliance between the Muscovite realm, the crown of Poland and the grand principality of Lithuania, to be directed against all enemies. (10) On the Tatar frontier there should be a co-ordinated defense, to be discussed between the boyars of the council and the lords of the Sejm. (11) Nobody shall be put to death without prior judgement by the boyars and other members of the council. The property of those executed shall pass to their heirs, and the king might not compel by force anyone to come to Lithuania or Poland. Men of high rank shall not be demoted without cause, and lesser servitors advanced according to the service they rendered.

In the latter provision the influence of the crown secretaries and men such as Andronov, of whom there were many in the Tushino encampment, is inescapable. These were men of humble birth, plucked and raised up by the whirlwind of the Time of Troubles, who wished to preserve their status, demanding that the new government raise people of humbler origin according to the service they rendered. Yet another interesting condition was imposed: "Each man of the Muscovite nation shall be free to travel for the sake of learning to other Christian countries, but not to pagan or Muslim countries, and the ruler shall not take away any of their patrimonies, possessions or homesteads." Here it is necessary to point out that the authors of this treaty were Saltykov and Mosalsky, fanatical supporters of the first False Dmitry and, consequently, of his plans. We know that False Dmitry, while reproaching the boyars for their ignorance, promised to permit them to go abroad.

(12) Russian prisoners of war taken to Poland shall be repatriated. (13) Polish and Lithuanian lords shall not be given positions in the Muscovite government. Those Polish lords remaining with Wladyslaw were to be rewarded with money payments, service tenures and patrimonies, but solely by common consent of both governments. The king obligated himself to negotiate with the boyars the border fortresses the Polish lords shall occupy, pending complete pacification of the country. It was obvious with what aim this last condition was inserted by the Poles. In the event of opposition in the eastern provinces, the king at least could retain the borderland places in his hands.

(14) Taxes shall be collected according to ancient custom. The king shall not impose any new tax without the consent of the members of the boyar council. Taxes shall be imposed upon inhabited places only. (15) There shall be free trade between the two realms. Russians shall be free to travel to foreign lands through Poland and Lithuania, and tolls shall remain the same as of old. (16) Movement of peasants was forbidden in the Muscovite provinces, and also between the Muscovite provinces and

Lithuania. (17) Slaves and bonded servitors belonging to lords shall remain their former status, and the king shall not grant them freedom. (18) Concerning the Volga, Don, Yaik and Terek cossacks, the king shall take counsel with the boyars and members of the council to decide whether or not their services were required.

In the foregoing treaty it is plain to see that it is the king, and not the prince, who stands in the foreground. The following words are appended to the treaty: "Concerning whatsoever is not defined in these articles, when it pleases God that his royal grace is before Moscow, or in Moscow, and the patriarch, with all the Holy Synod, boyars, gentry and all ranks of people do obeisance to him, the sovereign shall speak and rule upon these matters according to the Muscovite custom, together with the patriarch, the Holy Synod, the boyars and all the land."

It was plain that the name of Wladyslaw served merely as a cloak for the designs of Sigismund, since it was impossible to act directly in the name of the old king. The merchants of southwestern Russia who happened to be in Moscow let it be known to the inhabitants that they did not trust the promises of the man who had brought about the Union of Brest[14]. Sigismund was hastening to accomplish the second stage of fulfillment of his plans. He demanded submission from the ambassadors, and the ambassadors agreed to submit to him, pending the arrival of Wladyslaw, and even went so far as to swear the following oath: "Until God gives us Wladyslaw as sovereign of the Muscovite realm, we will serve, respect and wish well to his sovereign father, Sigismund Ivanovich, king of Poland and grand prince of Lithuania."

Having achieved this purpose, the king sent a letter to the Polish senators informing them of the arrival of the Tushino emissaries and of their request in favor of Wladyslaw. He continued: "Although in face of the heartfelt desire of these people we, guided by the advice of the lords who were present, did not deem it prudent to dash abruptly their hopes in our son, so that we might not let slip the opportunity to attract to our side those Muscovites who hold to Shuisky, and might give our affairs a most favorable turn. Bearing in mind that the campaign was undertaken not for our personal advantage or for that of our descendants but for the general good of the Commonwealth, we did not see fit to come to any definitive conclusion with them without the consent of all ranks."

Averting thus from himself the accusation that he had only his dynastic ambitions in mind, the king turned to the senators with the question of aid in the form of men and treasure for, he wrote, only lack of money could hinder this flourishing of their affairs for the way was open to the flowering of the glories of the gentry, to extension of the boundaries of the Commonwealth, and even to the conquest of the whole of the Muscovite monarchy.

MARINA'S PREDICAMENT IN TUSHINO

Meanwhile in Tushino, despite the fact that after the pretender's flight Rozynski and his companions were obliged to come to some agreement with the king, the greater part of the army wished to seek out the fugitive tsarlet and help him conquer Moscow.

Marina remained in Tushino. Pale, sighing and with dishevelled hair, she went from tent to tent pleading with the soldiers once again to embrace the cause of her husband, even though her position with the pretender was very precarious, as can be seen from her letters to her father. From one letter it is evident that the elder Mniszech had left Tushino at odds with his daughter, and had not given her his blessing. The same letter provides an insight into her relationship with her second husband. She begs her father to remember her to False Dmitry, and remind him of the love and respect he ought to have towards his wife. In another letter, Marina states: "I do not know what to write concerning my affairs, except that every day I go from one crisis to another. Nothing is ever resolved. People treat me the same as they did when you were here, and not as they promised they would at the time of your departure. I wanted to send some of my own people to you, but I need to give them some money for their subsistence, and I have none."

But her spirit did not weaken, nor did she want to renounce the goal for which she had sacrificed herself when she had left Sapieha's encampment for Tushino. The very magnitude of the sacrifices she had been forced to make rendered it impossible for her to turn back. In reply to her kinsman Stadnicki, who had informed her of the king's advance into Muscovite territory, she wrote: "I firmly rely upon God, the protector of the oppressed, that He soon will render judgement on our treacherous foe Shuisky."

She appended the following words to this letter in her own hand: "Whomsoever God has enlightened once, He has enlightened for ever. The sun does not lose its radiance simply because sometimes dark clouds obscure its countenance." Marina added these words because Stadnicki had not accorded her the imperial title in his letter. Equally amazing is her letter to the king in which she places herself under his protection, and wishes him a fortunate conclusion to his enterprise. "It is plain that fate never has played so cruelly as it has with me. From a mere noble family, it has raised me up to the Muscovite throne, and has cast me down from the throne into a cruel predicament. Subsequently, as if to comfort me with some degree of freedom, fate then led me into a situation worse than slavery itself. In my present situation I cannot live peacefully according to my dignity. If fate has deprived me of everything else, I still retain my right to the Muscovite throne, confirmed by my coronation, which recognized me as the true and lawful heiress, a recognition sealed by the twofold oath of allegiance of all the estates and provinces of the Muscovite realm."

From this letter it is evident, first, the terrible situation in which Marina found herself in Tushino during the time of the second pretender and, secondly, that Marina based her title to the Muscovite throne not on the right of her husbands but on her own coronation and the oath which the inhabitants of Muscovy had sworn to recognize her as their tsaritsa in the event that the first False Dmitry should die without issue. Consequently, Marina was drawing a distinction between her own cause and that of the second Pretender. He might indeed have been an impostor, as he was held to be by the Polish government, but she did not thereby lose any of her own rights.

THE PRETENDER IN KALUGA

Marina was premature in abandoning hope in the cause of her second husband. His rupture with the Poles had some advantages for him, for until now the chief reproach which could be levelled against him was that the Poles were devastating the Russian land. Now his quarrel with the Poles absolved him from this reproach. Arriving before Kaluga the pretender remained in a suburban monastery, and sent some monks into the town with the assurance that he had left Tushino, escaping the death which had been prepared for him by the Polish king, who was angered at his refusal to cede Smolensk and the Severian land to Poland. He was prepared, if need be, to lay down his life for the Orthodox faith and for the fatherland. His proclamation ended with the following words: "We will not allow heresy to triumph, nor will we cede either house or home to the king."

The inhabitants of Kaluga hastened to the monastery with bread and salt, escorted Dmitry into the town in triumph, and gave him the means to surround himself with imperial pomp. But they soon found out that, even though he had separated himself from the Poles, the pretender continued to be the brigand tsar because his power was based upon the cossacks. Prince Shakhovskoy, the inveterate intriguer, remained loyal to the pretender and brought to him the cossacks who were with him at Tsarevo-Zaimishche. Shakhovskoy probably was drawn to Kaluga by the prospect of playing the leading role at False Dmitry's court, in the absence of Rozynski.

In order to render the latter powerless False Dmitry wished to sow dissension in Tushino, with particular malice towards the Tushino Russians. Since they had shown little devotion to him, he wished to incite the Poles against them. To this end False Dmitry dispatched the Pole Kazimierski to Tushino with a letter to Marina and other persons in which he asserted that he was prepared to return to the encampment if the Poles would bind themselves by a new oath to serve him, and provided that the Russians who had deserted him were executed.

But these letters were taken from Kazimierski and he was forbidden, under pain of death, to sow dissension in the army. Rozynski wanted to pay the pretender in the same coin. He gave Kazimierski a letter to the former governor of Kaluga, the Pole Skotnicki,[15] in which he urged the latter, with the aid of the Poles who happened to be in Kaluga, to seize False Dmitry and return him to Tushino. But Kazimierski, on his arrival at Kaluga, handed the letter to False Dmitry, who immediately ordered Skotnicki to be thrown into the Oka even though he had no way of knowing whether this unfortunate would have done Rozynski's bidding. His fate was shared by Lord-in-waiting Ivan Ivanovich Godunov.

Fearing treason from both sides, no longer trusting either the Poles or the Russian nobility, the pretender wished to forestall plans harmful to him by means of cruelty. But if the pretender did not trust the Russian nobility, he did trust the slaves and cossacks for their interests were bound so closely to his. Thus the Don Cossacks did not heed Mlocki when he urged them to enter the king's service, but left for Kaluga. Those of the Tushino Poles who did not wish to join the king, and thought once again to come to an understanding with False Dmitry, relied principally upon the Don Cossacks, urged them to initiate the move, and openly set out from

Tushino for Kaluga with the assurance that if Rozynski pursued them, they, the Poles, would strike him in the rear. Despite the misgivings of their chief commander, Zarutsky, the cossacks, under the leadership of Princes Trubetskoy and Zasetsky, left Tushino, and Rozynski gave pursuit. They halted and gave battle, in the hope of receiving aid from the Poles, but the latter left them in the lurch and Rozynski left more than two thousand cossacks dead on the field, while the remainder dispersed to various localities, although a few returned to Zarutsky in Tushino.

MARINA FLEES TUSHINO

New disturbances in Tushino were caused by Marina's departure. On the night of February 11 she fled on horseback in a hussar's uniform, accompanied by a single servant girl and several hundred Don Cossacks. The next morning a letter from her to the army was discovered: "I am compelled to flee in order to escape utter misfortune and humiliation. Not even my good fame and dignity, given to me by God, have been spared! In conversations I have been compared to shameless women, and my name has been used as a reproach against the Poles. God forbid that I should ever have dealings with, or give myself to a man who has no right whatsoever to me or the Muscovite throne. Abandoned, without family, without friends, without subjects and defenseless, in my grief I commend myself to God, and I must of necessity go to my husband. I call God to witness that I shall not yield any of my rights, both for the defense of my own glory and inheritance, for because I am sovereign lady over nations and tsaritsa of Moscow, I cannot once again become a mere Polish subject; but also for the good of the Polish gentry which, being enamoured of glory and praise, will be mindful of its oath."

In this letter Marina declared that of necessity she must go to her husband, but soon it was learned that she was staying at Dmitrov, in Sapieha's encampment. Rozynski wrote to the king that Marina had lost her way and for that reason had ended up in Dmitrov, but Marchocki, one of his companions in Tushino, tells a different story. According to his account, Sapieha enticed Marina to his camp with a promise that he would champion her cause. We cannot discount this explanation when we remember what kind of life Marina had led with the brigand, to whom she would turn only as a last resort.

POLES ABANDON TUSHINO

Whatever the case may have been, there was unrest in Tushino. A council of war was held close to Rozynski's headquarters. The people who took his side, namely those who wanted to join the king, came on foot, armed only with sabres, not anticipating any violence from their own people. But Rozynski's opponents, about a hundred men, came on horseback with firearms, and some in full armor. They began to debate as to whom it was better to turn, to the king or to Dmitry. Those who advocated joining up with the king said that it was out of the question to support Dmitry. Moscow hated him, and would be more inclined to support the king than Dmitry. Several of Rozynski's opponents declared that it would be better to enter into negotiations with Shuisky, but they were contradicted by those who said: "Shuisky is not so simpleminded that he would buy peace from you while he is at war with the king." Others said: "Let us go beyond the Volga and turn the flank of the royal army if it is hostile to us." The others disagreed, saying that this would be futile, and the king would in no wise be harmed because the Muscovites, who had them in their territory, in any case would be obliged to divide their forces.

Finally several cried out that they must return to Poland. This argument was easy to refute: "If we disperse, the king will not call off the war, and we will not be able to avoid further service. Having lost our reward for so much service, we will have to serve again at a lower rate of pay." Not being able to counter these arguments with better ones, Rozynski's opponents took up the refrain. Their spokesman was Tyskiewicz, a personal enemy of Rozynski. They let fly a salvo of musketry in the direction of the hetman. His supporters responded with a volley, and the council broke up.

Rozynski's opponents, with the cry "Let all good people follow me!" went out of the encampment into the open field and decided to join False Dmitry in Kaluga. But the more prudent dissuaded them, in order that for the time being things remain peaceful at Tushino and then, if the royal conditions were unsatisfactory, they should withdraw a few miles from the capital in harmony and good order, and from there disperse to wherever they wished. All agreed to this.

In these circumstances Rozynski wrote a letter to Sigismund informing the king of Marina's flight and the mutiny in the army, saying that if within a certain time he received no news which would satisfy the gentry, it would be difficult to prevent further disorder. In order to save himself from the dangers threatening from all sides, from his own army, from False Dmitry in Kaluga, and from Skopin, Rozynski urged the king to come immediately to his aid. He urged Sigismund to undertake a rapid advance to Tushino. He also wrote that the Muscovites greatly desired this, since Tsar Vasily was at odds with Skopin. He therefore advised the king to write a letter to Skopin, whom, according to certain information received, it would not be difficult to attract to the Polish side. The Tushino Russians, particularly Patriarch Filaret, were very offended at being neglected by the king, who had yet to send them a single letter, and were perturbed by the lawlessness of the cossacks in Zubtsov province.

But the king did not budge from Smolensk nor did he send anyone to Tushino for definitive talks with the Polish gentry. As a result, Rozynski was compelled to abandon Tushino. Early in March 1610 he set fire to the encampment and marched along the highway to the monastery of St. Joseph of Volokolamsk.[16] A few of the Tushino Russians followed him, but most went with their submissions either to Moscow or to Kaluga. Saltykov and his companions remained with the king outside Smolensk.

Thus Moscow was rid of Tushino. Skopin merely had to settle accounts with Sapieha's detachment. We left Skopin at Alexandrovskaia Sloboda where he was continuing his negotiations with the Swedes, who were demanding a new treaty and fresh concessions. Despite the resistance of its inhabitants, Korela had been handed over to the Swedes. Furthermore, Tsar Vasily had been obliged to make the following promise: "We, the tsar's majesty, on account of your love, friendship, help and sacrifices, which you have extended us, and will extend in the future, give to you, beloved sovereign King Karl, in full ownership, whatever within reason you demand of the tsar's majesty, whether towns, territories or provinces."

This promise purchased the aid of an additional detachment of three thousand Swedes. Sapieha no longer could remain before the Trinity monastery and on January 12 he lifted the famous siege, taking up his headquarters at Dmitrov with a small force since the greater part of his forces had crossed the Volga in search of supplies. By mid-February the Russians and Swedes were advancing on Dmitrov. Sapieha advanced to intercept them, but was defeated. Dmitrov would have been taken but for the resistance of the Don Cossacks, who held out in a special fortification they had built near the town.

Here also Marina displayed great firmness of spirit. When the Poles, panic-stricken because of their defeat, half-heartedly set about the defense of their fortifications, she ran out of her lodging, crying out: "What are you doing, you cowards? Though I am a woman, I have not lost courage!" Seeing that Sapieha's cause was going badly, she decided to make for Kaluga. Sapieha did not wish to let her go, and she suspected that he was intending to hand her over to the king. Therefore she said to him: "Do not think of trading me off, as I have my Don cossacks here with me. If you try and stop me, I shall fight you."

Thereafter Sapieha did not try to stop her and she went to Kaluga, once again in male attire, part of the way on horseback, the rest of the way by sled. Sapieha remained in Dmitrov only for a short while after her departure; as soon as detachments returned with supplies from across the Volga he moved off to Volokolamsk, and Skopin could enter Moscow unhindered.

PRINCE SKOPIN'S POPULARITY

The famous commander was twenty-four-years old. In one year he had won as much renown as the other commanders had gained by heroic deeds spanning many years and, moreover, had won the great love of all good citizens, all the people of the land, who wished the country to be free of unrest, from the furor of the homeless, the cossacks, and all this Skopin had accomplished, not simply by a single brilliant feat, nor alone by those victories which had so captured the popular imagination whenever his memory was recalled. What was the cause of the popular acclaim and love which Skopin attracted? We have seen how, stirred and shaken to its foundation, Russian society was suffering from lack of a focal point, from the absence of a man to whom the people could attach themselves, around whom they could rally. At last such a man had appeared in the person of Prince Skopin.

Moscow, under siege by the brigand, was suffering famine, and within its walls witnessed unprecedented unrest, while the Tushino people raged around the countryside. Amidst all these troubles there was only one name which could rekindle all hopes, and that name was Skopin. Prince Mikhail Vasilievich was in Novgorod, he had come to an agreement with the Swedes, he was coming with them to the relief of Moscow. He was coming slowly, but he was coming all the same, and the Tushinites were melting before him. Skopin was now in Torzhok, now in Tver, and now in Alexandrovskaia Sloboda. In Moscow there were severe famine and riots, but suddenly all was quiet, the bells pealed, people hurried to the churches, and services of thanksgiving were sung, for it was heard that Prince Mikhail Vasilievich was nigh! In the Kremlin palace the unprepossessing old man was unloved and inactive because there there was nothing for him to do while he sat under siege, while all the vital matters of state had fallen into the hands of Skopin, who was acting alone, who alone was on the move, and upon whom alone depended the great task of deliverance.

There was no speculation, no conjecture about how Skopin's power, which rested on the skillful foreign soldiers, without whom he could do nothing, would survive after they had departed. There was no speculation, neither was it known for sure what influence Sigismund's invasion of Muscovite territory would have now that the Russians had chased Rozynski and False Dmitry away from Tushino, and had forced Sapieha to lift the siege of the Trinity monastery. Sigismund was far away, outside Smolensk; from a nearer perspective it could be seen that Tushino was abandoned, and that Sapieha had retreated from the Trinity monastery, just as Skopin happened to be approaching Moscow, and so they ascribed all these successes to him, as well as the panic and flight of the enemy. It is justly said that fame increases with distance, and the approach of the famed person diminishes his glory. The very remoteness of Skopin's activity, which was directed at the aim desired by most good people, and reached their ears, not in details, but as a whole, could not but enhance his glory, and strengthen the people's love towards him.

But it should also be added that his nearness, the actual presence of the famous commander, could not dispel the impression he had created by his distant triumphs. According to the testimony of contemporaries, he was a handsome young man, equipped with a lucid mind, a maturity of judgement beyond his years, skillful in military matters, brave and cautious at the same time, adroit in his dealings with foreigners; whosoever met him praised him to the skies.

Such was the man who appeared destined to liberate the Muscovite realm from the brigands and Poles, support the tottering throne of his old uncle, reconcile the Russian people with the Shuisky family and establish it on the throne of the tsars since, with the death of the childless Vasily, the voice of the whole land could hardly fail to be in favor of the popular favorite. But if the peaceful citizens, finding themselves a focal point in the tsar's kinsman, were prepared for the good of the land and of Skopin himself patiently to await the demise of Tsar Vasily in order to raise to the throne their favorite, who was innocent of any ambitious self-seeking,

the same was not true of Liapunov, who was unable to subordinate his
personal aspirations to the common good, and who did not recognize that
it was essential to employ honest means towards the attainment of so
lofty a goal, so that it would be lasting.

While Skopin was still at Alexandrovskaia Sloboda emissaries came
to him from Liapunov, greeting him as tsar in the name of the latter, and
giving him a letter full of damaging accusations against Tsar Vasily.
Skopin immediately tore up the letter and ordered the emissaries arrested,
but later allowed them to make their apologies and sent them back to Riazan without reporting the matter. The incident caused his uncle to suspect
Skopin. The tsar was convinced that if Prince Mikhail really had been
displeased with Liapunov's proposal he would have sent to Moscow the
Riazan people who had brought the letter. From then on, adds the chronicler,[17] the tsar and his brothers had evil intentions towards Prince Skopin.

SKOPIN'S TRIUMPHAL ENTRY INTO MOSCOW

On March 12 Skopin and De la Gardie made their triumphal entry into
Moscow. By order of the tsar, the magnates met Mikhail at the gates with
bread and salt. But the simple townsmen outstripped them, fell down before him and with tears pleaded with him to liberate the Muscovite realm.
Contemporary writers compare Skopin's reception to the triumph of
David, whom the Israelites considered to be greater than Saul. Tsar Vasily
gave no indication of displeasure; on the contrary, he met his kinsman with
tears of joy. His brother, Prince Dmitry, behaved very differently. Tsar
Vasily, who had married late, had only one or two daughters, who had
died in infancy. Consequently his brother Dmitry considered himself to
be heir apparent to the throne, and saw a deadly rival in Skopin to whom,
in view of the still uncertain order of succession, the love of the populace
virtually guaranteed the crown.

Prince Dmitry was the most eager calumniator of his kinsman at the
tsar's court. The tsar, either mindful of Skopin's unpretentiousness, and
not considering him a personal rival, had no reason for wishing to bar him
from the succession, or at least was motivated by prudence, not wishing
to quarrel with the popular favorite. He grew angry at his brother for his
bothersome accusations and even, it was said, on one occasion chased him
away with blows from his staff! It was said as well that the tsar had a frank
talk with his kinsman, in the course of which Skopin managed to prove
his innocence, pointing out the dangers of such rancor in troubled times.

But despite the fact that the tsar did not display the slightest animosity towards Skopin the people, who disliked the older Shuisky brothers, were speaking of enmity between uncle and nephew. De la Gardie, hearing tales of envy and hatred, urged him to leave Moscow as soon as possible and set out for Smolensk to confront Sigismund.

SIGISMUND'S DIFFICULT SITUATION

Sigismund's situation was not particularly alluring. If at first the Poles had managed to conquer Rzhev, Volodimirov and Zubtsov, which had been surrendered by the governors of the pretender, a few of the towns of the pre-ruined northern Ukraine put up a desperate resistance to the Zaporozhian Cossacks. The inhabitants of Starodub fought fiercely against them, and when their town was engulfed in flames they first threw their possessions into the fire and then plunged into it themselves. The inhabitants of Pochep displayed similar bravery; four thousand perished in a stiff defense. At Chernigov the enemy met with less resistance. Novgorod Seversk also swore allegiance to Wladyslaw. Mosalsk had to be taken by storm, and Belaia had to be starved into submission.

But Smolensk continued to hold out, and the inhabitants had good reason to hold out so resolutely. Despite the king's promises the Poles, and especially the Zaporozhian cossacks, raged furiously against the inhabitants of those towns which had surrendered in the name of Wladyslaw. In the Polish camp deserters confirmed that in the city of Smolensk there was famine and plague, and that Governor Shein himself was in favor of surrendering to the king, but that Archbishop Sergius[18] would not let him. On one occasion the community, headed by the governor, had come to urge the archbishop to surrender; but the archbishop, taking off his vestments and casting down his staff, said that he was prepared to suffer torture, but would not betray his church, and much rather would allow himself to be killed than agree to the surrender of the city. The people, swayed by these words, renounced their intention and, clothing Sergius once again in his vestments, swore to resist the Poles to the last drop of blood.

The governor proposed to make a sortie but the archbishop would not agree to this since he suspected that Shein wished to lead the people out of the city in order to do obeisance to the king. Wilczek, the Tushino Pole in command at Mozhaisk, sold that town to Tsar Vasily for a hundred rubles (three hundred and thirty-three and a third rubles in present-day currency). In the monastery of St. Joseph, where Rozynski had his

Fortifications of Smolensk
Built by F. Savelev Kon, 1596–1602

headquarters, yet another uprising against him had erupted. Fleeing from the mutineers, the hetman stumbled on the stone steps and fell on the side in which he had been shot and wounded outside Moscow. From this accident, and from grief that matters had gone completely awry, Rozynski died on April 4, new style, being barely thirty-five years old.

After his death Zborowski, with the greater part of the army, went on to Smolensk, others with Rucki and Marchocki remained in the St. Joseph monastery, but on May 21 they were driven out by Russian and foreign troops led by Valuev, Horn and Delaville. Leaving the monastery at great peril to themselves, the Poles were obliged to leave behind the Russians whom they had brought from Tushino, including Metropolitan Filaret, who thus had the opportunity to leave for Moscow. Of the fifteen hundred Poles and Don cossacks who had been in the St. Joseph monastery only about three hundred escaped, having lost all their banners. During this fight, according to the Poles themselves, they were greatly assisted by Don Cossacks. All the Tushino Poles now were grouped together on the Ugra river and from there they carried on their correspondence with False Dmitry, who came to them twice in person from Kaluga because they would not budge unless he paid them money. He succeeded in attracting many to his cause, bringing the pretender's army to the strength of 6,200 men. But Zborowski, acting in the name of the remaining Poles, moved to the environs of Smolensk in order to declare his loyalty to the king. Jan Sapieha also arrived there, as well as the khan of Kasimov. Lisowski, who was outlawed, did not dare come. He could not remain in the east after the fall of Tushino, so he moved westwards from Suzdal, concentrating his forces in Velikie Luki.

Both False Dmitry and the king found themselves in an awkward situation. The former, with his six thousand troops, could do nothing against Moscow; on the contrary, Muscovite detachments were advancing on Kaluga. The advance of Skopin and the Swedes towards Smolensk against the Poles in all probability would resolve the conflict in favor of Tsar Vasily. In that case, what remained for the Kaluga tsar? On the other hand, the king saw that his invasion of the Muscovite territories had only benefitted Shuisky, who had expelled the brigand from Tushino, and had scattered his forces. Shuisky had triumphed, and had at his disposal a large army under the command of a famous leader, with Swedish help in addition, while the king had hastened to Smolensk in the hope that his presence alone would be sufficient to subdue the Muscovite realm, torn apart by the Troubles. Now he confronted an unequal contest with a powerful and angry foe.

Given these circumstances, it was only natural that a rapprochement should take place between the king and the Kaluga tsarlet. Marina's brother, the governor of Sanock, who happened to be outside Smolensk, received from Kaluga reliable information that False Dmitry wished to place himself under the king's protection, but was waiting for the king to make the first move. Consequently the king summoned a secret council, at which he resolved to send the governor of Sanok to Kaluga in order to persuade the tsarlet to throw himself on the king's mercy. Meanwhile it was desirable to enter into direct negotiations with the Muscovite tsar, but Vasily, seeing that fortune had turned in his favor, forbade his governors to allow Polish ambassadors to pass until the king had evacuated Muscovite territory. But fortune smiled on Shuisky for only a short while.

SKOPIN'S DEATH

On April 23 Skopin, while attending a christening at the house of Prince Ivan Mikhailovich Vorotynsky, collapsed with blood pouring from his nostrils and, after an illness lasting more than two weeks, he died. There was a general rumor that he had been poisoned. The hatred of his uncle Prince Dmitry towards him was well known, and generally he was pointed to as the murderer. Crowds would have advanced on the house of the tsar's brother, but were chased away by troops. Concerning the veracity of the rumor that Skopin was poisoned, Russian contemporaries do not go so far as to make an outright accusation. The chronicle states: "Many said in Moscow that he was brought to ruin by his aunt, Princess Catherine, the wife of Prince Dmitry Shuisky (a daughter of Maliuta Skuratov and sister to Maria Grigorievna Godunova),[19] but God only knows the truth of the matter."[20] Palitsyn uses almost identical words: "We do not know how to say this, whether this was the result of God's judgement, or through the designs of evil men. Only our Creator knows."[21] Zolkiewski, who while living in Moscow had ample opportunity to find out the truth, discounts the accusation, and attributes Skopin's death to natural causes.[22] This important testimony is contradicted by that of another foreigner, Bussow, who was not favorably disposed towards Tsar Vasily.[23] The Pskov chronicle, which for reasons well known was also hostile to Shuisky, strongly asserts that Skopin was poisoned, relating in detail how, at the feast, the wife of Dmitry Shuisky herself handed Skopin the poisoned chalice. But in this account there is a ridiculous mistake. The murderess in this account is called Christina.[24] In all probability this name is fabricated from the word "christening", alluding to the baptismal feast at which Skopin collapsed.

LIAPUNOV RISES AGAINST TSAR VASILY

Whatever may have been, Skopin's death was the heaviest and most decisive blow against Shuisky. Previously the people had not loved or trusted Tsar Vasily and had seen him as an ill-fated tsar, unblessed by God. But Skopin had reconciled the tsar with the people, and had given them hope of a happier future. Now the man of reconciliation was no more and, what was worse, rumor had it that the tsar himself, out of envy and spite, had deprived himself and the tsardom of its strong support. This blow was all the heavier for the people, as it came at a time when hopes had been rekindled of a happier future, of divine mercy.

Such blows extinguish the last breath of spirit, the last ounce of strength. For the people the future no longer in any way was bound up with the Shuisky family. The tsar was old and childless, and his successor, Prince Dmitry, had not been loved or trusted even before he was accused of having poisoned his nephew. It is well known how, when someone who is loved dies, people begin to love all those whom he loved and to persecute all those unfriendly or hostile towards him. This makes understandable the feelings about Dmitry Shuisky after the death of Skopin. It is said that the people wept for Prince Mikhail just as they had wept for Tsar Fedor Ivanovich. In fact it could be said that Skopin was the last of the Rurikids enthroned in the hearts of the people. For a second time the house of Rurik had been cut off from the Russian throne.

As the link between the Russian people and Shuisky had been ruptured in this manner, as the gaze of many involuntarily and fearfully cast around on all sides, a voice was heard summoning them to a way out of their difficult, cheerless situation. This was a familiar voice, that of Liapunov. A short time previously, when the majority had shown their devotion to Skopin as their desired successor to the throne, Liapunov had not wanted to wait, but offered Skopin the throne during the lifetime of Tsar Vasily when such an action, if Skopin had agreed to it, would have served only to intensify the Troubles, not to calm them. Here Liapunov showed more than anything else that his goal, whether he aimed at it consciously or not, was not the ending of the Time of Troubles.

Now that Skopin was no more and discontent against Shuisky was growing, Liapunov was the first to rise against Tsar Vasily, but he only set the rising in motion, without specifying its aim. He demanded the deposition of Shuisky as an unworthy tsar who had destroyed his famous nephew, but he did not name Shuisky's successor. He carried on negotiations with the Kaluga tsarlet, and in Moscow he conferred with Prince Vasily Vasilievich Golitsyn, in order to dethrone Shuisky, according to the expression used by the chronicler,[25] but in the meantime he fell away from Moscow, ceased to obey its tsar, and sent messages inciting against the tsar those towns which had been loyal.

ZOLKIEWSKI'S VICTORY AT KLUSHINO

While Liapunov was raising rebellion at Riazan the Muscovite army, numbering about forty thousand, together with about eight thousand Swedes, was advancing against the Poles in the direction of Smolensk. Who was it that took Skopin's place as chief commander? None other than Prince Dmitry Shuisky, who was accused of having poisoned his kinsman, and who quite apart from that was hated by the soldiers for his haughtiness!

The king, who had learned that a large Muscovite army was assembling at Mozhaisk, sent against it Hetman Zolkiewski, who on June 14 besieged Tsarevo-Zaimishche where the Muscovite commanders, Eletsky and Valuev, were stationed. Here he joined Hetman Zborowski, who had brought thither those Tushino Russians who had preferred the service of the king to that of the Kaluga tsar. Despite these reinforcements, Zolkiewski did not wish to take Tsarevo-Zaimishche by storm, knowing that the Russians, who were weak in the open field, were impregnable when defending fortified places. Eletsky and Valuev, seeing that Zolkiewski was preparing to starve them out, sent to Prince Dmitry Shuisky in Mozhaisk asking him to relieve them. Shuisky moved forward and took position at Klushino, tiring out his army by a march in the intense heat. Two Germans from De la Gardie's contingent deserted to the Poles, and informed the hetman of Shuisky's movements. Zolkiewski summoned a council of war, which decided that it would be dangerous to await the enemy, since Eletsky and Valuev were in the rear. They decided to divide their forces. Part would remain near Tsarevo-Zaimishche to contain Eletsky and Valuev while the remainder would advance to Klushino to engage Shuisky.

On the night of June 23-24 the Polish army left its bivouac and on the next morning attacked Shuisky, having by reason of the narrowness of the terrain divided its forces into two concentrations. One group engaged the Swedes and compelled De la Gardie to retreat. The other detachment of Poles attacked the Muscovite army and chased away part of it, namely the cavalry; but Shuisky, with the infantry, stood fast in the village of Klushino and defended himself valiantly, while his cannon caused great casualties among the Poles. The outcome of the battle was therefore very doubtful when suddenly the German mercenaries began to surrender to the Poles, first two, then six, and then increasingly more and more of them. The Poles approached their regiments, crying out *"Komm! Komm!"*, and the Germans flew like birds in response to a call, and finally declared that they wished to enter into negotiations with the hetman. Both sides had given hostages, and negotiations had begun, when De la Gardie returned and wished to call off the negotiations, but he could do nothing. The foreign mercenaries agreed to join the hetman, while De la Gardie and Horn, with a small force of Swedes, received permission to withdraw to the north, to the borders of their country.

Meanwhile the Russians, seeing that the Germans were betraying them, began to prepare to move off and regroup their forces. The Swedes informed the Poles that the Russians were fleeing, so the Poles set off in pursuit and captured their baggage train. Dmitry Shuisky, in the words of the chronicler, "was a commander with a craven heart, encumbered with effeminate things, loving beauty and food, and not the drawing of the bow." The chronicle ascribes the treason of the Germans to the shortcomings of the chief commander. The Germans demanded money but he put them off with the excuse that there was none, when in fact there was. The Germans grew angry and sent to Zolkiewski outside Tsarevo-Zaimishche, saying that he should come without delay, since they would not oppose him.[26]

ZOLKIEWSKI'S MOSCOW CAMPAIGN

From outside Moscow Zolkiewski returned to the outskirts of Tsarevo-Zaimishche, informing Eletsky and Valuev of his victory. For a long time the commanders did not believe him, so the hetman showed them some noble prisoners who had been captured at Klushino. Convinced of the terrible truth, they still did not wish to surrender in the name of the prince, but said to Zolkiewski: "Advance on Moscow, and when Moscow is yours we will be willing to swear allegiance to the prince." The hetman replied: "If I take you, then Moscow will be ours."

The commanders unwillingly kissed the cross to Wladyslaw, but for his part the hetman had to swear to the following conditions: not to deprive the Muscovite people of the Christian faith; not to destroy the thrones of God or establish Roman churches within the Muscovite realm; Wladyslaw would be ruler under the same conditions as previous natural rulers; boyars and all ranks would remain secure in their positions as before; neither Polish nor Lithuanian governors would be sent to Muscovite towns, neither would military governors be appointed to towns; not to take away salaries, land grants or patrimonies from gentry, junior boyars or any servitors; not to have common dealings with the Kaluga tsarlet. The final clause is particularly significant: "If God grants that the town of Smolensk submit to our most glorious sovereign, Prince Wladyslaw Sigismundovich, then King Sigismund shall come directly from Smolensk with all his forces, both Polish and Lithuanian, and shall make no raids or acts of violence in the suburbs or in the countryside, and the land grants and patrimonies in Smolensk and in the provinces pertaining to the towns which have submitted to our sovereign prince shall be evacuated, and all border towns shall belong to the Muscovite realm as before."

Zolkiewski realized that Muscovy could be conquered only in the name of Wladyslaw, and only on condition that the latter ruled in the same manner as previous natural sovereigns. He understood that the slightest hint at the debasement of Muscovy before Poland, any breach of its integrity, would ruin the entire cause. The hetman agreed to conditions which guaranteed the integrity and independence of the Muscovite realm, for his aim was to overthrow Shuisky as quickly as possible and set up Wladyslaw in his place. Zolkiewski had to choose between two courses; either to agree to the conditions, take Moscow away from Shuisky and give it to Wladyslaw, or not to agree to the conditions, act in accordance with the king's intentions, strengthen Shuisky, and arm against himself the entire land, thus placing himself between two fires, Moscow and Kaluga. Naturally he chose the first alternative.

When Eletsky and Valuev swore allegiance to Wladyslaw and when Mozhaisk, Borisov, Borovsk, the St. Joseph monastery of Volokolamsk, Pogoreloe Gorodishche and Rzhev followed their example, the hetman's army was swelled by tens of thousands of Russians. Zolkiewski himself says that these new subjects of the prince were fairly loyal and well disposed, frequently brought him news from the capital, entered into correspondence with their relatives, and transmitted letters which the hetman wrote to various people in Moscow, together with proclamations urging Shuisky's deposition. A postscript dictated by the commanders of Tsarevo-Zaimishche was added by Zolkiewski himself to these proclamations, as he thought that this action would serve the Muscovites as a full guarantee of their future under Wladyslaw's rule. But here is the reply from Moscow which the servicemen from Smolensk and Briansk, to whom he had sent the proclamations and the postscript, sent the hetman: "We ourselves have read through these letters, and the replies and postscripts to them, and have given them to be read by the gentry, junior boyars and many men of all ranks from the various towns who are here in Moscow, and they, having read these documents, reply that there is no mention in these letters that our lord Prince Wladyslaw Sigismundovich is ready to be baptized into our Christian faith and then, having been baptized, will be placed upon the throne of our Muscovite realm."

The hetman replied that the baptism of the prince was an ecclesiastical matter, which was the concern of the patriarch and the clergy. But in Moscow it was thought that it concerned not only the patriarch but all the land, and that some in Moscow, if they saw that Shuisky no longer sat upon the throne, would be more inclined towards Kaluga than towards Wladyslaw.

THE PRETENDER BEFORE MOSCOW

The pretender took stock of his situation. He knew that after Klushino Shuisky's cause was lost, so he won over Sapieha's force with money, and advanced towards Moscow. On his way he was obliged to capture the St. Paphnutius monastery of Borovsk,[27] where there was a Muscovite commander, Prince Mikhail Volkonsky, and his two companions. The latter, observing the uncompromising attitude of the chief commander, resolved to surrender the monastery secretly, and opened the stockade gates, through which streamed the forces of False Dmitry. Volkonsky, becoming aware of this treason, rushed into the church. His companions who had betrayed him called upon him in vain to come out and submit to the victors. "I will die at the tomb of St. Paphnutius," answered Volkonsky. Taking his stand at the church doors, he fought his enemies until he collapsed from his wounds, and fell by the left choir, where he was finished off.

Having plundered the monastery the pretender proceeded to Serpukhov, which surrendered. The Crimean Tatars, who were on their way to aid Tsar Vasily, and who had received great gifts from him, could not withstand Sapieha's army and, instead of providing help, dispersed in search of plunder, rounding up captives like cattle into their encampments. Kolomna and Kashira surrendered to False Dmitry, but Zaraisk, commanded by Prince Dmitry Mikhailovich Pozharsky, did not surrender. Even prior to this Liapunov, rising against Tsar Vasily after the death of Skopin, had sent to Pozharsky his kinsman Fedor Liapunov, appealing to him to join with the people of the Riazan land against Shuisky, but Pozharsky, having sent a message on to Moscow, demanded reinforcements from Tsar Vasily, and received them. Now the inhabitants of Zaraisk came as a body to the commander, asking him to kiss the cross to the pretender. Pozharsky refused, and shut himself up in the citadel with a few people. Archpriest Dmitry encouraged him, and blessed him for being willing to sacrifice his life for the Orthodox faith, which further encouraged Pozharsky. Finally he came to an agreement with the inhabitants of Zaraisk: "If Tsar Vasily remains as before upon the throne, we will serve him, but if someone else attains the throne, him also will we serve." Having sealed this agreement by kissing the cross, all wavering ceased in the town of Zaraisk, and they began to attack the brigand's followers. The town of Kolomna also returned to its allegiance to Tsar Vasily.

False Dmitry, advanced and halted at the village of Kolomenskoe. Shuisky still had thirty thousand troops, but who was willing to fight on his behalf? It has been seen how servicemen had been negotiating with Zolkiewski concerning the conditions under which Wladyslaw was to rule. Golitsyn was in correspondence with Liapunov, who sent Alexis Peshkov to Moscow with a message to his brother Zakhar, and to all those in league with him, urging them to depose Shuisky. Servitors also entered into correspondence with False Dmitry's Poles, not with the aim of accepting the brigand in place of Shuisky, but to reach an agreement with the Tushinites that they would abandon their tsar and the Muscovites would depose theirs. The Tushinites already were pointing to Sapieha as a man worthy to be a Muscovite sovereign. Shuisky saw that it was going to be difficult to maintain his throne and therefore wished to negotiate with Hetman Zolkiewski, but when one faces a difficult task the tendency is to put it off under various pretexts. So Shuisky postponed an embassy to

the hetman, thinking that it would be more opportune to wait until the
hetman contacted him.

THE FALL OF SHUISKY

But Zakhar Liapunov and his companions did not want to wait. On July
17 they came in a great crowd to the palace. First Zakhar Liapunov
approached the tsar and demanded: "How long will you continue to shed
Christian blood? The land is devastated and nothing favorable has been
done during your reign. Have pity upon our ruin, and lay aside the tsar's
staff, for we have decided already what to do with you." Shuisky was quite
accustomed to such scenes. He saw before him a crowd of insignificant
people, and thought he could intimidate them by shouting, and so with
unfittingly querulous words he answered Liapunov: "How dare you utter
such words to me, when even the boyars would not address me in such
a manner?" He attempted to draw his dagger in order to intimidate the
insurgents further. But Zakhar Liapunov was not so easily frightened;
abuse and threats merely served to provoke him to retaliation. Liapunov
was a tall, strong man. Having heard Shuisky's abuse, having seen his
threatening gesture, he cried out to him: "Do not attack me. If I get my
hands on you, I'll throttle you." But his companions did not share
Liapunov's ardor. Seeing that Shuisky was not intimidated, and would not
accede willingly to their demands, Khomutov and Ivan Nikitich Saltykov
cried out: "Let us get out of here!" and immediately proceeded to the
platform on Red Square.[28]

It was known already throughout Moscow that something was afoot
in the Kremlin and crowds rushed towards the platform just as the patriarch
arrived there. It was necessary to explain what was happening, for people
were overflowing the square. Liapunov, Khomutov and Saltykov cried
that they should find a more spacious location, beyond the Moscow river
near the Serpukhov gates, whither they and the patriarch would accompany them. There the boyars, gentry, merchants and tradesmen took counsel about to end the devastation and plunder of the Muscovite realm. Poles
and Lithuanians were invading the Muscovite realm, and the Kaluga
brigand was coming upon them from the other side—danger threatened
the land of Muscovy from both sides.

The boyars and the people resolved that they would petition Lord Tsar
Vasily that he, the sovereign, renounce the tsardom because much blood
was being shed, among the people it was said that he was an ill-fated tsar,

and neither the Ukrainian towns which had gone over to the brigand wanted him as tsar. There was no opposition to this plea among the people; the only opposition came from a few of the boyars, but not for long. The patriarch was opposed, but nobody heeded him. The tsar's brother-in-law, Prince Ivan Mikhailovich Vorotynsky, went to the palace to beg Tsar Vasily to renounce the tsardom and accept Nizhny Novgorod as his appanage. Vasily had to agree to this request, coming from a boyar in the name of the Muscovite people, and so he and his wife moved from the palace to the house which he had occupied when he was still a mere boyar.

But hope of moving from that house back into the palace never left the old man. He communicated with his supporters, increased their number, and bribed the musketeers. The circumstances were propitious. The Tushinites had deceived the Muscovites, for when the latter sent to tell them that they had done their part and deposed Shuisky, and were waiting for the Tushinites to fulfill their part of the bargain and abandon the brigand, they received the ludicrous reply: "You do not remember the oath of allegiance which you have sworn to your sovereign, for you have cast him down from the tsardom, while we will die gladly for ours." The patriarch took advantage of this situation and demanded that Shuisky be restored to the throne, and many people were found to be agreeable to this.

Naturally the ringleaders of the July 17 plot could not agree. Fearful that their plans might be thwarted, they made haste to finish with Shuisky. On July 19 the same Zakhar Liapunov, with three princes—Zasekin, Tiufiakin and Merin-Volkonsky—and also a certain Mikhail Aksenov and others, took with them some monks from the Miracles monastery, went to the deposed tsar and declared that for the sake of pacifying the people he must become a monk. The thought of renouncing forever his pretensions to the throne, especially when these hopes were being rekindled, was intolerable for the old man. He struggled desperately against Liapunov and his companions, and had to held down by force throughout the ceremony. One of the conspirators, Tiufiakin, pronounced the monastic vows on his behalf, while Shuisky repeatedly denied that he desired the tonsure. This tonsure, which was forcibly administered, could not in any way be binding, and the patriarch would not recognize it. He called Prince Tiufiakin, and not Shuisky, a monk. Nevertheless the unwilling postulant was taken away to the Miracles monastery. His wife was forced to take the veil, and his brothers were placed under guard.

GOVERNMENT DURING SHUISKY'S REIGN

It is not reasonable to expect an abundance of governmental decrees from the short-lived, trouble-filled reign of Shuisky. A great part of Shuisky's reign was spent under siege, during which the action of the government was of necessity restricted to Moscow alone. He granted a few charters of immunity to churches and monasteries, and ordered that the monasteries give sustenance to ecclesiastical and monastic servitors of court villages who had fled from the brigands.

In the forefront stood the question concerning peasants and slaves. Godunov's temporary measure allowed the transfer of peasants between lesser landlords. Whether this measure remained in force for more than two years it is impossible to say, for in the peasant decree of False Dmitry nothing is said about it. On the other hand, it is impossible to assert on the basis of this decree that the Godunov decree was no longer in force because the decree of False Dmitry concerning the recovery of fugitive peasants could be applied to the same people between whom peasant transfer had been forbidden in Godunov's reign.[29]

In March 1607 Shuisky confirmed the enserfment of the peasants and ruled that those who had received peasants belonging to somebody else had to pay a fine of ten rubles a head, plus three rubles a year to their former lord. Apart from this, the recruiter was subject to punishment with the knout. If a married woman, a widow or an unmarried woman fled to another estate, and then married, the man who married such a woman would be awarded to her former lord, with all his possessions and any children born to her after her flight. A virgin less than seventeen years of age, or a widow more than two years after the death of her husband, or an unmarried youth over the age of twenty, detained without marriage or emancipation, might be given a certificate of manumission by the treasurer in Moscow, or by the lord lieutenant or magistrates in other towns. People shall not be kept unmarried, contrary to the law of God, lest fornication be encouraged.

The reinforcement of serfdom during Shuisky's reign also is explained by the same reasoning behind subsequent enactments of serfdom. Enserfment was to the advantage of the service gentry and small landholders and, even more important, the crown had need of the latter. Thus enserfment became all the more necessary. Boyars and rich landlords, who had so much power under Shuisky, did not wish to antagonize servicemen by restoring the right of peasant movement, thus depriving them of their means of livelihood, while these same servitors were protecting them from the cossacks and armed slaves under the banners of Bolotnikov and the Tushino brigand. We have noted that the Tushino Russians, in proposing conditions under which they would accept Prince Wladyslaw as their tsar, demanded that there be no peasant movement.

But if the powerful boyars under Shuisky could not, given the circumstances of the time, prevent a repetition of the decree concerning peasant enserfment nevertheless they might disregard the tsar's decrees concerning slaves inconvenient to them. On March 7, 1607 Vasily decreed that those slaves who had been in voluntary bondage for half a year, a year or more, and who had not been born into slavery, and were not longstanding proprietory slaves, and did not wish to enter into an indentured relationship, could not be made unfree. A slave could not be kept for even a day without an indenture, and if anyone maintained a slave without an indenture he was to have no recourse to the law.

But on September 12, 1609, when the boyars were instructed from above to reconsider this clause, they proposed that the enactment of 1607 be rescinded. They proposed instead that the legislation with regard to slaves should be the same as it had been under Tsar Fedor, namely that a slave who had served more than half a year would be bound definitively. In 1608 the boyars decreed that those slaves who had been in brigandage, and who had made their submission to the tsar, and had received their manumission, but once more had run away and reverted to brigandage, were they caught in the act or denounced either would be executed or handed over to their former lords. Gentry and junior boyars who had been disgraced during the reign of False Dmitry were denied the right to recover slaves set free due to their disgrace. It was specified that defendants in litigation concerning slavery who declared that the slaves in question, being sought by their former owners, had fled, were to kiss the cross to the fact that these slaves had fled without any enticement by the defendants. It was forbidden to give simple indentures for life. Such documents could be given only during the free years.[30]

Shuisky confirmed the charters given by Godunov to the townspeople, granting them self-government. The peasants of Ziuzdin district in Perm province were granted self-government following their petition, which contained the following words: "They live apart from the Perm towns, twenty versts or so from Kaigorodok, and are inscribed under a special heading in the cadastral surveys. They established their homesteads in the wild black forest, and are all newly-arrived people, yet there came to their district inhabitants of Kaigorod, both townsmen and peasants, who subsidized themselves by assessing tax against them, by unlawfully plundering them, by beating them and dishonoring their wives and children, and unjustly dragging them away to perform menial tasks in summer during ploughing time." The tsar granted their request and ordered them simply to make an annual lump sum payment of sixty rubles, separate from the inhabitants of Kaigorod, who were forbidden to visit them. In addition the inhabitants of Ziuzdin district received in their trading settlement the right to elect their own magistrate, who would settle their disputes.

The Ziuzdin peasants complained against those of Kaigorod and in the same way the inhabitants of Viatka complained against those of Perm. "According to the tsar's decree, forty-six postal couriers were sent from Viatka to Perm and in the direction of Solikamsk, but Prince Viazemsky, the governor of Perm, being in a dispute with the people of Viatka, beat the couriers from Viatka and tortured them without cause, to incite them to abandon their posts, whereas the people of Perm then would perform courier service, appropriating the courier tax. The governor of Perm tortured Viatka merchants almost to death to get money." The tsar wrote to Viazemsky that if the inhabitants of Viatka once more complained against him, he would order him to make double compensation *without process of law*.

Yet the very same year the tsar ordered the inhabitants of Perm to perform courier service alone, as they had before. It was not only against governors that complaints were levelled. A slave of Boyar Sheremetev presented a petition in which he wrote: "There was an ambush in Nizhny Novgorod by followers of the brigand. The tocsin began to sound, the townsmen rushed into town with their belongings, and a peasant of my lord, Boyar Sheremetev, also ran in with two new homespun coats, but as he ran in through the Ivanovsk gates the musketeers of the Kolzakov regiment apprehended him, and took the coats away from him. The next day I petitioned the governor to recover them. The captain, Kolzakov, sought out the coats, but drank them away in the tavern with the same musketeers, and then demanded ten altyns from the peasant to redeem them. About vespertide I went to the cathedral of Our Savior, and once again petitioned the governors, but then Captain Kolzakov accused me,

saying that I was slandering him. Then Secretary Vasily Semeonov said
to Kolzakov: 'Why didn't you cut this slave in two? Your own slaves are
so much better than he is.' And right there, in the cathedral, he abused
my master, Fedor Ivanovich Sheremetev. I stood up for my master, but
he abused me, and wanted to run me through, and cried out to Kolzakov:
'Wherever you or any of your musketeers meets with this slave or any
other of Fedor Sheremetev's slaves, strip them naked and beat them to
death. Do not fear any judgement, for I shall protect you.'"

Shuisky also concerned himself with the population of Siberia in various ways. Eight men were sent from the Moscow prisons to Pelym as agricultural peasants, but they fled, persuading two old peasants to accompany
them as guides. As a consequence the tsar wrote to Perm: "Henceforth
in Perm, both in the town and the province, this edict shall be firmly established. Whosoever travels or comes on foot to Perm from the Siberian
towns without a travel permit or authorization shall be arrested, interrogated and detained at our pleasure." At the same time it was ordered to
recruit in Perm agricultural peasants from among local people,[31]—from
a father a son, from an uncle a nephew, from a neighbor a neighbor, but
none from the tax-paying population.

The incessant failures of the Russian army, the superiority of foreign
soldiers over Russians, which became obvious when Skopin's regiments
joined the Swedes, and the necessity that commander saw of instructing
his men with the aid of the Swedes—all this compelled the Russians to
think of translating military manuals from foreign languages, to teach
Russians the skills for which foreign nations were famous. The transla-
tors were Mikhail Yuriev and Ivan Fomin.

The printing of books continued in Moscow. This was carried on by
Anisim Rodishevsky, a native of Volhynia, Ivan Andronikov Timofeev,
and Nikita Fedorov Fofanov, a native of Pskov. In the preface to the
Common Readings,[32] printed by the latter, it was stated that Shuisky had
ordered a new establishment for printing books, to be housed in a huge
edifice which was to be built.

Concerning the moral state of the Russian people, we have seen how
widespread was necromancy. It is plainly said of Shuisky that he strongly
believed in it. In his documents the tsar declared to the people that False
Dmitry had deceived everyone by means of sorcery, but it is easy to understand how the spread of such opinions must have had a damaging effect upon the moral qualities of the people. With such convictions the

people must have been like unto a frightened child, and thus standing to lose their moral strength. Wherein lay salvation when some sorcerer or other, with the aid of infernal forces, so easily might lead everyone astray? We must picture the pitiful situation of the typical Russian man at this time when at every step, with fearful vision, he must look around on all sides. Here an evil man is following his footsteps, there a plague is being borne along the wind. The absence of social solidarity has a dire effect upon the spirit where there is no defense against the violence of the strong or the ill-intentioned, when a man, emerging from his home, could not be certain whether he would return home safely.

But even more harmful was the fear, the conviction that everywhere hostile, etheral forces were directed against one. If the government assured the people that the renegade monk had led the people astray through sorcery and necromancy, there is nothing surprising in the fact that at Perm in 1606 the peasant Talev was burned and tortured three times on the rack for having caused the people the hiccups!

IV

THE INTERREGNUM
1610

OATH TO BOYARS

At the death of Fedor, before the election of Godunov, Irina had been considered the ruling tsaritsa but now, after the overthrow of Shuisky, no one could stand, or by any means be considered to be, at the head of government except the boyar council, and it was to this council that everyone had to swear allegiance. Until the election of a new tsar the people must subject themselves to the boyars. "All the people," it said in the instrument of allegiance, "did obeisance to Prince Mstislavsky and his companions, that they would be pleased to accept the governance of the Muscovite realm until God gives us a tsar."

Those who swore allegiance vowed "to obey the boyars, respect their judgement, and accept their ruling as to whosoever shall be sent on service or adjudged guilty; to be steadfast for the Russian realm and for them, the boyars, and to fight to the death against traitors; not to support the brigand who calls himself Tsarevich Dmitry; neither to contemplate nor to do evil against each other, but to elect a sovereign for the Muscovite realm for the boyars and the people of the land. The boyars shall give just judgement to all righteous people, and elect a sovereign with us and with all the people, throughout the entire land, in consultation with the towns. They shall reject their former sovereign Vasily Ivanovich. He shall no longer reside at the sovereign's court, neither shall he henceforth be enthroned over the realm. We have no murderous intentions towards the sovereign Vasily or his consort or his brothers, but Prince Dmitry or Ivan Shuisky shall not sit in judgement with the boyars."

LETTERS TO THE PROVINCES

In the documents sent throughout the towns dated July 20, 1610 Moscow declared: "Seeing the dissension among Orthodox Christians, Poles and Lithuanians have come into the territory of the Muscovite realm and shed much blood. They have destroyed churches and monasteries, defiled sanctuaries and tried to pervert the Orthodox faith into the Latin. The Polish king stands before Smolensk, Hetman Zolkiewski is at Mozhaisk, and the brigand is at Kolomenskoe. The Lithuanian people, in alliance with Zolkiewski, wish to conquer the Muscovite realm and destroy the Orthodox faith and introduce their own Latin faith. So we, speaking among ourselves and hearing from all of the people of the borderland towns that Lord Tsar Vasily Ivanovich upon the Russian throne is not loved, that no one takes any account of him or serves him, and that Christian blood has been shed for a long time, and that father has risen up against son, son against father, and friend against friend, all the people, seeing the ruin of the Muscovite realm, have petitioned him, the sovereign, together with all the land and all the people, that he relinquish the rulership because of internecine strife, and also for this reason, that the people who feared his disfavor, and did not love him or did not support him or the Muscovite realm, might all be in accord and stand as one in defense of the Orthodox Christian faith. The sovereign has abdicated and has moved to his former residence, and is now a monk, while we have kissed the cross and sworn that we will resist the rebels and refuse to recognize the brigand. And you, all people, must stand together with us and be united lest our Orthodox Christian faith perish, and our mothers, wives and children be subjected to the Latin faith."

THE BOYARS AND HETMAN ZOLKIEWSKI

From these documents it is evident that immediately after the overthrow of Shuisky the strongest party in Moscow was that which did not want as sovereign either the Polish prince or False Dmitry and consequently wished to elect somebody from their own most exalted people. The patriarch belonged to this party, and there is no doubt that the instrument of allegiance and the documents sent throughout the towns were written under his influence. This party had two candidates for the throne, Prince Vasily Vasilievich Golitsyn and the fourteen-year-old Michael Fedorovich Romanov, son of Metropolitan Filaret Nikitich. But because of the circumstances this party had to yield to another. Hetman Zolkiewski was at Mozhaisk, and was demanding that Moscow recognize Wladyslaw as tsar. He had with him a detachment of Russian servicemen who had sworn allegiance to the prince, and False Dmitry stood at Kolomenskoe.

The provisional government in Moscow could not rid itself of Zolkiewski and False Dmitry simultaneously, especially when the latter had supporters among the lesser people of the city. There was no way an assembly might be summoned to represent the entire land, and Moscow was compelled to choose between the two candidates for the throne at hand, False Dmitry and Wladyslaw. If the pretender had supporters among the lower strata of the Muscovite population, the boyars and the better people found it impossible to accept the brigand, who would bring into the boyar council his Tushino and Kaluga boyars, lords-in-waiting and conciliar secretaries, and give the possessions of the rich to plunder by his cossacks and the city rabble, his long-standing allies.

Hence for the boyars and the better people, for the cautious people who had something to preserve, the sole salvation from the brigand and his cossacks lay in Wladyslaw, that is to say, Hetman Zolkiewski and his army. The leader of False Dmitry's party was Zakhar Liapunov, who had been seduced by huge promises from the brigand. The leader of Wladyslaw's party was the leading boyar, Prince Mstislavsky, who declared that he personally had no wish to be tsar but neither did he wish to see as tsar anyone from among his brother-boyars. This meant that it was necessary to choose a tsar from a royal family.

Having learned that Zakhar Liapunov wished secretly to let the pretender's army into the city, Mstislavsky sent word to Zolkiewski that he immediately must make haste towards the city. The hetman advanced from Mozhaisk on July 20 and sent letters to Moscow in which he declared that he was coming to defend the city from the brigand. He forwarded a letter to Mstislavsky and his companions outlinging the advantages the boyar might expect from a close union with Poland.

This scion of the Polish magnates thought it necessary to convey an aristocratic message to the boyars: "We have heard rumors that Prince Vasily Shuisky has cast off the rulership and has taken religious vows, and that his brothers are kept under close guard. We are vexed and greatly grieved at this, and trust that nothing harmful will befall them. You yourselves know, and it is well known to us in Poland and Lithuania, that the Shuisky princes long have been great boyars in the Muscovite realm, that they served their natural sovereigns truly and faithfully, not sparing their own lives. Prince Ivan Petrovich Shuisky gloriously defended Pskov, and Prince Mikhail Vasilievich Skopin-Shuisky bravely defended the realm. All great realms value their great boyars. Now that they find themselves in your hands, you must protect the Shuisky princes, your brothers, as worthy men, entertaining no designs against their lives or health, nor allowing violence, ruination or persecution to be perpetrated against them. His grace, our most illustrious sovereign king, together with his crown prince, shall show his bounty even to the Shuisky princes, as to all your great boyars, when you serve our sovereign truly and faithfully, for he shall observe all this in faithfulness and trust, and grant his sovereign favor."

Despite the fact, that Mstislavsky had summoned the hetman, and that his aid was needed against the pretender, for the majority of Muscovites the thought of accepting as sovereign a foreign prince from Lithuania was fearfully burdensome. The patriarch was strongly opposed to recognition of Wladyslaw, and although the hetman was merely eight miles from Moscow the boyars nevertheless were writing to him that they did not need his help, and demanded that Polish troops not approach the capital.

But Zolkiewski had a powerful ally, the pretender, the bugbear of all the better people. "Better to serve the prince," they said, "than to be beaten by our own slaves, and to be tortured endlessly by laboring for them." Yet the patriarch insisted all the more on choosing a Russian Orthodox tsar. On one occasion he sought to persuade the people by an example from history. "Remember, Orthodox Christians, what Charles did in Great Rome!"[1] But the people did not care about Charles or Great Rome. "All the people smiled," says a contemporary, "they stopped up their clever and sensuous ears and dispersed."[2] Metropolitan Filaret Nikitich of Rostov stepped onto the stone platform on Red Square and said to the people: "Do not be tempted. I know personally of the evil intentions of the king towards the Muscovite realm. He and his son wish to rule it and destroy our true Christian faith, and establish their own Latin faith." But even this plea fell on deaf ears.

ACTIVITIES OF THE PRETENDER

On July 24 Zolkiewski stood only seven miles from Moscow at the Khoroshovsk Meadows and the pretender was about to enter Moscow. At the time of the battle with the pretender Mstislavsky, to make contact with Zolkiewski, sent to ask him: "Do you come to Moscow as an enemy or a friend?" Zolkiewski replied that he was prepared to help Moscow if the city recognized Wladyslaw as tsar.

At the moment emissaries from the pretender arrived at the hetman's encampment. The pretender, wishing to remove his rival, gave Sapieha a missive in which he promised immediately on attaining the throne to pay the Polish king three hundred thousand zlotys to pay annually into the treasury of the Commonwealth three hundred thousand zlotys for a period of ten years, furthermore to pay the prince a hundred thousand zlotys for a period of ten years, promised to conquer Livonia from the Swedes on behalf of Poland, and to provide fifteen thousand troops for the Swedish war. Concerning the Severian land he gave the evasive promise that he was not prepared for negotiations on this matter but that should this matter be pursued why should he not be given his due? It would, however, be better for each to keep to his own.

With this missive from Sapieha's encampment emissaries were sent to Smolensk to persuade the king to accept the Pretender's proposals. Visiting first the hetman's encampment, they declared to Zolkiewski the object of their mission to the king and said that False Dmitry wished to send gifts to him, the hetman. But Zolkiewski, while he allowed them free passage to the king, refused to have any dealings with the brigand.

AGREEMENT WITH ZOLKIEWSKI

Meanwhile communications continued with Moscow. When Mstislavsky sent his letter to the hetman he received no written reply. Zolkiewski sent word to him that written correspondence merely prolonged matters, to which there would be no end. Negotiations were opened but the matter dragged on because first of all it was necessary to remove the most powerful impediment, Wladyslaw's alien faith. The patriarch declared to the boyars concerning the election of the prince: "If he is baptized and received into the Orthodox faith, I shall bless you. If he is not baptized, a breach of the Orthodox Christian faith will occur throughout the Muscovite realm, nor will our blessing be upon you."

The boyars insisted that Wladyslaw's acceptance of Orthodoxy be established as the first condition of his election, but the hetman was unable to agree to this without instructions from the king. Personal negotiations between Mstislavsky and Zolkiewski, which took place on August 2, 1610, close by the New Virgin convent, were broken off by news that the pretender was approaching Moscow. The brigand was repulsed with the help of Russian troops who had arrived with Zolkiewski, under the command of Ivan Mikhailovich Saltykov, the son of Mikhail Glebovich.

The pretender's assault and the murmuring of the Polish army, which had received no pay and was threatening to go home, forced the hetman to hasten negotiations. He declared that he would accept only those conditions confirmed by the king and on which Saltykov and his companions had kissed the cross outside Smolensk. Additional conditions now proposed by the boyars in Moscow, among which the principal item was that Wladyslaw should receive the Orthodox faith in Mozhaisk, must be referred for the king's decision.

The boyars agreed. For his part, the hetman agreed immediately to introduce several changes and additions, which had not been in Saltykov's treaty. These alterations are very interesting, showing the difference in outlook between the Tushinites, who had concluded the treaty outside Smolensk, and the boyars who were now negotiating in Moscow. For example, in the Saltykov treaty the condition was included regarding free exit from the country for purposes of study. This condition is omitted from the Moscow treaty. The Saltykov treaty, compiled under the strong influence of people who could have received important rank only in Tushino, had demanded the promotion of non-nobles according to service. In the Moscow treaty the boyars introduced the condition: "Muscovite princely and boyar families are not to be displaced or disparaged in matters of precedence or honor by foreign immigrants." The Saltykov treaty was drawn by notorious supporters of the first False Dmitry who had no fear of vengeance for the events of May 17, 1606; but the compilers of the Moscow treaty considered it essential to add that there should be no reprisals for the slaughter of the Poles on May 17, 1606.[3]

The following conditions were added. Sapieha must be detached from the brigand. Moscow was to be helped against the latter, and as soon as the capital was delivered Zolkiewski must withdraw with the Polish troops to Mozhaisk, there to await the conclusion of negotiations with Sigismund. Marina must be repatriated to Poland and forbidden to declare her rights to the Muscovite throne. The towns of the Muscovite realm captured by the Poles and the brigands must be evacuated to match their status before the Time of Troubles. Concerning compensation for the king and the Polish military for their war expenses, Muscovite high ambassadors would discuss the matter with Sigismund. Finally, the hetman promised to write to the king with a petition that he raise the siege of Smolensk.

OATH OF ALLEGIANCE TO WLADYSLAW AND SIGISMUND'S CLAIM

On August 27, 1610, half way between the Polish encampment and Moscow, the solemn oath of allegiance of the inhabitants of Moscow to Prince Wladyslaw took place. Here, in two pavilions, where stood richly adorned lecterns, ten thousand men swore allegiance on the first day. The hetman for his part swore on behalf of Wladyslaw to observe the treaty. On the second day the ceremony of allegiance took place in the Dormition cathedral, in the presence of the patriarch. The Tushino Russians, Mikhail Saltykov, Prince Mosalsky and others, who had arrived before Moscow with Zolkiewski, also came. They approached the patriarch for his blessing, but the patriarch greeted them with these menacing words: "If you have come in righteousness and not in deceit, and if you are not plotting the ruin of the Orthodox faith, you have the blessing of all the ecumenical communion and of me, a sinner. But if you have come in deceit, with evil intentions towards the faith, then you shall be accursed." Saltykov with tears in his eyes assured Hermogen that they would have an honest and true sovereign, and so the patriarch blessed him. But when Mikhail Molchanov approached, Hermogen cried out at him: "Accursed heretic! You have no right to be within this church," and ordered him to be ejected. The hetman and the boyars entertained each other and exchanged gifts. They thought that the Time of Troubles had ended through the election of a tsar from a foreign nation, from a royal line.

But the Time of Troubles was far from over. The election of Wladyslaw was not accompanied by the fulfillment of the principal demand of the people, who could be pacified only through deception. Since it had not made the entire proceedings public, the provisional government was forced to deception. Writs were sent throughout the towns calling upon them to swear allegiance to Wladyslaw, and in these documents the governing boyars wrote that, since the delegates from the towns for the election of a tsar had not yet arrived, Moscow had kissed the cross to Prince Wladyslaw on the understanding that he would be sovereign in our Orthodox faith of the Greek dispensation. But naturally it was impossible to conceal the truth. Many people knew very well that the question of the prince's conversion to Orthodoxy had been postponed, and several of them felt strongly impelled to spread the word in Moscow, and convey the information to the pretender and around the towns.

So while other towns subjected themselves to Moscow and swore allegiance to Wladyslaw, other towns such as Suzdal, Vladimir, Yuriev, Galich and Rostov entered into secret correspondence with the pretender, expressing their readiness to go over to him. Previously these very towns had risen up against False Dmitry and had defended themselves valiantly against his supporters, whom they regarded as enemies of the realm. But now the highest interest, the religious interest, prevailed and overcame all others. For many it was better to submit to a man who called himself the Orthodox Tsar Dmitry, son of Ivan Vasilievich, than to a foreign Lithuanian prince. From that moment, from the proclamation of Wladyslaw as tsar, the popular movements in Muscovy assumed a religious character, and King Sigismund hastened to aggravate the situation.

Two days after the solemn oath of allegiance on both sides, Fedor Andronov[4] came to the hetman from Smolensk with a letter from the king in which he demanded that the Muscovite realm be subjected to him personally, and not to his son. After Andronov came Gasiewski with a more detailed order for the hetman. Yet the hetman and Gasiewski, aware of the state of affairs, considered it impossible to violate the treaty and fulfill the wish of the king, whose name was, as the Poles well knew, hateful to the Muscovite populace.

THE PRETENDER REPELLED

Resolving not to reveal the king's intention, Zolkiewski began to observe the clause of the treaty whereby he promised to detach Sapieha from the brigand and repel the latter from Moscow. He sent to Sapieha with the admonition not to hinder the business of king and Commonwealth and to persuade the pretender to declare his submission to Sigismund, in which case Zolkiewski promised to petition on his behalf for the governorship of Sambor or Grodno for his sustenance. Should the pretender refuse,

Sapieha was to deliver him to the hetman, or at least dissociate himself from him. Sapieha was prepared to obey the hetman's command, but his companions would in no wise agree.

Zolkiewski perceived the necessity of resorting to stronger measures than simple exhortations. He moved by night from his encampment and at crack of dawn stood before Sapieha's encampment in battle formation. Prince Mstislavsky assisted him with a Muscovite detachment fifteen thousand strong, placing another strong detachment within the city at the hetman's disposal to keep supporters of False Dmitry in check. Joining with Zolkiewski the foremost boyar of the realm, Prince Mstislavsky, came under the command of a Polish hetman! Sapieha's army was terrified, seeing before them the combined regiments of Zolkiewski and Mstislavsky. The Russians, noticing their timidity, wished immediately to strike at them, but the hetman did not wish to shed the blood of his own people and awaited a peaceful submission, which was not long in coming. Sapieha appeared for a personal interview with the hetman and promised either to persuade the pretender to submit, or to abandon him. But False Dmitry, or rather his wife, who were both at that time in the Ugresha monastery,[5] did not wish to listen to any such conditions. The refusal of several towns to accept the election of Wladyslaw promised them new disorders, a new opportunity to recoup their losses.

Then the hetman declared his intention to the boyars. He would pass through Moscow by night, approach the monastery and take the pretender unawares. The boyars agreed, and allowed the Polish army to pass through the city by night. The city was nearly deserted, since the boyars recently had put thirteen thousand troops into the field. Nevertheless, their trust was not betrayed. The Poles passed through the city expeditiously, without dismounting or causing any distress to the inhabitants. The Polish and Russian armies joined near the Kolomenskoe picquet lines and proceeded to the Ugresha monastery; but news of his peril had reached False Dmitry from Moscow he fled to Kaluga accompanied by his wife and Zarutsky, who had gone over to his side after quarrelling with the hetman, who had refused to give him supreme command of the Russian forces which had declared for the prince. Since he did not think he could pursue the pretender, the hetman returned to his encampment, and the boyars to Moscow.

The next day False Dmitry's Russian supporters who had not followed him to Kaluga visited the hetman and declared their desire to swear allegiance to Wladyslaw on condition that they retain those dignities they

had received from the pretender. Zolkiewski had no objections to satis-
fying these demands, but the Muscovite boyars would in no wise agree
to them. Informing the towns of the latest events, they wrote: "The
Lithuanians, Jan Sapieha and his companions, and the Russians, Prince
Mikhail Turenin and Prince Fedor Dolgoruky, and the brigand's counsellors Prince Aleksei Sitsky, Alexander Nagoy, Grigory Sunbulov, Fedor Pleshcheev, Prince Fedor Zasekin and the secretary Peter Tretiakov,
and all the service and non-service men have made their submissions to
the lord prince." Here it is interesting to note that the two boyars, Princes
Turenin and Dolgoruky, are singled out from the other supporters of False
Dmitry, who are described as the brigand's counsellors. Several of these
counsellors of the brigand, dissatisfied with the welcome they had received in Moscow, once again left to join the pretender.

EMBASSY TO THE KING BESIEGING SMOLENSK

Having repelled False Dmitry, the hetman insisted upon the early dispatch
of ambassadors to Sigismund, which would give him a pretext for removing from the Muscovite realm suspicious persons mistrusted by the
people as unworthy of occupying the throne. Zolkiewski persuaded
Golitsyn to take charge of the embassy, flattering him by saying that such
a vital matter should be accomplished only by such an important personage as himself, and assured him that the embassy would afford a favorable
opportunity to obtain special favor from the king and from the prince.
Golitsyn accepted the proposition.[6]

Zolkiewski received a dual benefit from his absence. First, having sent
him away from Moscow, he was placing a candidate for the throne in the
prince's hands. Second, by sending away from Moscow the most renowned boyar, by reason both of his talents and accomplishments, it
would be easier to deal with the remainder. Michael Fedorovich Romanov,
who at that time bore the rank of table attendant, was still very young
and for this reason could not be included in the embassy. Then the hetman
tried to nominate Michael's father, Metropolitan Filaret, as a representative from the clergy. Zolkiewski urged that for such an important matter
it was necessary to send a man who was eminent, not only in rank, but
also in ancestry, and that only Filaret could meet the latter criterion.
When he informed the king of the oath of allegiance Moscow had taken
to Wladyslaw, the hetman had written: "Only God knows what is hidden
in the hearts of men, but as far as can be observed the Muscovites sincerely

desire that the prince rule over them. To discuss the baptism and other conditions, they are sending Prince Vasily Golitsyn and his companions to your royal grace. These negotiations will not be difficult, since Prince Golitsyn, approaching the patriarch and the other boyars, declared that they would petition concerning the baptism, but that even were the king not to grant their request God and the sovereign are free to do as they please since they have kissed the cross to him, and we will settle the matter with him."

By means of the embassy having sent away Golitsyn and the father of Michael, Zolkiewski proceeded to deal with the former tsar, who also could be dangerous, for the patriarch did not consider him a monk. At the insistence of the hetman the boyars conveyed Vasily to the St. Joseph monastery of Volokolamsk, and his brothers to Belaia, in order that they might the more easily be sent into Poland. The patriarch apparently guessed at this intention, and insisted that Shuisky be dispatched to the Solovetsk monastery,[7] but all in vain. Tsaritsa Maria was imprisoned in the Intercession convent at Suzdal.[8]

Filaret and Golitsyn set off at the head of the embassy. Among the other members of the delegation were Lord-in-waiting Mezetsky, the conciliar noble Sukin, the conciliar secretary Tomilo Lugovskoy and the conciliar secretary Sydavny Vasiliev. Among the clergy were Archimandrite Evfimy of the Savior monastery, Avraamy Palitsyn, cellarer of the Trinity monastery, and others. They were joined by elected representatives of the various classes of people. The number of people in the embassy amounted to 1,246 persons.[9]

The ambassadors were given the following instructions: (1) To demand that Wladyslaw accept the Greek faith in Smolensk from Metropolitan Filaret and Archbishop Sergius of Smolensk so that he might come to Moscow as an Orthodox Christian. (2) That Wladyslaw, once upon the throne, must not entertain any relations with the Pope on matters of faith, but only on matters of state. (3) Should anyone from Muscovy wish through folly to apostasize from the Greek faith, they must be put to death and their property confiscated (an exception to the clause in the treaty whereby the possessions of a criminal were not to be confiscated, but passed to their heirs). (4) That the prince must bring with him from Poland only a few necessary persons. (5) The previous title of the Muscovite sovereigns must not be diminished. (6) That Wladyslaw marry in Muscovy a maiden of the Greek faith. (7) The towns and places occupied by the Poles and brigands must be returned to the Muscovite realm, as it existed before the Troubles and as agreed with the hetman. (8) Poles and Lithuanians who came with Wladyslaw shall be granted estates well within the borders, and not in borderland regions. (The aim of this condition is clear; Poles who owned borderland estates could easily transfer them to Poland). (9) All prisoners captured within Muscovite territory during the Troubles must be returned without ransom. (10) The king must withdraw from Smolensk, and do no violence to the suburbs or the surrounding countryside. (11) At a future meeting of the Sejm the Muscovite emissaries must attend and in their presence the Polish Commonwealth must confirm a solemn alliance between the two states.

In the event of invincible opposition on the part of the Poles the ambassadors were authorized to moderate their demands. With regard to the first clause, if the prince would not agree to accept Orthodoxy in Smolensk, but wished to postpone the matter until his arrival in Moscow, where he would receive a decision rendered by the Orthodox and Latin clergy, the ambassadors were to answer that they had no instructions on this matter, and would request permission to write to the patriarch, the boyars and the whole land, and beg the prince to come immediately to Moscow. Also the ambassadors should not dispute on matters of faith with the Polish lords or with Latin theologians.

Concerning the fourth clause, the ambassadors must insist that Wladyslaw not bring with him more than five hundred Poles. Concerning the title, the ambassadors might agree that the matter be decided finally in Moscow by the ruling of the patriarch, the clergy, boyars and members of the council. The ambassadors might amend the clause concerning the prince's marriage thus: Wladyslaw might not marry without the advice of the patriarch, the clergy, boyars and members of the council. The ambassadors were not to agree to any payment to the king for his expenses, or for the pay of Polish troops with the brigand in Sapieha's contingent. They were not to agree to building a Catholic church in Moscow, or placing of Polish officials in Russian borderland towns before the complete pacification of the realm. They were to refuse to discuss any frontier disputes "lest there be delays arising out of so great a matter." Should there be obstinate insistence by the Poles on any of the preceding points the ambassadors were to answer that they had no instructions on these matters, and that decision of these matters must be postponed until discussions could take place between Sigismund and his son, after Wladyslaw had become the Muscovite sovereign. In Moscow, as we have seen, it was hoped that as soon as Wladyslaw became tsar he would look of necessity to the welfare of his realm, which is why the ambassadors first and foremost insisted that Wladyslaw arrive in Moscow as soon as possible.

The patriarch sent with the ambassadors his own personal letter to Sigismund in which he begged the king to allow his son to embrace the Greek faith: "For the love of God, great sovereign, do not despise our request, and do not yourself mock God, nor insult our clergy and such innumerable peoples." But Sigismund first had to consider how not to insult his own people, and with the aim of emerging from the conflict either with the whole of the Muscovite realm, or at very least with a part of it, continued the siege of Smolensk. On the other hand Jan Potocki, chief commander of the besieging forces, seeing Zolkiewski's success in Moscow, wanted to capture Smolensk immediately. His wishes coincided with that of the army, irritated by the long siege. Despite the enthusiasm and bravery of the besiegers their attacks were continually repulsed by the besieged, even though among the latter there raged an epidemic. When news of Zolkiewski's agreement with the Muscovite provisional government was received, the people of Smolensk entered into negotiations with the king, but as soon as Sigismund declared to Shein that Smolensk was an ancient possession of Lithuania and must surrender not to the prince, but to the king himself, the commander refused to separate himself from Moscow without the consent of the whole land. The conclusion of the negotiations were postponed until the arrival of the high ambassadors from Moscow. At that time the town was divided, if we are to believe the reports of deserters. The gentry, of whom there were about two hundred, the musketeers, of whom there were about twelve thousand, and even the clergy and the governor, had agreed to surrender the city to the king, arguing that it made no difference whether they lived under the rule of the king or his son provided that their faith and rights were preserved. But the trading people and townsmen did not in any way wish to desert Moscow, and insisted that they await the ambassadors' arrival.

THE PRETENDER IN KALUGA

Meanwhile by reason of the election of Wladyslaw the Swedes of necessity were transformed from allies into enemies of the Muscovite realm. They captured Ladoga but were unsuccessful before Ivangorod, the inhabitants of which, despite the extremity of their situation, remained

Red Square in Moscow
Palm Sunday Procession

faithful to the pretender. Horn defeated Lisowski before Yama after which Lisowski and Prosovetsky, together with the Don Cossacks, moved off towards Pskov, but quarrelled because Lisowski wanted to serve Wladyslaw while Prosovetsky wanted to serve the pretender. As a result Lisowski proceeded to Ostrov, while Prosovetsky halted twenty versts from Pskov.

The pretender, as before, was fortifying himself in Kaluga and apparently found it needful to prepare for conflict with his former ally Sapieha, who had invaded the Severian land apparently with the intention of taking it away from him; but in fact his intention was quite otherwise. By agreement with his cousin, the chancellor Leo, Sapieha was to support False Dmitry, thus distracting the Muscovites' attention from the king's designs. The dominions of the Kaluga tsar were fairly widespread. For example, Serpukhov belonged to him; there the notorious Fedor Pleshcheev governed on his behalf.[10]

POLISH ARMY ADMITTED INTO MOSCOW

Remaining alone before Moscow with a small army, Zolkiewski clearly saw the danger of his situation. He saw that the Russians only under extreme duress had agreed to accept a foreign occupant of the throne, and would never accept one who professed an alien faith, while Sigismund would never allow his son to accept Orthodoxy. But even now, as before, the pretender aided the hetman. Through fear of the common people, who would not hesitate at the first opportunity to rise in favor of False Dmitry, the boyars themselves proposed to Zolkiewski to admit the Polish army into Moscow. The hetman gladly agreed, and sent to assign billets within the city. But in Moscow every move was watched. A monk sounded the tocsin and declared to the assembled people that the Poles were entering Moscow. The boyars were terrified by the disturbances, and requested Zolkiewski to wait another three days. But the hetman himself was perturbed, called a council of war in his army and said: "It is true that I myself wished to place my army in the capital, but now, having reviewed the situation carefully, I have reconsidered. In such a large and public assembly I cannot reveal the reasons which prevent me from placing my army there. Send to me in my headquarters two men from every regiment, and I shall explain."

When the deputies arrived, the hetman expounded the situation: "Moscow is a large and populous city. Nearly all inhabitants of the Muscovite realm gather together in the Kremlin for judicial matters, and all military headquarters are there. I myself will be quartered in the Kremlin, others of you in Kitai-quarter, the rest of you in White Quarter. But in the Kremlin there always gathers a multitude of people. There are sometimes fifteen or twenty thousand people, for whom it would be no trouble to choose a convenient time to destroy me there. I have no infantry, and you people are unskilled in infantry tactics, while the gates are in their hands." Citing the example of the first False Dmitry, who had perished together with his Poles, the hetman concluded: "It would be far better to quarter the army among the suburbs close to the city, which in this manner would be almost like conducting a siege."

But this plan was opposed strenuously by Zborowski's regiment, which consisted of Tushino Poles. The latter complained unceasingly that the booty had been snatched from their hands. They hoped that now at least, if Moscow fell into their hands, they would have the tsar's treasury. Yet the hetman hesitated, fearful, and wanted to take position in the suburbs.

The deputy from the Zborowski regiment, Marchocki,[11] replied to the hetman: "In vain does your grace consider Moscow as powerful as it was in the time of Dmitry, and us as weak as those who came to his wedding. Ask the Muscovites themselves and they will tell you that from the arrival of Rozynski to the present day three hundred thousand junior boyars have perished. At the time when they slew Dmitry and our people the forces of all the land were gathered in Moscow, because the tsar was preparing to make war against the Crimea; but although the Russians were many, and we had only three regiments, even then our people were brought to ruin only by treason. And now that you have come to make war, we will fight even on foot if it is necessary. Your grace complains that he has few infantry. We shall send you every day from each regiment to the Kremlin as many infantrymen with weapons as you require. If you are fearful of stationing the entire army in the capital, then place our regiment there. We will await in Moscow either death, or reward for our former labors. Concerning the deployment of the army in the suburbs, it seems to me that this would be even more perilous than placing them in the city proper. Recently we have entered into peaceful relations with Moscow, and even now they are unconcerned that most of our men are all the time in Moscow rather than in the encampment, and they go about within the city without trepidation, just as they would in Cracow. It would be the same if we were stationed in the suburbs. Most of our men would be within the city rather than with the regiments."

Zolkiewski answered heatedly: "I do not see what your grace sees. Why don't you take over as hetman. I hand over my command to you!" Marchocki answered: "I do not wish to be commander, but I want to make one point, namely that if you do not place the army within the capital not three days will pass before Moscow changes sides. On behalf of my own regiment, I declare that we have no intention of remaining before Moscow for yet another three years."

With that the deputation left the hetman. Zolkiewski was not persuaded by Marchocki's arguments, and sent Gasiewski to Moscow to propose to the boyars that they assign him the New Virgin convent and the suburbs. The boyars agreed, but the patriarch protested that it was not proper to leave the nuns in the convent together with the Poles, nor to send them away to make room for the Poles. The patriarch's sentiment evoked a strong response. Nobles, tradesmen, townsmen and musketeers began to gather around Hermogen. The patriarch twice sent to the boyars, summoning them to his presence. They excused themselves, pleading that they were concerned with matters of state. Then Hermogen sent a message to them, saying that if they would not come to him, he would come to them, and not alone, but with all the people.

The boyars were afraid, came to the patriarch, and argued with him for two hours, disagreeing with his words about the hetman's evil intentions. Hermogen said that Zolkiewski was violating the conditions. He had not sent anyone against the Kaluga brigand, he wanted to bring his troops into Moscow, and he would send Russian regiments on campaign against the Swedes. The boyars, for their part, maintained that the entry of Polish troops into Moscow was inevitable, otherwise the common people would betray the city to False Dmitry. Ivan Nikitich Romanov had told the patriarch that if the hetman withdrew from Moscow they, the boyars, would then have to follow him in order to preserve their lives; that if Moscow fell to the brigand the patriarch would be answerable for this catastrophe. They read the patriarch a stern order written by the hetman for the prevention and punishment of any disorderly conduct that the Poles might permit themselves.

At the same time Gasiewski, knowing the state of affairs between the patriarch and the boyars, sent a message to the latter saying that the very next day the hetman would send troops against the pretender, provided that the Muscovite regiments were at the ready. This news gave the boyars the edge in the dispute. Mstislavsky took advantage of this occasion to praise the hetman. It is also reported that the boyars in their triumph resolved to tell Hermogen to attend to church matters and not meddle in secular affairs, since never before had the clergy administered matters of state. Evidently the betrayal of the realm to heretics was no concern of the church!

In any case the patriarch gave in to the boyars, and so also did the people. Saltykov, Sheremetev, Andrei Golitsyn and Secretary Gramotin[12] in turn went about among the people, dissuading them from their uprising or from thinking of a fresh one, and so the people grew quieter. Gasiewski set off at a gallop to the hetman's encampment with news that there was no danger in quartering the army in the capital, and that the boyars themselves had requested it. The hetman agreed. On the night of September 20-21 the Poles quietly entered Moscow, took up quarters in the Kremlin, the Kitai-quarter and the White quarter and occupied the New Virgin convent. They also occupied Mozhaisk, Borisov and Vereia, in order to ensure their line of communication with the king.

Zolkiewski in his own interest wanted to fulfill scrupulously what he had promised. Disputes between Poles and Muscovites were to be settled by an equal number of judges from both nations. Justice was impartial and strict. For instance, when a drunken Pole fired at an icon of the Virgin the tribunal sentenced him to have his hands cut off and burned at the stake. Another Pole forcibly abducted the daughter of one the of the Muscovite burghers. The culprit was lashed with the knout. The duty of provisioning the Poles was placed upon the towns and districts around Moscow, which were assigned according to the various troops; but when the Poles sent to collect the supplies, according to their own admission, arbitrarily took everything they fancied and violently abducted the wives and daughters of the inhabitants, the latter agreed to pay the Poles in cash, the collection of which they themselves undertook. Most important for the hetman was to gather the musketeers into his own hands since a popular uprising depended on them, and with the agreement of the boyars he solved this problem by entrusting command of the musketeers to Gasiewski. The musketeers gladly agreed to this since Zolkiewski, by his pleasant manners, gifts and entertainments, so won them over that they were ready to fulfill any or all of his wishes, and themselves came to him and begged him not to suspect them of treason, calling upon him to arrest any suspects. The hetman even managed to come to an understanding with the patriarch. At first he dealt with him through intermediaries, but then visited him in person and gained his confidence.

ZOLKIEWSKI LEAVES MOSCOW

Notwithstanding all these amicable relations and skillful measures, Zolkiewski knew that rebellion would flare at the first news of the king's unwillingness to dispatch Wladyslaw to Moscow. He also knew that these tidings would arrive very soon, and therefore he made haste to quit the capital. On one hand he wished by his physical presence to strengthen those who believed as he did and persuade the king to abide by the treaty. On the other hand must depart Moscow to preserve his reputation, and extricate himself from a situation which threatened soon to become extremely complicated. He had concluded his campaign with extraordinary success, but now he could perish ingloriously with his negligible force amidst a general uprising. The boyars were terrified when the hetman announced he must leave, and begged him to remain, but Zolkiewski was adamant. The boyars accompanied him for a long distance from the city, and even the common people showed their affection for him by giving him one gift after another. When he travelled through the streets the inhabitants of Moscow rushed forward and wished him a safe journey. Gasiewski took over command from the hetman.

NEGOTIATIONS AT SMOLENSK

As he left Moscow Zolkiewski took with him the deposed Tsar Vasily, and also his two brothers. On October 20 the king wrote to the boyars: "In accordance with your agreement with Hetman Zolkiewski, we have ordered Princes Vasily, Dmitry and Ivan Shuisky to be sent into Lithuania lest they stir unrest in the Muscovite dominion. Wherefore we order that you confiscate their patrimonies and estates and give them to us, your sovereign."

Two other suspect persons, Filaret and Golitsyn, were already outside Smolensk and at the king's mercy. They had left Moscow on September 11 and on the way, on September 18, they had written to Moscow that the royal army had besieged Ostashkov and waste its environs. On September 21 they had written that, not being able to capture Ostashkov, the Poles had spread out through the districts of Rzhev and Zubtsov and had devastated them. On September 30 they had written that many Russian nobles were coming to the king before Smolensk and, according to the king's wish, were swearing allegiance not only to the prince, but also to the king himself, and that the king was rewarding them with charters for service tenures and patrimonies. As for those who had sworn allegiance to the prince, the king ordered them to take an additional oath to himself, and those who refused were placed under arrest.

Several times the king had sent to the inhabitants of Smolensk, calling upon them to swear allegiance to him as well as to his son. The inhabitants of Smolensk had not agreed, and now the king was devising every imaginable means against their city. On October 7 the ambassadors arrived outside Smolensk, and were received with honor. They were assigned fourteen tents within a verst of the king's headquarters, but they were given meagre rations. In response to the ambassadors' complaints the reply was that the king was not in his own land, but at war, and that there was nowhere that he could obtain supplies. On October 10 the high ambassadors presented themselves to the king and petitioned that he send his son to assume the Muscovite tsardom. Leo Sapieha, on behalf of the king, answered in vague terms that Sigismund was awaiting domestic peace and order in the Muscovite realm, and would specify a time for negotiations.

Meanwhile there were disputes within the royal council as to whether or not the prince should be sent to Moscow. At first Leo Sapieha, despairing of the capture of Smolensk, had been among those in favor of sending the prince to Moscow, but he quickly changed his mind, especially when he received a letter from Queen Constance, who wrote to him: "You are despairing of the capture of Smolensk and presently are advising the king to lift the siege. We adjure you not to give such advice, but join with other senators in urging the continuation of the siege. Not only is the honor of the king at stake, but also that of the whole army." Sapieha began to persuade the king that the oath of allegiance given by the Muscovite people to Wladyslaw was suspect. Were not the Muscovites merely seeking to gain time? This oath meant more harm than good in Poland, since because of the uncertainty of this matter it would be necessary to lift the siege of Smolensk and abandon hope of obtaining the provinces of Smolensk and Severia, which would add to the fearful injury and shame should the Muscovites betray Wladyslaw. It would be much better to persevere in what had been begun, and not let slip what was already within reach and, having conquered, lead Wladyslaw in triumph to Moscow.

Those who demanded fulfillment of the hetman's treaty argued thus: we cannot make oathbreakers of the king, the hetman and the army. The Muscovites are not accustomed to being without a sovereign. If they are not given the prince chosen by themselves then, being thereby absolved of their oath of allegiance, they will turn to another and, having seen our perfidy, resolutely resist us. We cannot conclude this war by force, since we do not have sufficient means to do so. If we do not conclude the war, we will suffer harm from two sides, from Moscow and from our own people; from Moscow because they will choose a different sovereign, and from our own people because there will arise military confederations by reason of arrears in pay. It will be difficult to obtain funds from Poland since there is nothing in the treasury, and the king above all must be solicitous of his own fame, for if his fame is lost he will lose everything, both at the hands of his own people and of foreigners. The war cannot go well because not only are the means lacking to continue it, but also because we do not have the wherewithal to discharge our debts. The soldiers will go in desperation to Poland for their pay, whence the hatred of the army for the king's welfare, and hatred from the gentry, and in the end rebellion, when his life and ruler will be at risk.

But if the prince is sent to Moscow we will have peaceful neighborly relations, we will easily be able to recover Livonia and Sweden easily, and there will be less damage from the Tatars. A large part of the gentry will obtain estates in Muscovy and as a result the Polish Commonwealth will be more secure against mutinies, for the cause of the late uprising was the poverty of the citizens. The king, having given his son to Moscow, will obtain for himself eternal glory, from his own people and abroad. If the death of the king should occur, which God forbid, and the election of his second son encounters difficulties, his elder brother, the Muscovite tsar, will help him.

The opposing side argued that the sovereign was young, still a child, and would be unable to govern without guardians, who would be either Poles or Muscovites, or a mixed group drawn from both peoples. If Poles were appointed, the Muscovites would be insulted, for the Muscovite people cannot abide foreigners, as witness the case of Dmitry, whom they killed because he admitted foreigners into his intimate counsels. To entrust the prince to Muscovite guardians would be difficult, first because there was nobody to guide the sovereign in a befitting manner. If they educated him in their customs they would defile with vulgarity a sovereign who had shown so much promise. The guardians naturally should be of the most noble people, but should not be in a position to take advantage of the inexperience of the sovereign (they revere their own sovereign like deity). The inexperience and youth of the sovereign, the share they would have in the government, would give rise among them to contempt for the tsar's authority, they would quarrel with one another, and whoever over-powered the others would have designs against the tsar himself. Examples of this are plentiful, not only among barbarians, but also in enlightened countries, for it is difficult to restrain ambition; this evil insinuates itself gradually, especially when fate is favorably disposed, and the Muscovites are very prone to this tendency because they are proud and envious.

Previous sovereigns had restrained this tendency among them by fear, but a young sovereign could not restrain it. Who then, should be chosen as guardians? Surely it was essential to recognize good qualities and habits in a man before he be permitted to assume such a position, but how to identify him? Candidates would hinder and denigrate each other and, were they to display such ludicrous rivalry even in meeting and bowing, what could be expected of them in such an important matter? Join the Poles and Muscovites together? For them to get along together would require the help of the Holy Spirit; men of the most moderate character would be needed. Under a young sovereign enmity must rise among them. Some, devoted to the father and the sovereign, would advise him in his good interest, but others would indulge and flatter the young man to their own advantage. Only the special mercy of God might preserve him from such fate. Harmony between Polish and Muscovite guardians is an impossibility by reason of difference in temperament.

The present state of the Muscovite realm demands a man to defend it against foreign enemies, to pacify domestic disorder, and to restore each man to his previous place, for if the disturbed vital juices of the sick body politic are not healed to return each man to his proper place the illness must flare once more. A young man cannot do this, and, failing, his life and authority must be imperiled. The common people must rise against the Polish noblesto seize all but absolute power. The boyars, the leaders of the people, would employ the people as a weapon to advance their own ambitious aims. They must be restrained, for otherwise an uprising can be expected at any time, this many-headed beast can be subdued only by the sword.

This a youth cannot do, and if he does it at someone else's prompting, there will be a mighty disturbance. Besides, it is dangerous to accustom a young sovereign to bloodshed. The priests have immense influence, they are the leaders of the popular movement, they would turn the heads even of a mature man. We must make them harmless, or their poison will be without remedy. In such event the sovereign cannot be safe, and only the

Poles can defend him. If they are too few they will not defend him, but rather destroy him. He will not be permitted to maintain a large army at his side; what kind of life would it be for the sovereign to spend all his time in the encampment, in a state of insecurity? We cannot believe in his election or the kissing of the cross.

If the Muscovites had chosen him of their own free will and after long deliberation we could hope that they had chosen freely and would serve him willingly, for the affection of subjects is the foundation of government. But there is none of this, only a mask and talk of free election. Necessity lies at the basis of their loyalty. How can there be a free election when a sword is held over the head? Necessity is being cloaked merely by a figleaf, for if the prince is beloved by them why did they not choose him before, when they were in a position of strength? Why did they oppose the hetman, why did they sacrifice their lives for Shuisky? They sought help on every side against the father, called him a perjurer and said that he had violated his oath to them and to their sovereign. A fine indication of a favorable disposition!

Love was not the cause of the prince's election, but necessity, for when you are drowning you are glad when even the wickedest enemy extends a helping hand. From the conditions of the election it is easy to see what they thought of us. In two of these we can see their unfavorable disposition; that the prince be baptized into the Greek faith, and that Poles not be given borderland estates. If they require a Christian to be baptized this signifies that they do not consider him to be a Christian, and how could they possibly have a favorable attitude towards a non-Christian? They say that the prince must be rebaptized. They must think well of their candidate, that for a crust of bread he must agree to be an apostate and commit desecration before all peoples and before them. They say that this condition was introduced by the patriarch. So much the worse! They say that Poles must not be given lands close to the borders; but why should they fear them? Is it possible to love those whom we fear? Why give them estates only in the interior? They don't trust Poles, but whom do they choose as tsar? A Polish prince!

We are asked to believe in kissing the cross, but let us see how they have dealt with other sovereigns. Did not Ivan die of poison?[13] They say that he was a tyrant, yet Fedor and his little brother Dmitry were not guilty of anything, but they also perished. They say that Godunov did these things, yet they elected Godunov as tsar, and if God had not punished him his son would now be reigning; but they accepted him as tsar, kissed the cross to him, and straight away killed him, calling him a traitor.[14] The Russians swore allegiance to Shuisky and stood by him as long as matters were favorable. In this manner they will betray our prince, first of all because he is a Catholic, and the patriarch will condone it. It is difficult to trust a people already so accustomed to violating oaths. Let us take as an example the Roman Republic, where change of rulers became the custom. This legacy has descended to the present-day Italians. It is said that the hetman, all the army and the king have promised, and that they must fulfill the promise. So they should, but not unintelligently, not losing sight of the circumstances, which are as important as the principal matter. We must hand over the prince after removing all impediments, since we have promised him a land at peace.

The Muscovites say that if we do not give them the prince they will turn to another sovereign. But to whom can they turn? Nobody will abandon his own country, and nobody except the English king has a son, and even he is a heretic, and there is little hope that he will be rebaptized. We are the closest of all, and we can act the most conveniently. The capital is in our hands and they cannot know our shortcomings since, judging by our successes, they esteem us higher than we esteem ourselves. It is true that it will be hard for the army, but even so it will not necessarily mutiny. There will be money from the Polish requisitions, although not the full amount. If they receive part payment, they will wait for the balance. After all they are not foreigners, but native sons, laboring for their own gain, not for that of a foreign sovereign.

You say that when we hand over the prince Moscow will pay in full and compensate the Polish Commonwealth. But there is nothing, or only very little, in the Muscovite treasury, so where is the money coming from? If they try to take the money from private persons an uprising will flare all the sooner. They promise to return Livonia, to defend us against the Tatars, but make no mention of the Severian land, which we shall surely lose. It will be difficult to regain Livonia, since we cannot use the Muscovite army soon for this; it is exhausted, and we must give it time to recuperate. There would be an insurrection against the king if we handed over his son without the consent of the Poles. Since he cannot even conclude alliances without the consent of the Commonwealth, how can he give a ruler to a neighboring state? The king has the right to look after the interests of his descendants, but not to the detriment of the Commonwealth, and it is certainly harmful if he gives his son to a foreign people without the Commonwealth's consent.

Weighing all the arguments for and against, it is difficult to decide which course to follow. If the prince were of full age and the Commonwealth gave its consent, we could agree quickly to send the prince to Moscow. But at present we must adopt a middle course. It would be better to chose the king as sovereign since he is a man of mature years and experienced in administration. But it would be dangerous to propose this to the Muscovites. It would arouse their suspicions and alarm the clergy, which knows well that the king is an ardent Catholic. As far as the prince is concerned, in view of his tender years they can hope to train him in everything according to their own customs, but they can have no such hopes with regard to the king. Thus we cannot propose the king to them directly, but in a good cause the most direct path does not always lead to success, especially when dealing with a devious people.

If it is presently inopportune to give the king the title of tsar, at least the administration of the realm rests with us, and this eventually will open the way to achieve our purposes. We will not refuse them in the matter of the prince. We will abide by our previous undertaking, but will demonstrate to the boyar council why we cannot send the prince immediately. We will demonstrate that the obstacles originate not with us but with them, that delay works not to our advantage but to theirs, and for this the nobility must be detached from the common multitude. We must tell one person one thing, another something different. It will be possible to demonstrate to both the nobility and the common people that the realm is not yet pacified. It is swarming with enemies, both foreign and domestic, and it would be difficult to overcome this with such an impoverished tsar. Much money must be disbursed by the treasury to pay the army, but if Wladyslaw comes immediately funds for the army must be diverted to the tsar, to maintain the splendor of a court.

The tsar's revenues now are dissipated in various directions, appointments are held by unworthy persons. All this must be set in order before the the tsar arrives so that he might enter a prosperous realm. Noble men must be attracted by private promises and it pointed out clearly to them that the prince is young; that for establishment of tranquillity in such a disorganized realm reason and time are needed. If the realm is not pacified there will be further unrest, this time worse than before. Attention must be devoted to the security of the sovereign, for evil persons called brigands have multiplied in the land. The tsar would be secure only with a numerous detachment of bodyguards, which would compound the exhaustion of the treasury and of the land, whereas when the prince attains full age and reason bodyguards would not be needed.

We have to await the convocation of the Sejm in order to ask the Commonwealth concerning the dispatch of the prince, and all this needs time. In the meantime how can a disorganized state remain without a head? The enemy will take advantage of this and become stronger. A young sovereign cannot rule or enter into their way of doing things, since he would not know them. Let them send their sons and nobility to the royal court, that the prince may acquaint himself with their customs, and they can get to know his ways. Then he will come to Moscow as a well-known person, and will rule according to the customs of the land. Meanwhile men must be attracted to him individually by promises, and the same with regard to the clergy because even among them there is ambition. If they agree to postpone the prince's arrival, then say that during this time the realm should not be without a head, and who is closer at hand to be recognized as that head than the king, the sole guardian of his son? Naturally the most sensible people will be quite content to live peacefully in their own homes and eat their bread until it is time for the prince to arrive on attaining full age. We should not talk of this to the ambassadors who are here present (Filaret and Golitsyn). They were sent away from Moscow as suspect persons. It would be better to send emissaries to Moscow, there to negotiate with well-disposed people; but if one of these ambassadors is well-disposed to us, it would be a good idea to send him also to Moscow.

These arguments prevailed. It was decided not to send the prince. The first session between the ambassadors and the lords of the council took place on October 15, 1610. The lords declared that the king could not withdraw from Smolensk and evacuate the army from the Muscovite realm, for he had come thither to pacify that realm, to destroy the brigand, to liberate the towns, and to place his son upon the Muscovite throne. The ambassadors replied that the realm would be pacified far more quickly if the king evacuated his army from it; that in order to destroy the brigand, Zolkiewski's detachment alone was sufficient, for the strength of the brigand consisted solely of Polish troops; that the king's campaign against the brigand would devastate the Muscovite realm, which had been laid waste enough already.

The ambassadors said that it was strange to them to be negotiating about this since the condition of the king's withdrawal from Smolensk had been confirmed by the hetman's oath in the treaty with Valuev and Eletsky at

Tsarevo-Zaimishche. In the same treaty the evacuation of all towns belonging to the Muscovite realm was mentioned explicitly, and the hetman had undertaken to petition the king concerning the lifting of the siege of Smolensk; consequently there could be no discussion on this matter. The Polish lords answered that the king could not give his fifteen-year-old son to the Muscovite throne, but wished to pursue the brigand himself, after which he would appear before the Sejm, without whose consent he could not send his son to Moscow.

A second session took place on October 17. The Polish lords repeated what they had said before, but in a sharper tone, and finally pronounced directly with regard to Smolensk: "Why have you not yet shown any respect to the king, and separate the son from the father? Why do you not immediately surrender Smolensk to the king? You could order the inhabitants of Smolensk to swear allegiance to the king and the prince together, and in this way you would show respect to the king." The ambassadors, having heard this out, asked the Polish lords: "When you elected your king, and he had a father in Sweden, King Johann, you separated the father from the son, kissed the cross to the son but you did not kiss the cross to the father." The Polish lords retorted that King Johann was not pacifying their realm, and concluded thus: "Until our sovereign has captured Smolensk, we can hardly leave." Then, wishing to avoid discussion concerning Smolensk, and to conclude more expeditiously the principal matter of their discussions, the ambassadors said: "The king must fulfill the treaty and his son, the Muscovite tsar, must immediately negotiate with him concerning Smolensk, if the king considers it such a great dishonor not to obtain this city." "In any case," added the ambassadors, "the honor of the sovereign lies in the inviolability of his word, and the king has declared more than once that he has not undertaken this campaign for the conquest of cities."

The third session took place on October 20. Here the Polish lords openly declared: "Even if the king agreed to retreat from Smolensk the Polish lords and knights would not agree to this, but would rather die, and inherit their eternal patrimony." The ambassadors in answer to this ordered the hetman's treaty to be read. The Polish lords vehemently cried out: "We have told you more than once that we are not bound by the hetman's treaty." Despite this they immediately began to negotiate compensation for the king and army, as stipulated in the hetman's treaty. The ambassadors replied that it would be strange for the tsar's treasury to pay for the devastation of the Muscovite realm, and that on the matter of compensation Tsar Wladyslaw could deal later with his father. In conclusion the ambassadors requested the Polish lords to report to the king that so far no one had discussed the principal matter. More than anything they wished to know whether the king would give his son to the tsardom, and whether the prince would accept the Orthodox faith of the Greek dispensation. The Polish lords promised to report to the king concerning this.

The fourth session took place on October 23. The Polish lords declared that the king would grant his son but would not send him before the meeting of the Sejm. They read through the articles to which the king had agreed. (1) Concerning the faith and marriage of the prince, let it be as God and he himself willed. (2) The prince will not correspond with the Pope over matters of faith. (3) The king orders prisoners of war to be released. (4) Concerning the number of people accompanying the prince and their payment, the ambassadors must reach agreement with Wladyslaw himself. (5) With regard to the execution of apostates from the faith, the king agreed with that clause of the declaration. Concerning other clauses, there would have to be a decision by the Sejm.

As for withdrawal from Smolensk there was emphatic refusal. The Polish lords concluded their answer thus: "As soon as Smolensk surrenders and swears allegiance to the king, his majesty himself will pursue the brigand, will destroy him and, having pacified the realm, set out with all his army and with you, the ambassadors, for the Sejm. There he will give you as your tsar his son, with whom you may then depart for Moscow." The ambassadors replied that to capture Smolensk, pursue the brigand, pacify the realm and proceed to the Sejm would demand much time, whereas for the Muscovite realm each minute of the king's dilatoriness was costly, giving rise to doubt and leading to unrest. Therefore they, the ambassadors, begged the Polish lords to turn the king aside from his intention, and insisted that the hetman's treaty be fulfilled.

The ambassadors also requested permission to correspond with the inhabitants of Smolensk, with whom hitherto they were forbidden to communicate. At the same time Metropolitan Filaret held a conversation with Leo Sapieha on whether it was necessary for the prince to be baptized. Sapieha concluded this conversation thus: "Concerning this matter, most holy father, I shall speak on another occasion, for at present it would be pointless for me to speak about it. For now I will say only one thing: the prince already has been baptized, and nowhere is there anything written about a second baptism."

To this the ambassadors replied: "We beg the king and the prince with tears that the prince be baptized into our Orthodox faith of the Greek dispensation. You yourselves know, lords, that the Greek faith is the mother of all Christian faiths, and that all other faiths have fallen away from her and established themselves separately. Faith is a gift of God, and we trust that God will by His grace touch the heart of the prince, and desire that he be baptized into our Orthodox faith, and therefore you, lords of the council, must not lead the prince away from this and resist the grace of God. It is in no way feasible that a sovereign be of one faith and his people of another, nor do you yourselves tolerate your rulers being of another faith. And you in particular, Leo Ivanovich, should rejoice that our sovereign Wladyslaw, son of Sigismund, should be in our Orthodox faith of the Greek dispensation, since your grandfather, your father, yourself and many of your other kinsfolk were in our Orthodox faith of the Greek dispensation, but for some reason or other have separated from us.[15] You should therefore be an advocate of our faith."

The fifth session took place on October 21. The Polish lords, wishing to intimidate the ambassadors and show them the necessity of submitting to Sigismund's will, informed them of the successes of the Swedes in the northwest, and of the strengthening of the pretender, to whom three hundred gentry from Moscow had deserted. The ambassadors replied that they doubted the veracity of these tidings, since nobody had written concerning this from Moscow. If indeed there was treason among the people of Moscow, and because of this the hetman was unable to pursue the brigand with his troops, the king could send the troops who were occupying Mozhaisk, Borovsk, Viazma, Dorogobuzh and Belaia, which troops presently were doing nothing but laying waste and devastating the realm. If the king commanded these troops to be sent against the brigand, and we write to these towns concerning this royal favor, and also mentioning that he soon will send his son to assume the tsardom, all the people will rejoice, and will forsake the brigand. On the other hand, were the king to advance with his troops into Muscovite territory, the people will have doubts, all that has been agreed upon will be nullified, and things will be even worse than before."

The Polish lords answered heatedly: "We have given you accurate news concerning the Swedes and the brigand, nor do you yourselves know what you are asking. Even should the king desire to leave Smolensk and return to his own country, his army, which consists of free men, will not obey him, and those who are occupying the various Muscovite places (and there are eighty thousand of them altogether) will go over to the brigand if they do not receive their pay, and that will be the end of the Muscovite realm."

The ambassadors replied: "We beg the king's majesty to take pity upon the Muscovite realm and order his soldiers to pursue the brigand, and order to be evacuated from the country those Cherkassians[16] and Tatars who, stationed in towns which have sworn allegiance to the prince, are burning, devastating and taking captives." The Polish lords cried out in answer to this: "You have come not to give, but to receive orders. You have not come from your sovereign, but have come from Moscow with a petition to our sovereign, and whatsoever our sovereign orders, you must do it. We are giving you accurate tidings that the Swedes have captured Ivangorod and Ladoga, and wish to advance upon Pskov and other towns, and that from the other side the brigand is rallying with many people, and that many people are deserting and coming to him from Moscow, and also Turks and Crimeans are seeking to come to his aid. There is more that we have not told you. The Danish king wishes to annex Archangel and Kola. You yourselves see how many enemies are fastening their eyes on your realm; each wants to seize something for himself. You should rejoice for your realm that this the evil hour has not yet come, so do not dissuade the sovereign from his campaign. Even if our sovereign himself wished to return to his country you should still petition him to pacify your realm. Our sovereign, taking pity upon your realm, wishes personally to pursue the brigand but you do not understand the sovereign's graciousness, and want to dissuade him from his campaign."

The ambassadors replied: "We cannot give orders to his majesty. He will do whatever he wishes. But since we are instructed to petition on behalf of the patriarch, the boyars and all the people of the Muscovite realm, this is what we are doing. We are seeking to dissuade the king from the campaign because even without it our realm is devastated and ruined, and since the arrival of the prince has been postponed, the land will be brought into dejection and doubt. We ask permission to write to the patriarch, the boyars and all the people in Moscow that henceforth we should act according to their instructions, for without this we cannot agree to anything."

The Polish lords replied: "Even without instructions from Moscow you can do anything, since you are high ambassadors. For a start, in order to pacify the king, see to it that the inhabitants of Smolensk kiss the cross to the king and the prince. You call the prince your sovereign, yet you dishonor his father the king. What will it cost you to yield to his majesty Smolensk, which he wishes to conquer, not for himself, but for his son? The king will bequeath to him not only Smolensk, but also Poland and Lithuania, after which Poland, Lithuania and Moscow will all be one."

"We call upon God to witness," the ambassadors replied, "that there is nothing concerning this written in our instructions. Neither now, nor later at the Sejm, will we consent to yield any town whatsoever to Poland or Lithuania. The Muscovite realm all belongs to God and our sovereign, Wladyslaw the son of Sigismund. When he is enthroned as tsar God and our sovereign are perfectly free to do as they wish; otherwise we may not speak about or even consider such a matter."

Sapieha replied: "We wish Smolensk to kiss the cross to the king simply for the sake of honor." "The king's honor," retorted the ambassadors, "will be much greater in all the world, and God's favor will be manifest, if he pacifies the Muscovite realm, if Christian blood is spared, and he places his son upon the Russian throne. Then not only Smolensk but all of the Russian realm will be under his son."

The Polish lords cried out: "We have heard many vain words from you. Tell us one thing. Do you wish to send to the inhabitants of Smolensk, calling upon them to do honor to the sovereign and kiss the cross?" "You yourselves know," replied the ambassadors, "that our instructions were written with the agreement of the hetman, and the hetman kissed the cross on this on behalf of the king and also you, my lords. But how can we kiss the cross to the king since not only is this not in our instructions but is not the intention of all the people? How can we do this without the consent of the whole land?" "If that is so, then Smolensk is finished!" the Polish lords exclaimed.

The ambassadors once again asked permission to correspond with the patriarch and the boyars, complaining that the gentry who had accompanied them lacked the wherewithal to support themselves and would die of hunger since their estates and patrimonies were occupied by Lithuanian soldiers, the ambassadors themselves, were suffering great privation, and half their horses were perishing through lack of fodder. The Polish lords replied: "All this is your own fault. If only you would fulfill the king's wish, both you and your gentry would have everything you need."

At that time Hetman Zolkiewski arrived before Smolensk and on October 30 made a triumphal entry into the encampment. He brought the deposed Tsar Vasily and his brothers, and presented them to Sigismund. It is said that when it was demanded of Vasily that he bow to the king, he replied: "A sovereign of Moscow and All Russia cannot bow before a king. By the just decrees of God I am brought a prisoner here, not by your hands, but betrayed by Muscovite traitors, my own slaves."

On November 6 the sixth session took place in Zolkiewski's presence. The ambassadors began with the words: "We are glad that the hetman, Stanislaw Stanislavich has arrived. With his presence God will grant that royal business will be completed more successfully since the hetman wrote to Moscow concerning the king's grant more than once, and pronounced the king's grant of the prince to all the people of the Muscovite realm. On behalf of the great sovereign king, on behalf of the Polish and Lithuanian land he kissed the cross to the Muscovite realm, and all the people trusted the hetman's word. Concerning which we also petitioned you and spoke with you, the lords of the council, but you believed otherwise and disbelieved us. But now Hetman Stanislaw Stanislavich, according to his oath, also can speak on our behalf."

Leo Sapieha answered: "We have met with you many times, but no good has come of it. We have insisted without end that you do honor to the king, and order the inhabitants of Smolensk to kiss the cross to his majesty and his son the prince. But you senselessly refuse, saying that you cannot do this without the consent of the Muscovite boyars, although you have been given plenipotentiary powers to speak and resolve on all matters."

The ambassadors replied to this: "We had hoped on the same day that we arrived here we would receive everything according to the hetman's treaty. But up to now not a single clause of this treaty has been fulfilled. You yourself know, Stanislaw Stanislavich! Can we undertake anything new on our own initiative? You yourself saw in Moscow how the patriarch and boyars took counsel with all the people on every clause of the treaty, and read out all the clauses to them more than once, and explained whatsover seemed offensive to them, and concerning other clauses they referred them to you. Not only did the patriarch take counsel with the boyars, but also with all the people of every rank. How can we alter anything in these clauses without consultation with the whole land? As for surrendering Smolensk to the king, not only is this not in any of the clauses, but also not in your memory or in that of anyone else. More than once you told all of us that as soon as we came to the king, his majesty would withdraw all his forces from Smolensk, and would return to Poland."

The hetman spoke to the lords of the council for a long time in Latin, and then replied to the ambassadors: "The treaty which I concluded with the Muscovite realm was according to the command and will of the king, and the king will observe all of that treaty. But in order that his majesty might withdraw from Smolensk (concerning which I did not speak with you, but advised you to send a petition concerning this), how can I give orders to my sovereign? And where is it confirmed in the proceedings that I should pursue the brigand? And if I did not do so, that is not my fault. It was resolved to send the boyars Prince Ivan Mikhaikovich Vorotynsky, Ivan Nikitich Romanov and Lord-in-waiting Golovin to me with the Muscovite army. I had detailed off my army for this, and had placed it in Borisov, Mozhaisk and Borovsk, but your men did not arrive to join with them. At that time the brigand was corresponding secretly with several Muscovites. These people were investigated, and the brigand's documents were discovered in Moscow in many places.

"Prince Fedor Ivanovich Mstislavsky and his companions then came to me in my encampment and asked me to come with all my army to Moscow, and that if I did not come to Moscow I should pursue the brigand. Then many boyars, seeing the instability among the Muscovite people, did not remain in Moscow, but followed me with their wives and children. For this reason I did not enter Moscow, but sent Jan-Piotr Sapieha after the brigand. Perhaps he is still occupied with him. Then, when I was with the boyars, many clauses pertaining to the treaty were changed. Concerning this, ask the nobleman Ivan Izmailov and his companions, who have come with me to the king to present petitions concerning estates. They will tell you how the boyars in Moscow dealt with me and took counsel with me.

"In just such a manner you are dealing here with the lords of the council, so that it may redound to the king's honor and to your advantage. The document which was sent from Moscow to Smolensk is here with me, but in it is written that which you desired. It was not I who commanded that it be written. I know my treaty, namely that no cannon shall fire upon Smolensk, there shall be no siege maintained, and the king is fulfilling the agreement. In order that the inhabitants of Smolensk not separate father from son, and kiss the cross to both, you should do this for the sake of the king's honor. If you do not command the inhabitants of Smolensk to do this, our senators will say that the king must avenge his honor. We are prepared to die for the honor of our sovereign, and so it will go badly for Smolensk. Do not quibble, fulfill the king's desire, and when Smolensk submits we will write an agreement concerning the king's withdrawal."

"Be mindful of God and your soul, Stanislaw Stanislavich!" the ambassadors answered. "In the rescript given to Eletsky and Valuev it is written explicitly that when the inhabitants of Smolensk kiss the cross to the prince the king will withdraw from Smolensk, neither will there be any destruction or violence done to the city, and all borderland towns shall pertain to the Muscovite realm as before. We expected help from you, that you would abide by your oath, petition the king on behalf of the Muscovite realm, and tell your brothers the Polish senators that they themselves should persuade the king to desist from shedding blood. You say that after our departure you and the boyars changed many things in the treaty, and make reference to the courtiers Ivan Izmailov and his companions, but we do not even wish to ask them about this. We need a document from the boyars, for it is impossible to believe the word of people who are coming to the king seeking estates. In the treaty clauses were written that Poles and Lithuanians should not be present, nor administer the affairs of the land in the chancelleries; yet even before the sovereign has arrived estates and patrimonies are being distributed. We have reminded you of this, so that doubt and grief should not spread among the people." Sapieha answered: "The lord king does not chase away those who seek his favor, and who is there to grant them favors prior to the arrival of the prince but his majesty? And now the sovereign has granted Prince Mstislavsky the rank of master of the horse and Prince Yury Trubetskoy boyardom, and for this all boyars are grateful to his majesty."

To return to the principal matter, the ambassadors ordered Conciliar Secretary Tomila Lugovskoy to read out the hetman's treaty with Eletsky and Valuev, concluded near Tsarevo-Zaimishche. But Sapieha did not allow him to read it, and cried out: "You have long since been forbidden to make reference to that rescript; you are only trying thereby to embarrass the hetman. Should you once more refer to that rescript, things will go badly for you." Lugovskoy answered: "Even though I should die, I shall speak the truth. You set no store by this rescript, but we shall both now and in the future stand by it."

Zolkiewski then intervened in the dispute. "I am prepared," he said, "to swear that I remember nothing that was written in that rescript. It was written by the Russians whom I had with me and who slipped it in front of me. Not having read it, I set my hand and seal to it, and therefore it would be better to set this rescript aside and concentrate upon the Moscow treaty, which his majesty himself has confirmed."

Other Polish lords cried out: "Concerning Smolensk, we are telling you for the last time: if you do not compel the inhabitants of Smolensk to swear allegiance to the king and the prince, the oath of the hetman is void, and his majesty and we no longer shall have any patience with Smolensk. We will not leave one stone standing upon another, and it will suffer the same fate as Jerusalem."

The ambassadors made the same reply as before, that they could not violate the treaty on their own initiative, and asked to send a messenger to the patriarch, the boyars and all ranks, when they would do whatsoever the whole land decided. "You, Leo Ivanovich," they said, "have yourself been an ambassador, so you know whether an ambassador might exceed his instructions. You were an amabssador from one sovereign to another, but we have been sent by the whole land, so how can we do anything that is not in our instructions without the consent of the whole land?" The ambassadors turned to Zolkiewski, urging him to use all his influence to save Smolensk. "Will not all the people say," they said, "that before your arrival at Smolensk the king observed the treaty but as soon as you arrived Smolensk was captured?" The hetman gave his word to strive with all his might to prevent any assault upon Smolensk until the return of a messenger sent by the ambassadors to the patriarch and the boyars, asking for fresh instructions.

The hetman was informed that Filaret was angry at him for having brought the deposed Tsar Vasily to Smolensk, and for having presented him to the king in secular garb. This is why before the end of the session Zolkiewski approached the metropolitan with excuses. "I took the former tsar," he said, "not of my own free will, but at the request of the boyars, to prevent potential unrest among the people. Furthermore he was almost starving to death in the St. Joseph monastery. The reason I brought him in secular dress is because he himself does not wish to be a monk. He was tonsured against his will, and involuntary tonsure is contrary to both your canon law and ours, and the patriarch agrees."

Filaret replied: "It is true that the boyars wished to banish Prince Vasily under Polish and Muscovite guard to some fortified monastery, but you insisted that he be sent to the St. Joseph monastery. You should not have brought him and his brothers to Poland because you gave your word that you would not take him out of the St. Joseph monastery, and it was confirmed in the treaty that you would not deport or exile a single Russian to Poland or Lithuania. You kissed the cross on this, but you have violated your oath. You should fear God, for it is not fitting to part a man from his wife. As for the fact that he was not being fed at the St. Joseph monastery, this is the fault of your officials, since the boyars surrendered him into your hands."

Fearing for Smolensk, the next day the ambassadors went to Zolkiewski to remind him of his promise. The hetman declared to them, apparently on his own initiative, that there was only one way to save Smolensk: to let the Polish army enter, as had been done in Moscow, and then *perhaps* the king would not compel Smolensk to swear allegiance, and would not himself go after the brigand at Kaluga. In answer the ambassadors read out to him the clause in the treaty that no Polish troops were to be placed in a single town, and once again insisted that they be allowed to dispatch a messenger to Moscow. The hetman promised to intercede to this effect. In order to learn the result of his petition, the ambassadors visited him once again the following day. Zolkiewski declared that the king was agreeable to the dispatch of a messenger, but first demanded that his soldiers be admitted into Smolensk. The ambassadors replied as before that they could not consent to this on their own authority. The next day the hetman sent to the ambassadors one of his kinsmen, who told them that the king had agreed to the dispatch of a messenger to Moscow, but on condition that within two weeks he return with plenipotentiary powers.

Then it was announced to the ambassadors that they should attend upon the hetman on November 18. There they encountered all the lords of the council, and Sapieha demanded that the king's soldiers immediately be admitted into Smolensk, since Shein and the inhabitants of Smolensk could not be trusted. The leading merchant Shorin[17] and some junior boyars had approached Smolensk, and Shein had asked questions of them concerning the brigand—where was he, and how strong? It is evident that they wished to communicate with the brigand and allow him into the city. The ambassadors repeated that they could do nothing without fresh instructions from Moscow. Concerning the inhabitants of Smolensk, it was impossible to believe Shorin and such other criminals. "They did not approach Smolensk at our instigation, but were deceiving and tempting the inhabitants of Smolensk, and you, the senators, are being misinformed about them." The Polish lords replied that they could not await consultations with Moscow. "You will see what will happen to Smolensk tomorrow!" The ambassadors replied that they at least be allowed to consult with the metropolitan, who could not be present at this meeting by reason of infirmity. The Polish lords agreed.

Arriving at their encampment, the ambassadors took counsel. Filaret said: "There is no way in which we can consent to the king's men being allowed into Smolensk. If ever even a few of the king's men are allowed into Smolensk, the city is lost to us. But if the king captures Smolensk by assault, we must submit to the judgement of God, only let not the city be surrendered by our own faint-heartedness." Then the gentry and the ambassadorial staff were summoned to the council, and were asked: "If Smolensk is captured by assault, will not the ambassadors be accursed and hated by the patriarch, the boyars and all the people?" All replied: "As one body we must resolve on this: that not one Pole or Lithuanian shall be admitted into Smolensk. If even a few of the king's men are admitted into Smolensk, then the city is lost. Whatever blood is shed, or whatever happens to Smolensk, let it not be our fault. Only let us not lose Smolensk through our own faint-heartedness." Gentry and junior boyars from Smolensk who happened to be with the embassy said: "Even though our mothers, wives and children perish in Smolensk, let us nevertheless firmly resolve that not one Pole or Lithuanian be allowed to enter Smolensk."

The next day the ambassadors declared to the Polish lords their decision, and begged with tears that the king not assault Smolensk, but not even tears prevailed. On November 21 the whole army advanced upon the city, detonated a mine, and blew up a tower and a section of the wall about ten sazhens in length. Three times the Poles penetrated the city, but three times they were repulsed.

On November 29 the ambassadors were ordered to attend Zolkiewski, at whose quarters they encountered all the other Polish lords. The same proposals came from the Poles, and the same answers from the ambassadors. Another session took place on December 2. Sapieha confronted the ambassadors with these words: "Have you considered? Will you allow the king's soldiers to enter Smolensk? Know that, because of the king's mercy, Smolensk has not been reduced in order that innocent blood not be shed along with the guilty."

The same answer came from the ambassadors. The Polish lords continued: "The king grants your requests and has allowed you to write to Moscow, only write the truth and do not add anything superfluous. In any case you have written to Moscow a number of times, and this you were doing improperly by writing secretly and alienating people from the king, telling them not to come to the king to petition concerning estates and other matters. Who indeed can favor them, if not the king?"

The ambassadors replied: "Do not let these brigands who come to you from Moscow tell you untruths and slanders about us, instead let Christian blood cease to be shed, and let Christians on both sides be in peace and tranquillity. Concerning estates, we wrote and told you that this could lead to distrust among the people."

On December 4 the ambassadors were informed that they might send to Moscow a messenger, who would be accompanied by the king's bailiff, Isakowski. On December 6 Isakowski and the messenger actually departed, but in the meantime there entered into force the resolution we have discussed, the clause stating the impossibility of sending the prince to Moscow immediately. Seeing the intractibility of the principal ambassadors, the Poles turned their attention to the secondary figures and by promises induced them to betray their cause, abandon the principal ambassadors and set off for Moscow, there to act in the king's interest.

Filaret and Golitsyn learned that the conciliar noble, Sukin, Crown Secretary Sydavnoy Vasiliev, Archimandrite Evfimy of the Savior monastery, Cellarer Avraamy Palitsyn of the Trinity monastery, and many other nobles and men of various ranks, having accepted from the king charters for estates and other grants, had been sent back to their homes.

They also wished to sway the conciliar secretary Tomilo Lugovskoy. Sapieha summoned him and when he arrived he found the chancellor together with Sukin and Sydavnoy, clothed in rich garments. Sapieha said to Lugovskoy: "Wait a while. I shall just present these gentlemen and other nobles to the king that he may take leave of them, since Sukin is old, and the others living here have run short of food."

Tomilo interrupted Sapieha, saying: "Leo Ivanovich! It is unheard of anywhere that ambassadors behave as Sukin and Sydavnoy are doing. They are travelling to Moscow, abandoning the business of the realm and the land and their colleagues! How will they be able to look upon the miraculous image of the Mother of God, in whose name they were dispatched? For our sins we are engaged in such a weighty matter as never before in the history of the Muscovite realm. Christian blood is being shed incessantly, and henceforth we do not know how it will cease to flow. Even though Vasily Sukin expires, it is better for him to die here, where he has been ordered, and not abandon his charge. There are older men living here who do not desert their posts. If Sydavnoy is dismissed because he has run short of provisions, all of us ought to have been dismissed long ago since we all have run short of rations, as we all were given the same subsistence allowance. May God judge them for what they are doing! I declare to you, Leo Ivanovich! As soon as these people arrive in Moscow there will be distrust and grief among the people, and in the other towns we may expect great unrest as a result of this. Henceforth the metropolitan and Prince Vasily Vasilievich will not be able to achieve anything. Five clergymen were sent with the metropolitan, and also five of us sent with Prince Vasily Vasilievich. Half are being dismissed, while the other half remains. Let things be according to the will of God and the sovereign, King Sigismund, for henceforth we can achieve nothing."

Sapieha answered: "You should not be perturbed about this. You are all at the disposal of the sovereign. His majesty granted their request and dismissed them in accordance with their petitions, but the business of the embassy can proceed without them. There can be no evil consequences in Moscow as a result of their arrival, but only good results, for they will serve our sovereign faithfully. Perhaps when you observe them, some of you will wish to serve truly and faithfully, and the sovereign will reward these men with his great favor, with estates and patrimonies, and whosoever wishes to go, he will order sent back to Moscow." Lugovskoy answered to this: "We must ask God and King Sigismund that Christian blood cease to be shed and the realm be pacified. We were sent to his majesty not to promote our own interests, or to present petitions on our own behalf, but for the sake of the entire Muscovite realm."

Sapieha broke off the discussion, went to the king, but ordered Lugovskoy to wait. Coming back from the king, he took Tomilo into a separate room and spoke with him privately. "I wish you all the best, only listen to me and serve the sovereign with upright service and his majesty will reward you with all that you can desire. I, relying upon you, have assured the sovereign that you will obey him. The inhabitants of Smolensk demand that you, the ambassadors, send to them one of your number so they might ask what they should do. They will listen to you, and will fulfill the sovereign's will. So Vasily Sukin is ready, and is awaiting you. Go with him to Smolensk, and say to the inhabitants that they should kiss the cross to the king and the prince, or allow the king's men into Smolensk."

Lugovskoy answered: "I cannot in any way do this. Metropolitan Filaret and Boyar Prince Vasily Vasilievich Golitsyn and their companions were sent from the patriarch, boyars and all the people of the

Muscovite realm, and I can do nothing without consulting them, nor can I contemplate doing anything. How can I do this and bring down an everlasting curse upon myself? Not only would the Lord God and the people of the Muscovite realm not suffer this from me, neither will the earth bear me up. I was sent among the petitioners on behalf of the Muscovite realm, and am I the first to be led into temptation? According to the word of Christ, it were better if a stone were tied to me and I were cast into the sea. There will be no profit to the cause of the realm in this. I know for certain that many people better than I have gone to Smolensk and spoken of the king's grace, but these people were not heeded; if therefore we go now and it is evident that we are lying, the inhabitants of Smolensk henceforth will be all the more obstinate, and will not heed anyone. We must all meet with them openly, and not below the walls under guard. This they already know."

Sapieha continued as before: "Just go and declare yourself to him, and let Sukin do the talking. Go, do not be obstinate, and seek the king's favor for yourself." Lugovskoy answered: "I should be glad of the king's favor, and am prepared to serve the sovereign insofar as I am able; but for what I cannot do, let not his majesty the king lay his disfavor upon me. For what I cannot do is to go before the city on my own initiative. Indeed it is improper even for Sukin to go, nor will God disregard this action of his." With this the interview ended. Sapieha went to see the king while Lugovskoy returned to his headquarters in the encampment and related everything to the senior ambassadors.

The next day Filaret and Golitsyn summoned Sukin, Sydavnoy and the archimandrite of the Savior monastery, telling them that they should be mindful of God and their souls, and remember that they had been sent from the shrine of the Immaculate Mother of God and with the blessing of the patriarch. Sukin and his companions answered: "The king has sent us with his papers to Moscow for his own royal business, so how can we not go?" These people were speaking honestly, but even so Cellarer Palitsyn was dissimulating. He did not wish to explain himself to the metropolitan on matters which might embarrass him and did not attend him, pleading sickness which, however, did not prevent him from setting out for Moscow.

Accordingly forty-three men were left in the ambassadors' encampment. Zakhar Liapunov also left the ambassadors, although he did not proceed to Moscow, but went over to the Polish encampment. He daily feasted with the Polish lords, amused them with jests concerning the ambassadors, and asserted that the senior ambassadors were acting independently, were not consulting with the gentry, but were concealing everything from them. In these last words we see why Liapunov left the ambassadors. Filaret and Golitsyn declared to the Polish lords that the arrival of Sukin and his companions would give rise to unrest and the collapse of the whole enterprise. But the enterprise collapsed even without this.

SALTYKOV AND ANDRONOV AID THE KING IN MOSCOW

We have seen how it was that the boyars and wealthier people in general were fearful of the brigand and his followers, and strongly supported Wladyslaw, and at their behest the Poles were admitted into Moscow. Particularly conspicuous for his devotion to Wladyslaw was the first-ranking boyar, Prince Fedor Ivanovich Mstislavsky. As early as August 1610 Sigismund sent to Mstislavsky and his companions a letter of commendation which specifically referred to Mstislavsky's long-standing devotion to the king and the prince. "The boyars and councillors spoke concerning your previous zeal and goodwill. We and our son will call to mind your amity and zeal for us before all the people, according to your lineage and dignity, higher than that of all your brother boyars."

Mstislavsky was not ashamed to accept the rank of master of the horse[18] from the Smolensk encampment. Another boyar, Fedor Ivanovich Sheremetev,[19] wrote an obsequious letter to Leo Sapieha, requesting his favor. He did obeisance to the king and the prince concerning his small patrimonial hamlet. On September 21 [New Style], 1610 Sigismund sent the boyars a document in which he ordered that Mikhail Saltykov and his companions be rewarded as the first to arrive from Tushino to swear allegiance to him. The reward consisted in restoring the moveable and immoveable property confiscated by Shuisky into the treasury for treason. In this document there is not a word concerning the prince. Sigismund explicitly states that Saltykov and his companions had come "to our royal majesty, began to serve first of all, and did obeisance to us, that we should reward them, our faithful subjects, for their loyal service to us." Mikhail Glebovich was given the district of Charonda (which previously belonged to Dmitry Godunov and then to Prince Skopin), the district of Totma and, in the district of Kostroma, Krasnoe Selo and Reshma. To Saltykov's son, Ivan Mikhailovich, was given the Vaga district, which formerly belonged to Boris Godunov and later to Dmitry Shuisky.[20]

Many petitioners went in person to the king at the Smolensk encampment. Many documents and charters issued by Sigismund have come down to us, grants to various people concerning estates, titles and appointments. Everywhere expressions such as "our boyars" or "we have ordered" are used. Among the petitioners was Tsaritsa Martha, concerning whom the king wrote to the boyars: "There also arrived our nun Martha, consort of the great sovereign Ivan Vasilievich, of blessed memory, presenting her petition to the effect that Vasily Shuisky, whilst occupying the great sovereign dignity of Moscow, had plundered her, had taken away that which the great sovereign Ivan Vasilievich had granted her, and ordered her to be fed with meagre rations from the palace. Those people who dwell with her are given no allowance of money or grain, she is in everything impoverished and in debt. You should order an allowance be given her and her people, according to what is customarily allowed to ladies of the ruling family who have entered the religious life."

There also emerged all those who had been disgraced during the previous reign. Vasily Yakovlevich Shchelkalov[21] requested a charter for his service estate and patrimony. Afanasy Vlasiev did obeisance, requesting that he be given back his house and his possessions, which had been taken away by Shuisky.[22] Archpriest Terenty, who is well known to us, requested that he be reinstated in the Annunciation cathedral.[23]

But the documents issued in the name of the king were addressed only to Moscow; letters to the other towns were written in the name of Wladyslaw. Thus the Muscovite provisional government, the boyar council, tacitly recognized Sigismund as ruler, pending Wladyslaw's arrival. In all probability the boyars, or at least the majority of them, went no further than this. But this did not satisfy Mikhail Glebovich Saltykov, who was working with the direct purpose that not Wladyslaw, but Sigismund, be proclaimed tsar.

But Saltykov did not amount to much and therefore in the Smolensk encampment it was recognized that it would be advantageous to acknowledge the services of another species of people, namely those Tushinites prepared to do anything to raise themselves above the common herd. They, in concluding a treaty before Smolensk, announced that a future government would elevate people of lowly birth according to their deserts. At the forefront of these people, by reason of his abilities and energy, was Fedor Andronov, of whom it was known only that he was a merchant tanner who had attracted the attention of Godunov (through sorcery, as

Andronov's enemies asserted) and was transferred from Pogoreloe Gorodishche to Moscow. Then, during the Troubles, we see him at Tushino
and before Smolensk. Here he was able to ingratiate himself with the king
or his advisers to such an extent that Sigismund sent him to Moscow with
the title of conciliar noble, although there is reason to think that he had
acquired this title even in Tushino.

At the end of October 1610 the king wrote to the boyars: "Fedor
Andronov has served us and our son truly and faithfully, and has served
us to this moment. Now we wish to reward him for this service, and order
you to command him that he be among the associates of our Treasurer
Vasily Petrovich Golovin." Andronov continued to serve the king truly
and faithfully. He fulfilled every command of Gasiewski without question,
if indeed he had not anticipated them. The best articles from the tsar's
treasury were and sent to the king, although several of these Gasiewski
took for himself. For example, Gasiewski ordered the boyars to take an
inventory of the treasury and affix their seals to it, but when later the boyars
visited the treasury they found not their seals but the seal of Andronov,
and asked him what this meant. Andronov replied that Gasiewski had
ordered the seals to be broken. According to the Poles there were in the
treasury images cast in gold of the Savior and the Twelve Apostles. The
latter had been melted by Shuisky for coin to pay the Swedish mercenaries. For Gasiewski's Poles there remained only the image of the Savior,
valued at thirty thousand gold pieces. Some wished to send it to the
Catholic church in Cracow, but the greed of the majority prevailed and
the sacred image was broken into pieces.

Andronov was not content with the duties of treasurer; he wanted to
render other services to the king. On his arrival in Moscow he wrote to
Leo Sapieha, excusing Zolkiewski for having conceded the demands of
the Muscovites. "If you had not drawn up the treaties according to their
wishes," wrote Andronov, "naturally it would have been necessary to have
obtained your objective by fire and sword. The lord hetman judged that
for the present it was better to accept their tricks but that when we take
them into our hands these tricks will avail them little. We trust in God
that in time their tricks all will come to naught, and their designs will be
diverted to the right course." Andronov wrote of the necessity of keeping
in the vicinity of Moscow a detachment of Polish troops, of whom not
a single man must be permitted to leave the encampment and all held
instantly ready in the event of an uprising, while the servants of the king's

grace, Andronov and his companions, would keep several thousand musketeers and cossacks at hand. Andronov also proposed to expel from the chancelleries people remaining from the previous reigns, the "clients" of Shuisky as he called them, and give their positions to people devoted to the king. He wrote: "A decree immediately must be sent about what to do with those who were here during Shuisky's reign, and were even more incompetent than Shuisky himself."

A list of these people, probably compiled by Andronov himself, has survived in fragments. Several references are interesting. For example: "Crown Secretary Grigory Elizarov held an appointment in the Chancellery for Novgorod. He is a heretic, and heretics were assigned to him (let us not forget that Andronov himself had been accused of necromancy); Crown Secretary Smolianin had been a junior boyar; Mikhailo Begichev's appointment was given to him for having acted as an informer; the crown secretaries, Filipp and Anfinogen Fedorov, sons of Golenishchev, are evil gossips."

Andronov's wishes were fulfilled. His companions from the Tushino and Smolensk encampments were appointed to the chancelleries. Stepan Solovetsky was appointed to the Chancellery for Novgorod, Vasily Yuriev to the Chancellery of Crown Revenues, Evdoky Vitovtov was appointed to the foremost ranks of the conciliar secretaries, Ivan Gramotin was appointed keeper of the seal and secretary to the Chancellery of Foreign Affairs, as well as crown secretary in the Chancellery of Military Tenures. In the Chancellery for Crown Revenues, Prince Fedor Meshchersky was appointed. Prince Yury Khvorostinin was appointed to the Chancellery of Artillery, while Mikhail Molchanov was appointed to the special chancellery dealing with relations with the Polish lords. Ivan Saltykov was appointed to the Chancellery for Kazan.[24]

The boyars were greatly insulted when they saw in their company in the council the tradesman Andronov with the high-sounding title of treasurer. They considered it a particular dishonor that this common tradesman dared to debate with Mstislavsky and Vorotynsky, was in full command, and enjoyed the complete confidence of the king and Gasiewski inasmuch as he acted openly and agitated to for Sigismund as tsar, whereas the boyars were wavering or were holding to Wladyslaw.

Gasiewski, together with the people who had sworn allegiance to the king, was in complete charge. At council meetings he received numerous petitions. He referred them to the boyars, who did not see them, because at Gasiewski's side sat Mikhail Saltykov, Prince Vasily Mosalsky, Fedor Andronov and Ivan Gramotin. The boyars did not hear what he said to these personal counsellors. All resolutions and petitions were signed by Gramotin, Vitovtov, Chicherin and Solovetsky because all senior conciliar secretaries had been dismissed. Whereas the senior boyars were angry because they were jealously guarding their rank, Golitsyn and Vorotynsky were angry because the king slighted them, placing next to them in council the common tradesman Andronov.

Saltykov was the more angry at Andronov because he felt his service record entitled him to the principal role, yet he must share the perquisites of service with a common tradesman. Conflict and rivalry immediately broke out between these individuals. Andronov wrote to Sapieha: "Good care must be taken, lord hetman, that estates not be granted without consultation, because both the lord hetman and Ivan Saltykov issue charters granting estates. Previously it was the practice that they were issued at the single office designated by the sovereign. Now I fear lest everyone be given a rich reward for a trifling service. I appeal, as I am accustomed to do, to your generosity (since none of my petitions have been denied), and ask that you be so kind, your grace, to ask of his majesty the king that he grant me the small village of Ramenie and the small village of Shubino in the province of Zubtsov, which had been given to Zarutsky."

Saltykov also wrote to Sapieha: "I am pleased to serve and direct matters, and lead many people to support his royal majesty. May all traitors be driven from his presence! Nevertheless the governor of Velizh, Aleksandr Ivanovich Gasiewski, listens to them and inclines unto them, dishonors me and does not allow me to conduct my business. He accepts everything according to their decisions and at his own responsibility, without regard to Muscovite custom. The Muscovite people are insulted greatly that the king's grace has altered grants and offended many people through persecution and ruin thanks to the common tradesman Fedor Andronov, and has taken authority from Mstislavsky and his companions, and from us, and has placed governance and trust in such a person. There were similar favorites under Shuisky, namely the Izmailovs and such a commoner as Mikhailka Smyvalov, on whose account hitherto much blood has flowed. And now, given these counsellors and regents, not one town shall be subject to Moscow unless they are removed. What does such a person know about government? His father traded in sandals in Pogoreloe Gorodishche, and he was brought from Pogoreloe to Moscow at the order of Boris Godunov for his sorcery and heresy, and was a common tradesman in Moscow. Have pity upon us, Leo Ivanovich! Do not let the Muscovite realm be lost to the king. Send someone trustworthy, and order them to oversee the activities of these men. Much of the treasury is in arrears in that Andronov frequently intervenes and excuses people from torture in exchange for promises. Others not subject to his jurisdiction he forcibly brings before him for trial yet fails to pay the sovereign's money into the treasury."

Saltykov accused Andronov of arbitrariness, and people were found (probably including Andronov himself) who accused Saltykov of the same. The accusation was that allegedly Saltykov called himself governor or regent in Moscow, conducted business without decisions by the boyars, expelled some and rewarded others, spoke disrespectful words to the boyars, namely that the sovereign had granted him full responsibility in all matters and had ordered them to obey him. Saltykov, in his letter to Sapieha, denied these charges and cited Prince Mstislavsky, the boyars and many others.

They in turn reported to the king that the rich districts given to Saltykov (Vaga, Charonda, Totma and Reshma, the revenues of which alone amounted to sixty thousand rubles) caused envy and murmuring among the boyars and the people. Saltykov replied that these districts belonged of old to his brothers, and that the revenues from them did not exceed three thousand. "And I, sovereign, and Leo Ivanovich! I went to the sovereign king, leaving my wife, children and possessions, valued at above sixty thousand rubles, relying upon the sovereign's favor and upon your solicitude in your capacity as a senator. I and my son Ivan served and were devoted to the king and the prince, and you, the great senators, and the great realm of the Polish crown and Grand Principality of Lithuania, and everywhere spoke up on your behalf, expecting favor for myself. God has entrusted the Muscovite and Novgorod realms to the sovereigns, the king and the prince, by their sovereign fortune, your senatorial diligence and our humble services; but others accompanied me to the sovereign, and they were given towns with provinces, not merely districts, yet our own family is of senatorial rank."

Concerning his actions in favor of Sigismund in Moscow, Saltykov wrote to Sapieha: "I wrote to incline the boyars and all the people of Moscow to you, that the sovereign king should come to Moscow, that he would obtain much glory if he were to pursue the brigand at Kaluga. Now

I have persuaded the boyars and the people of Moscow to send Prince Mosalsky to petition the king to purge his son's realm and attack the Kaluga brigand. Thus the king should proceed without delay and earn glory by moving against the brigand at Kaluga. As soon as the king is in Mozhaisk, please write to me immediately, and I will persuade the boyars and all the people of Moscow to petition the king to purge his son's realm and attack the brigand. The king should come to Moscow immediately and without delay, for much dissension is arising in Moscow on account of the brigand, and people are tempted to join him. Why does the king remain outside Smolensk? If the king is in Moscow, Smolensk in any case will be his." In another document to the same Leo Sapieha, Saltykov wrote: "Here in Moscow many people hate me because I favor the king and the prince in many matters."

Saltykov was writing the truth. At the time of Zolkiewski's departure unrest began among the inhabitants of Moscow. "We spent several weeks," says one Polish eyewitness, "in mutual distrustfulness, with friendship in words, but stone in our bosoms. We indulged each other in feasts, but our thoughts were otherwise. We observed the utmost caution. We placed a guard day and night upon the gates and intersections. In order to forestall evil, at the advice of the boyars who were well-disposed towards us Gasiewski deployed throughout the towns eighteen thousand musketeers under the pretext of protecting those places against the Swedes, but really for our own security. Through these measures we weakened the power of the enemy. The Muscovites were tiring of us but simply did not know how to get rid of us and, plotting mischief, frequently raised the alarm so that two, three or four times a day we had to mount up, and hardly ever could unsaddle our horses."

On November 21, 1610 Sigismund informed the boyars that first he must destroy the Kaluga brigand and his supporters, bring out the Poles and Lithuanians, liberate the towns and, thus having pacified the Muscovite realm, meet with the Sejm and decide the fate of Wladyslaw. The king in this missive included Smolensk in the list of towns supporting the brigand, and for this reason wrote: "Until the inhabitants of Smolensk swear allegiance to us it is not our pleasure to withdraw, nor is it safe for the Muscovite realm."

On November 30 Saltykov and Andronov, coming at eventide to the patriarch, asked him to bless the people for swearing allegiance to the king. So says a letter from Kazan to Khlynov; it adds that the next day

Mstislavsky came concerning the same matter but that the patriarch would not grant his request, and that a quarrel with the patriarch began, for they wished to stab the patriarch, who then sent around the hundreds to the leading merchants and trading people, summoning them to the cathedral church. The leading merchants, traders and the populace, arrived at the Dormition cathedral, refused to kiss the cross to the king despite the fact that hordes of armed Poles stood around the cathedral.

We cannot rely entirely upon the foregoing information since it was written by the inhabitants of Kazan, who wished to justify their own oath of allegiance to False Dmitry. Nowhere is it evident that Saltykov thought it possible or useful to bring matters so bluntly to a head, and directly demand an oath of allegiance to the king. Taking into consideration the designs of Saltykov as expressed in his letters to Sapieha, we may surmise that he, together with Mstislavsky, went to Hermogen to ask his consent to their inviting the king to Moscow, and the patriarch did not agree.

Whatever the case, the people clearly saw that Wladyslaw's cause was going badly whereas the movement in favor of the brigand was gaining momentum. The priest Khariton was arrested while journeying to Kaluga in the name of the inhabitants of Moscow to summon the pretender to the capital, and when first interrogated accused the following princes of having relations with the brigand: Vasily and Andrei Vasilievich Golitsyn, Ivan Mikhailovich Vorotynsky and Zasekin. On being interrogated a second time, he exculpated Prince Andrei Golitsyn, saying that he had not corresponded with the brigand.

Nevertheless Golitsyn was placed under arrest along with Vorotynsky and Zasekin because he had provoked the hatred of the Poles. Once, when Gasiewski was seated in the council with the boyars, and the noble Rzhevsky appeared there with the announcement that the king had granted him the rank of lord-in-waiting, Golitsyn addressed the following words to Gasiewski: "Your Polish lordships! We are suffering many wrongs at your hands. We have accepted the prince as our sovereign, but you do not give him to us. Letters are written to us, not in his name, but in the name of the king, and rewards are distributed under the royal title, as you can see. People of humble birth are made equal to us, who are highly born. Either cease to deal with us in this manner, or release us from our oath of allegiance, and we will look out for ourselves." The Khariton affair, and the news that Ivan Pleshcheev wished to attack the Poles in Moscow, gave Gasiewski an excuse to admit foreign mercenaries into the Kremlin and to take complete charge.

Matters in the northwest were going badly for the Poles and their supporters. Ivan, the son of Mikhail Saltykov, was sent with an army to
Novgorod to protect it from the Swedes and brigands. Saltykov, calling
himself a subject of the king, reported to his sovereign Sigismund that on
the road to Novgorod he had sent to its inhabitants a missive urging them
to kiss the cross to Prince Wladyslaw, not to secede from the Muscovite
realm, and serve and render everything in favor of the great sovereign.
The inhabitants of Novgorod answered that they had sent to Moscow to
find out about the real oath of allegiance and to bring back a copy of the
confirmatory charter, and that on the return of their emissaries they, the
inhabitants of Novgorod, would kiss the cross to Wladyslaw, but until
then they would not allow Saltykov into the city because other towns
which had sworn allegiance to Wladyslaw had admitted Poles, Lithuanians and Cherkassians who had beaten, robbed and burned out the better
people.

At the same time Saltykov learned that letters were being sent from
Pskov to Novgorod urging that it would be better to submit to the Kaluga
tsarlet rather than an infidel Pole, and that many of the inhabitants of
Novgorod were swayed by this argument. Thus Saltykov sent one letter
after another to Moscow urging that the boyars immediately release the
Novgorod emissaries in order to prevent disturbances in favor of the brigand. Finally these emissaries returned, but even then the inhabitants
allowed Saltykov entry only after they had extracted an oath that he would
enter the town accompanied only by Russians, and would not allow any
Lithuanians into the city. Saltykov administered to the inhabitants of
Novgorod the oath of allegiance to Wladyslaw, and sent documents to the
surrounding towns urging them to follow the example of Novgorod, and
not secede from the Muscovite realm. The inhabitants of Toropets obeyed
but promptly informed Saltykov that, notwithstanding their oath of allegiance to Wladyslaw, Lithuanians were devastating their countryside,
torturing, beating and leading people off into captivity. Seeing this, other
towns decided not to kiss the cross to the Pole, and declared a state of siege.
Saltykov, in the name of the nobles and junior boyars, petitioned Sigismund to control his subjects, as if the king had any means at his disposal
to do so.

KAZAN AND VIATKA SWEAR ALLEGIANCE TO THE PRETENDER
Matters were going even worse for Wladyslaw in the east. Here Kazan
openly swore allegiance to the pretender, and its example was followed

by Viatka. The chronicle says that when the inhabitants of Kazan agreed to kiss the cross to False Dmitry the deputy governor, the well-known Bogdan Belsky, was opposed, and for this reason was killed.[25] But the documents sent out from Kazan were issued in the names of the governors, Morozov and Belsky. Nevertheless Belsky could have declared his opposition after the documents were sent out, and have been killed for this reason. Along with the documents were distributed copies of the oath of allegiance according to which the inhabitants of Kazan had kissed the cross. Those who pledged allegiance must swear "that we will not obey any orders coming from the Lithuanians, and will not enter into any correspondence with them, but will resist them and fight them to the death. We will not admit any Don, Terek or Yaik cossacks, or musketeers from Archangel into the city in large numbers, nor will we obey their orders, but we will admit cossacks in small numbers for the purposes of trade, twenty or thirty at a time, but not allow them to remain in the city for very long."

These words are very puzzling. The inhabitants of Kazan swear allegiance to False Dmitry, for they see that Moscow is being occupied by the Poles, but at the very same time they do not want the cossacks. This is a sinister portent for the pretenders, the cossack tsars, signifying that Kazan's involuntary loyalty will be shortlived. The answer of Perm to the urging of the inhabitants of Viatka, that they recognize Dmitry, was that, as they stated in their rescript, they had received the documents and sent them throughout the towns, but there is not a word about any desire on their part to swear allegiance to Dmitry. They wrote merely: "We are glad to be at one with you and resist the plunderers for the sake of the Orthodox Christian faith. And you, gentlemen, should be in counsel with us as before, and send us traders and others from Viatka with merchandise, grain, meat and all kinds of goods, and we will visit you as before with our goods. And henceforth whatever news we have we will write and send you. And you, gentlemen, whatever news you hear from anywhere at all, write it down and send it to us." Thus the inhabitants of Perm remained constant in their former cautious attitude, prepared to correspond with their neighbors concerning matters to their advantage but not oaths of allegiance.

DEATH OF THE PRETENDER

But the towns were corresponding with one another about swearing allegiance to False Dmitry when he was no longer among the living. When he was forced to flee the Moscow area to Kaluga because of Zolkiewski, among those who deserted him in favor of Wladyslaw was the Kasimov tsar. Then the old Tatar begged the hetman that he might go to Kaluga to visit his son, who had remained with the brigand, and promised to bring his son back with him. But the moment the old tsar appeared in Kaluga he was drowned on False Dmitry's orders. Then the baptized Tatar Peter Urusov, commander of False Dmitry's Tatar bodyguard, swore to avenge the tsar's death.

On December 11 they invited the pretender outside the town to hunt hares. They killed him and fled to the steppe. The pretender's inseparable companion, the jester Koshelev, who witnessed his master's death, rushed with news of it to Kaluga. Marina, who had reached the last days of her pregnancy, in desperation rushed about the town crying out for vengeance, but there was nobody on whom to take revenge since the assassins were far away. About two hundred Tatars remained in Kaluga. The cossacks threw themselves upon them, hunted them like hares, killed the richer murzas and plundered their houses.

Zarutsky wished to flee but was seized by the populace and not allowed to leave. Prince Grigory Shakhovskoy asked the commune that he be allowed to proceed to Moscow with their submission but they did not trust him and refused. Then, when Marina gave birth to her son Ivan they proclaimed him as their tsarevich. But in the context of the Troubles a newborn infant was a poor leader and inhabitants of Kaluga were obliged to comply with the demand of the Muscovite government and kiss the cross to Wladyslaw. Nevertheless at first they replied that they would swear allegiance only when the prince was in Moscow and had accepted the Orthodox faith. But then they unconditionally received Prince Yury Trubetskoy and all the town kissed the cross.

END OF THE INTERREGNUM
1610–1613

MOVEMENT AGAINST THE POLES

The death of the brigand was the second cardinal event in the history of the Time of Troubles if we consider the first to be Sigismund's incursion into the Muscovite realm. Now, with the death of the pretender, the king and his Muscovite supporters had no pretext for further movement by Sigismund into Russian territories, nor was there any further excuse for remaining outside Smolensk. The more substantial people, who had agreed to recognize Wladyslaw as tsar in fear of being subject to the cossack tsar now were liberated from that fear and might act more freely against the Poles.

As soon as it was known in Moscow that the brigand had been killed then, in the words of a contemporary account, the Russian people rejoiced, saying to one another that the people must unite to resist the Lithuanians so that they departed the Muscovite land, and on this they kissed the cross. Saltykov and Andronov wrote to Sigismund that the patriarch was summoning many different people openly, saying that were the prince not baptized into the Christian faith and all Lithuanians did not leave the Muscovite land the prince would not be our sovereign.[1] The patriarch wrote the very same words in letters to many towns; and the people of the towns and of every station, great and small, received them and wished to rise up.

LIAPUNOV'S UPRISING

But even here, amid the general readiness to rise against the Poles, the first to move was Liapunov. Until the death of the brigand, Prokopy had been loyal to Wladyslaw. In October he had captured Pronsk from the pretender in the name of the prince. But in January 1611 the Muscovite boyars wrote to Sigismund concerning Liapunov's uprising in Riazan, saying that Zarutsky was acting in concert with him, and was advancing upon Tula with his cossacks. The boyars demanded that the king arrest

Zakhar Liapunov, who was at that time with him outside Smolensk, and was in correspondence with his brother.[2]

CORRESPONDENCE BETWEEN TOWNS

Once again the towns corresponded with each other, but this time their letters were of quite a different nature. Earlier they persuaded each other to wait, not to hasten to swear allegiance to the man who called himself Dmitry, since his supporters were plundering in the towns which had sworn allegiance. But now this reason existed no longer. The towns exhorted one another to stand up for the Orthodox faith, to arm against the Poles who threatened its destruction.

The first to raise their voices were the inhabitants of the district around Smolensk, which was being occupied and plundered by the Poles. They wrote many letters to their brethren, the other inhabitants of the Muscovite realm, but for them this brotherhood was national nor political, but religious. "We are brothers and kinsmen because we were begotten at the sacred font by holy baptism."[3] The people of the Smolensk region wrote that they had submitted to the Poles in order not to depart from Orthodox Christianity and not to suffer utter ruin, but even so this they had suffered. "Where are our leaders?" the Smolensk countrymen wrote. "Where are our wives and children, brothers, kinsmen and friends? Who among us went to Lithuania or Poland to ransom our mothers, wives and children, and lost their lives? The ransom was collected in the name of Christ, yet all of this was plundered! If any of you wishes to die a Christian there arises a great cause for your souls and lives, that we all may be Christians in unity. Doubtless you think that you can live in peace and tranquillity? We did not resist, we entrusted our lives, yet we all perished and entered eternal travail by reason of Latinism. If you do not unite now, in common with the whole land, you will weep bitterly and sigh with inconsolable, everlasting grief. The Christian faith will be replaced by Latinism, the churches of God will be ruined in all their beauty, and your Christian race will be slain by a savage death, your mothers, wives and children will be enslaved, dishonored and led off into captivity." The Smolensk inhabitants also wrote that they had lost all hope of ever having Wladyslaw as tsar for the Sejm had resolved "to deport the better people, lay waste the entire land, and rule over all the Muscovite land."[4]

The people of Moscow, receiving this document, sent it to the various towns, adding their own hortatory epistle, in which they wrote: "We,

Orthodox Christians, write to you, to all the peoples of the Muscovite realm, to our lord brethren, Orthodox Christians. Our brothers write to us that we, all the remaining Orthodox Christians, must not perish at the hands of the foes of Orthodox Christendom, the Lithuanians. For the sake of God, the judge of the quick and the dead, do not despise our poor and tearful sighing, be united with us against our common foe. Be mindful of one thing: only if the root and foundation is strong will the tree be immovable. If there is no root, how shall anything hold together?"[5]

By these words the inhabitants of Moscow wished to emphasize the importance of their city, the root of the realm, but even they, true to the dominant interest of the time, hastened to demonstrate the significance of Moscow from a religious point of view: "Here is the image of the Mother of God, the eternal defender of Christians, painted by Luke the Evangelist.[6] Here are the great illuminators and defenders, Peter, Alexis and Jonas the miracle-workers.[7] Or is all this in vain for you, Orthodox Christians? Our brethren wrote us the truth, and now we see the Christian faith being changed to Latinism and the churches of God ruined. Need we write much concerning our own lives? For here among us the most holy Patriarch Hermogen is steadfast, as a true pastor, unfailingly offering his life for the Christian faith, and all Orthodox Christians are following him, only they do not openly declare themselves."[8]

The inhabitants of other regions did openly declare themselves. At the beginning of January 1611 Nizhny Novgorod sent to Moscow to find out what was going on there. The emissaries visited with the patriarch, received from him his blessing for an uprising, but did not bring any documents from him, as the patriarch had no opportunity to write. The secretaries, clerks and all the people of his household had been removed, and his palace plundered. Previously the inhabitants of Nizhny Novgorod had urged those of Balakhna to remain faithful to the tsar in Moscow, and not engage in internecine disputes over the various claimants to the throne. But now there was no tsar in Moscow, his place was held by the patriarch, the custodian of the faith, and the patriarch was calling for an uprising.

Nizhny Novgorod deferred to him. Together with the inhabitants of Balakhna they swore to defend the Muscovite realm, and called upon the other towns to be mindful of God, the Immaculate Mother of God and the Muscovite miracle-workers, and to stand together as one with them. The inhabitants of Nizhny Novgorod also sent a letter to Riazan. Liapunov answered them: "We, my lords, know this for sure, that in Moscow our most holy Patriarch Hermogen, all the Holy Synod and the people marked by Christ have suffered great persecution and oppression from their own apostates and from the Poles and Lithuanians. For a long time we have renounced the Moscow boyars, and have written to them that they, tempted by the glory of this world, have denied God, have thrown in their lot with hard-hearted westerners, and turned against their own flock. Nor have they achieved anything by the words of the treaty or by the oath on which the hetman kissed the cross to them."

The insurgent Russian people even now did not refuse their allegiance to Wladyslaw, but swore "to defend the Orthodox faith and the Muscovite realm, not to kiss the cross to the Polish king, not to serve or favor him, to clear the Muscovite realm of all Poles or Lithuanians, and fight unfalteringly against the king, the prince, the Poles and Lithuanians and against whomsoever shall stand with them against the Muscovite realm; in no wise to correspond with the king, the Poles and the Russian people who favor the king; not to begin any internecine strife among ourselves. And whomsoever God gives us as sovereign over the Muscovite realm and the lands of the Muscovite tsardom, him will we serve and favor and wish well in all faithfulness by this our oath. And if the boyars send from Moscow concerning anyone, that we should arrest him and send him to Moscow or any town whatsoever, or inflict any penalty or execution upon him, we will stand together unanimously and defend these people, and will not surrender them until God has granted us a sovereign over the Muscovite realm. And if the king does not yield us his son to rule the Muscovite realm, and does not withdraw the Poles and Lithuanians from Moscow and all the Muscovite and Ukrainian towns, and does not retire from Smolensk and withdraw his soldiers, we will fight to the death."

The inhabitants of Yaroslavl, in their missive to Kazan, refer to the bravery of Patriarch Hermogen as a miracle whereby God manifested His will to the Russian people, and called upon everyone to follow this divine portent. "The unexpected has come to pass. The most holy Patriarch Hermogen has defended the Orthodox faith unwaveringly and, not fearing death, summoning all Orthodox Christians, has spoken and exhorted them and, ordering them all to defend and die for the Orthodox faith, accused the heretics before all the people. If he had not been sent by God, to what pass things would have come, and who would have begun to resist? The heretics not only trampled the faith underfoot, but even vaunted the fact to everyone, and nobody dared say a word in fear of the many of

Lithuanians and Russian malefactors who, renouncing God, had become their allies. But the patriarch sent his command to the towns to defend the Orthodox faith, saying that whosoever died would be new martyrs. Hearing this from the patriarch, and seeing with their own eyes, the towns corresponded with each other and marched upon Moscow."[9]

At this time when dreadful hardship had overtaken the Russian land three men, according to the words of the people of Yaroslavl, the consoled an insulted people: Patriarch Hermogen, Archbishop Sergius of Smolensk and Governor Shein. The inhabitants of Yaroslavl made it known that they had sent three detachments towards Moscow, that the inhabitants of the towns had met the soldiers with icons and had given them provisions. There was a strong movement in the towns. The soldiers recruited to clear the realm visited the monasteries and the cathedral churches, with weeping attended services for deliverance from the present humiliation and, receiving blessings from the clergy, left the town accompanied by salvoes from cannon and small arms, so that the campaign mightbe made known to the inhabitants of the neighboring towns.

When governor Ivan Ivanovich Volynsky moved out of Yaroslavl with his troops his kinsman, another Volynsky, stayed in the town with the older gentry "to conduct all business, recruit servicemen for the campaign, and to write to the towns. They all signed a strict pledge that if anybody did not go, or returned without leave, he would be shown no mercy. This resolution was drawn up in all the other towns.

Where towns had not renounced completely their allegiance to Wladyslaw the clergy spoke the most decisively. Abbot Anthony of the Solovetsk monastery wrote to the Swedish king, Karl IX: "By the mercy of God, in the Muscovite realm the most holy patriarch, the boyars and all the people from all the towns are corresponding, are gathering for a council in Moscow, are taking counsel, and with one mind are resisting the Lithuanians, wishing to choose for the Muscovite realm a tsar from among the native boyars, whom God wishes, neither do we wish for anyone from another land with an alien faith. We are unanimous here in the Solovetsk monastery, in the Suma fortress[10] and throughout the seaboard region, that we want no one of alien faith upon the Muscovite throne as tsar, other than one of our own native Muscovite boyars."[11]

The inhabitants of Perm also rose up, having been inactive up to this point, when the struggle was between such contenders for the throne as Dmitry, Shuisky and Wladyslaw. But now they moved their detachments, after the patriarch had blessed the uprising against the blasphemous Lithuanians. The inhabitants of Perm knew of only one patriarch, and they received a missive from him concerning the uprising, and to him they sent a list with the names of their soldiers.[12] The inhabitants of Great Novgorod also rose up and, through the blessing of Isidore their metropolitan, swore to aid the Muscovite realm against the despoilers of the Orthodox faith,[13] and to resist them with one mind. Having sworn this, Novgorod imprisoned the governors appointed by Wladyslaw, namely Saltykov and Kornilo Choglokov, for their innumerable injustices and dishonesty.[14]

FAILURE OF THE FIRST MILITIA

Despite general inspiration and enthusiasm for liberation of the realm from foes of an alien faith, the undertaking could not succeed for two reasons. First, at the head of this enterprise stood Liapunov, a passionate man, who was far too self-centered to sacrifice his personal ambitions for the sake of the common cause. According to the standards of that time a man of humble origin, pushed forward from the crowd by the upheavals of this turbulent time, striving passionately for leadership, Liapunov hated the people who held him back, who relied upon ancient custom and wished to preserve their standing. At a time when the towns were urging each other to rise against the enemies of the faith, Liapunov alone did not restrain himself, and in his missive launched an attack upon the boyars. Having lately become the leader of the militia force, he not only refused to make concessions to people of birth and rank but derived particular satisfaction from humiliating them, exalting himself before them through his new position, and thereby caused indignation, enmity and unrest.

The second, even more important reason for the failure of the movement was that Liapunov, long unscrupulous as to means, in the uprising of the land to liberate the realm and establish of order, extended his hand— to whom? To the enemies of all order, the people who throve on unrest, namely the cossacks! He was joined by cossacks under the command of Zarutsky, Prosovetsky and Prince Dmitry Timofeevich Trubetskoy, all of them Tushino boyars and commanders. It is said that Liapunov deceived Zarutsky with the understanding that, after the Poles had been expelled, they would proclaim as tsar the son of Marina, with whom Zarutsky already was involved. Worse still Sapieha, who had shed so much Russian blood, who had fought so long against the Trinity monastery, declared his desire to fight for the Orthodox faith against his own Polish countrymen, and Liapunov accepted his offer!

This is what Sapieha wrote to Prince Trubetskoy, governor of Kaluga: "We have written to you (my lord!) many times in Kaluga for advice, but you avoid and deride us. We have done you no evil, neither do we wish to do any in the future. We have expressed our wish to sacrifice our lives for your Christian faith and for fame in your service, so you ought to consult with us and tell us your intentions. Know through us that we are free people, we do not serve the king or the prince, we stand by our service, and intend no harm to you, neither do we wish for any reward from you, for whosoever is tsar in Moscow will reward our services. Therefore you ought to take us into your confidence and communicate with us as soon as possible and tell us your intention, and we will offer no objection to you, but will defend with you the Orthodox Christian faith and the holy churches, and will sacrifice our lives in your service. We are told that in Kaluga certain idle persons are spreading the rumor that we are destroying the holy churches and forbid services to be sung, and stable our horses in them, but you will not find such things in all our cavalry. These idlers are lying to you, they are sowing dissension between us. Of our cavalry more than half are Russians, and we have ordered and taken strong precautions that there be no damage to the churches of God. We are also on guard against the brigand, for remember who did what on his departure?"

The former Tushino governor, Fedor Pleshcheev, wrote to Sapieha: "Emissaries are coming to you from Prokopy Liapunov with favorable news and counsel. I advise you that Prokopy and the towns are content, and say that they will not wait to pay you for your services until there is a tsar in Moscow, but will be pleased to pay you immediately."[15]

At the same time Liapunov wrote to the Polish lord, Czernacki, urging him to send emissaries on behalf of Sapieha to conclude terms, and at the same time displayed a fearful misuse of the reading of Holy Scripture: "As of old the great Moses agreed that it was better to suffer with God's people than to have the temporary sweetness of sin, so you also seek to do the will, in the words of the apostle, not of an earthly lord, but of the eternal ruler, wishing to be champions of the truth, seeing the unjust attack of the Polish king against the Muscovite realm and the universal ruination of the present time."[16]

But at least this unlawful union did not last for long. Within a month Sapieha was writing to Kostroma, urging the inhabitants once more to recognize Wladyslaw. "Now for some unknown reason you have betrayed your sovereign, and wish to have goodness knows whom upon the

Muscovite throne. You yourselves know the might and strength of the Poles and Lithuanians. Who can fight against them?"

But there were many who would fight. They came from the Riazan and Severian lands with Liapunov, from Murom with Prince Litvin-Mosalsky, from Suzdal with Artemy Izmailov, from the Vologda land and the seaboard towns with Nashchokin and Princes Pronsky and Kozlovsky, from the Galich land with Mansurov, from the lands of Yaroslavl and Kostroma with Volynsky and Prince Volkonsky. All these were civil regiments, regiments of people of the land, primarily people of the free north. Yet also converging on Moscow for the same purpose of liberating the land came the cossack host of Prosovetsky from the north; from the south came the cossack hosts of the Tushino boyars, Prince Dmitry Trubetskoy and Zarutsky. Trubetskoy and Zarutsky everywhere invited "those from outside the plain," in other words non-steppe cossacks, promising them pay. In the invitation the following words were used: "Whosoever belongs to the boyars, whether serfs or long-standing peasants, let them come with no hesitation or fear, they will be given freedom and pay like any other cossacks, and they will be given documents in the name of the boyars and commanders of all the land." Thus the cossack leaders tried to enlarge their numbers within the Muscovite realm.

At this time of general uprising, when from all directions armed formations were approaching the walls of Moscow, led by men of humble birth who were pushed to the forefront because those of the first rank were absent, what were the members of the tsar's council, the rulers of Moscow, doing? At the beginning of the uprising, as early as 1610, Saltykov and his companions had proposed to the boyars that they beg the king to send Wladyslaw to Moscow, that they write to the ambassadors, Filaret and Golitsyn, telling them to submit entirely to the king's will, and to Liapunov forbidding him to incite the rising or muster troops. The boyars drafted the documents and brought them to the patriarch to be sealed, but Hermogen answered them: "I shall write letters to the king and order them to be signed with my spiritual authority if the king gives his son to the Muscovite realm, if the prince be baptized into the Orthodox faith, and if the Lithuanians depart from Moscow. As for those who rely upon the king's word, it is well known that they wish us to kiss the cross to the king, and not to the prince, and I will not bless but curse you who write such letters. I am writing to Prokopy Liapunov that if the prince is not placed upon the Muscovite throne, and if he is not baptized into the Orthodox faith, and if the Lithuanians do not depart from Moscow, I will bless all who have kissed the cross to the prince and urge them instead to come to Moscow and sacrifice their lives for the Orthodox faith."

The chronicle says that Saltykov began to defame and abuse Hermogen and, seizing his dagger, tried to stab him. But the patriarch, overshadowing him with the banner of the cross, loudly said to him: "Let the banner of the cross be against your accursed dagger, and may you be accursed in this world and in the next." But Mstislavsky quietly said: "Go about your business and suffer for the Orthodox faith, for if you are seduced by diabolical temptation your stem shall be uprooted from the land of the living."[17]

In this manner the letters were dispatched without the signature of the patriarch. Prince Ivan Mikhailovich Vorotynsky and Andrey Vasilievich Golitsyn, who were under arrest, were forced to set their seals to them.

PARLEYS OUTSIDE SMOLENSK

These documents were brought before Smolensk on December 23 and the next day presented to the ambassadors with the demand that the order of the boyars immediately be carried out, otherwise things would go badly for them. When the documents were read out Filaret replied that they could not comply. "We were sent by the patriarch, the Holy Synod, the boyars, all ranks of people and all the land, but these documents were inscribed without the agreement of the patriarch and the Holy Synod and without the consent of the whole land. How can we obey them? And there is written in them about ecclesiastical matters, concerning the kissing of the cross by the inhabitants of Smolensk to the king and the prince. This is all the more reason why we can do nothing without the sanction of the patriarch." Golitsyn and the remaining members of the embassy declared these documents unlawful.

On December 27 the ambassadors were summoned to the Polish lords, in whose company they encountered Secretary Chicherin, who had been sent from Moscow with tidings of the death of the pretender. The Polish lords declared to the ambassadors that to the king's good fortune the brigand had been slain at Kaluga. With a bow the ambassadors gave thanks for these tidings. "Now," the Polish lords asked mockingly, "what do you say concerning the boyars' document?" Golitsyn replied that their delegation had not been sent by the boyars alone that they were accountable not only to the boyars but first and foremost to the patriarch and the spiritual authorities, and only then to the boyars and the whole land; the letters had been written on behalf of the boyars alone, and even then not all of them. The Polish lords said: "You have been making the excuse all the time that you did not have any orders from Moscow concerning Smolensk; yet now you have received the order to submit entirely to the king's will, and you still prevaricate?" Sapieha read through the boyars' document and said: "See, the Holy Ghost has inspired the boyars with the very same things of which we spoke to you in our sessions. In the very same words they order you to fufill what we have demanded of you. This means that God himself has revealed this to them."

Golitsyn replied: "Be so good as to hear out my petition without interruption, and convey it to his royal highness. You say that we must obey the boyars' decree. In truth I should be glad to obey their decree and do as God will help me to do, but the boyars must deal justly with us, and not as they are doing. It was the patriarch, the boyars and all the people of the Muscovite realm who sent us to petition the great sovereigns, and not the boyars alone. I would not have come on behalf of the boyars alone, and yet they alone are writing to us on such a great matter, disregarding the patriarch and the Holy Synod, and without the counsel of all the people of the Muscovite realm. This is the first disservice they have done us, yea, and all the people of the Muscovite realm, and we think that on account of this there will be great doubt and grief. May Christian blood not be shed on account of this! There is another disservice that the boyars have done us. It was written in our instructions, and we were ordered to petition his majesty the king to withdraw from Smolensk and to evacuate all his troops from the Muscovite realm, and we were ordered quite emphatically to present this petition. But now they inform us that they have written to the king by the hand of Prince Andrei Mosalsky, and petitioning the king to pursue the brigand at Kaluga. We petition the king, on the basis of our instructions, that he return to his realm, yet Mosalsky petitions that he should proceed to Kaluga. We knew nothing of this, we bring on ourselves the king's anger and hear many cruel words from him. For Prince Mosalsky could have come to us concerning this matter, about which we could have petitioned the king ourselves. They further write to us that we must not negotiate about the brigand, where he is, and how strong. As if we wished him well! And for this we shall complain about the boyars to God. They themselves know that we have not sought any good for the brigand, but wrote to the boyars concerning the brigand precisely what you mentioned to us in our sessions, that many people had rallied to the brigand. We did not know what to reply to you, and so it is unbefitting for them to cast aspersions on me on account of this. They themselves know that, by the mercy of God, my father and grandfather were not expelled from the council, they took part in all the proceedings, their boyardom was not purchased, they were not appointed to the council outside Moscow, they sought no benefit for the brigand, they did not kiss the cross to him, they were never with the brigand nor wished anything from him; our concern was that for the sake of the image of the Mother of God and our oath of allegiance we opposed the brigand and unsparingly sacrificed our lives. Yet now they have placed my brother Andrei under arrest, for some unknown reason, and write to me concerning an idle tale, that allegedly I, while before Smolensk, was in communication with the brigand, and for this reason they defame me. When God grants that I see upon the Muscovite throne our sovereign Wladyslaw Sigismundovich, I shall present my petition to him concerning all this calumny, and for the present, senators, I pray that you will transmit my petition to his majesty the king."

The Polish lords promised but demanded as before that the boyars' decree be fulfilled with regard to Smolensk. The ambassadors refused as before on grounds that they had no instructions from the patriarch. The Polish lords argued that the patriarch was a spiritual figure who did not interfere in the concerns of the land. The ambassadors replied: "With us, from the beginning of the Russian tsardom under previous great sovereigns things were ordered thus: if great matters pertaining to the realm or the land arise, our great sovereigns summon to an assembly the patriarch, metropolitans and archbishops, and take counsel with them concerning all matters, and nothing is resolved without their counsel, and our sovereigns accord the patriarchs great respect, they meet them and accompany them, and assign them a place by their side. To such an extent are the patriarchs honored among us, as were the metropolitans before them.[18] Now that we are bereft of a sovereign, the patriarch is the principal dignitary among us, so it is not befitting to take counsel on such a great matter. When we were in Moscow the boyars conducted no business without the approval of the patriarch, they took counsel with him in everything, and the patriarch as well as the boyars dispatched us, as Hetman Stanislaw Stanislavich well knows. Furthermore, our letters of credence, our instructions and all related matters from the first were written in the name of the patriarch, and therefore we cannot act without the patriarch's letters, on the basis of those issued by the boyars alone. As letters issued by the patriarch without the boyars are not valid, so also are letters issued by the boyars without the patriarch. It is now necessary to act according to the general counsel of all the people. A sovereign is needed, not only by the boyars, but by everybody, and the present matter affects everybody, for it is unprecedented in Moscow. Furthermore, lords of the council, please state the answer of the inhabitants of Smolensk to the boyars' missive?"

"The inhabitants of Smolensk are persisting in their obstinacy" the Polish lords replied. "They do not obey the boyars' letters, they demand that they be allowed to meet with you, and they say that they will do as you bid, so consequently everything depends on you." The ambassadors replied: "You yourselves, my lords, can judge how the inhabitants of Smolensk will heed us, if they do not even obey the boyars' letters. It is now clearly obvious that in Moscow things are not being done as they ought to be. If the patriarch, the boyars and all the people of the Muscovite realm in common counsel had written, and not the boyars alone, the inhabitants of Smolensk could not have refused them. But we ourselves do not know what to do. Only half of us are left here, the other half have been dismissed to Moscow, and the principal person here among us is the metropolitan, and he does not wish to do anything without a document from the patriarch; nor does he wish to speak, and we can do nothing without him."

The Polish lords dismissed the ambassadors saying that the next day, December 28, they must come accompanied by Filaret for a final session. At that session Filaret said to the Polish lords: "I have heard your speeches of yesterday from Prince Vasily Vasilievich. He said the very same to you as I would have said. I, as metropolitan, on such a matter would not dare to dream of saying to the inhabitants of Smolensk that they must kiss the cross to the king without a document from the patriarch." Golitsyn added, "And we cannot act on such a great matter without the metropolitan." The Polish lords dismissed the ambassadors angrily. As they left the room, the Polish lords cried out: "These are not ambassadors, these are brigands!" Following this Ivan Bestuzhev visited the Polish lords with some words or other from the inhabitants of Smolensk, but the Polish lords would not give him a hearing and ejected him. When he was outside Sapieha shouted at him through a window: "You do not obey the will of the sovereign, you ignore the boyars' letters. See what will happen to you!" Bestuzhev turned around and said: "We are all in God's hands. Whatever is His pleasure, so let it be. We petition the king that all the people of the Muscovite realm resolve and favor him; we wish this for his royal majesty, but we do not wish to break with Moscow."

Meanwhile Zakhar Liapunov and Kirill Sozonov kept trying to persuade the Polish lords that the principal ambassadors were the culprits since they did not explain anything to the gentry. The Polish lords summoned the gentry, and said to them: "It is known to us that the ambassadors do not consult with you about anything, and even conceal the boyars' letters from you." The gentry replied: "Some idle person, some brigand, who wishes to see a quarrel between you and the ambassadors, told you this. Place him before us, so that we may challenge him face to face. The ambassadors read the boyars' document to us, and we said to them that we could not comply with it, since it was written without the patriarch and without the consent of the whole land."

For almost a whole month after that the ambassadors were not invited to a session. Golitsyn thought up a way to come to an agreement with the king: to persuade the inhabitants of Smolensk to allow a small detachment to enter the city while at the same time the king would not demand of them an oath of allegiance in his own name, and would lift the siege immediately. The Polish lords were informed of this, and a session took place on January 17, 1611. Golitsyn proposed to the Polish lords that about fifty or sixty Poles be admitted into the city. The Polish lords replied: "This would only be an insult to the king. He has besieged Smolensk for a year and a half, and it would be ludicrous to admit only fifty or sixty men!" The ambassadors replied that they would not agree to admit more than a hundred men, and with that the session ended.

Meanwhile, on January 23, Ivan Nikitich Saltykov had arrived before Smolensk with new letters from the boyars confirming the previous position. The inhabitants of Smolensk replied that henceforth if any such criminal letters were sent to them, they would order the bearer to be shot. There were with the king ambassadors from the entire Muscovite realm, and it was through them that they the boyars must speak. On January 29 a new document to the ambassadors was compiled, and on the 30th they were summoned for another session with the Polish lords, with whom they encountered Saltykov. The ambassadors declared that the document lacked the patriarch's signature, so they had only one option, to continue the matter of the admission of the king's men into Smolensk, and furthermore they hoped that the king, in accordance with his promise, would not order the inhabitants of Smolensk to swear allegiance in his name. The Poles exclaimed that this was a falsehood, that there never had been any question of conceding the oath of allegiance in the king's name. "You yourselves at the last session declared to us," the ambassadors replied, "that the king had conceded the oath of allegiance to himself, and had ordered that it should be simply a matter of how many men must be admitted into the city, and we had thanked the king already for this." "Falsehood! Falsehood!" the Polish lords continued to exclaim. "If you had perceived any untruthfulness in us," said Filaret, "the king would have ordered us sent back to Moscow, and that others be chosen in our place. We have never lied about anything, and we remember everything that we have said and that we have heard from you. The business of an ambassador is not to go back upon his word, and the word of an ambassador is firm. If we deviate from our own words, what can henceforth be believed? We cannot do any more business if you accuse us of untruthfulness."

It was not the Polish lords who replied to Filaret, but Saltykov. "You ambassadors," he exclaimed, "must believe the Polish lords, in their graciousness, for they do not lie. It is not befitting to antagonize the lords of the council and cause the great sovereign king to be angry. You must without question fulfill the king's wish according to the boyars' decree, and not look for anything to the patriarch. He is not responsible for matters of state, only for his own priestly functions. His majesty is not inclined, for two years having besieged this insignificant place and not having taken it, to go away ignominiously. You ambassadors must intervene for the sake of the king's honor and order the inhabitants of Smolensk to kiss the cross to the king." The ambassadors replied that Saltykov should remember to whom he was speaking, that he had no business meddling in the deliberations of ambassadors chosen by the entire realm, and insult them with unbefitting words. Turning to the Polish lords, Filaret said: "If you, my lords, wish to deal with us on this matter, speak to us yourselves and do not allow to intervene in the discussion unauthorized persons with whom we do not wish to waste words." The Polish lords ordered Saltykov to be silent, and asked the ambassadors: "Once and for all, do you wish to act in accordance with the boyars' document?" Filaret replied: "You yourselves know that our father and leader of the clerical estate is the most holy patriarch, and he who is bound by his word is not unbound by the tsar or even by God himself. Without the patriarch's document I cannot in any way negotiate concerning the oath of allegiance to the king, and you should not vex me with this. I vow to you in the name of God that even if I should suffer death, I cannot negotiate concerning this without a document from the patriarch." "Then you will go immediately to the prince at Wilno!"[19] exclaimed the Polish lords, and dismissed the ambassadors.

On February 1 the ambassadors once again were summoned to the Polish lords where the previous question, the previous reply, the previous threat were restated. "Make ready to travel to Wilno." "We have not been instructed to travel to Wilno" said the ambassadors. "If his majesty the king orders us taken to Lithuania and Poland against our will, let it be as the king wishes. But we cannot travel on nothing and with nothing. Everything has been consumed, our comrades have been sent back to Moscow, and we can do nothing here." On February 7 once more they summoned the ambassadors and declared that the king, being merciful to the inhabitants of Smolensk, had granted their petition and would permit them to swear allegiance to the prince alone. But in order not to insult the king's honor it was necessary to admit into Smolensk at least seven hundred men. If they sent only a hundred men Shein would order them to be cast into prison or killed. The ambassadors replied that they would not agree to admit more than two hundred men. The next day it was declared to the ambassadors that they should enter into discussions with the inhabitants of Smolensk regarding the admission into the city of the king's men without specifying the number. The ambassadors could hardly persuade them to admit two hundred men since the inhabitants of Smolensk understood only too well that this would be merely the first step towards conquest of their town, and therefore set the unalterable condition that before any Poles be admitted into Smolensk the king must withdraw beyond the frontier with all his forces, and that the detachment entering the city must have no authority and behave in a disciplined fashion.

But in the king's council quite a different set of conditions was written down. (1) The guard on the city gates must be composed half of the king's men and half from the citizenry. One key would be with the governor, and another with the commander of the Polish detachment. (2) The king promised to bear no malice against the citizens for their opposition or for their impudence, and would not exile anyone without due cause. (3) When the inhabitants of Smolensk conveyed their submission and complied with all his demands the king would lift the siege, and the city would be subject to the Muscovite realm until matters were further decided. (4) The inhabitants of Smolensk who previously submitted to the king would be subject not to the city tribunal but to the Polish command. (5) The inhabitants of Smolensk were to pay to the king all war damages caused by their lengthy resistance.

Naturally Smolensk could not accept these conditions, which all too clearly revealed the king's intentions. They demanded that the city keys remain with the governor of Smolensk alone, that Smolensk and the province of Smolensk pertain to the Muscovite realm as before, that when they kissed the cross to Wladyslaw the king withdraw from their city and evacuate the whole province and, when he had returned to Lithuania with all his forces they would admit his entire detachment. The inhabitants of Smolensk also refused to pay any indemnity, pleading poverty, and promising only to send the king gifts.[20]

Hearing these demands, the Poles decided to employ means to make the ambassadors more tractable. On March 26, 1611 Filaret, Golitsyn and their companions were summoned for discussions. Since the spring thaw had come and the ice on the Dnieper was thin, they were obliged to come on foot. The Polish lords declared to them that without fail they would be sent to Wilno. They declared that they would not be sent back to their previous quarters, but would remain on this side of the river. The ambassadors begged at least to be permitted to return to their previous quarters to gather up their necessities, but this request was refused. As soon as they emerged from the meeting they were surrounded by soldiers with loaded weapons, and were conducted to the place designated. The metropolitan was provided with one hut, Prince Golitsyn, Mezetsky and Tomilo Lugovskoy another. Outside and around a guard was placed, and access to the ambassadors was forbidden to the gentry of the embassy. In this manner they spent Easter Sunday. On that day the king sent to them a side of beef, a carcass of aged mutton, two lambs, one kid, four hares, one grouse, four suckling pigs, two geese and seven chickens. All this the ambassadors shared with their servitors. Discussions concerning Smolensk were re-opened. The Polish lords repeated their previous proposals, except for the clause concerning war indemnities. The ambassadors also made a concession, and promised to persuade the inhabitants of Smolensk to admit the entire Polish detachment into the city two or three days before

Sigismund's withdrawal, provided that the king designate the date of his departure, and inscribe it in the memorandum of agreement. But at that point there came news of the destruction of Moscow.

BURNING OF MOSCOW

At the very moment when Sigismund was considering it essential to capture Smolensk for Poland by any means whatsoever, and was wasting time in discussions which were fruitless and humiliating to his dignity, the uprising against his son was not weakening in the Muscovite realm, and the conduct of the Poles was adding more and more fuel to the flames. The Ukrainian towns which had sworn to the brigand—Orel, Bolkhov, Belev, Karachev, Aleksin and others—on the death of the brigand kissed the cross to the prince despite the fact that the king's men, under the leadership of a certain Polish lord, Zaprojski, burned them, killed the people and led them off into captivity. Gasiewski ordered a detachment of Zaporozhian Cossacks to proceed to the Riazan towns in order to prevent Liapunov from setting out for Moscow. The Cherkassians gathered under Isaak Sunbulov, a commander devoted to Wladyslaw, and besieged Liapunov in Pronsk, but the governor of Zaraisk, Prince Dmitry Mikhailovich Pozharsky, came to his aid with men from Kolomna and Riazan. The Cherkassians, hearing of his approach, withdrew from Pronsk. Liapunov, now liberated, proceeded to Riazan, while Pozharsky himself soon was besieged in Zaraisk by the Cherkassians and the same Sunbulov; but he effected a sortie, expelled the enemy from their fortress and inflicted a heavy defeat on them. The Cherkassians hastily retreated to the Ukraine, and Sunbulov towards Moscow. There was no longer any obstacle in the way of the uprising in the south.

The prime mover of this uprising, the principal personage in the state during this time without a ruler, was still in Moscow. This was the patriarch, at whose bidding the whole land rose up and rallied in the name of the faith. Saltykov came to him with the boyars and said: "You wrote that the soldiers should come to Moscow. Now write and tell them to turn back." "I shall write," Hermogen replied, "if you, traitor, together with the Lithuanians, get out of Moscow. If you remain, I shall bless everybody to die for the Orthodox faith. I see it mocked, I see the destruction of the holy churches, I hear Latin chants in the Kremlin, and I cannot endure it."[21] The patriarch was placed under arrest, and it was ordered that he receive no one.

The patriarch did not tell all. As soon as Zolkiewski departed insults to the inhabitants of Moscow began, aggravated all the more by the perilous situation of the Poles who saw themselves encircled amidst an agitated populace. As soon as the hetman left Gasiewski moved into Boris's old palace. Saltykov, abandoning his own home, occupied the palace of Ivan Vasilievich Godunov. Andronov took up residence in the house of the archpriest of the Annunciation cathedral.[22] Everywhere Polish guards stood at the gates, and street barriers were demolished. Russians were forbidden to go about with swords, axes were confiscated from merchants offering them for sale, and carpenters who came with them to work were prohibited even to carry knives. Fearing that through lack of weapons the people would arm themselves with cudgels, peasants were even forbidden to bring small pieces of timber for sale. The hetman's prohibitions against the rowdiness of the Poles were abandoned. Women and maidens were raped. During the evenings they assaulted people passing through the streets visiting each other's houses. At the hour of matins they stopped not only ordinary people, but even priests.

On March 17, on Palm Sunday, they released the patriarch for the customary ride upon a donkey, but none of the people came to receive palms.[23] The patriarch was placed under arrest, and it was ordered spread that Saltykov and the Poles wished at that time to massacre the patriarch and the unarmed populace, that Lithuanian troops stood all around the squares, both cavalry and infantry at the ready. In fact Polish eyewitnesses wrote that Saltykov had told them: "You have just had your opportunity, and you did not punish Moscow. Now they will punish you on Tuesday, and I am not going to wait around for that. I shall take my wife and go to the king." He wished to anticipate the inhabitants of Moscow and attack them before help could come to them from Liapunov, whom they were expecting that Tuesday.

The Poles prepared for the Tuesday, mounting cannon on the towers of the Kremlin and the Kitai quarter. In fact in the Moscow suburbs the soldiers from Liapunov's regiments were gathering secretly in order to support the inhabitants should there arise an affray with the Poles, and the principal leaders also were gathering—Prince Pozharsky, Buturlin and Koltovskoy. But Tuesday began peacefully, the inhabitants of Moscow were quiet, the merchants peacefully opened their shops in the Kitai quarter and did business. Then Nikolaj Kozakowski began to force carters in the market to help haul cannon up onto the tower. The carters refused, a dispute broke out, and clamor. Then a detachment of foreign mercenaries, eight thousand strong, which had gone over to the Poles after Klushino and now was stationed in the Kremlin, thinking that the popular uprising had begun, rushed in a crowd and assaulted the Russians. The Poles followed the example of the foreign mercenaries and began a fearful slaughter of the unarmed populace. In the Kitai quarter up to seven thousand perished. Prince Andrei Vasilievich Golitsyn, under arrest in his own home, was murdered by the enraged Poles. But in the White quarter the Russians had time to rally and arm themselves. They sounded the tocsin, raised a fearful clamor, barricaded the streets with tables, benches and beams, and fired at the Poles and foreign mercenaries from behind these fortifications. They shot out of windows, threw rocks, beams and planks.

The soldiers who earlier had previously gathered in the suburbs gave active help. On Presentation Street the Poles were halted by Prince Dmitry Mikhailovich Pozharsky, who joined the artillerymen and repulsed the enemy, drove them into Kitai quarter, and established a small fortress near the church of the Presentation on the Lubianka. Ivan Matveevich Buturlin stood by the Yauza gates, and Ivan Koltovskoy in the Trans River quarter.[24] The Poles, who had been chased into the Kremlin and the Kitai quarter, besieged on all sides by the insurgent populace, thought up a stratagem—to smoke out the enemy by fire. They tried to set fire to Moscow in several places but this the inhabitants prevented, making it necessary to exchange shots with them and launch sorties. At last they managed to set fire in several places. It is said that Mikhail Saltykov was the first to set the fire, and to his own home. A fearful wind arose, towards the evening flames swept through the White quarter, and fire began in the Kitai quarter amongst the Poles, but did not spread for the wind was not blowing in that direction. The night was illuminated; one could see a pin, and the tocsin sounded incessantly from all the belfries.

The next day, Wednesday, the Poles took counsel as to what to do. The boyars said: "Even though you burn the entire city, it is still enclosed within walls. You must try by all means to set fire to the Trans River quarter, around which there are no walls. Then you can withdraw easily, and may easily receive help." Following this advice the Poles went to Trans River quarter, and there met with stiff opposition. The musketeer settlements were situated there, and they had people to defend them. However, despite great difficulty and losses, the Poles eventually succeeded in setting fire to the Trans River quarter. On the other side they renewed their attack on Pozharsky, who repelled them all day from his small fort, but at last fell from his wounds and was carried off to the Trinity monastery. The populace was forced out of doors into the cruel frost. In Moscow there was no longer anywhere to live. On Maunday Thursday several of the inhabitants of Moscow came to Gasiewski to plead for mercy. He ordered them to kiss the cross to Wladyslaw once again, and issued a command to his men to cease the slaughter. The inhabitants of Moscow who had submitted were ordered to wear a special badge—a towel round the waist.

THE POLES BESIEGED IN MOSCOW'S RUINS

Maunday Thursday passed peacefully for the Poles but on Friday came news that Prosovetsky was approaching Moscow with thirty thousand troops. Gasiewski sent Zborowski and Struys[25] against him. Prosovetsky, having lost in a skirmish with them about two hundred of his cossacks, settled down in his malvoisins, which the Poles did not dare attack, but withdrew to Moscow. Prosovetsky also retreated several miles where Liapunov, Zarutsky and other commanders were waiting. On Easter Monday the entire militia force, numbering a hundred thousand men, approached Moscow and took up positions near the Simonov monastery, surrounding themselves with malvoisins. Several days later Gasiewski led out his entire army to the Russian encampment, but the Russians did not come out to fight. He sent the mercenaries to flush the Russian musketeers out of a small hamlet situated near the encampment, but they were repulsed with heavy losses. Having beaten them off, the musketeers advanced upon the Poles, whose cavalry had to hasten and exchange fire with them. The Russian cavalry during all this time did not leave the encampment, but when the Poles retreated towards Moscow the Russians came out of their encampment and pursued them. The Poles halted in order to drive them back, and the Russians retreated to the encampment. The Poles resumed their retreat, and the Russians once more gave pursuit. It became very difficult for the Poles, who scarcely managed to regain Moscow, and never again ventured out of the city.

On April 1 the militia force approached the walls of the White quarter. Liapunov stood by the Yauza gates, Prince Trubetskoy and Zarutsky close by the Vorontsovsk Field, the commanders of Kostroma and Yaroslavl by the Intercession gates, Izmailov by the Presentation gates, and Prince Mosalsky by the Tver gates. On April 6, early in the morning, the Poles heard a noise, looked out, and already the Russians were occupying the greater part of the walls of the White quarter. To the Poles there remained only five gates or towers. Daily clashes commenced. Liapunov distinguished himself among the commanders by his bravery and good management. As the chronicler described him: "As the commander of all the Muscovite forces, he glides everywhere among the regiments, roaring like a lion."[26] The Poles were in a severe predicament. "The knights are suffering great hardship in Moscow," they wrote to Potocki[27] before Smolensk. "They are besieged in the Kitai quarter and the Kremlin, the gates are all removed and there is nothing to eat." Provisions for themselves and fodder for their horses had to be obtained by fighting. At the beginning of May, on Poklonnaia Hill, the encampment of the famous knight Jan Sapieha wavered. He conducted parleys with the Russians, and displayed unfriendly intentions towards the besieged. Then, not having come to terms with the militia force, he armed himself against but was repulsed and came over to the side of Gasiewski. But the latter obtained little advantage from him. Sapieha's knights grew weary of remaining outside Moscow where there was nothing to plunder, and they withdrew to Pereiaslavl Zalessky.[28] Gasiewski sent part of his army with them. Why he weakened himself in such a way, the Poles who were with him do not explain. In all probability he was compelled to do so through lack of provisions.

After that there remained very few of the besieged Poles, perhaps three thousand or so, apart from the mercenaries and Polish infantry who, as we know, were very few in number. In order to conceal their lack of strength from the eyes of the besiegers the Poles spread the rumor that the Lithuanian hetman was coming to their aid with large forces, whereas the Russians knew better than they who was or was not coming to aid them. As a sign of joy the Poles fired their cannon and weapons. "It seemed to us," one of them wrote, "that the gunfire among us was very dense, but from this very gunfire Moscow noticed that only a handful of us remained within the walls of the Kremlin and the Kitai quarter." Having fired their weapons, and thinking that they had caused great consternation in Moscow, the Poles dispersed to their quarters and slept peacefully on the night of May 21-22.

But the besiegers did not sleep. Three hours before dawn they placed a ladder and scaled the wall of the Kitai quarter. The guard on the tower, the trusty Marchocki, hearing a noise, at first did not know whence it came—from humans or from dogs, of which at the time there were many in burnt-out Moscow. But then he saw that it came from humans, and cried "Moscow! Sound the alarm!" Marchocki leapt up and ordered the alarm sounded since the Russians have a practice, he says, of placing a bell on every tower. When the besiegers heard the bell they knew they were discovered and with a shout rushed upon the walls. Hearing the alarm, the Poles rushed out of their houses and repulsed the Russians from the Kitai quarter. Then the besiegers turned to the other side, to the towers of the White quarter held by the Poles, and in the course of the day captured them all. The next day the Russians besieged the mercenaries in the New Virgin convent and compelled them to surrender. After that the Russians laughed at the Poles. "The Lithuanian hetman is coming to aid you with a large force," they shouted at them. "He is coming with five hundred troops! You will not find any more, that is all that Lithuania can send! Koniecpolski is coming, he is bringing you food, he is bringing you one sausage [kiszka]." (The names of the troop commanders were Kiszka and Koniecpolski).[29] But Chodkiewicz, the Lithuanian hetman, did not come.[30] Sigismund was not as yet concerned with Moscow. First he had to finish his business with Smolensk.

INTERNMENT OF THE AMBASSADORS

On April 8 Filaret and Golitsyn were summoned to Sapieha and the chancellor announced to them that on Tuesday of Holy Week the Russians had opened hostilities, the king's men had moved against them, burned the city, and much Christian blood had been shed on both sides. At the same time Sapieha announced that the patriarch, for having provoked the uprising, had been placed under arrest and confined in the St. Cyril monastery.[31] The ambassadors wept bitterly, and Filaret said: "This has happened because of the sins of all Orthodox Christendom, and for whatever reason this has occurred, and who intended such ruin, God will not tolerate it, and such unmercifulness will be called to account in all realms. Call to mind our words. In all our sessions we have said that his royal majesty should have ordered all clauses be confirmed according to his own promise and in accordance with the treaty, otherwise there would be great doubt and grief among the people. This is what has happened. Thus even now, if his royal majesty has mercy, and you, lords of the council, are pleased to spare Christian blood, all will receive peace and tranquillity."

Sapieha replied that it was precisely for that reason that the king had entered the Muscovite realm, in order to pacify it, but the Russians themselves were to blame for everything. The Poles could not have avoided burning Moscow, otherwise they themselves would have been killed. "But tell me," he added, "how can we alleviate this evil and spare the shedding of blood?" The ambassadors replied: "At present we ourselves do not know what to do. We were sent by the whole land, and first and foremost by the patriarch. But we hear from you that our principal leader is now your prisoner, the boyars and all the people of the Muscovite realm are now before Moscow and are fighting the king's men. Exactly who we are here, or ambassadors from whom—we do not know. Those who have sent us are, you say, now against the purpose of our embassy. And now we do not know how to negotiate concerning Smolensk because if the inhabitants hear that the Poles whom the citizens of Moscow admitted now have burned Moscow, they will fear that the same will happen to them the moment they admit the king's men." Sapieha replied: "There is no need to speak of what has happened in Moscow. Tell us what we are to do now." The ambassadors replied: "There is no other way to proceed than this: the king must confirm our clause with regard to Smolensk, and specify the time he will withdraw into Poland in a letter under your senatorial signatures. We will inform the patriarch, the boyars and all the people of the Muscovite realm in Moscow of the king's mercy, and we will write to those who have gathered before Moscow that they desist, that they not fight the king's forces, and that as soon as possible they write from Moscow to summon people from all ranks."

Sapieha agreed, but demanded that the treaty concerning Smolensk be concluded immediately, and that the king's men be admitted into the city without delay. The ambassadors replied that they could not do this without corresponding with Moscow, since the inhabitants of Smolensk would not comply. Sapieha ordered the ambassadors to write two letters, one to the patriarch and boyars, the other to the commanders of the militia force standing before Moscow. But when the next day Lugovskoy brought these letters to Sapieha the latter demanded of him: "Will you immediately admit the king's men into Smolensk?" Lugovskoy replied that it had been decided to await a reply from Moscow. "If that is so," said Sapieha, "you will all be sent to Wilno." Lugovskoy replied: "It is necessary to spare Christian blood, but we are not frightened by Poland. Poland we know."

On April 12 the ambassadors were informed that the next day they were being taken to Poland. In vain did Filaret and Golitsyn point out that they had no instructions from Moscow to travel to Poland, and they had no supplies for the journey. The Poles paid no heed, brought up a boat to their quarters and bade them make ready. When the servants of the ambassadors began to transfer into the boat the belongings and provisions of their lords, the Polish bailliffs began to assault the servants, ordered the supplies to be thrown out of the boat, and took the better articles for themselves. The plundered ambassadors were conveyed together in one boat in which were posted soldiers with loaded weapons, and behind the boat went yet two more boats with the ambassadors' servants. On the way the ambassadors suffered extreme privation in all things. While they were travelling through the estates of Hetman Zolkiewski the latter, who happened to be there at the time, sent to enquire as to their health. The ambassadors answered him that he should be mindful of his soul and his solemn oath.[32]

CAPTURE OF SMOLENSK

Shortly after the ambassadors concluded their business did the inhabitants of Smolensk did likewise. Disease had ravaged the city, which was deprived of salt. Of eighty thousand inhabitants estimated at the beginning of the siege, barely eight thousand remained, but those who survived had no thought of surrender. Andrei Dedeshin, who is known to us, having defected to the king, pointed out to him a sector of the wall constructed hastily in the damp autumn time, which was therefore weak. The king ordered the cannon aimed on that side, and the wall was breached. On the night of June 3 the Poles carried out an assault and went through the breach into the city. Shein and fifteen of his companions stood above the clamor and declared that he would sooner die than surrender to anyone from the common soldiery. Then Jakob Potocki hurried to him, and Shein surrendered to him. The inhabitants shut themselves up in the cathedral church of the Mother of God and detonated the gunpowder stored below in the crypt, and were blown to pieces, following the example of the inhabitants of Saguntum, as the Polish historians put it.[33]

Shein was brought to the king's encampment, and was interrogated on 27 points. (1) Why, and hoping for what, after the surrender of the capital, did he not wish to surrender Smolensk in the name of the king? Answer: He only hoped that the king would withdraw from Smolensk, having given his son to the tsardom of Moscow, as had been written in the document which had been sent from Moscow. (2) Whence had he received the information? If from the king's encampment, from whom, how many times, and by what means? Shein named all the defectors. (3) Through whom had he corresponded with Golitsyn, and concerning what? Answer: Concerning nothing. (4) What correspondence had he carried on with Liapunov and other traitors? Answer: None. (5) Why had he not heeded the counsel of the archbishop and Deputy Governor Gorchakov that he surrender Smolensk? Answer: He had heard nothing from Gorchakov. The archbishop had spoken only once, when correspondence had begun with the Muscovite ambassadors, and the conditions laid down by the senators had been brought. He had said: "The wrath of God has descended upon the whole land and upon them. What the sword does not destroy will perish by the plague. It would be better for us to surrender and swear allegiance to them, even though they might later destroy us." Such words he only spoke once amid a great multitude of people. Nobody paid attention to them, and subsequently he did not at any time recall any of this, but previously, from the beginning of the siege, the archbishop frequently reproached him, Shein, asking why he had not ordered any activity against the enemy, why he did not obtain informers and not allow sorties to be made. (6) What did you intend to do if you had managed to hold out in Smolensk? Answer: I am devoted to the prince with my whole heart. But if the king had not given his son to the tsardom, then, since a land cannot be without a sovereign, I would have submitted to him who became tsar in Moscow. (7) Who advised him and helped him to maintain himself for so long in Smolensk? Answer: Nobody in particular, because nobody wished to surrender. (8) Before the king came before Smolensk from whom did he, Shein, receive news from Poland and Lithuania? Answer: From the serfs living along the border.

Questions 9-16 were questions of a similar nature, namely concerning relations with various persons and places. The answers are insignificant. (17) How much was the revenue from the Smolensk districts before the siege, and where where they expended? To this question Shein replied in detail. According to him there were 900 rubles in the treasury. (18) Where were concealed the possessions left behind by those who had died? Answer: I did not take any of these possessions. (19) Is not money buried somewhere or other in Smolensk? I do not know. (20) With what did Vaska Polochanin arrive in Smolensk? He said that the king had sent him to Riga for artillery. (21) Did he not correspond with somebody among the merchants in the king's encampment? Answer: With nobody. (22) Who brought salt and other supplies from the king's encampment into Smolensk? Answer: The kinsmen of the inhabitants, who had been in the encampment. (23) With whom among the Smolensk junior boyars had he been in correspondence, and how did they advise him? Answer: With nobody. (24) How many pieces of artillery were there in Smolensk? 170 pieces and 8,500 puds of powder at the commencement of the siege. (25) Through whom had he corresponded with Ivan Nikitich Saltykov? Answer: He had not corresponded through anybody; but when Saltykov betrayed the king he had sent a letter, to which an answer was given with the approval of the archbishop. (26) What had he been in the reign of the first pretender, Grishka Otrepiev, and how much in favor? Answer: I was at Novgorod Seversky at the command of Tsar Boris. When the others submitted to Grishka, I also submitted. At first he was angry with me, but then he began to favor me and call me to service. I was not present at his death. (27) When did he begin to correspond with the Kaluga tsarlet, and what was the nature of his correspondence? Answer: I had no correspondence whatsoever with the pretender. On one occasion he sent Ivan Zubtsov to Smolensk with a lengthy document, in which all the Bible and Psalter was cited, urging that the inhabitants of Smolensk submit to him, that they overthrow their governors and set Zubtsov in their place, that they send their whole treasury to him at Tushino, and that the merchants send all their wares to him. When he was enthroned in Moscow, he would reimburse everything. Instead of accepting Zubtsov as governor, they cast him into prison.

After they had interrogated Shein they sent him to Lithuania, where at first they kept him in close confinement, in shackles. Shein's family was divided between the king and Sapieha. Sigismund took his son, Sapieha his wife and daughter. Joy over the capture of Smolensk in Lithuania and Poland was indescribable. The king gave a speech full of gratitude to the knighthood, the main thrust of which was contained in the following words: "You have defeated a stubborn enemy. You have defeated them, not by starving them out, but by your own valorous deeds. Your steadfast hearts have defeated the stubborn by bravery." Skarga[34] preached a sermon. "First of all, let us rejoice, in that God has shown the path to the spreading of His church and the Catholic truth, to the salvation of people's souls. This people, burdened by its ancient schism from the church of God, had fallen into superstition and sin, crying out to heaven. On them had fallen such stupid pride, that they regarded the Latins as pagans, like unto the Jews and infidels, but the Lord God, by calamities and humiliations, has brought them to recognize their blasphemies." The famous preacher did not consider it necessary to trouble himself that the facts he cited were only half-truths. For example, according to him, Patriarch Hermogen, not wishing to swear allegiance to Wladyslaw, had requested the aid of Skopin, but Skopin had led his men away. The patriarch had summoned the False Dmitry but the latter, when he had rallied before Moscow, had been killed by his own men. And so on.

VASILY SHUISKY AND HIS BROTHERS IN WARSAW

After the capture of Smolensk, instead of proceeding immediately towards Moscow, the king was compelled to leave to attend the Diet in Warsaw. There, in the intoxication of triumph, it was thought that with the capture of Smolensk all was over. They forgot that in Moscow a handful of Poles was surrounded by a large number of enemies. They hastened to indulge themselves with the solemn entry into Warsaw of the captive Muscovite tsar. On October 29, 1611 Zolkiewski, accompanied by a few lords who were deputies of the land, with the household of knights in his service, travelled through the Krakowski suburb to the king's castle. Behind him travelled an open cart, drawn by six horses. In that cart sat the deposed tsar of Moscow, in a white brocaded robe and a fur cap. He was a gray-haired old man, of not very tall stature, round-faced, with a long and somewhat misshapen nose, a large mouth and a long beard. He stared straight ahead and sternly. In front of him sat his two brothers, and in the middle of them a bailliff. When the three Shuisky brothers were brought before the king, they bowed down low, holding their caps in their hands.

Zolkiewski began a long speech about the fickleness of fortune, praised the bravery of the king, referring to the fruits of his heroic deeds—the capture of Smolensk and Moscow. He expatiated on the might of the Muscovite tsars, the last of whom now stood before the king and was bowing low. Then Vasily Shuisky, bowing his head low, touched the ground with his right hand, and then kissed that hand. The second brother, Dmitry, struck the same ground with his forehead, and the third brother, Ivan, thrice bowed low and wept. The hetman continued that he was delivering the Shuiskys to the king not as prisoners but as examples of human fortune, and asked him to show them kindness. Then the Shuiskys silently bowed their heads. When the hetman had concluded his speech the Shuiskys were permitted to approach the king. This was a great spectacle, giving rise to amazement and pity, say contemporaries. But among the throng of lords of the council there were heard voices which demanded, not pity, but revenge upon Shuisky, who had been guilty of the deaths of many Poles. Particularly prominent was the voice of Jerzy Mniszech, who demanded vengeance on behalf of his daughter. The Shuiskys were imprisoned in the castle of Gostynsk, several miles from Warsaw.

THE MILITIA TROIKA

A certain Yury Potemkin brought to the encampment outside Moscow news of the capture of Smolensk but the boyars, Mstislavsky and his companions, received these tidings directly from the king. The king wrote that one of the reasons which had prompted him to capture Smolensk was the treason of the gentry of the Smolensk district, who had deserted the king's cause along with Ivan Nikitich Saltykov. The king had sent Saltykov with the Smolensk gentry to Dorogobuzh, but these gentry had begun to take counsel, intending to desert to the Muscovite regiments, until one of them informed Sigismund of their intentions. Saltykov must have been denounced at the same time, but subsequently he contrived to justify himself to the king, and came to him enjoying his previous favor.

The boyars, calling themselves loyal subjects of the king, replied that they, hearing of the slaughter of many innocent Christian souls, simple people, women and children, who had departed this world wretchedly on account of the recalcitrance of Shein and other evil men, grieved according to Christian custom and brotherly love, as if they were their own kinsfolk. "Concerning this, great sovereigns, that God has given you victory and conquest over those who were disobedient to you, we give praise to God, and we greet you, great sovereigns, in your glorious and newly acquired realms." The boyars informed the king that the inhabitants of Great Novgorod, in the name of his sovereign majesty, had interrogated Boyar Ivan Mikhailovich Saltykov under torture, and after torturing him had impaled him.

We have seen how the inhabitants of Novgorod had informed the commanders of the insurgent militia force of Saltykov's imprisonment. The chronicler provides the details: Saltykov captured Ladoga from the Swedes, and from there wished immediately to proceed towards Moscow because he feared the hostile attitude of Novgorod. The latter had sent to him and had begged him to return to them in Novgorod, and kissed the cross that they would do him no harm. Saltykov believed them and returned but soon afterwards the inhabitants of Novgorod forgot their oath, arrested him and, not content with imprisoning him, subjected him to the torture. In vain did Saltykov swear that he had no designs against the Muscovite realm, in vain did he promise that even if his father came with the Lithuanians, he would fight against him. They did not believe the younger Saltykov, and he atoned by a terrible death for the conduct of his father. It is said that the principal instigator of the affair was Secretary Semeon Samsonov.

The boyars also informed Sigismund that they had written many times to the insurgent militia force, urging it to turn back. "But these criminals would not desist from their brigandage, and do not address themselves to your sovereign grace, nor do they obey our letters and commands in anything. They abuse and dishonor us through all manner of unbefitting speech, they threaten us with savage and shameful death, and those of our people stationed in the towns have been tormented with evil death and torture, and they have redistributed and laid waste our estates and patrimonies."[35] Finally, the insurgent militia force provided information about relations between themselves and the Swedish king, with the intention of electing one of his sons as the Muscovite sovereign. According to the words of the chronicler, the leaders of the militia force decided they could not be without a sovereign, and resolved to send to the Swedes to ask for a king's son to reign over the Muscovite realm.[36]

In conducting negotiations about a future tsar the militia force had to give thought to the matter of forming a provisional government and establishing some order in administration of the army and the land. We have observed that many commanders from various sides had come before Moscow with their own detachments. To whom among them was it fitting to give first place? The highest title, that of boyar, was borne by Prince Dmitry Timofeevich Trubetskoy and Zarutsky, although they had received their boyardom at Tushino. Yet the lesser-ranking noble Liapunov could not, by reason of his abilities and energy, yield place to these boyars. On June 30, 1611 the tsareviches, boyars, lords-in-waiting, and the servicemen and gentry of the various lands of the Muscovite realm who stood before Moscow in defense of the house of the Most Holy Mother of God and for the Orthodox Christian faith against the despoilers of the Christian faith, the Poles and Lithuanians, resolved and chose on behalf of the whole land the boyars and commanders Prince Dmitry Timofeevich Trubetskoy, Ivan Martynovich Zarutsky and the conciliar noble and commander Prokopy Petrovich Liapunov, to the end that they, in charge of government, conduct all affairs of the land and the army, justly settle disputes between all people, and all the army and the land would obey these boyars in everything.

"The resolution confirms that with regard to granting of estates, these shall be meted out as it was in the time of previous legitimate Russian sovereigns. Estates and patrimonies taken away by the boyars for themselves and given out to others without the decree of the land shall be taken back, and their crown and black lands[37] shall be ascribed to the crown, and estates and patrimonial lands shall be given to junior boyars who are without estates or who are destitute. Crown villages and black districts, and money payments to all who, having served in Moscow, Tushino or Kaluga, have received them in excess of the proper measure, are to be resumed. Estates given, no matter to whom, in the name of the king or the prince are to be taken away, but they shall not be taken from gentry who have no other estates or allowances. Gentry and junior boyars sent from Moscow with the ambassadors before Smolensk, and who now are held hostage in Lithuania, shall not have their estates confiscated, and their wives and children shall be treated in the same way as those who endured the siege of Smolensk.

"Church lands are not to be taken and distributed, and those previously granted out must be given back. Estates are not to be seized from the wives and children of gentry who have died or been slain, neither are patrimonies to be taken away from the supporters of Skopin. The boyars, in consultation with the whole land, are free to grant patrimonies provided that they do not violate the previous decree of Patriarch Hermogen. (What the nature of that decree was, or when it was issued, is unknown). Gentry, junior boyars and all ranks who left Moscow, were in Tushino or Kaluga and were placed in various towns are to exchange their patrimonies with those who were besieged in Moscow, and not for grants issued by Tushino. Soldiers whose estates are in borderland locations and devastated by the Lithuanians or Tatars shall be given estates in other towns around Moscow to the extent that it is possible to satisfy them. If gentry and junior boyars who had not reported for service outside Moscow by May 29, and who for that reason had forfeited their estates in accordance with the previous boyar decree, present their petition to the boyars and all the land, saying that hitherto they had not come by reason of poverty, there shall be an investigation concerning this and if it appears they are telling the truth their estates shall be restored to them in the same manner as those who were deprived of their estates because of a false petition, or who were in Moscow involuntarily. Gentry and junior boyars sent to the towns as governors or on other missions, and are fit for service, shall return and are ordered to join the regiments immediately, and be replaced by gentry who are not fit for active service. In the Chancellery of Crown Service and Appointments shall be placed one of the senior gentry, and with him secretaries chosen by the whole land, and they shall be ordered henceforth to give estates to gentry and junior boyars who are poor, destitute, have no estate or only a small one.

"If the atamans and cossacks have served for a long time and wish to be granted estates and salaries, and wish to be assigned to the towns, their wish shall be fulfilled. Those who do not wish to be so rewarded shall be given an allowance of grain and money. Atamans and cossacks are to be withdrawn from the towns and districts, and are forbidden to plunder or murder. Junior boyars, cossacks and musketeers shall be sent to the districts for supplies, and it is commanded that supplies be collected in an orderly fashion. If any of the soldiers commits brigandage in any of the towns or districts, or along the highways, such incidents shall be investigated, stopped and punished, even by death, and to this end the Chancellery for Criminal Affairs and the Land Chancellery[38] shall be reconstructed as before. Deputy governors shall not dispose arbitrarily of revenues and take them for themselves, but must send them to the treasury. A seal of the land must be designed for letters on all official matters, and letters concerning all important affairs of the realm must bear the signature of a boyar. All vital military matters must be supervised by a boyar and the secretary for crown appointments in the Great Chancellery. Those soldiers presently outside Moscow who are killed or disabled by the Lithuanians for the sake of the Orthodox Christian faith shall have their names inscribed in the muster roll,[39] and their services shall be written about by the commanders and captains of the regiments, and shall be sent by hand to the great muster roll, so that the service of all soldiers shall not be forgotten.

"Peasants and people who have fled or have been abducted by other landlords in the Time of Troubles shall be sought out and be given back to their previous landlords. The boyars selected for this by the resolution of the whole land are responsible for governing the land and all matters pertaining to the land and the army. The boyars shall neither execute anybody nor exile them to the towns without the resolution of the whole land. There shall be no riotous assembly or conspiracy by anyone, nor shall anyone conceive enmity against another. If anyone has such a complaint, let him present a petition to the boyars and to the whole land. And whosoever goes about in a mob and in conspiracy, or whosoever says to anyone any treasonable words against the whole land, these matters shall be investigated fairly and punishment and execution pronounced by the boyars, consulting with the whole land, according to their guilt. But without informing the whole land, nobody may be executed or exiled to the towns. And he who kills without the resolution of the land shall himself be executed. If the boyars now elected by the whole land to conduct the affairs of the land and the army are not mindful of the affairs of the land and the army, do not resolve disputes fairly, and do not conduct the affairs of the land and the army according to the decree of the whole land, and if under their leadership all the affairs of the land fail to progress, or if any of the commanders disobey the boyars in all things, the whole land shall be free to replace these boyars and commanders, and choose others in their place, consulting with the whole land as to who is fit for the business of the land and the army."

In this resolution we see, on one hand, a judicious obliviousness of the past. Those who had served Shuisky in Moscow and the tsarlet in Tushino and Kaluga were placed on an equal footing, but restricted by the desire that reconciliation be combined with an attempt to reconstitute strict justice. Those who had received in excess of their just deserts for whatever service they had rendered were called upon to give it back. There was also clearly the conservative inclination, that everything should be as it was of old, a tendency to moderation, as it had been under previous sovereigns. But this tendency towards re-establishment of order, so clearly expressed by the militia force, on this occasion was fruitless for the reasons already cited, namely the character of the man who stood at the head of the better people of the land in opposition to the cossacks, the character of Liapunov; and because the pure was mingled with the impure, for alongside the people of the land stood the cossacks. The chronicles have preserved for us the interesting information that the soldiers did obeisance to the three leaders, urging that they not reproach each other with Tushino.[40] It stands to reason that such reproach could be levelled only by Liapunov at Trubetskoy and Zarutsky, who had been Tushino boyars; although they were equal in their capacity as triumvirs, because of their boyar rank Trubetskoy and Zarutsky took precedence over him, and he signed himself third, yet it pleased him to remind his senior colleagues that they had no right to exalt themselves because of their boyar rank, which they had obtained at Tushino. Among the leaders there was great hatred and pride, says the chronicle.[41] One wished for honor and primacy above the other, one did not wish to be less than the other, and each wished to have sole command. Prokopy Liapunov exalted himself above his proper station, and on account of his pride there was much shame and dishonor to men of lineage, not only to junior boyars, but even among the boyars themselves. They came to pay their respects to him, and stood before his hut for a long time, for he admitted no man to his presence immediately, was very cruel to the cossacks, and on account of this there was great hatred towards him.

It stands further to reason that the man who hated Liapunov most was Zarutsky, who also wished to have exclusive command. Trubetskoy played no overt role for he was in the shadows, and the chronicle explicitly states that he enjoyed no respect whatsoever from Liapunov and Zarutsky. Thus properly speaking in the Moscow encampment there was dual power and not a triumvirate in the leadership, that is to say, there was rivalry between Liapunov and Zarutsky. Liapunov, despite the fact that he antagonized men of lineage, relied upon the gentry and junior boyars, on the untainted militia force of the northern or northeastern provinces, in a word upon the non-cossacks. Zarutsky relied upon the cossacks, and was their chief commander and representative. The decree of the land was written by gentry and junior boyars. The chronicle says that Liapunov inclined to their counsel and ordered the decree to be written whereas for Trubetskoy and Zarutsky, the cossack commanders, this matter was distasteful, and it is easy to understand why. The decree was directed against the cossacks, threatened them with severe punishments for lawlessness and plunder, and was aimed directly at Zarutsky, who had seized many towns and districts and now, according to the decree, he must return them. And from that time, says the chronicle, when Liapunov ordered the decree to be written, they took counsel on how to kill him.[42]

DEATH OF LIAPUNOV

The affair began when Matvei Pleshcheev, having seized twenty-eight cossacks by the monastery of St. Nicholas on the Ugresha,[43] cast them in the water. The cossacks rescued their comrades from the water, brought them to the encampment, called a council of war and raised an outcry against Liapunov, wishing to kill him. The chronicle is silent about the details, but it is apparent that the cossacks had the law on their side. If Pleshcheev caught the cossacks in the act of plundering he was obliged to bring them to the encampment and hand them over to the tribunal, but he arbitrarily threw them into the water even though it had been confirmed in the decree that the death penalty was subject to the counsel of the whole land. Liapunov left the encampment to flee to the Riazan land but the cossacks caught up with him close to the Simonov monastery,[44] and persuaded him to halt. The cossacks must have understood how dangerous it would have been to let Liapunov quit the encampment and give him opportunity to collect his own new militia force, to which naturally all the gentry and junior boyars would rally. Liapunov spent the night in the small fortress of Nikitsk. The next morning the whole army came to him and persuaded him to return to the encampment.

But if the cossacks so strongly desired the death of Liapunov, even more so did Gasiewski within Moscow desire it. The cossacks under Trubetskoy and Zarutsky were no threat to him; he feared the militia force of the people of the land when they had such an active and talented leader as Liapunov. In one of the skirmishes the Poles had taken captive a Don Cossack who was an adoptive brother of the ataman, Isidore Zavarzin. This Zavarzin tried to find a way to liberate his comrade, and asked Gasiewski permission to meet with him, having given a hostage. Gasiewski availed himself of this opportunity, and ordered letters to be written in the name of Liapunov, in which he wrote to all the towns: "Wherever cossacks are captured they are to be killed and drowned, and when God grants that the Muscovite realm is pacified, we will destroy all these evil people." Liapunov's signature was cleverly forged on the document. The captive cossack gave this document to Zavarzin. "Here, brother, see what treachery Liapunov is plotting against our cossack brethren!" Having taken the document, Zavarzin replied: "Now we will kill the bastard!" When Zavarzin arrived at the encampment and showed the letters, the cossacks called a council of war. Trubetskoy and Zarutsky did not attend the council of war. They sent for Liapunov twice, but he did not come. On the third occasion they sent to him non-cossacks, Sylvester Tolstoy and Yury Potemkin, and they guaranteed that no harm would come to him. Liapunov came to the council of war. Ataman Karamyshev cried out that he was a traitor, and showed him the document bearing the signature. Liapunov examined the document, and said: "The signature is similar to mine, only I did not write it." There began a quarrel which ended with Liapunov lying dead under cossack sabres. With him they killed Ivan Nikitich Rzhevsky. Rzhevsky was a bitter foe of Liapunov, but seeing that he was in the right, he defended him and died with him.[45] According to some accounts, Rzhevsky said to the cossacks: "Prokopy was killed on account of a hoax, Prokopy is innocent."

With the death of Liapunov the gentry and junior boyars were left without a leader, in the power of the cossack chieftains. The chronicler relates that shortly after the death of Liapunov a copy of the Kazan Virgin was brought from Kazan to the encampment. The clergy and the servicemen came out on foot to greet the icon, while Zarutsky and the cossacks came on horseback. The cossacks were displeased that the servicemen wished to excel them in piety, and began to abuse them. The chronicler adds that the gentry and table attendants sought death for themselves because of the violence and their shame, many were killed and many were mutilated. Others returned to their towns and to their homes, fearing that they would be murdered by Zarutsky and the cossacks. There were also some among them who bought governorships and other appointments from Zarutsky, and went to the towns to recoup the money they had paid. Most of those who remained outside Moscow were those accustomed to living alongside the cossacks in Tushino and Kaluga. The encampment also was filled with inhabitants of Moscow, tradesmen, merchants and all kinds of common people, who made a living by supplying various foodstuffs. In the encampment there were chancelleries manned by secretaries and clerks. Provisions were collected from the towns and districts and brought before Moscow, but the cossacks did not desist from their brigandage, ranging in groups of a hundred or so along the highways, looting and killing.

NOVGOROD CAPTURED BY SWEDES

At the same time that the cossacks, by the murder of Liapunov and the dispersal of the better servicemen, had halted the progress of the national cause around Moscow, in the northwest Great Novgorod had fallen into the hands of the Swedes. We have observed how the latter had met little success, capturing only Korela. They had lost Ladoga and a second advance on it was unsuccessful, as was their advance on Oreshek. In the month of March De la Gardie[46] approached Novgorod, stood seven versts from it at the Khutinsk monastery, and sent to ask the inhabitants of Novgorod whether they were friends or foes of the Swedes, and whether they wished to observe the Vyborg treaty. Naturally Novgorod replied that this was not their concern, that everything depended on the future sovereign in Moscow. Learning that the land had risen against Wladyslaw, that Moscow had been burned out by the Poles besieged by the militia force of the land, Karl IX had written to the latter's commanders urging that henceforth they must not elect foreign sovereigns, but choose one of their own.

In answer to this Governor Vasily Ivanovich Buturlin, sent to Novgorod by Liapunov, proposed a conference with De la Gardie, at which he declared that the whole land had requested the king to grant one of his sons to rule the Muscovite realm. Negotiations began and dragged out because the Swedes, like the Poles, first demanded money and towns, and because in Novgorod events occurred which gave De la Gardie hope that he might conquer it easily. According to Swedish accounts Buturlin himself, who hated the Poles and had become friendly with De la Gardie even in Moscow, now advised him to conquer Novgorod. According to Russian accounts there was disagreement between Buturlin and the senior governor, Prince Ivan Nikitich Odoevsky the Elder,[47] which prevented the latter from taking active measures for the security of the city. Buturlin corresponded with the Swedes, the traders brought them various supplies, and when De la Gardie crossed the Volkhov and stood by the Kolmovsky monastery Buturlin continued to negotiate with him. To complete the misfortune, there was no communication between the soldiers and the townsmen, who took alarm and rushed into the city with their possessions. On July 8 De la Gardie ordered an assault but after a cruel slaughter failed to break into the city. On Buturlin's order the suburbs were burned. The Swedes then stood inactive for seven days. This encouraged the inhabitants of Novgorod. While some prayed day and night, others began to drink, encouraging one another. "Do not fear the arrival of the foreigners, they cannot capture the city, there are many people within it." Drunken people climbed the walls and shamelessly abused the Swedes. The latter had a prisoner, Ivan Shaval, a bondsman of Lutokhin. Shaval, knowing how poorly the city was guarded, promised to lead the Swedes into it. On July 15 (as De la Gardie later recounted it) Secretary Anfinogen Golenishchev came to the Swedish encampment from Buturlin, who had ordered that De la Gardie be told to leave Novgorod, and not come as had been planned. De la Gardie ordered this reply: "Buturlin deceives me in everything, he sends to me with threats, he wants to draw me away from Novgorod, but let him know that I will call him to account for these words in Novgorod." On the night of July 16 Shaval led the Swedes to the Miracle gates without being observed.

The inhabitants only became aware that the enemy was within the city when the Swedes attacked the sentries along the walls and before the houses. The Swedes encountered the first resistance on the square where Buturlin was deployed with his detachment, but this resistance was short-lived. Buturlin left the city and during the retreat the cossacks and musketeers plundered the shops and houses under the pretext that otherwise the Swedes would take everything. There was yet another, but futile, act of resistance in two places. The musketeer captain Vasily Gaiutin, Secretary Anfinogen Golenishchev, Vasily Orlov, and the cossack ataman Timofey Sharov with forty cossacks, decided to defend themselves to the last extremity. Many times the Swedes called upon them to surrender, but to no avail, and all died together for the Orthodox faith.

Archpriest Amos of the Holy Wisdom cathedral[48] shut himself in his house with several citizens, fought for a long time against the Swedes and killed many of them. Amos at that time was under an interdict from Metropolitan Isidore. The metropolitan was conducting prayers on the wall, saw the heroic deed of Amos, and in his absence forgave and blessed him. The Swedes, enraged by his resistance, finally set fire to the archpriest's house, and he perished in the flames with his companions. Not one of them fell alive into the hands of the Swedes.[49]

These were the last defenders of Great Novgorod. Isidore and Odoevsky, seeing that there were no soldiers in the city, sent to De la Gardie to sue for terms. The first condition was an oath of allegiance by the inhabitants of Novgorod to a Swedish prince. De la Gardie on his part agreed not to plunder Novgorod, and was admitted into the citadel. The details of the treaty were as follows: (1) There would be sincere friendship and eternal peace between Novgorod and Sweden on the basis of the treaty of Teusen[50] and the treaties concluded under Tsar Vasily. The inhabitants of Novgorod agreed to sever all relations with Poland, accept the Swedish king as their protector and defender, without whose consent they would conclude no alliance or peace with anybody. (2) The inhabitants of Novgorod shall elect and request as tsar one of the sons of King Karl, and would confirm his election by an oath of allegiance, as a consequence of which the Muscovite realm also would recognize King Karl as its protector and one of his sons as its tsar. (3) Until the arrival of the prince, the inhabitants of Novgorod shall subject themselves to De la Gardie, undertake together with him to bring the nearby towns into allegiance to the king, in this not sparing their lives. They undertook not to conceal anything from De la Gardie, and that they inform him in good time of any tidings from Moscow or anywhere else, nor would they undertake any important enterprise without his knowledge or consent, and more especially would not harbor any hostile designs towards him. They promised to declare without concealment all revenues of Novgorod and its districts, and all money presently in the treasury.

(4) De la Gardie promised that if the realms of Novgorod and Muscovy recognized King Karl and his successors as their protectors, the king would send to rule over them one of his sons as soon as both realms through their plenipotentiaries requested his majesty to do so. De la Gardie promised that after the accession of the prince, as also now before his arrival, he would commit no act of oppression against the Orthodox faith, not touch the churches or monasteries, and not appropriate their revenues. (5) None of the towns or districts of Novgorod would be annexed to Sweden, except for Korela and its district. Concerning compensation for expenses incurred in sending the auxiliary army to aid Shuisky, the king would confer with the boyars and the Russian people as soon as his son came to assume the tsardom. (6) It shall be forbidden to take out of Russia into Sweden money, bells or military equipment without the knowledge or consent of the Russians. Russians would not be deported to Sweden, nor would Swedes be detained in Russia. Men of all ranks would retain their former rights. Their possessions would remain inviolate. Judgment would be rendered as before. In order to ensure impartial justice, in places of judgment there shall be equal numbers of Russian and Swedish officials. For injuries inflicted on Russians by Swedes, or vice versa, punishment shall be meted without favoritism.

(7) Deserters were to be surrendered. (8) Swedish soldiers who had rendered service to Russia with the consent of the Russian magnates shall receive rewards in the form of possessions (patrimonies?), salaries and

estates. There shall be free trade between the two countries with the usual customs dues. (9) Cossacks may cross the frontier as they wished but servitors of boyars shall remain bound to their owners as before. (10) These conditions shall be preserved inviolate always, not only in relation to the realm of Novgorod but also in relation to those of Vladimir and Moscow if their inhabitants, together with those of Novgorod, recognized the king as their protector and the prince as their sovereign. (11) The Swedish army shall not be billetted in the outer parts of the city where they might be a burden to the inhabitants, but the latter shall help with money for their provisioning. No inhabitant might leave the city to live in the countryside or remove possessions without the knowledge and consent of De la Gardie.

The latter swore to observe the treaty. The inhabitants of Novgorod also swore to fulfill the conditions, even if the realms of Vladimir and Moscow did not agree to do so. By this clause, consequently, Novgorod dissociated its cause from that of Muscovy. From the treaty it is clear that it was written by the victor. The Muscovite realm could not accept it in this form since with the election of the prince as tsar was tied the obligation to recognize his father the king and his successors as protectors of the Russian tsardom, whereas the chief condition for the Russians, namely the acceptance of the Orthodox faith by the prince, was omitted in the treaty.

FURTHER CIVIL STRIFE IN PSKOV

Novgorod now had separated from the Muscovite realm as long since had Pskov, which had not acted with the purpose of recognizing a foreigner as sovereign. Here was the last corner where a pretender might still appear. We left Pskov when it was in the power of the lesser citizens, who were persecuting the clergy and the better people as traitors. At first this was based on evidence of clear treason but later there people were found who appeared to profit personally from the Troubles by accusing both the innocent and the guilty. There was much turbulence and bloodshed, both justly and unjustly, says the chronicler. Some brought denunciations of brigandage, corruption and false promises, while others, because of their simple-mindedness, looking upon the others, joined in the chorus and tortured many people. And if someone spoke on behalf of anyone, saying he was being tortured unjustifiably, they would seize him also, crying "What sort of a man are you, to speak up for a traitor?" The prison was always full. But, as usually happens, the rule of the multitude, having been transformed into the insane tyranny of a few, provoked strong opposition even among the majority of the most humble citizens. Their patience being exhausted by the violent acts of the musketeers and Kudekusha, they allied themselves with the clergy and the better people.[51]

In August 1609 the musketeers ordered a certain Alexis Khozin to be executed, and this arbitrary act served as the pretext for an uprising. All the people rose up, the greater and the less, even those who had joined the chorus, profited from their own people and accepted false promises. Now, seeing the pass to which things had come, seeing that there was neither security for the innocent nor judgment for the guilty, they rose up against the musketeers. Why did the musketeers rule without the consent of the town and execute someone without the general consent of all? Why did they take it into their heads to act in their own arbitrariness and take no account of Pskov? They all pushed their way to the musketeers, wishing to take Alexis Khozin from them. The musketeers refused to yield, armed themselves and sounded the bell on the Romanikha tower; thus the news spread that the musketeers were attacking the inhabitants of Pskov, and various townsmen advanced on them. The latter, realizing that they had no chance against all the people of Pskov, laid hold of Alexis Khozin, struck off his head and fled to their own settlement, whereupon the inhabitants of Pskov shut off the town to them. Then the better people, seeing the majority in their favor, wished to take advantage of the situation, seized Timofey Kudekusha and seven of his supporters and stoned them, but at this point the better people did not know how to exercise moderation. They began indiscriminately to call all the lesser people conspirators, the guilty along with the innocent. Priests meddled in matters which were not their concern, the leaders interrogated humble people with severe tortures in the city hall, beat others with the knout in the marketplace, beheaded scores of people and cast their heads into the moat. The prisons were filled once again , but this time with humble folk. Other lesser people dispersed to the bytowns and villages.

When the news arrived in Pskov that Tsar Vasily had triumphed, that the Tushino encampment had been destroyed, and the lesser people realized they could expect no help from their own tsar, Dmitry, the better people wished to settle accounts with their opponents. They shut up the city. Boyars, leading merchants, junior boyars and monastic servitors armed themselves and mounted up. All their supporters, helpers and sympathizers rallied around them. All the square and the citadel were filled with armed men. All the bells of the Trinity church pealed. They chanted prayers for Tsar Vasily, they congratulated and embraced each other, and talked of finally pacifying the lesser people and bringing them into allegiance, and killing the dissidents and musketeers in their settlement. The lesser people, seeing that for them the hour of decision had come, went to the Zapskovie river district,[52] rang the bells of the church of SS Cosmas and Damian,[53] and a huge crowd gathered. The inhabitants of Polonishche, hearing the bells, came to the aid of Zapskovie. The better people ordered the musketeers' settlement bombarded from the Intercession tower but the inhabitants of Polonishche did not let them fire, dislodging them from the tower. Then the better people decided to go and fight for control of Zapskovie but the inhabitants trained the regimental cannon on the square, demolished the tower by the Vozvozsk gates and sent word to the musketeers in the settlement that they should come to the aid of the lesser people in Zapskovie. The better people, hearing that the inhabitants of Zapskovie were talking with the musketeers, were alarmed, and communicated with the lesser people, begging that the musketeers not be admitted into the city and promising that all would live together as before, neither kissing the cross to Novgorod nor harming anyone. The inhabitants of Zapskovie replied: "The musketeers have not betrayed us, why do you not allow them into the city?" The better people, seeing that it would be difficult to dissuade the lesser people, rushed on Polonishche to prevent the musketeers from entering the city but the inhabitants of Polonishche repelled the better people from the gates. Then the two governors, the junior boyars and the better people, altogether about three hundred, left for Novgorod, others to Pechory.[54] still others hid for the while in their houses, and the people admitted the musketeers into the city. This time the lesser people used their victory with moderation. They took an inventory of the possessions of those who had departed for Novgorod but did not touch the possessions of those who had hidden in Pechory or in Pskov.

After that there began enmity between Novgorod and Pskov, recalling ancient times. Inhabitants of Novgorod, with Swedes and exiles from Pskov, suddenly descended upon the Pskov region, chased off livestock, took peasants captive and spoiled grainfields and meadows. But this was only the beginning of the hardships. In Moscow, Novgorod and Toropets people kissed the cross to the Lithuanian prince. In Pskov arrived a letter from Moscow from the patriarch and the boyars, telling them to kiss the cross to Wladyslaw. "How can you resist the Muscovite, Lithuanian and Polish tsardom?" But the inhabitants of Pskov were not daunted, and did not kiss the cross. Lisowski came and for almost four days ravaged the Pskov region, and like a wolf systematically plundered and devoured. In March 1611 the Lithuanian Hetman Chodkiewicz arrived before Pechory from Livonia, besieged Pechory for six weeks, and there were seven assaults.

On March 23 in Ivangorod there appeared Sidorka, the last brigand calling himself Tsarevich Dmitry.[55] The cossacks aroused themselves, obeying the summons of one of their own. On April 15 they left Pskov, saying that they were going after Lisowski, but instead joined the brigand at Ivangorod. In these years of the Troubles, says the chronicler, there was no governor in Pskov, only Secretary Ivan Leontovich Lugovskoy, and the townsmen assigned to help him, and with these people the secretary looked after all matters, both military and civil; and by the grace of God the foreigners did not conquer one town belonging to Pskov, but they conquered them when governors began to multiply in Pskov. As early as the beginning of spring Pskov sent petitioners to the whole land, to the commanders outside Moscow, saying that Lisowski was devastating the region, Chodkiewicz was besieging Pechory, the inhabitants of Novgorod were setting out with a number of foreigners, and from Ivangorod the brigand was taking up arms against Pskov. Many attacks were converging from all quarters, and there was no help from anywhere. But the encampment outside Moscow could not afford this aid nor could it be concerned with Pskov.

SCARCITY AMONG POLES AND RUSSIANS

We left that encampment at the time when, because of the death of Liapunov, the cossacks were in the ascendant and the more substantial people in the militia force either had to quit the common cause or tolerate the turbulence of the cossacks. On August 14, 1611 (New Style)[56] Sapieha once more arrived before Moscow with provisions, and fought against members of the militia force. The besieged Poles effected a sortie to the White quarter, but unsuccessfully. The next day they were more fortunate. The Poles under Sapieha managed to cross the Moscow river and get supplies to the besieged. The besieged on their part staged another sortie, and managed to capture four of the gates of the White quarter from the Russians. The stiffest fight took place by the Nikita gates, but the Poles managed to hold onto these. The Tver gates remained in the hands of the Russians. The Poles say that the Russians were seized with such panic that the next day not only did they fail to make any attempt to recapture the lost gates, but even poorly guarded those that remained in their hands. But although the militia force of Trubetskoy and Zarutsky was intimidated, notwithstanding this fear it was saved by lack of discipline among the Poles. While those of them who had fought all day for control of the gates grew weary towards evening, and sent to ask Gasiewski for reinforcements, not one regiment moved, despite Gasiewski's order. The next day Gasiewski called together his army and declared that it was necessary to take advantage of the situation, strike with all their forces, and capture the remaining fortifications of the White quarter. Sapieha let it be known that as soon as the besieged reached the walls of the White quarter, he would attack the militia force from the open field. Most of the army was in agreement with Gasiewski but some, who were envious of him, said that Chodkiewicz, the Lithuanian hetman, was coming, and it was pointless to take the glory away from him and give it to Gasiewski, and the majority agreed to do nothing. Sapieha fell sick and on September 14 died within the Kremlin in Shuisky's house.

On October 6 (New Style) Hetman Chodkiewicz finally arrived outside Moscow, took position by the Andronov monastery, and fought a few skirmishes with the members of the militia force, but not with a very fortunate outcome. According to the testimony of the Poles themselves, who also explain the reason for this misfortune, there was enmity between Potocki, the governor of Smolensk, and Chodkiewicz. Potocki did not wish credit for the conquest of Moscow to go to Chodkiewicz. Consequently, in the army which was moving upon Moscow there were two factions, those of Potocki and Chodkiewicz. Furthermore the Poles did not wish to be subordinate to Chodkiewicz, a Lithuanian hetman. Finally the Russian soldiers had every justification for laughing at the paucity of the hetman's forces. With him there came no more than two thousand troops, weakened in morale by disputes and physically weakened by their previous labors in Livonia. There was no infantry at all.

So passed the autumn of the year 1611. When winter came the Poles lacked provisions. For hay they had to travel several miles accompanied by armed detachments for safety, and Chodkiewicz retreated from Moscow to the Rogachev monastery (between the Pugaia and Volga rivers, twenty versts from Rzhev). A few of those Poles who had been under siege in the Kremlin and Kitai quarter also left with him. Those who remained in Moscow, as well as the chasseurs from Sapieha's regiments who wished to remain with them, were given a special reward, and as surety were given valuables from the tsar's treasury. First two crowns were given, those of Godunov and False Dmitry, the tsar's rhinoceros staff with precious stones, the rich hussar's saddle of False Dmitry, several rhinoceros horns, which at that time were very highly valued.[57] The followers of Sapieha were given two caps belonging to the tsars, a golden staff and an orb decorated with precious stones.

The boyars, besieged in the Kremlin, saw that only the immediate arrival of the king or the prince with an army could save them and so, at the beginning of October, they sent to Sigismund a new embassy, consisting of Prince Yury Nikitich Trubetskoy, Mikhail Glebovich Saltykov and Secretary Yanov. The new embassy, it said in their letters of credence, had been sent because the former ambassadors, as the king himself had written, had acted not according to the instructions had been given, had corresponded with the Kaluga brigand, with the besieged in Smolensk, with Liapunov and other traitors. The document addressed to Sigismund begins thus: "To the most illustrious sovereign Sigismund III, etc., from your clergy of the Muscovite realm, Archbishop Arsenius of Archangel and all the Holy Synod, and the faithful subjects of you, the sovereign, boyars and lords-in waiting," and so forth. Hermogen was imprisoned, and in such a case would not have agreed to sign a document where the boyars had described themselves as the most faithful subjects of Sigismund. The former patriarch, Ignaty, appointed by False Dmitry, had taken advantage of Zolkiewski's entry into Moscow to make good his escape, and had departed into the Polish territories.[58] At the head of the Kremlin clergy there remained Arsenius, a Greek who had been appointed to serve in the cathedral of the Archangel, and who thus styled himself archbishop of Archangel.[59]

Thanks to lack of arms among the Poles, the unarmed militia force of Trubetskoy and Zarutsky was able to maintain itself outside Moscow, making themselves out to be, as previously, men who had come to fight for the Orthodox faith against the sacrilegious Poles and Lithuanians. But the Russians did not at all regard this militia force in this way after the death of Liapunov. Thus the inhabitants of Kazan wrote to those of Perm: "The cossacks, violating their sacred oath have, my lords, killed the fighter and champion of Christ's faith, Prokopy Petrovich Liapunov outside

Moscow, him who was defending the Orthodox Christian faith, the house of the Most Holy Mother of God and the Muscovite realm against the Poles and Lithuanians and the Russian brigands. We, the metropolitan and all the people of the realm of Kazan have agreed with Nizhny Novgorod and all the towns of the Volga region, on the high and the low bank, and the Cheremis of the low bank, that we all will be in counsel and unity, defend the Muscovite and Kazan realms, not fight against each other or do harm to one another. And if anyone commits a crime he shall be punished by due process of law, according to his guilt. We shall not admit into the towns any new governors, captains or any officials, nor replace the previous ones, and everything shall be as before. Neither will we admit cossacks into the town, and we will stand firmly to this until God grants a sovereign to the Muscovite realm. And we will choose for ourselves over the Muscovite realm a sovereign by election of the whole land of the Russian dominion. But if the cossacks elect a sovereign according to their desire, on their own, without agreeing with the whole land, we will not accept such a sovereign."[60]

From this document we see that the people of the land, the inhabitants of the untainted half of the Muscovite realm, the dwellers of the Volga region, as opposed to the Ukraine, earlier ruined by the cossacks, were not at all dismayed by the death of Liapunov and the triumph of the cossacks outside Moscow, nor did they identify at all the cause of liberating the land with one man, one commander. Sorrowfully alluding to the slaying of their leader, at the same time they let it be known that the common cause was not lost thereby, that among them reigned common counsel and unity, let it be known that they would not allow any change, any novelty, until the restoration of lawful order, until the election of a tsar by the whole land, and repeated their first resolution concerning the cossacks— they would not allow cossacks into the towns nor would they accept a sovereign elected by them alone.

APPEALS FROM TRINITY MONASTERY

The moral force represented by the untainted, communally-minded part of the population was as strained as earlier, and as before promises were made of a unanimous stand for the faith of their fathers against sacreligious foes. Earlier the call to rise originated with the principal personage of the time when there was no sovereign, the patriarch. Now his voice could not be heard from his Kremlin dungeon. Instead of letters from the patriarch there rang the summons in letters from the glorious Trinity monastery, which recently had acquired new fame, from Archimandrite Dionysius and the cellarer, Avraamy Palitsyn.[61] The latter is well known to us. We have seen how the cunning cellarer was unwilling to suffer hardship outside Smolensk, or wait for imprisonment in the depths of Poland, and left without taking leave of the ambassadors. On arrival at his monastery he saw that Wladyslaw's cause was lost, and grew eager the cause of liberation. As Liapunov's defense force approached Moscow, Avraamy appeared before it with holy water. The man whose name stands together with that of Palitsyn in the famous missives of the Trinity monastery, Archimandrite Dionysius, was distinguished by a different character. We must now become acquainted with him.

ARCHIMANDRITE DIONYSIUS

Once, at the beginning of the Time of Troubles, in Moscow, in the marketplace where books were sold, there arrived a young monk, tall, well-built and handsome. All eyes were turned upon him and one of those who were present, calling to mind the conduct of certain monks, addressed ungracious words to him. The monk, instead of becoming angry at this, took a deep breath, burst into tears, and said to him: "Yes, brother! I am in this respect such a sinner as you have thought me to be. God has revealed to you the truth about me. If I were a proper monk I would not be strolling around this market, I would not be wandering among the people, but would be sitting in my cell. Forgive me, a sinner, for my thoughtlessness, for the sake of God." All those present, affected by these words, turned with shouts upon the man who had dared abuse the worthy monk, calling him an impertinent ignoramus. "No, brothers," the monk said to them, "that am I, not he. All his words concerning me are justified. He was sent by God to remind me that I must not wander about the marketplace, but sit in my cell." With these words the monk left. The man who had wronged him rushed after him and begged his forgiveness. This monk was from the monastery at Staritsa, and his name was Dionysius.

Soon Dionysius was seen again in the squares of Moscow in the dignity of archimandrite of his monastery, and there he did not say this time that it was unbefitting to show himself among the people, for here he was in his proper place. When giving instructions to the clergy Patriarch Hermogen cited Dionysius as an example. "See," he said, "the archimandrite of Staritsa. At no time does he absent himself from the cathedral church, he is always present at councils of the tsar and of the community." By the councils of all the community the patriarch meant those turbulent gatherings of the people where the opponents of Tsar Vasily demanded his deposition, where the patriarch defended the tsar, and where Dionysius was at the side of the patriarch and persuaded the people, regardless of the insults the turbulent crown rained upon them.

From the Staritsa monastery Dionysius was transferred to the post of archimandrite of the Trinity monastery. When Moscow was destroyed and the cossacks and followers of Sapieha were running amok in the surrounding districts, crowds of refugees swarmed to the Trinity monastery from all sides, and it was fearful to look upon them. Some had broken bones and others were burned, others had their limbs torn from their sockets, hair torn from their heads, others had their arms and legs cut off, while others simply came to make confession, receive the sacrament and die. Many never succeeded in reaching the monastery, but died on the way. The monastery, the settlements and the surrounding hamlets were full of the dead and the dying.

Dionysius summoned the cellarer, the treasurer and all the brethren, servitors and monastic peasants, and spoke to them, saying that in this time of need it was necessary to give everyone seeking sanctuary at the shrine of St. Sergius all the help in their power. They replied unanimously: "Who, lord archimandrite, in such a misfortune can gather his wits? There is nobody we can turn to except the one God." Dionysius burst into tears and once more said to them: "Know that this is a trial sent us by God. God delivered us from the great siege, and now on account of our laxity and miserliness He humbles and reproaches us even without a siege." "What are we to do?" asked the cellarer, brethren and servitors. Dionysius replied: "The house of the Holy Trinity will not be laid to waste if we pray to God that He give us wisdom. Only rely upon this, and each will do what he can." The servitors and peasants took counsel among themselves, and said to the archimandrite and the brethren: "If you, my lords, will give to the poor from the monastic treasury for food, clothing and medicine, and will give to the workers who are hired to prepare food, serve, heal, collect and bury the dead, we will not spare our lives." And so they ministered to all the poor, living and dying. First of all they built houses, hospitals for the wounded, huts for hospitality to all ranks who had fled Moscow and other towns, separate houses for men and women, in the settlements of Sluzhanaia and Klementievo. Monastic servitors travelled around the village and along the highways, gathering up the wounded and dead. The women to whom the monastery gave refuge and sustenance incessantly sewed and washed shirts for the living and shrouds for the dead. And within the monastery, in the archimandrite's cell, sat dexterous scribes, among whom Alexis Tikhonov was particularly distinguished. They collected instructive words from holy scriptures, composed exhortatory letters, and sent them among the towns and regiments, calling for the liberation of the land.

In the summer of 1611, while Liapunov was still alive, letters were sent by Dionysius to Kazan, to all the lower towns,[62] to Great Novgorod, to the maritime regions, to Vologda and Perm. "Orthodox Christians!" it said in the document, "be mindful of the true Orthodox Christian faith, that we were all born of Christian parents, and were signed with the seal of holy baptism, promising to believe in the Holy Trinity. Place your hope in the sign of the Lord's cross, and show your valorous deeds, beseech your servicemen to be at one with all Orthodox Christians, and in common stand against the betrayers of Christians, Mikhail Saltykov and Fedka Andronov, and against the ancient foes of Christianity, the Poles and Lithuanians. You have seen the utter ruin that Christians have suffered from them; you have seen what devastation they have wrought within the Muscovite realm. Where are the holy churches of God, the images of God? Where are the monks, flourishing in their gray hair? The nuns, adorned as benefactresses, are they not all utterly ruined and insulted with evil abuse? Neither old men nor babes at the breast are spared. Be mindful and have pity upon the universal deadly ruin you have seen, so that a savage death may not also overtake you. Let the servicemen without delay hasten towards Moscow, and meet with the boyars and all Orthodox Christians. You yourselves know that every cause has its proper time, and that any untimely undertaking simply results in bustle and inactivity. Even though there be certain disaffection in your lands, for the sake of God lay this aside for the time being, so that you may together work for the deliverance of the Orthodox Christian faith, before aid comes to the enemy. Have pity, set about this cause more expeditiously, send aid in the form of soldiers and contributions to the treasury lest the army now gathered outside Moscow be dispersed through scarcity."[63]

On October 6 the authorities of the Trinity monastery sent letters throughout the provinces with the news that "Chodkiewicz has come to Moscow to aid the Lithuanians, and with him have come more than two thousand men, and have taken up their positions along the highways in

Krasnoe Selo[64] and along the Kolomna road, to prevent supplies reaching the boyars, commanders and soldiers who are defending the Orthodox Christian faith, so that through hunger they may be driven from Moscow, leading us, Orthodox Christians, to utter destruction. But the boyars, commanders and the soldiers are standing firmly and steadfastly outside Moscow, they wish to suffer for the Orthodox Christian faith as they have vowed, and by their death receive eternal life. But gentry, junior boyars and all ranks of servicemen from Kashira, Kaluga, Tula and other towns around Moscow have come towards Moscow, and from the Severian towns Yury Bezzubtsov and his men are hastening to Moscow, while from the other side gentry, junior boyars and all ranks of servicemen and soldiers from many towns are gathering in Pereiaslavl Zalessky and also wish to advance on Moscow." The document concludes with the same exhortation we have seen in previous letters. Naturally in the Trinity monastery the conduct of the cossacks in the encampment outside Moscow was all too well known, but even so that force stood under the banner of the Orthodox faith and the Muscovite realm, was keeping under siege the ancient foes of the cross of Christ, and was fighting successfully against them. It is not surprising that the authorities of the Trinity monastery considered it their obligation in the hour of danger to summon the Russian people to the aid of the militia force of Trubetskoy and Zarutsky. The small number of the regular army was cause for concern. Meanwhile among the Russians, bereft of their leader and their focus, numerous detachments were forming and causing fearful harm to the Poles, not giving them any rest, capturing booty and supplies. Among the Poles these partisans bore the name "*sziszi*".

SIGNS OF A POPULAR LIBERATION MOVEMENT

The nation was ready to rise up as one man. The uninterrupted series of troubles and hardships had not crushed the mighty powers of the young nation. They had purified society, brought it to realize the necessity to sacrifice everything for the salvation of the faith, threatened by foreign enemies, and for public order, threatened by internal foes, the brigands. Signs appeared of understanding the need for moral cleansing, for the heroic deed of freeing the land from its enemies; signs that the people, seeing no help from outside, had searched its inner spiritual world in order thence to draw out the means of salvation. The word spread through the districts, the towns sent letters to one another saying that in Nizhny

Novgorod there had been a divine revelation to some pious man or other, whose name was Grigory. He was commanded to preach the word of God throughout the whole Russian realm. They said that this Grigory was favored with a vision at midnight. He saw the roof snatched from his house and a great light illuminated the room, where there appeared unto him two men preaching repentance, of purifying the realm. There also had been a vision in Vladimir. Following this, according to the counsel of all the land of the Muscovite realm, all the Orthodox nation in all the towns resolved to fast, to abstain from food and drink for three days, even babes at the breast, and according to this resolution Orthodox Christians fasted. For three days—Monday, Tuesday and Wednesday—they neither ate nor drank anything, and on Thursday and Friday they ate sparingly. Thus, dominated by religious feeling, the thought welled among the people of the need to purify the whole land, to look beyond the troubled and profane social degeneracy of their time. We have seen that even Shuisky thought of this purification, and how two patriarchs wished to cleanse the nation of the sin of their recent perfidy, but theirs were personal gestures, and for this reason premature. Now the nation had learned by experience to think of the need for purification. Orthodox Christians fasted, says the document, of their own free will.[65]

MININ IN NIZHNY NOVGOROD

Now everything was ready, only the beginning of the movement was awaited. The movement declared itself in Nizhny Novgorod. The representatives of the government here at the time in question were the governors, Prince Vasily Andreevich Zvenigorodsky[66] and Andrei Semonovich Aliabiev,[67] the crown agent Ivan Ivanovich Birkin[68] and Secretary Vasily Semeonov. Among the number of territorial elders was Kuzma Minin Sukhoruky, a butcher.[69] Birkin had served Shuisky, then the Tushino brigand, then Shuisky again, and once again betrayed him in the company of Liapunov, who had sent him to Nizhny Novgorod. Here he was regarded as an unreliable person, and the territorial elder had called him to his face a vessel of Satan. When, in October 1611, the inhabitants of Nizhny Novgorod received the letters from the Trinity monastery, the senior people of the town, together with the clergy, gathered to take counsel, and Minin said: "St. Sergius has appeared to me in a dream and ordered me to awake those who were asleep. Read the letter of Dionysius in the cathedral, and wherever it is pleasing to God." The crown agent

Birkin contradicted him, but Minin halted him, pointing out that the people had guessed his intentions.

The next day the inhabitants of Nizhny Novgorod gathered in the cathedral church. There Archpriest Savva urged them to stand firm for the faith, and read the document from the Trinity monastery. After the archpriest, Minin spoke: "We wish to aid the Muscovite realm, so let us not spare our possessions, let us sell our houses, pledge our wives and children, and do obeisance to him who shall come forward for the true Orthodox faith and be our leader." After that there were private consultations, and Minin continued his exhortation. "What are we here to do?" they asked him. "Take up arms," Minin replied, "we ourselves are not skilled in military matters, so let us put out the call among the free servicemen." "And where shall we obtain the funds to engage servicemen?" the question was heard once again. "I, a sinner, have taken up a collection among my companions, numbering altogether 2,500 men, and we have collected 1,700 rubles. We have given a third of our wealth. I had 300 rubles, and I gave a hundred rubles into the fund. You should do likewise." "Let it be so! Let it be so!" they all cried. A collection was taken up. There came a widow who said: "I was left childless after the death of my husband, and I have twelve thousand rubles. I give ten thousand into the fund, and shall keep two thousand for myself." Those who would not give voluntarily were forced to contribute. But before they could hire soldiers they must first find a commander.

PRINCE POZHARSKY

At that time there lived in the province of Suzdal the well-known table attendant and commander Prince Dmitry Mikhailovich Pozharsky, who had arrived there from the Trinity monastery and had recovered from his wounds, sustained during the destruction of Moscow. Minin corresponded with him, made an agreement, and announced to the people that they must not summon anyone but Prince Pozharsky. Feodosy, archimandrite of the Caves monastery,[70] the senior noble Zhdan Petrovich Boltin and senior men of all ranks were sent to him. Pozharsky answered the emissaries: "I rejoice in your counsel, I am ready to travel immediately, but first choose from the people my coadjutor in this great cause who will gather together the treasury." The emissaries said that there was no such man in their town. Pozharsky answered: "You have Kuzma Minin with you, he has been an official, he is accustomed to such matters."

Dmitry Pozharsky
Spasso-Efimiev Monastery, Suzdal

When the emissaries returned and announced to the inhabitants of
Nizhny Novgorod what Pozharsky had said, they did obeisance to Kuzma,
urging him to accept the task. Minin refused, except on condition that the
inhabitants of Nizhny Novgorod submit entirely to his will. "I will agree,"
he said, "if you will write out a resolution that in everything you will be
obedient and submissive, and give money for the soldiers." The inhabitants of Nizhny Novgorod agreed, and Minin wrote into the resolution his
previous words, that they must give up not only their possessions, but also
sell their wives and children. When the resolution was signed Kuzma took
it and sent it off immediately to Pozharsky lest the inhabitants of Nizhny
Novgorod, their ardor cooled, revoke it.

SECOND MILITIA FORCE

News that the inhabitants of Nizhny Novgorod had risen and were ready
to make any sacrifice for the soldiers quickly spread among the nearby
towns. Gentry from Smolensk who had lost estates in their own region because of conquest by the Poles, and who had received lands in the province of Arzamas, sent to petition the inhabitants of Nizhny Novgorod
to receive them, for Zarutsky had expelled them from their new estates,
forbidding their peasants to obey them. The inhabitants of Nizhny Novgorod sent these petitioners to Pozharsky to request him to come to Nizhny
Novgorod immediately. He came, and on his way picked up servicemen
from Dorogobuzh and Viazma, who had been given estates in Yaropolch,
but who also had been dispossessed by Zarutsky, and together with them
entered Nizhny Novgorod, where he was received with great honor.

First of all the new leader of the militia force occupied himself with
the distribution of pay to the soldiers, but the treasury of Nizhny Novgorod grew insufficient. It was necessary to write around all the towns and
request their co-operation. These letters were written in the names of Dmitry Pozharsky, Ivan Birkin, Vasily (Semonov?) Yudin and the soldiers
and people of the land of Nizhny Novgorod. In these it was written that
"according to the word of Christ there have arisen many false Christs and,
seduced by their charms, all our land has been crushed, there has arisen
internecine strife in the Russian realm, and this has lasted for some considerable time. Seeing such strife among us, the predators of our salvation,
the Poles and Lithuanians, have sought to destroy the Muscovite realm,
and God has allowed this insidious design to be accomplished. Seeing
themselves such injustice, all the towns of the Muscovite realm, having

corresponded with one another, have resolved by kissing the cross that we, all Orthodox Christians, will be in love and unity, and not begin anew our previous internecine strife, will liberate the Muscovite realm from its enemies, and will elect no sovereign on our own initiative without consultation with the whole land, so that God may give us a pious tsar, like unto our previous legitimate Christian sovereigns. Gentry and junior boyars from all the towns have been outside Moscow, they strongly besieged the Poles and Lithuanians, but then the gentry and junior boyars dispersed from outside Moscow in search of transient pleasures, plunder and theft. Many are striving to the end that the Polish lady Marina and her illegitimate son rule over the Muscovite realm. But now we, all the people of Nizhny Novgorod, have corresponded with Kazan and all the lower towns and the towns of the Volga basin, and have gathered together with many soldiers. We see the utter ruin of the Muscovite realm, we beg God for mercy, and we all will come and pledge our lives for the Muscovite realm.

"Furthermore there also have come to us in Nizhny Novgorod from Arzamas natives of Smolensk, Dorogobuzh and Viatka, and gentry and junior boyars from many other towns. And we, all the people of Nizhny Novgorod, have taken counsel among ourselves, and have resolved to share our goods and houses with them, to give them pay and assistance, and send them to the aid of the Muscovite realm. And you, my lords, also must be mindful of your solemn oath to resist our foes to the death. You must all the sooner pursue the Lithuanians. If you, my lords, gentry and junior boyars, fear some oppression from the cossacks or some acts of brigandage or other, you must have no such fear. When all the upper and lower towns are in accord, we will as all the land take counsel concerning this, and not allow brigands to inflict any harm. You yourselves know that we hitherto have inflicted harm on no one, neither henceforth do we wish to inflict any harm. You must be immediately in one counsel together, and the soldiers together shall pursue the Poles and Lithuanians so that as before the cossacks cannot overcome the forces of the lower towns by brigandage, plunder, other criminal acts or support of Marina's son. And when we are in accord with you let us deal with the Poles and Lithuanians as one, as far as the merciful God gives us aid. And whosoever around Moscow or in any of the towns wishes to do harm or shed new blood on behalf of Marina and her son, we shall not allow them to inflict any harm. We, all the people of Nizhny Novgorod, have resolved on this, and have written to the boyars and all the people of the land in Moscow, that unto our death we shall reject Marina and her son, and that brigand who stands before Pskov, as well as the Lithuanian king."[71]

This document, which called for a second uprising of all the land, differs from the letters written at the time of the first uprising in that in it is declared a movement purely pertaining to the land, directed as much, if not more, against the cossacks as against the Poles and Lithuanians. The basic intent of the document is this: we must unite and act together, so as not to allow the cossacks to do anything harmful. The document had a strong influence because in the districts everyone was ready for the uprising, and awaiting only the beginning. From everywhere delegates to the council were sent to Nizhny Novgorod. Funds also were sent, and soldiers came. The first to arrive were the inhabitants of Kolomna. At first there resided in Kolomna, in accordance with the king's decree, Vasily Sukin, who is known to us as having left the negotiations of the embassy outside Smolensk; but as early as August 26, 1611 the king had written to the boyars in Moscow that Sukin, together with his son, had departed to join the traitor-boyars. It appears that Sukin had fled to the Trinity monastery, since we encounter his name in the letters of the Trinity monastery alongside the names of Dionysius and Palitsyn. The inhabitants of Kolomna were followed by those of Riazan, who in turn were followed by servicemen from the Ukrainian towns. There came loyal cossacks and musketeers who had been under siege in Moscow with Tsar Vasily. All these received pay. Between all these visitors and the inhabitants of Nizhny Novgorod there was great common purpose and love, says the chronicler.[72]

But bad news came from a quarter whence it was least expected. Kazan, which hitherto so strongly had urged the other towns to support the common cause now, at the instigation of the secretary, Nikanor Shulgin, declined to participate in it. Apparently Shulgin was dissatisfied that royal Kazan, the chief of the lower towns, and he, who had seized all power therein, did not stand at the head of the uprising instead of the second-rank Nizhny Novgorod with its own local elder. Shulgin was supported by the father of his son-in-law, the builder Amfilokhy Rybushkin, who did not obey the letters of the Trinity monastery. Then the authorities of the Trinity monastery summoned his father, Pimen, archimandrite of the monastery of the Mother of God at Staritsa, and inflicted heavy labor upon him, forcing him to bake bread. Shulgin was joined in Kazan by Ivan

Birkin, who also was discomfited at the ascendancy of Pozharsky and Minin in Nizhny Novgorod.

Having received news of the evil counsels of Shulgin and Birkin, Prince Dmitry, Kuzma and the soldiers placed their trust in God and even as Jerusalem, says the chronicle, was cleansed by the last people, so also in the Muscovite realm the last people gathered together and went against the godless Latins and their own traitors. They were in fact the last people of the Muscovite realm, the basic, fundamental people. When the whirlwinds of the Time of Troubles struck many belonging to highest society shook and trembled, but when they touched the social foundations they encountered the fundamental people, against whose power their force shattered.

Thus ended the year 1611 and the year 1612 began. At the end of January in Kostroma and Yaroslavl there appeared letters from the Moscow boyars urging them to break with Zarutsky and be loyal to Tsar Wladyslaw. "You yourselves see," the boyars wrote, "God's favor upon our sovereign, his sovereign justice and good fortune. Prokopy Liapunov, the principal instigator of the Troubles, on whose account Christian blood was shed, was killed by the brigands who were with him, and Ivashka Zarutsky and his companions were party to this, and they kept his body for three days on the square to be eaten by dogs. Now Prince Dmitry Trubetskoy and Ivan Zarutsky stand before Moscow for the shedding of Christian blood and the utter ruin of all the towns. Cossacks incessantly travel from the encampment around the towns. They plunder, slaughter indiscriminately, they take boyars' wives and simple womenfolk for fornication, they deflower virgins by hideous violence, they destroy the churches, desecrate sacred icons, they do such scurrilous things to icons that our minds fear to write. And the Poles and Lithuanians, seeing our slackness, also lay waste and make war upon our towns. Much of this is known to you; how soldiers sent by us from Moscow were quartered in the New Virgin convent, protecting God's church as the apple of their eye. But when Ivashka Zarutsky and his companions captured the New Virgin convent they destroyed the church of God, and stripped the nuns —the daughter of Prince Vladimir Andrevich, and Olga, the daughter of Tsar Boris, upon previously they dared not look—completely naked, and plundered other poor nuns and virgins and took them for fornication, and they came out of the convent and burned the church and convent. Is this Christianity? They are worse than the Jews, they execute and abuse their own people. They, these brigand cossacks, our bondsmen and yours, plunder, kill and insult you, the gentry, junior boyars, leading merchants and better trading people, and henceforth they wish to own our houses and yours, as you yourselves know better than us.

"And once again these same brigands—Ivan Zarutsky and his companions—choose as sovereigns these same cossacks, calling themselves the sons of sovereigns. They also support the son of the Kaluga brigand, whom it is not befitting to call to mind. Then the same brigands and godless ones, Kazarin Begichev and Nekhoroshko Lopukhin, have summoned yet another brigand from outside Pskov. Still another brigand, also Dmitry, declared himself in Astrakhan in the company of Peter Urusov, who killed the Kaluga brigand. And with these brigand sovereigns shall the Muscovite realm be strong, and shall Christian blood cease to be spilled, shall the Muscovite realm henceforth cease to be laid waste? Can the Muscovite realm stand firm with such regents as Prince Dmitry Trubetskoy and Ivashka Zarutsky? Even in their own houses they never had the skill to administer anything, yet they rule and decree everything in such a great and glorious realm, and for no other purpose than their own idle self-interest, brigandage and sodomy, and the utter ruin of the Muscovite realm.

"And the great sovereign, King Sigismund, together with the great Sejm, in accordance with the counsel of the Polish and Lithuanian land, has sent his son, the great sovereign Prince Wladyslaw, to reign over the realm of Vladimir and Moscow, and himself accompanied him to Smolensk with an army consisting of numerous cavalry and infantry, for the greater pacification of the Muscovite realm, and we joyfully await his approach to Moscow. You yourselves may judge that it is only with King Sigismund and his son that we may bring peace to the Muscovite realm and spare Christian blood. Seeing our want and utter ruin, the disorganization and lack of counsel among us, who would not marvel, who would not burst into tears and sigh? On all sides the enemy rends the Muscovite realm, and we have become a laughing stock and a shame and a reproach to all neighboring countries. And this is all because of you, because of your looseness and perfidy."[73]

The boyars wrote the truth. The cossacks of the encampment outside Moscow in fact entered into correspondence with the Ivangorod pretender, who by that time succeeded in establishing himself in Pskov, for which reason he is usually referred to as the Pskov pretender. Kazarin Begichev, who arrived at Pskov from outside Moscow, was unmindful of his soul and his old age when he caught sight of the brigand, and immediately cried out: "Here is our true sovereign from Kaluga!" But on March 2 the encampment outside Moscow swore allegiance to the pretender at the instigation of Ivan Pleshcheev. Meanwhile from Yaroslavl it was made known in Nizhny Novgorod that Zarutsky had sent many cossacks to Yaroslavl, that Prosovetsky was coming with an army, that they wanted to seize Yaroslavl and the seaboard towns to prevent the forces of Nizhny Novgorod from joining the inhabitants of Yaroslavl. Having received these tidings Pozharsky immediately sent his cousin, Prince Dmitry Petrovich Lopata-Pozharsky, and the secretary, Semeon Samsonov, to occupy Yaroslavl before Prosovetsky's arrival, in which aim they succeeded. The main army followed Lopata in the same direction. The treasuries of Nizhny Novgorod were insufficient to pay this force, and therefore money was levied from the merchants of other towns who were trading in Nizhny Novgorod, altogether 5,207 rubles, of which 4,116 were taken from officials of the Stroganov family.

In Balakhna and Yurevets-on-the-Volga the inhabitants met the army joyfully, gave money and honorably escorted it. At Reshma, Kirill Choglokov appeared before Pozharsky and gave him a document from Trubetskoy, Zarutsky and the army outside Moscow. The cossacks wrote that they had violated the oath of the whole community not to choose a sovereign without the counsel of the whole land, and had kissed the cross to the brigand who was in Pskov, but then learned that the one in Pskov was a common brigand and not the man of Tushino and Kaluga. They had forsaken him and kissed the cross that henceforth they would suport no brigand but would join in counsel and unity with the Nizhny Novgorod militia force, would resist the enemy and liberate the Muscovite realm. Pozharsky and Minin did not believe in the cossacks' repentance. They firmly resolved not to ally themselves with the cossacks yet, not wishing to antagonize them prematurely, dismissed Choglokov with honor and conveyed word to the cossacks that they need not fear in the least, that they were hastening to their aid outside Moscow.

Allowing the army to rest for a little time at Kineshma, Pozharsky moved towards Kostroma but on the river Ples received news that the governor of Kostroma, Ivan [Petrovich] Sheremetev[74] favored Wladyslaw, and did not wish the Nizhny Novgorod force to enter the city. Pozharsky consulted with Minin, and decided to advance to Kostroma without halting. Here there were two factions among the inhabitants. One supported the governor, the other did not wish to have Wladyslaw. The latter was more numerous, and as soon as Pozharsky reached the outskirts of Kostroma the people rose up against Sheremetev, took away his governorship, and would have killed him if he had not been protected by Pozharsky, from whom the inhabitants of Kostroma requested another governor, Roman Gagarin, who is well known to us.[75] At the same time the inhabitants of Suzdal sent to request protection from Prosovetsky. They were sent Lopata's brother, Prince Roman Petrovich Pozharsky.

MILITIA FORCE HALTS IN YAROSLAVL

During the early days of April the militia force finally reached Yaroslavl, where they received a document from the Trinity authorities. Dionysius, Avraamy Palitsyn, Sukin and Andrei Palitsyn informed them that "on March 2 the evildoer and apostate Ivan Pleshcheev and his companions, through the criminal agency of the cossacks, had brought about in the regiments an oath of allegiance. They kissed the cross to the brigand, who in Pskov calls himself Tsar Dmitry. They induced Boyar Prince Dmitry Timofeevich Trubetskoy, the gentry, junior boyars, musketeers and the inhabitants of Moscow to swear allegiance against their will. They had kissed the cross, fearing that they would be done to death by the cossacks. Now Prince Dmitry was living amongst these evildoers in great oppression, and would be glad to unite with you. On March 28 the two Pushkin brothers arrived at the monastery of St. Sergius. Prince Dmitry Timofeevich Trubetskoy sent them to us for consultation, so that we might send to you, in order to deal with the Poles and Lithuanians and those enemies who presently are fomenting disorder.

"And now you should consider this: can even a small hut stand firm without a householder, can even one town stand firm without someone in authority? Still less can a great realm be without a sovereign. Gather together, my lords, in one place, wherever God wills, and take good counsel. Let us beg the Almighty to avert His just anger and give His flock their own pastor, until the workers of evil and insulters of us his remaining Orthodox Christians are scattered. It is well known that the towns around Moscow—Kaluga, Serpukhov, Tula and Riazan—have not kissed the cross at the instigation of the brigands, and rejoice and await our counsel. Also on March 28 there came to us a man from Tver, who said to us that in Tver, Torzhok, Staritsa, Rzhev and Pogoreloe Gorodishche they did not kiss the cross, and are awaiting communication and advice from you. They did not allow Ivan Pleshcheev into Tver, nor did they allow his companions or his cossacks to buy bread. We cordially pray you, hasten and come to us in the Trinity monastery so that those now outside Moscow may not on account of their own discord lose the Great Stone City, the forts and the artillery."[76]

In the same document the first mention is made of the martyr's death of Patriarch Hermogen ("He died in disgrace and in want"). The chronicle recounts that the Poles sent to Hermogen some Russians who urged him to write to the Nizhny Novgorod militia force, telling it not to come to Moscow. Hermogen replied: "Let those be blessed who have come for the liberation of the Muscovite realm. But as for you, you traitors, may you be accursed."[77] The Poles ordered him starved to death. He died on February 17, 1612 and was buried in the Miracles monastery.

On April 7 there came from Yaroslavl letters to the towns. "The boyars and lords-in-waiting, and Dmitry Pozharsky, and the table attendants and the greater nobles and crown agents, town dwellers, captains, gentry and junior boyars of all towns, and the princes, murzas[78] and Tatars of the Kazan realm, and the musketeers, cannoneers and all service and townsmen of the various towns present their petition. Because of the multiplication of the sins of all Orthodox Christendom, God has brought His unquenchable wrath upon our land. First He cut short the well-born stem of the imperial family (and so forth: there follows a recitation of the misfortunes of the Time of Troubles, concluding with the murder of Liapunov, and the turbulence of the cossacks consequent thereupon). From outside Moscow Prince Dmitry Trubetskoy and Ivan Zarutsky, and the atamans and cossacks wrote to us and all the towns that they had kissed the cross not to choose a sovereign without the consultation of the whole land, that they would not serve Marina or her son, yet now they have kissed the cross to the brigand Sidorka, wishing to kill the boyars, gentry and all the better people, to plunder treacherously and rule according to their criminal cossack custom. How Satan has clouded their eyes! Before them their Kaluga tsar was killed, and lay headless for all the people to see for six weeks, and they wrote about it to Moscow from Kaluga for the benefit of all the towns!

"Now we, all Orthodox Christians, in common counsel, have agreed with the whole land, and have given our answer and entrusted our souls to God, that we will not serve their brigand tsar Sidorka, nor Marina and her son, and will firmly and immoveably shall resist the Poles and

Lithuanians. And you, my lords, be pleased to consult with all the people in common counsel how in the present utter ruin we may cease to be without a sovereign, how we may choose a sovereign by common counsel, so that the Muscovite realm be not destroyed utterly in the present misfortunes without a sovereign. You, my lords, know how at present we fare without a sovereign against the common foes, the Polish, Lithuanian and German people and the Russian brigands, who are beginning to shed blood anew. And how are we to deal with neighboring realms about the affairs of the realm and the land without a sovereign? And how henceforth will our realm be able to stand strongly and immoveably?

"And so, according to the counsel of your whole community, be so good as to send us in Yaroslavl, from all ranks of the people, two men each, and with them write down your advice, under your own hand. You should write also on your own behalf to the regiments outside Moscow that they forsake the brigand Sidorka, and cause no dissension between themselves and the whole land. In Nizhny Novgorod the leading merchants and all the townsmen of the land, not sparing their possessions, have furnished the gentry and junior boyars with pay, and now from all the towns there have come servicemen, who have petitioned all the land for pay, but we cannot give it to them. Thus you, my lords, should send to us in Yaroslavl the money in your treasury to pay the soldiers."[79]

The document bears signatures, among which we recognize the principal personages of the army. The first signature belongs to Boyar Morozov, the second to Boyar Prince Vladimir Timofeevich Dolgorukov, the third to Lord-in-waiting Golovin, the fourth to Prince Ivan Nikitich Odoevsky, the fifth to Prince Pronsky, the sixth to Prince Volkonsky, the seventh to Matvey Pleshcheev, the eighth to Prince Lvov, the ninth to Miron Veliaminov, the tenth to Prince Pozharsky. In the fifteenth place we read: "On behalf of the chosen man of all the land, in the place of Kuzma Minin, Prince Pozharsky has set his hand." Following that of Minin, there are thirty-four signatures, among which are those of Princes Dolgorukov and Turenin, the Sheremetevs, Saltykov and Buturlin.

THE MILITIA FORCE AND NOVGOROD

Crowds of servicemen arrived at Yaroslavl to join the militia force, townsmen brought cash from their treasury, but it was impossible to undertake a campaign against Moscow immediately. The cossacks seized Uglich and Poshekhonie and ran riot through the districts, while the

Swedes stood in Tikhvin. It was impossible to move southwards, leaving these enemies in the rear. Prince Dmitry Mikhailovich Pozharsky and Kuzma took counsel with the whole army, clergy and townsmen as to how the cause of the land might best be served, and resolved to send emissaries to Novgorod, keep the Swedes occupied with peace negotiations and send the army against the cossacks. Stepan Tatishchev, with one man chosen from each town, was sent to Novgorod, bearing letters to Metropolitan Isidore, Prince Odoevsky and De la Gardie. The militia force asked the metropolitan and Odoevsky how they were getting along with the Swedes. To De la Gardie they wrote that if the Swedish king would give his brother to rule the realm, and if he were baptized into the Orthodox Christian faith, they would be glad to be of one counsel with the inhabitants of Novgorod. This was written, says the chronicle, so that when they came before Moscow for the liberation of the Muscovite realm, the Swedes should not come to make war on the seaboard towns.[80]

The letters for Novgorod were written on May 13. On May 19 Isidore, Odoevsky and De la Gardie dismissed Tatishchev with the answer that they would send their emissaries to Yaroslavl, but Tatishchev declared that nothing good could be expected in Novgorod.[81] Despite this, in June the leaders of the militia force sent letters throughout the Ukrainian towns loyal to the Pskov brigand, Marina and her son, that they might forsake this known brigand. "Only forsake this brigand, and be in common counsel and unity with us, and our enemies, the Poles and Lithuanians, will leave the Muscovite realm. If you do not forsake the brigand, the Poles and Lithuanians will destroy utterly Moscow and all the towns, will slaughter all of us and all of you, our land will be empty and its memory erased, and all this God will inflict upon us, yea, and all neighboring realms shall call you traitors to your own faith and fatherland and, most of all, how will you give answer at the second coming of the just Judge? And Metropolitan Isidore and Prince Odoevsky have written to us from Great Novgorod that among them there has been no harm from the foreigners to the Orthodox faith and no ruin to Orthodox Christians. Karl the Swedish king has died, and has been succeeded as ruler by his son Gustavus Adolphus, and his second son Karl Philipp soon will come to rule in Novgorod, and place himself completely at the disposal of the people of the Novgorod realm. He wishes to be baptized into our Orthodox Christian faith of the Greek dispensation. And you, my lords, knew all about this, and were to have sent to us, for the common counsel of all the land, two or three men from all ranks, and were to have written to us your advice as to how we are to resist our common enemies, the Poles and Lithuanians, and as to how in this evil time we are not to be without a sovereign, and how we are to choose ourselves a sovereign in consultation with the whole land. But if you, my lords, do not send quickly to take counsel with us, do not join in counsel with the whole land, and do not in common counsel with us choose a sovereign, with heartfelt tears we shall part from you, and by consultation with the whole community, with the towns of the seaboard, the lower towns and the towns around Moscow, we shall choose a sovereign. We also declare to you that on June 6, from outside Moscow, Prince Dmitry Trubetskoy, Ivan Zarutsky and all the people sent to us a document of submission. They write that they had rebelled, they had kissed the cross to the Pskov brigand, but now they have found that he is truly a brigand, and have forsaken him and kissed the cross that henceforth they will not promote any other brigand, and will be in common counsel with us and the whole community. They wrote concerning this to us and to you in all the Ukrainian towns."[82]

This time they wrote the truth from the encampment outside Moscow. On April 11 Ivan Pleshcheev arrived thence at Pskov to find out about the brigand. Pleshcheev, in the words of the chronicle, turned to the true path, did not wish there to be enmity in the land, and told everyone that this was truly a brigand. It is quite possible that the disagreement of many in the encampment outside Moscow itself, the disagreement in the northwestern towns, and also the refusal of the inhabitants of Tver to receive him into their city, induced Pleshcheev to follow the true path. Whatever the truth of the matter, his refusal to recognize the brigand had its effect in Pskov. On May 18 the brigand had to flee from the city with the governor, Prince Khovansky, but Pleshcheev entered into negotiations with Khovansky and convinced him to surrender the brigand. Consequently, on May 20 they brought the pretender back into the city and imprisoned him in the town hall, and on July 1 they sent him off for Moscow.

Pozharsky sent to distant Siberia letters with information about dealings with Novgorod, and with the demand that they send delegates to the council concerning the election of the prince. He informed the towns that the detachments he had sent against the cossacks and the Cherkassians were everywhere successful. Prince Dmitry Lopata-Pozharsky had expelled the cossacks from Poshekhonie, Prince Dmitry Mamstriukovich Cherkassky had expelled the cossacks of Little Russia, or Cherkassians, from the monastery of St. Anthony in the Bezhetsk district, and then had expelled the cossacks of Great Russia from Uglich. Governor Naumov had repelled the detachments of Zarutsky from Pereiaslavl.[83] But amid all these successes unrest appeared in Yaroslavl itself. Here, with the levies from Kazan, there appeared Ivan Birkin, who is well known to us, with the Tatar captain Lukian Miasnoy. Even on the way they had quarrelled with each other. Birkin behaved as an enemy in the towns and districts, and when he arrived at Yaroslavl the quarrel with Miasnoy over who should be the principal leader broke out afresh, and the matter almost came to blows; but, what was even worse, this quarrel found echoes in the militia force of Pozharsky. The majority were opposed to Birkin and deserted him, but the natives of Smolensk took his side. Birkin went back with the greater part of his men, but Lukian Miasnoy remained with twenty princes and murzas, thirty gentry and a hundred musketeers. The unrest did not end even with Birkin's departure. Quarrels about seniority broke out between the leaders. Each of the soldiers sided with his own commander, and there was no way to resolve the matter until they decided to settle it according to ancient custom through a mediator, a clerical third party, and sent to Cyril, the former metropolitan of Rostov who was living in the Trinity monastery, urging that he occupy his former throne in Rostov. Cyril agreed, came to Rostov and then to Yaroslavl, and moved the people to agree that whenever a quarrel broke out among the leaders, they must report everything to him.[84]

Burdened by the great and difficult task, casting uneasy glances on all sides, wondering where they might find help, the leaders of the militia force called to mind the country with which previous Muscovite tsars had been in constant friendly relations, which had given subsidies during the perilous war with Turkey. That country was Austria. The leaders of the militia force, in their inexperience, thought that now Austria wished to be generous, would help the Muscovite realm in its hour of need, and on August 20 they wrote a letter to Emperor Rudolph in which, setting forth all the hardships suffered by the Russian people from the Poles, they wrote: "When you, great sovereign, graciously hear out our letter, you may judge whether the cause of King Sigismund is just in that he, having violated his oath, has ruined such a great Christian realm, and has utterly destroyed it, and whether it is right to do thus to a Christian realm! And among you, the great sovereigns, how can anything be confirmed except by a solemn oath? We petition your imperial highness, on behalf of the whole land, that you, calling to mind the friendship and love of our great sovereigns towards you, must look upon us in our present humiliations, and shall write the Polish king that he desist from his present injustice, and order his men of war to be withdrawn from the Muscovite realm."[85] In July there arrived at Yaroslavl the promised emissaries from Novgorod; from the clergy Abbot Gennady of the Viazhitsk monastery, from the city gentry Prince Fedor Obolensky, and one man from each of the districts of the Novgorod territories. On the 26th this mission appeared before Pozharsky and, according to custom, began their speech with a rehearsal of the causes of the Troubles. "After the extinction of the imperial stem, all unanimously elected Boris Fedorovich Godunov to rule over the realm because he had been regent over the Russian state, and all were in obedience to him. Afterwards, because of the denunciations of evil persons, the wrath of the sovereign fell upon the privy boyars and on more distant people, as you yourselves know. And a certain brigand monk fled from the Muscovite realm and declared himself...," and so on. Here it cannot help but be noticed that the emissaries explicitly linked Boris's wrath at the privy and more distant people with the appearance of the pretender, as cause and effect. Calling to mind subsequent events concerning the negotiations of the first militia force with De la Gardie, in the course of which Buturlin "on account of certain measures failed to reach an agreement and Jakob Pontus seized the wooden town of Novgorod by force, and the inhabitants of Novgorod agreed with him to ask a Swedish prince to rule over them," the emissaries gave information that this prince, Karl Phillip, in fact had been sent by his mother and his brother, was now on the way, and they thought he must soon be in Novgorod. The emissaries concluded their speech with the words: "You yourselves know that Great Novgorod has never been separated from the Muscovite realm, and so now you also, taking common counsel with one another, be in love and unity with us under the hand of a single sovereign."

These words could not fail to perturb the leaders of the militia force, the representatives of the Muscovite realm. Novgorod, of old a part of the latter, demanded that the entire realm be in amity and unity with it, and accept the sovereign whom it had chosen. Pozharsky replied with bitter words: "Under previous sovereigns ambassadors came from other realms, and now you are ambassadors from Great Novgorod! Of old, since sovereigns began to rule over the Russian realm, Great Novgorod was never separated from the Russian realm. So now let Novgorod be together with the Russian land as before." After these words Pozharsky went on to say how treasonable and improper it was to elect foreign sovereigns. "We have been tempted by this already," said he, "let not the Swedish king do as the Polish king has done. Sigismund of Poland wished to give his son the prince to rule over the Russian realm, yet he has betrayed the oath of Hetman Zolkiewski and his own rescript for a year, and has not given his son. And you yourselves know what the Poles and Lithuanians have done to the Muscovite realm. And Karl, the Swedish king, wished to send his son the prince quickly to rule over the Novgorod realm, and yet nearly a year has passed and the prince has not been in Novgorod."

Prince Odoevsky attempted to excuse the dilatoriness of Prince [Karl] Phillip by the death of his father, news of which had reached him when he was on his way to Novgorod, and then by the war with Denmark. He concluded thus: "Such incidents as the Lithuanian king has inflicted upon the Muscovite realm we do not expect from the Swedish kingdom." Pozharsky replied emphatically that, having learned from experience, he would not expose himself to treachery a second time, and would recognize [Karl] Phillip as tsar only after he had come to Novgorod and had accepted the Greek faith. "And we cannot in any way send ambassadors to Sweden," concluded Pozharsky, "you yourselves know what people were sent to King Sigismund of Poland, Prince Vasily Golitsyn and his companions! And now they are held in captivity as prisoners of war, and they are perishing through hardship and dishonor, being in a foreign land." The emissaries objected that the Swedish king would not repeat the action of Sigismund, since he himself had learned by experience its futility. "Sigismund has committed an injustice, yet what has he gained by holding the ambassadors? Now, even without them, are not you, boyars and commanders, gathered together against our enemies, the Poles and Lithuanians, and are you not resisting them?"

Pozharsky's answer to that is important for us, firstly because it shows his attitude towards one of the most remarkable men of the Time of Troubles and, secondly because it demonstrates the character of Pozharsky himself, as opposed to that of Liapunov, which could not fail to have an influence upon the success of the second militia force. Pozharsky replied: "People are also needed at present. If such a pillar as Prince Vasily Vasilievich were now here, all would adhere to him, and I should not have undertaken such a great matter in place of him, but now the boyars and all the land have compelled me to undertake this great matter against my will. And seeing what was done on the Lithuanian side, we shall not send ambassadors to Sweden, nor will we wish for a sovereign who is not of our Orthodox faith of the Greek dispensation." Pozharsky's last words strongly affected the Novgorod emissaries. The insistence, namely on not electing a non-Orthodox sovereign evoked in them a feeling which served as the strongest bond between all Russian people, which had raised the whole land against the Poles and Lithuanians. Obolensky said: "We have not fallen away from the true Orthodox faith, we will petition Prince Karl Phillip to join our Orthodox faith of the Greek dispensation. We will stand together with you, boyars and commanders, and with all the Muscovite realm, but even if you desert us, we will wish to die alone for our true Orthodox faith, nor do we wish for a sovereign not of our faith, the Greek faith."

The negotiations concluded with Pozharsky refusing to enter any obligations with the Swedes. But lest by an open breach they provoke the latter against the militia force they resolved to send an emissary, Perfily Sekerin, to Novgorod, to gain time. They sent him, says the chronicler, so that they should not provoke foreigners into coming to liberate the Muscovite realm. "If, my lords," wrote the leaders of the militia force to the inhabitants of Novgorod, "the prince does not grant your request, and does not reach Novgorod by the present summer travelling season, all the people in all the towns will have doubts concerning this. And we cannot be without a sovereign. You yourselves know that such a great realm cannot remain for so long without a sovereign. And for the present, until the prince arrives in Novgorod, the people of Novgorod shall be in love and common counsel with us, will not begin war, will not annex the towns and provinces of the Muscovite realm to that of Novgorod, will not compel the people to take any oath of allegiance, and will not commit any provocations."[86]

THE MILITIA MARCHES ON MOSCOW

When, at the time the second emissary was sent to Novgorod and, the militia force was preparing to set out on campaign from Yaroslavl, a cossack conspiracy against Pozharsky's life was discovered. From the encampment outside Moscow there arrived in Yaroslavl two cossacks, Obreska and Stepan, who had co-conspirators there, Ivan Dovodchikov, a native of Smolensk, and Semeon Khvalov, a native of Riazan. The latter lived in the household of Prince Pozharsky, who fed and clothed him. They thought up various means, for example stabbing Pozharsky in his sleep, but finally decided to murder him somewhere in the street, among the crowd. On one occasion the prince was in the meeting hall, whence he proceeded to inspect the artillery, which had been ordered to march on Moscow, and was compelled on account of the crowd to stand by the doors of the Chancellery of Military Appointments. A certain cossack, whose name was Roman, took his arm, probably to help him get free of the crowd. At that time a conspirator, the cossack Stepan, darted between them, tried to strike with his dagger at the prince's stomach but missed, and struck Roman in the leg, so that he fell and began to groan. Pozharsky did not in the least imagine that the blow had been directed at him; he thought that this misfortune had occurred because of the lack of security in the crowd, and even wished to continue on, when the crowd rushed towards him with a shout, saying that it was him whom the assassins wished to stab. They began to search, found the dagger, seized the assassin, who under interrogation confessed everything, and named his accomplices, who also confessed. According to the sentence of the whole land the culprits were distributed to the prisons among the towns, and some were taken to Moscow to reveal the plot. There they confessed a second time in the presence of the whole army, but were forgiven because Pozharsky had requested it on their behalf.

Naturally, after that, Pozharsky and the militia force were reluctant to set out on campaign to the environs of Moscow where under the guise of allies they might encounter assassins. But they could delay no longer because news had come of Chodkiewicz's approach to Moscow. Pozharsky sent some advance detachments, the first under the leadership of the commander Mikhail Samsonovich Dmitrievich and Fedor Levashev. They were ordered that when they arrived outside Moscow they must not enter the encampment of Trubetskoy and Zarutsky, but establish themselves in a separate small fortress by the Petrovsk gates. A second detachment was sent under the leadership of Prince Dmitry Petrovich Lopata-Pozharsky and Secretary Semeon Samsonov, who were ordered to take position by the Tver gates.

Apart from news of Chodkiewicz's movements there was yet another reason to hasten in their campaigns towards Moscow. It was necessary to rescue the gentry and junior boyars outside Moscow from slaughter by the cossacks. The Ukrainian towns, prompted by the letters of the militia force, had sent their soldiers, who had arrived in Trubetskoy's encampment and were stationed in the fort by the Nikita gates. But Zarutsky and his cossacks gave them no rest. The unfortunate Ukrainians Kondyrev and Begichev and their companions sent a plea to Yaroslavl that the militia force come to Moscow immediately to save them from the cossacks. When the emissaries saw the peace and good order the soldiers of the new militia force enjoyed, and called to mind their own oppression by the cossacks, they could not utter a word of their petition by reason of their tears. Prince Pozharsky and the others knew Kondyrev and Begichev personally, but now they could scarcely recognize them, in such a wretched state did they appear at Yaroslavl! They rewarded them with money and cloth, and sent them back to their own people with the joyful news that the militia force was on its way to Moscow.

But as soon as Zarutsky and his cossacks found out the news Kondyrev and Begichev returned with, they wished to kill them. They scarcely managed to escape to the regiment in Dmitriev while their comrades, the remaining Ukrainians, were forced to disperse to their own towns. Having scattered the Ukrainians, Zarutsky now wished to hinder the movement of the militia force. He sent numerous cossacks detachments to obstruct Prince Lopata-Pozharsky, to scatter his regiment, and slay the commander, but this design did not succeed. Lopata's detachment bravely encountered the cossacks and put them to flight.

Finally the main militia force advanced out of Yaroslavl. Having heard prayers at the Savior Monastery, at the tombs of the Yaroslavl miracle-workers (the famous Prince Fedor Rostislavich the Black and his sons David and Constantine),[87] and having received the blessing from Metropolitan Cyril and all the clergymen, Pozharsky led his militia force out of Yaroslavl. Advancing seven versts out of the town, the army encamped for the night. Here Pozharsky handed the army over to Prince Ivan Andreevich Khovansky and Kuzma Minin, ordering them to proceed to Rostov to await him there, while he himself with a few men proceeded to Suzdal, to the Savior-Evfimy monastery,[88] where he begged forgiveness at the tombs of his ancestors and then, as agreed, caught up with the army in Rostov. In this town the militia force was joined by even more soldiers from various districts, allowing Pozharsky to send a detachment under the command of Obraztsov to Belozersk to forestall hostile actions by the Swedes.

It was necessary to make one more important arrangement. Metropolitan Cyril, who in Yaroslavl was mediator in the quarrels between the commanders, remained in his eparchy. It was necessary to have just such a figure outside Moscow, even more so as quarrels were foreseen, given the proximity of Trubetskoy and Zarutsky. And so, on July 29, Pozharsky wrote on behalf of all ranks of people to Metropolitan Ephraim of Kazan:[89] "Because of the great multiplication of the sins of all of us Orthodox Christians, Almighty God has vented the fury of His anger among the nation, he has extinguished the two great luminaries in the world. He has taken from us the head of the Muscovite realm and leader of the people, the sovereign tsar and grand prince of All Russia, and also has taken away the pastor and teacher of the spiritual sheep of his flock, the most holy patriarch of Moscow and All Russia. Yea, and throughout the towns many pastors and teachers, metropolitans, archbishops and bishops, who were like illustrious stars, have been extinguished, and now He has left us orphaned, and we have been abused and derided and a reproach among peoples. But He has not left us completely orphaned, He has given us one consolation, namely you, great lord, as the certain great light to be placed upon a candlestick to shine in the Russian realm. And now, great lord! there is considerable grief among us, that the whole land is in counsel outside Moscow, yet we have no pastor and teacher among us. Only the cathedral church of the Mother of God remains in Krutitsa, and it is widowed.[90] And we, according to the counsel of the whole land, have decreed that Isaiah, the hegumen of the Storozhevsky monastery, shall be metropolitan of the house of the Mother of God in Krutitsa. Many can bear witness that this Isaiah leads his life according to God. And we have sent Abbot Isaiah to you, great lord, to Kazan, and we pray your worthiness that you, great lord, not leave us in utter grief and without a pastor, but create Abbot Isaiah metropolitan of Krutitsa, and send him to Moscow quickly to us in the regiments, and shall give him a full set of vestments for the church of Krutitsa is extremely impoverished and ruined."

According to the accounts of the Russian chronicles Zarutsky, hearing that the militia force was moving out of Yaroslavl, gathered with the cossacks entrusted to him, that is to say, almost half the entire army, and moved off to Kolomna, where Marina and her son were living. Having captured them, and having sacked the town utterly, he proceeded to the Riazan localities and, laying them waste, established himself in Mikhailov. The Poles give quite a different account of what prompted

Zarutsky to quit the encampment outside Moscow. According to their words Chodkiewicz, who was situated in Rogachev, carried on correspondence with Zarutsky, inducing him by various promises to come to the king's side. One of Sapieha's army, named Borislawski, acted as intermediary. He appeared in the encampment outside Moscow, declaring he was dissatisfied with the hetman and the king's service and wanted to serve with the Russians. The latter believed him but a certain Pole, Chmeliewski, who also had fled the Polish encampment, revealed to Trubetskoy the negotiations between Borislawski and Zarutsky. Borislawski was handed over for interrogation, they burned him with fire and he died under torture, and Zarutsky thought it best to leave the encampment and go to Kolomna. The cossacks remaining with Trubetskoy sent Ataman Vnukov to Rostov to ask Pozharsky to make haste to Moscow. But this mission also had another aim. The cossacks wanted to know whether the militia force was planning anything against them. But Pozharsky and Minin conversed with Vnukov and his companions very graciously, gave them gifts of money and cloth, and sent them to Moscow with news that they were coming immediately; and in fact they followed immediately after them, moving through Pereiaslavl towards the Trinity monastery.

Arrived at the Trinity monastery on August 14, the militia force deployed between the monastery and the settlement of Klementievo. This was the last encampment before Moscow, the last step was at hand, and hesitation seized the militia. They did not fear the besieged Poles, neither Hetman Chodkiewicz, but they did fear the cossacks. Pozharsky and Minin wanted immediately to assure themselves about the cossacks by some kind of covenant, to agree with them, in the contemporary phrase, not to intend any evil against each other. Disagreement arose within the militia force. Some wished to go to Moscow. Others disagreed, saying that the cossacks were enticing Prince Dmitry to Moscow to kill him as they had killed Liapunov.

At that time there was a proposal from other unexpected allies, from the foreign mercenaries Margeret[91] and three of his comrades, who wrote to say that they had recruited soldiers and were prepared to come to the aid of the militia force. The boyars, commanders and the selectmen of all ranks in the Muscovite realm, both military and civil, addressed this answer to Margeret's companions only. "We do obeisance to your great sovereign kings, and rejoice on account of their generosity, in that they generously display solicitude for the Muscovite realm, and order soldiers recruited for our aid. We praise you, the leading men, for your benevolence, and through our love we wish to reward you wherever it is possible. "But we are surprised that you are in counsel with the Frenchman, Jacques Margeret, of whom we know only too well. He came from the Holy Roman empire during the reign of Tsar Boris Fedorovich, and the sovereign rewarded him with an estate, patrimonies and a salary. But later, under Tsar Vasily Ivanovich, Margeret joined the brigand and did much evil to the Muscovite realm, and when the Polish king sent Hetman Zolkiewski, Margeret returned with the hetman; and when the Poles and Lithuanians, deceiving the Muscovite boyars, destroyed Moscow, burned it and slaughtered the people, at that time Margeret shed Christian blood worse than the Poles and, having plundered the sovereign's treasury departed Moscow into Poland with the traitor Mikhail Saltykov. We know very well that the Polish king ordered this same Margeret to be with him in the council. And we wonder in what manner this Margeret wishes to help us against the Poles. We imagine that Margeret desires to enter the Muscovite realm at the instigation of the Polish king, to do some kind of evil. We are on our guard against this, and for this reason we are sending soldiers to the town of Archangel as a safeguard.

"Also we do not now need mercenary troops from other countries. Hitherto we have not been able to settle with the Poles because the Muscovite realm was in dissension, but now all the Russian realm has chosen on account of his wisdom, justice, ancestry and bravery the table attendant and commander Prince Dmitry Mikhailovich Pozharsky-Starodubsky to be at the head of military and civil affairs. Also those people who were in brigandage with the Poles and Lithuanians now have begun to be of one mind with us, and are fighting the Poles and Lithuanians and are liberating the towns. Wherever revenue is collected, we are giving it to our soldiers, musketeers and cossacks and we, the boyars and commanders, gentry and junior boyars, are serving and fighting without pay for the holy churches of God, for the Orthodox faith and for our own fatherland.

"And God's wrath has come upon the Poles and Lithuanians for their injustice. The Turks and Crimeans have utterly devastated Volhynia and Podolia, and according to our correspondence the Crimeans now wish to lay waste the Polish and Lithuanian lands. And so, relying upon the mercy of God, we are arming ourselves, without any mercenaries. And if by chance we do not defeat our enemies, we will send our own people to you, instructing them explicitly how many men to hire, and how much to pay them. And you shall demonstrate to us your affection by writing to us concerning Jacques Margeret, stating by what means he left the Polish land and appeared among you, and how he now stands with you, in what honor. We had thought that on account of his injustice there would be no place for him in any land except Poland."[92]

THE MILITIA AND THE COSSACKS

It proved possible to get rid of the foreign mercenaries, but not the cossacks in the encampment outside Moscow. The news came that they hourly expected Chodkiewicz around Moscow. Pozharsky was not swayed by the cossacks. He promptly sent ahead Prince Turenin with a detachment, ordering him to take position by the Chertole gates, and designated August 18 as the day for the whole militia force advance on Moscow. Having chanted prayers at the shrine of the miracle-worker, and having been blessed by the archimandrite, the army set out. The monks accompanied them in procession and there, when the last people had set forth on the great mission, a strong wind blew from Moscow in the face of the militia force! Another portent! Hearts fell, and with fear and langor the warriors approached the icons of the Holy Trinity and miracle-workers Sergius and Nikon and kissed the cross in the hands of the archimandrite, who sprinkled them with holy water. Then, when this sacred ceremony was ended, the wind suddenly changed direction and blew with such force in the rear of the army that the horsemen could scarcely stay mounted. At that moment all faces lit up, everywhere vows were heard that they would sacrifice their lives for the house of the Immaculate Mother of God and for the Orthodox Christian faith.

It was already towards evening when, reaching not less than five versts from Moscow, the militia force halted on the Yauza river. Detachments were sent to the Arbat gates to reconnoitre convenient places for an encampment. When they returned, having fulfilled their mission, night had already fallen, and Pozharsky decided to spend the night where they stood. Trubetskoy incessantly sent to summon Pozharsky to his encampment, but the commander and all the army replied: "Henceforth we shall not take positions alongside the cossacks." The next morning, when the militia had crept a little closer towards Moscow, Trubetskoy met him with his soldiers, proposing that they take positions together in a single encampment close by the Yauza gates, but once again received the previous reply: "Henceforth we shall not take positions alongside the cossacks," and Pozharsky took position in a separate fortification by the Arbat gates. Trubetskoy and the cossacks were angry.

In this manner there was revealed outside Moscow an interesting spectacle. Before its walls stood two militia forces having, apparently, a single aim—to expel the enemy from the capital—but at the same time sharply divided and hostile to each other. The old militia force, composed principally of cossacks and led by a Tushino boyar, was representative of a diseased Russia, of the population of the pre-ruined southern Ukraine, a population with anarchic tendencies. The second force, under the leadership of a commander noted for his loyalty to the established order, was representative of the healthy, clean half of Russia, of a population of patriotic character which at the very beginning of the Troubles resisted its renegades and brigand servitors and now, mindless of its apparently hopeless situation in the aftermath of the cossack triumph following the death of Liapunov, had gathered with great sacrifices their last forces and dispatched them for the liberation of the realm. The guarantee of their success lay in the fact that this healthy half of the Russian population, realizing the need to sacrifice everything for salvation of the faith and the fatherland, and knowing, clearly the source of the evil, the principal enemy of the Russian realm, cut away the diseased, infected half. Minin's words in Nizhny Novgorod—"Let us desire to aid the Muscovite realm, let us not spare anything"—and the words of the militia outside Moscow— "Henceforth we will not take up our positions alongside the cossacks"— these words expressed the inward purification, the recovery of the Muscovite realm. The pure separated itself from the impure, whereupon the purging from the realm of the its domestic enemies became an easy matter.

BATTLE WITH THE POLES

Liberation was all the easier because the state it must combat was suffering from the grave, unhealed sickness of domestic disorder. As early as the autumn of 1611 the Poles in Moscow sent word to the king that they would not remain after January 6, 1612. When the deadline expired, they kept their word. They called a council of war, chose as marshal of the confederacy Jozef Celinski and, numbering seven thousand mounted troops, left for Poland to demand the pay they had earned. In Moscow there remained part of Sapieha's army and the detachment sent from Smolensk under the two Koniecpolskis. The chief commander in place of Gasiewski, Jakob Potocki, sent his kinsman Nicholas Struys to urge Chodkiewicz on.

Four thousand followers of Sapieha, who had joined Chodkiewicz, allegedly through the intrigues of Potocki's party, abandoned the hetman's encampment, formed a confederation, elected as their marshal Jan Zalinski, and left for Lithuania. With matters in such a state, we need not be surprised at Chodkiewicz's inactivity, lasting more than half a year. All that he could do was supply the besieged with provisions.

On August 21 Pozharsky became aware of Chodkiewicz's movement from Viazma towards Moscow. By the evening of that day the enemy was in position on Poklonnaia hill. In order to bar his way to the Kremlin, the army stood on both banks of the Moscow river, Pozharsky's force on the left bank near the New Virgin convent, and Trubetskoy's force on the right bank near the Crimean Courtyard. Trubetskoy sent word to Pozharsky that to make a successful flanking attack against the hetman he needed several hundred horsemen. Pozharsky selected five squadrons of his best cavalry and sent them over to the other bank.

At dawn on the 22nd the hetman crossed the Moscow river near the New Virgin convent and attacked Pozharsky. The battle continued from the first hour of sunlight until the eighth, and threatened to end badly for Pozharsky. He had been driven back to the Chertole gates and, seeing that the Russian cavalry was not fit to fight the Polish, he ordered his army to dismount, but during this change in formation the Russians barely managed to withstand the onslaught of the enemy.

On the other bank Trubetskoy's forces stood completely inactive. The cossacks looked calmly on the battle, and mocked the gentry. "The rich have come from Yaroslavl, and they alone are fleeing from the hetman," they cried. But the captains of those squadrons lent to Trubetskoy from Pozharsky's force could not look calmly on the battle. They moved to the aid of their own people. Trubetskoy did not wish to let them go, but they paid him no heed and quickly forded the river. Their example even influenced a few of the cossacks. Atamans Filat Mezhakov, Afanasy Kolomna, Druzhina Romanov and Marko Kozlov followed them, crying out at Trubetskoy: "Because of your quarrels ruin threatens the Muscovite realm and the soldiers!" The arrival of fresh detachments decided the matter for Pozharsky. The hetman, no longer hoping to break through to the Kremlin from that side, retreated to Poklonnaia hill. On the other side the Poles in the Kremlin, making a sortie to free the Watergate, were repulsed and lost their banners. But at night four hundred waggons with supplies under the convoy of a detachment of six hundred men entered the city. The way was shown by a Russian, Grigory Orlov. The guards moving ahead of the waggons had succeeded in entering the city when the Russians appeared, commenced a strong crossfire and captured the waggons. On the 23rd the besieged once again sortied from Kitai quarter, this time successfully. They crossed the Moscow river, captured a Russian fort situated close to the church of St. George (on Yandov street) and established themselves there, raising Polish banners on the belfries. There was no other action on the 23rd. The hetman used this day to move his army from Poklonnaia hill towards the Donskoy monastery in order to penetrate towards the city by way of the Trans River quarter through the present-day Ordynskaia and Piatnitskaia streets. Possibly he counted on not meeting strong resistance from Trubetskoy's cossacks who were positioned there, since he had observed their indifference on the day before. He possibly hoped that Pozharsky's force wished to avenge itself upon the cossacks, and would not come to their aid. On this occasion Trubetskoy was deployed along the Moscow river along the (old) Luzhniki, and his own cossack detachment was in a fort by the church of St. Clement (on Piatnitskaia street). Pozharsky's encampment was, as before, on the left bank close to the church of St. Elias the Wronged, but Pozharsky himself, with the greater part of his army, crossed over to the Trans River quarter, in order with Trubetskoy to bar the hetman's way into the city.

On the 24th, a Monday, once again at dawn, battle commenced and continued until the sixth hour from sunrise. The Poles overran the Russians and plunged them into the river, while Pozharsky and his regiment scarcely stood their ground and were forced to cross over to the left bank. Trubetskoy and his cossacks went into the encampments beyond the river. The cossacks even abandoned the little fort by the church of St. Clement, which was captured immediately by Poles coming out of Kitai quarter. The Poles, according to their custom, raised their banners on the church of St. Clement. This sight of Lithuanian banners on an Orthodox church enraged the cossacks. They rushed furiously back to the little fort and drove out the Poles. But one sentiment among these savage people quickly gave way to another. Seeing that they were fighting alone against the enemy, unaided by the gentry under Pozharsky, the cossacks quickly abandoned the fort again, insulting the gentry thus: "These rich people do not wish to do anything. We are naked and hungry and fight alone. Therefore we shall never again come out and fight." The fort once more was captured by the Poles, and the hetman laid out his encampment near the church of St. Catherine the Great Martyr (on the Ordynka).

Seeing the success of the enemy, and knowing they could not decide the battle unassisted, Pozharsky and Minin sent Prince Dmitry Petrovich Lopata-Pozharsky to seek out the cellarer Avraamy Palitsyn, who was at the encampment conducting prayers by the church of St. Elias the Wronged. Pozharsky requested Avraamy, under the escort of many gentry, to visit to the cossacks in their encampment and sway them to go against the Poles, and attempt to bar supplies from reaching Kitai quarter and the Kremlin. The cellarer proceeded straight away to the most important place, to the fort by the church of St. Clement, close to which there still stood a crowd of Poles, and said to the cossacks: "By you a good deed has commenced, you have stood strongly for the Orthodox church, and have won renown in many distant realms by reason of your bravery. And now, brethren, do you wish to destroy such a good beginning at one blow?" These words affected the cossacks. They replied that they stood ready to pursue the enemy, yield up their lives, and would not return without victory. Only let the cellarer go into the encampments to the other cossacks, and move them also to join the cause. The cellarer went, and on the bank caught sight of many cossacks preparing to cross over to that side of their encampments. Palitsyn persuaded them also to turn back. Other cossacks, standing on the other bank, seeing their brethren turn back, not knowing yet what was happening, also rushed back across the river, some by way of the ford, others through the flood. Seeing that matters were taking a turn for the better, Palitsyn crossed the river into the cossack encampments proper. There some cossacks were nonchalantly drinking, others were playing dice, but Palitsyn managed to sway them as well until this whole crowd of ragamuffins, barefooted and naked people (they had drunk and gambled away all their booty) rushed across the river in the steps of their comrades, crying "St. Sergius! St. Sergius!" Seeing the general movement of the cossacks, Pozharsky's force also advanced, the St. Clement's fort once again was won from the Poles, and Russian infantry lay in the ditches among the nettles along the roads to prevent the hetman from approaching the city.[93]

Dusk had begun to fall but still there was no decisive action. Among the regiments arose tearful prayers that God preserve the Muscovite realm from destruction, and they vowed to build three shrines, dedicated to the Purification of the Mother of God, John the Evangelist and Metropolitan Peter. The man who had sparked the great cause was destined to take the decisive step. Minin approached Pozharsky, requesting from him troops to deal with the hetman. "Take whomsoever you wish," Prince Dmitry answered. Minin took the deserter well known to us, the troop commander Chmeliewski, and three squadrons of gentry, crossed the river and went against two Polish troops, one cavalry and one infantry, positioned by the Crimean Courtyard. These panicked and, without awaiting the onslaught of the Russians hastily fled towards the hetman's encampment, in the course of which the two troops collided. Seeing this, the Russian infantry leaped out of the ditches and advanced on the Polish encampments, and after them moved all the cavalry of the militia force. The Poles could not withstand this combined onslaught. Having lost five hundred men—a fearful loss in view of the smallness of their army—the hetman left the St. Catherine encampment and retreated to the Sparrow hills. The Russian soldiers were eager to pursue the enemy but the cautious commanders halted them, saying that it was too much to expect two joyous events on the same day. Only a strong fusillade continued for two hours. In the regiments it was impossible to make out any human voice, and the sky was aglow because of the conflagration. The next day the rising sun found the hetman on the road to Mozhaisk.

LIBERATION OF MOSCOW

The hetman had been repulsed by the combined numbers of both militia forces, and supplies were not allowed to get through to the Poles besieged in the Kremlin and Kitai quarter. Now it was necessary to take counsel as to how to drive them out for good, but once again dissension flared between the forces of Trubetskoy and Pozharsky; that is to say, between the cossacks and the gentry. Prince Trubetskoy, a boyar, demanded that Table Attendant Prince Pozharsky and the trader Minin must visit him in his encampment to take counsel. But they did not agree not because, says the chronicler, they found this demeaning, but because they feared they would be murdered by the cossacks.[94]

Soon fresh sowers of discord made their appearance, whose activities are described in this document, sent through all the towns from Pozharsky. "Through the blessing of the great lord, the most holy Cyril, metropolitan of Rostov and Yaroslavl and all the Holy Synod, according to the counsel and resolution of the whole land, we have arrived at Moscow, and following the hetman's arrival we fought for four days and four nights against the Poles and Lithuanians, Cherkassians and Hungarians. By the grace of God, and by the prayers of the Immaculate Mother of God, the

Muscovite miracle-workers Peter, Alexis and Jonas,[95] and the miracle-worker Sergius, intercessor for the Russian land, we have repelled the enemies of all our community, Hetman Chodkiewicz, together with the Poles and Lithuanians, Cherkassians and Hungarians, from the forts, and did not allow them to come with supplies into the city, and the hetman with all his forces went to Mozhaisk. Ivan and Vasily Sheremetev were not with us before September 5, but on September 5 they arrived, stayed in the regiments of Prince Dmitry Timofeevich Pozharsky, and Ivan Sheremetev, together with the fomentors of all evil, Prince Grigory Shakhovskoy, Ivan Pleshcheev and Prince Ivan Zasekin, began to urge the atamans and cossacks to every manner of evil, in order to cause division and dissension in the land. They began urge the atamans and cossacks to go through the towns, to Yaroslavl, Vologda and other towns, to plunder Orthodox Christians. This same Ivan Sheremetev, together with Prince Grigory Shakhovskoy, urge the atamans and cossacks to kill our leader, Prince Dmitry Mikhailovich Pozharsky, as they killed Prokopy Liapunov, for Prokopy was killed at the instigation of this same Ivan Sheremetev, and thoroughly plunder the soldiers and drive them away from Moscow. Ivan Sheremetev, his companions, the atamans and cossacks intend that the Lithuanians remain in Moscow, and do everything according to the criminal instigation of the cossack encampment, destroy the realm and kill Orthodox Christians. So you, my lords, should be aware of these evil designs, and live in great caution, and write to us concerning everything, advising us how to resist these criminal machinations."

Most important of all, naturally, was not to allow the cossacks to depart the environs of Moscow and gain possession of the northern towns. The cossacks cried out that they were hungry and cold, and no longer could remain outside Moscow. Let the rich gentry remain there. Hearing that the good works done before Moscow were being wasted, Archimandrite Dionysius of the Trinity monastery called the brethren into assembly to take counsel. There was no money in the monastery, nor was there anything to send the cossacks. What honor might they show them, imploring them not to disperse from Moscow without vanquishing the enemies of Christian blood? They resolved to send to the cossacks the church treasury, the vestments, chasubles and jewelled stoles, as a short-term pledge for a thousand rubles, and addressed a letter to them. The missive affected the cossacks. They felt in their consciences that it would be terrible to take as a pledge ecclesiastical articles from the monastery of St. Sergius, and they returned them to the monastery with two atamans, and in a letter promised to endure all, and not depart from Moscow.[96]

After this it was necessary to reconcile matters between the commanders. On behalf of the whole army it was resolved that Pozharsky and Minin would not visit the cossack encampments and that the commanders assemble at a neutral place on the Neglinnaia and deliberate on the cause of the land. The commanders sent letters around the towns. "Until now there have been among us various commands but now, through the mercy of God we, Dmitry Trubetskoy and Dmitry Pozharsky, in accordance with the petition and resolution of all ranks have become as one and have resolved that we, together with the chosen man Kuzma Minin, shall approach Moscow, and will wish the Russian realm well in all things, without any treachery, and we have placed our headquarters and the chancelleries on the Neglinnaia, on the Pipe.[97] We have brought everything together in one place, and carry out all business together. And we intend the following with regard to the besieged in Moscow: we have placed gabions by the Cannoneers' Courtyard, in the Egorievsky monastery and by the church of All Saints on Kulishki street, and from there we shall bombard the city incessantly and achieve all that we desire. Refugees have come out of the city to us, Russian, Lithuanian and German people, and have told us that within the city many are killed by our cannon, and many are dying through oppression and hunger. The Lithuanians are eating human flesh, and no bread or other supplies remain to them, so we hope to gain control of Moscow soon. And you, my lords, must in everything heed the letters coming from us, Dmitry Trubetskoy and Dmitry Pozharsky, and write concerning all matters to us both, and if letters come to you from only one of us, you shall not believe them."

Whereas in this way the cause was going well outside Moscow, evil tidings arrived from the north. The Little Russian Cossacks, or Cherkassians, having separated from Chodkiewicz, had crept up unexpectedly on Vologda and captured it. Archbishop Sylvester of Vologda described this occurrence in a letter to Pozharsky: "On September 22, about an hour before sunrise, the destroyers of the Orthodox faith arrived in Vologda without warning, captured the city, insulted the churches of God and burned the city and its suburbs to the ground. The governor, Prince Ivan Odoevsky the Younger,[98] went away and they killed the other governor, Prince Grigory Dolgoruky, and Secretary Kortashev. They took me, a sinner, captive and held me in their quarters for four nights. Many times they led me to execution, but the Lord had mercy, and they released me barely alive. When they approached Vologda, because of the carelessness and negligence of the governor, there were no patrols sent out of the city, there were no sentries on the towers, in the fort or on the city walls, there were no captains or sergeants with the musketeers, nor were there any cannoneers or helpers with the artillery. Only a few were on guard at the gates, and they did not hear the Lithuanians entering the city, and the main gates were not locked. The Poles and Lithuanians left Vologda on September 25. And now, my lords, the town of Vologda is a burnt-out place; it is impossible to fortify it for a siege or bring up artillery. The inhabitants of Vologda who have fled do not dare gather in the town. The commander Obraztsov came from Beloozero with his regiment and established himself in Vologda, but nobody heeds him, they all rob each other. Thus you, my lords, must send to Vologda a strong commander and a secretary. And all this came about through drunkenness. The commanders drank away the city of Vologda."

On the other hand news came to Moscow that Chodkiewicz wished to move his detachments suddenly and push through to the besieged in Kitai quarter and the Kremlin. The commanders took counsel as to how to prevent the Poles from getting through, ordered the army to weave wattle fences and dig a ditch across the Trans River quarter peninsula, from one shore to the other. The commanders stood in turn day and night supervising the labors. As early as mid-September, Pozharsky sent a missive to the Kremlin: "Prince Dmitry Pozharsky pays his respects to the colonels and all the knighthood, the Germans, Cherkassians and haiduks[99] who are besieged in the Kremlin. It is known to us that you, who are under siege in the city, are suffering immeasurable hunger and great privation, day by day awaiting your ruin, and you are being fortified and encouraged by Nicholas Struys and the traitors to the Muscovite realm, Fedka Andronov and his companions, who are together with you to save their own skins. You know that in the past year (reckoning from September) Karol Chodkiewicz was here with his army, Lord Sapieha with a large gathering, and in Moscow the Poles were there with Zborowski and many other colonels, and the Polish and Lithuanian army at that time was numerous. But we, relying upon the mercy of God, did not fear the Poles and Lithuanians. Now you yourselves have seen the approach of the hetman, and how the hetman has fled before us, yet we did not fight with all our forces. Do not expect the hetman a second time. The Cherkassians who were with him have left him and have gone to Lithuania. The hetman has gone away to Smolensk, whither no new forces have come, as Sapieha's army is all in Poland. You yourselves know how much injustice has arisen in Moscow on account of King Sigismund and the Poles and Lithuanians. You should not destroy your souls on account of this injustice. There is no need for you to suffer such hunger and privation on account of injustice. Send to us without delay, preserve your heads and your lives intact. And I will take this upon my soul, and will beseech the soldiers. Whichever of you wishes to return to his own land, we will let him go without any hindrance, while those who wish to serve the Muscovite realm will be rewarded according to their worth."

The answer was a haughty and rude refusal despite the fact that the famine was fearful. Fathers ate their children, one haiduk ate his son, another ate his mother, one comrade ate his own servant. The troop commander who was reputed to judge the guilty fled from the place of judgment so that the accused would not devour the judge.

Finally, on October 22 the cossacks moved to the attack and captured the Kitai quarter. The Poles held out in the Kremlin for yet another month. In order to get rid of superfluous mouths to feed, they ordered the boyars and the Russians to send their wives out of the Kremlin. The boyars were greatly distressed, and sent to Pozharsky with the request that their wives be received without being humiliated. Pozharsky sent word to them that they might send their wives without fear, and he himself went to receive them. He received them all honorably and conducted each to her own kinsfolk, ordering everyone to take care of their needs. The cossacks were perturbed, and once more among them were heard the usual threats. "Kill Prince Dmitry! Why did he not allow us to plunder the boyars' wives?"

Led by hunger to extremity the Poles at last entered into negotiations with the militia force, demanding only that their lives be spared, and this was promised. The first to come out were the boyars, Fedor Ivanovich Mstislavsky, Ivan Mikhailovich Vorotynsky, Ivan Nikitich Romanov with his kinsman Michael Fedorovich Romanov and the latter's mother, Martha Ivanovna and all the other Russians. When the cossacks saw the boyars gathering on the Stone bridge[100] which leads from the Kremlin over the Neglinnaia, they wished to attack them, but were restrained by Pozharsky's force and compelled to return to their encampments, after which the boyars were received with great honour. The next day the Poles surrendered. Struys and his regiment fell to Trubetskoy's cossacks, who plundered and killed many of the prisoners. Budzilo with his regiment was led off to Pozharsky's soldiers, who did not touch a single Pole. Struys was interrogated and Andronov was tortured to find out how many of the tsar's valuables had been lost, and how many remained. They discovered the ancient tsars' caps which had been given as a pledge to Sapieha's followers who had remained in the Kremlin.

On November 27 Trubetskoy's force gathered by the church of Our Lady of Kazan behind the Intercession gates, and Pozharsky's force by the church of St. John the Merciful in the Arbat and, having taken up crosses and images, they moved into Kitai quarter from opposite sides, accompanied by all the inhabitants of Moscow. The two forces joined near the stone platform on Red Square, where Archimandrite Dionysius of the Trinity monastery was conducting prayers, when another procession appeared, coming out of the Kremlin by the Frolov (Savior) Gates. Archbishop Arsenius of Elasson (or Archangel)[101] came with the Kremlin clergy, bearing the icon of Our Lady of Vladimir. Wailing and sighing spread among the people, who had lost hope of ever seeing again this image so beloved by the inhabitants of Moscow and all Russians.[102] After prayers the army moved into the Kremlin and there joy turned into grief when they saw in what a state the resentful schismatics had left the churches. Everywhere was filth, images were defaced, eyes gouged out, thrones stripped bare. In the vats a horrible meal had been prepared— human corpses! The great national triumph, similar to that our fathers have observed constantly through two centuries, ended with mass and prayers in the Dormition cathedral.

Trubetskoy took up quarters in the Kremlin, in Godunov's house, where Pozharsky visited him for consultation, having deployed his forces in the Arbat, in the Holy Cross monastery. The cossacks, as before, gave him no rest, all of them demanding pay. They had forgotten, says the chronicler, that they had plundered all the treasury in many towns.[103] On one occasion they burst into the Kremlin, crying out that they would kill the leaders. The gentry halted them, and fighting almost broke out between them. Meanwhile they had arrested some suspicious persons or other. It appeared that these were junior boyars from Viazma. Letters were taken from them, and from them it appeared that King Sigismund himself was in Viazma.

KING SIGISMUND MARCHES ON MOSCOW

When it became known in Warsaw that things were going badly for the Poles in Moscow many were found who placed all the blame on the king, reproaching him for dilatoriness and lack of skill in taking advantage of the circumstances. They demanded that as soon as possible he must march towards Moscow and set the matter right, but no one suggested the means or the army the king must have. The king, however, went. In August he arrived at Wilno and awaited his army, but it made no appearance, for the king had no money. Somehow the king hired three thousand Germans, organized two infantry regiments, and proceeded with them towards Smolensk, where he arrived in the month of October. He hoped that the cavalry, or knighthood, which happened to be in Smolensk, would rally around him, but he met with refusal. He called a council of war and in an ardent speech implored the army to follow him, but all in vain.

The sorrowful king moved from Smolensk with only his German infantry and an evil portent appeared. As soon as he entered the gates, called the Tsar's gates, the barriers broke from their hinges, fell and blocked his way. The king had to make his exit through another gate. A few of the knights felt ashamed that they had permitted their king to march with a mere handful of mercenaries into a hostile land, and twelve hundred cavalrymen caught up with the king on the road to Viazma. On the way they joined Chodkiewicz and marched to besiege Pogoreloe Gorodishche. Here the governor was Yury Shakhovskoy, who countered the king's demand to surrender with the words: "Go to Moscow. If Moscow belongs to you, we will be yours!" The king obeyed, and went on. Arrived outside Volokolamsk, he sent on towards Moscow a detachment of soldiers under the leadership of the young Adam Zolkiewski. With him was sent Prince Daniel Mezetsky, a companion of Filaret and Golitsyn in the embassy, and Secretary Gramotin, who were to sway the inhabitants of Moscow into subjection to Wladyslaw.

In Moscow, when they learned of the king's approach, a great fear fell upon the commanders. The soldiers nearly all had dispersed, and there was no one to go against the enemy. Neither could they withstand a siege, for they had not sufficient provisions. Notwithstanding, they resolved to die together and when Zolkiewski's detachment approached Moscow, they met it bravely and chased it away. In this skirmish Ivan Filosofov, a native of Smolensk, was taken prisoner. Zolkiewski ordered the prisoner inter-rogated as to whether Moscow wished to accept the prince to rule the tsardom, whether Moscow was populated, and whether there were food supplies. Filosofov replied with conviction that Moscow was full of peo-ple and grain, and that all had vowed to die for the Orthodox faith and not accept the prince as tsar. The same Filosofov uttered the very same words before the king himself. In fact not one town surrendered, and not one Russian fled to the encampment to do obeisance to the prince.

Abandoning all hope of conquering Moscow, Sigismund wanted at least to capture Volokolamsk and ordered it attacked with cruel on-slaughts. The governors there were Karamyshev and Chemesov but, according to the chronicler,[104] there was little activity on their part in the city. All activity was organized by the atamans Neliub Markov and Ivan Epanchin. Under their leadership the besieged fought with ferocity during the assaults, and during the three assaults they killed many Lithuanians and Germans.

KING SIGISMUND RETREATS

The king, finding further failure there, raised the siege of Volokolamsk and retreated. Now new losses occurred in his small army from hunger and cold. Prince Daniel Mezetsky fled from the king on the road and, arriving in Moscow, gave news that King Sigismund was marching di-rectly into Poland with all his men.

Great as was the fear evoked by Sigismund's approach to Moscow, now it was matched by the joy of the news of his retreat from Voloko-lamsk. The great charge of liberating the realm was ended. News arrived that the enemy within also had suffered a reverse. Zarutsky and his brigand cossacks had departed Mikhailov and had assaulted Pereiaslavl-in-Riazan.[105] But Mikhail Matveevich Buturlin defeated him head on and forced him to flee.

ELECTION OF MICHAEL FEDOROVICH ROMANOV

Sigismund's withdrawal gave a breathing space in which to attend to the election of a tsar by the whole land. Letters were sent throughout the towns with the invitation to send men in authority and selectmen to Moscow for vital business. They wrote that Moscow was liberated from the Poles and Lithuanians, the churches of God were adorned in all their previous beauty, and God's name was glorified in them as of old. But the

Tsar Michael Fedorovich Romanov

Muscovite realm must not be without a sovereign. The people of God had nobody to whom to be devoted, without a sovereign the inheritance of the Muscovite realm must be ruined utterly. Without a sovereign the realm in no way could be rebuilt, criminal scheming everywhere must multiply; therefore the boyars and commanders invited the clergy to come to them in Moscow, and the gentry, junior boyars, leading merchants, tradesmen and inhabitants of all the towns and districts must choose the best, strongest and wisest men, as many as were needed for the affairs of the land and the election of a sovereign. All towns must send them to Moscow, and all officials and all delegates must agree firmly in their towns, and exact firm agreement from everyone about election of a sovereign. When sufficient officials and delegates had gathered, a three-day fast was fixed, after which the meetings began.

First they deliberated whether they should choose a prince from foreign ruling houses, or one of their own native-born Russians, and they resolved: "Not to elect the Lithuanian or Swedish king or any of their children, or men of the German faiths, or anyone of a foreign tongue, or not of the Christian faith of the Greek dispensation to rule over the realms of Vladimir and Moscow, nor to desire Marina or her son because we have seen the injustice committed against us by the Polish and Swedish kings, the violation of their oaths and disruption of the peace. The Lithuanian king has devastated the Muscovite realm, and the Swedish king has taken Great Novgorod by deceit."

They began to choose among their own number. Then there began disagreement, confusion and unrest. Each wished to act according to personal opinion, several even wanted the throne for themselves, and they gave bribes and canvassed support. Factions formed, but not one gained the upper hand. On one occasion, says the chronograph,[106] a member of the Galich gentry brought to the assembly a written submission stating that the closest by family ties to the previous tsars was Michael Fedorovich Romanov, and it was fitting to elect him as tsar. Dissenting voices were raised. "Who has brought such a document, who, and whence?" Then a Don ataman came forward and handed in a written submission. "What is this you have given?" Prince Dmitry Mikhailovich Pozharsky asked of him. "It concerns our lawful tsar, Michael Fedorovich," the ataman replied.

This opinion, offered by a member of the gentry and an ataman from the Don decided the matter. Michael Fedorovich was proclaimed tsar. But not all delegates had reached Moscow. The most notable boyars were not there. Prince Mstislavsky and his companions immediately after their liberation had dispersed. They found the company of gentry who had liberated them embarrassing. Now they were summoned to Moscow for the common cause. Reliable men were sent to the towns and districts to learn the opinion of the population about the new election, and final decision was postponed for two weeks, from February 8, 1613 until the 21st. Finally Mstislavsky and his companions arrived, the late delegates made their appearance, and the emissaries dispatched to the districts returned with news that the people joyfully acknowledged Michael as tsar. On February 21, during the week of the Feast of Orthodoxy, that is to say, on the first Sunday of Lent, the final assembly took place. Each rank gave its written voice and all opinions agreed, all ranks indicated one figure— Michael Fedorovich Romanov. When Archbishop Feodorit of Riazan, Cellarer Avraamy Palitsyn of the Trinity monastery, Archimandrite Joseph of the New Savior monastery and Boyar Vasily Petrovich Morozov stepped on the platform on Red Square and asked the overflowing square their choice as tsar, the answer resounded "Michael Fedorovich Romanov."[107]

NOTES

Additional information on personalities and topics found in the text and notes is available in Joseph L. Wieczynski, ed., *The Modern Encyclopedia of Russian and Soviet History* (MERSH); Harry B. Weber, ed., *The Modern Encyclopedia of Russian and Soviet Literatures (Including Non-Russian and Emigre Literatures)* (MERSL); David R. Jones, ed., *The Military-Naval Encyclopedia of Russia and the Soviet Union* (MNERSU); Paul D. Steeves, *The Modern Encyclopedia of Religions in Russia and the Soviet Union* (MERRSU), all published by Academic International Press.

The most recent comprehensive account of this era is R.G. Skrynnikov, *The Time of Troubles. Russia in Crisis, 1604-1618*. Edited and Translated by Hugh F. Graham (Gulf Breeze, Fla., Academic International Press, 1987).

CHAPTER I

1. The Holy Synod (*Osviashchenyi sobor*) was an assembly of the bishops, heads of monasteries and other prominent clergy of the Russian Orthodox church, and is not to be confused with the lay board of the same name set up by Peter the Great to administer church affairs.

2. Alexander Nevsky (1220-1263) was prince of Novgorod, grand prince of Vladimir, and also since the reign of Ivan the Terrible a saint of the Russian Orthodox church. His surname derives from his victory over the Swedes on the Neva river in 1240, and he is celebrated also for his victory over the Teutonic Knights on the ice of Lake Peipus on April 5, 1242.

3. The Shuisky clan was descended from Prince Andrei, the second son of Grand Prince Alexander Nevsky (1220-1263), whereas the house of Moscow was descended from the third son, Prince Daniel. Despite this seniority, Vasily Shuisky was the only member of the clan ever to become tsar. The family had been prominent in Muscovite service in the sixteenth century, although at the same time they frequently came into conflict with the rulers of Moscow. In 1536 Prince Ivan Dmitrevich Shuisky fled to Lithuania and founded a branch of the house which long outlasted its Russian counterparts. The name is derived from Shuia, one of its seats east of Moscow. See the entry by Hugh F. Graham, "The Shuiskii Family," MERSH, Vol. 35, pp. 53-58; also Gustave Alef, "Bel'skies and Shuiskies in the XVI Century," *Forschungen zur Osteuropaische Geschichte*, Bd. 38 (1986), pp. 221-240.

4. The Dormition cathedral, built by the Italian architect Aristotle Fiorovanti between 1475 and 1479, was the main cathedral of the Kremlin, in which such ceremonies as coronations and royal weddings were conducted.

5. This account is taken from the *Letopis' o mnogikh matezhakh* (Chronicle of Many Rebellions), pp.102-103, which was composed about 1658 at the court of Patriarch Nikon, and was based largely upon the earlier *Novyi letopisets* (New Chronicler), the official court chronicle of the Romanovs, compiled about 1630. The text of the *Letopis' o mnogikh matezhakh* was printed and published by N. I. Novikov in 1771, and it is from this rather than the *Novyi letopisets* that Soloviev cites, since the latter was not printed until 1910 in the fourteenth volume of the *Polnoe sobranie russkikh letopisei* (Complete Collection of Russian Chronicles PSRL), although one variant of it, the copy owned by Prince Mikhail Obolensky, was printed in 1853, and Soloviev occasionally cites from it. I have preferred to cite from the 1910 edition, which is more widely used by modern scholars.

6. The Assembly of the Land (Zemskii sobor) wan an institution in which representatives of various strata of society met to discuss matters of national importance. Some historians have seen it as an abortive step towards a permanent limited monarchy, but this view is generally discounted. Ivan IV used it sobor several times to gain public approval for his fiscal and military policies, and such assemblies also met for the election of Fedor Ivanovich, Boris Godunov and Michael Romanov. Here we see some kind of rump Assembly to legitimize Vasily Shuisky's seizure of power in June 1606. The Assembly remained in more or less continuous session from the election of Michael Romanov in 1613 until the return of Filaret from Polish captivity in 1619. Thereafter the Assembly was convoked only infrequently. See entry by Richard Hellie, MERSH, Vol. 45, pp. 226-234.

7. The father-in-law of False Dmitry.

8. Grishka Otrepiev was the runaway monk who allegedly assumed the identity of Tsarevich Dmitry (presumed dead since 1591), in 1603 appeared in Poland and successfully asserted his claim to the Muscovite rulership. His murder in a sedition led by Shuisky opened the way for the latter to the throne.

9. Ivan IV's last wife, Maria Nagaia, after the death of Tsarevich Dmitry and the ensuing tumult in Uglich was forced to take the veil under the name Martha. The accession to power of False Dmitry released her from monastic confinement, and so while Dmitry was alive she willingly played the part but, as we see here, changed her tune again after his death.

10. This latter assertion by Shuisky was completely false. All eyewitness accounts of the death of False Dmitry assert that to the very end he maintained his identity as the true son of Tsar Ivan Vasilievich.

11. This and the succeeding documents are quoted almost verbatim from *Sobranie gosudarstvennykh gramot i dogovorov* (Collection of State Documents and Treaties, Vol. 2 (St. Petersburg, 1819), No. 140-142. Hereafter SGGD.

12. The Buczynski brothers were two Protestant Poles in the entourage of False Dmitry who served as his personal secretaries.

13. N. M. Karamzin, *History of the Russian State* (Istoriia gosudarstva rossiiskogo), Vol. 12, col. 5: "This testimony is scarcely of sufficient value, and even if not imagined, was extracted by fear from two pusillanimous servitors

who, wishing to preserve themselves from the wrath of the Russians, did not fear to slander the ashes of their benefactor, which had been scattered to the winds! They were believed by contemporaries, but it is difficult to convince their descendants that False Dmitry, even though he was not very judicious, could dream of such a terrible and insane scheme, for it would have been easy to predict that the boyars and Muscovites would not allow themselves to be led like lambs to the slaughter, and that the bloodshed would end in the slaughter of the Lithuanians, together with their chieftain." (Soloviev's note)

14. M. V. Skopin-Shuisky (1586-1610) had been raised to the rank of lord-in-waiting in 1604, and had been given the task of escorting Martha from her distant convent to Moscow during the first month of the reign of False Dmitry. He was also appointed one of the "High Swordbearers," a new court rank created by False Dmitry. On the accession of Vasily Shuisky, who was his uncle fourth-removed, he was given a series of promiment military commands, as will be seen later in this volume.

15. He was 53 or 54 years old at the time of his coronation. An inscription in the Archangel cathedral in the Kremlin states that he died in Poland in 1612, in his sixtieth year.

16. The Golitsyn family was of Lithuanian origin, which can be traced back to Patrikei, who in 1408 came to serve Grand Prince Vasily I of Moscow, and became the ancestor of the Patrikeev family. His son became the ancestor of the Golitsyn and Kurakin families. The Golitsyn family contributed many illustrious statesmen and soldiers in the seventeenth and eighteenth centuries, the most famous being the favorite of the regent Sophia in the late seventeenth century. Concerning the subject of this note, there is tantalizingly little information, despite the fact that more than once he was considered as a candidate for the throne. The earlier Vasily Vasilievich Golitsyn was among the Muscovite forces besieging Kromy in the spring of 1605, together with his brother Ivan. Sources conflict as to whether Basmanov's desertion took place upon his own initiative, or at the urging of Mikhail Glebovich Saltykov and the Golitsyn brothers. Golitsyn is also notorious as one of the murderers of the young Tsar Fedor and his mother. On May 1, 1608, he and the tsar's brother, Dmitry Shuisky, were defeated by the Bolotnikov rebels at the battle of Bolkhov. The Liapunovs, vainly having approached Skopin with a view to displacing his uncle, apparently envisaged Golitsyn as a back-up candidate, but Golitsyn refused. He seemed more responsive when his name was put forward after the deposition of Vasily Shuisky in July 1610, but his candidature evoked little popular response. Later Hetman Zolkiewski named him to lead the grand embassy to King Sigismund. Since the bulk of this embassy later was interned in Poland, Golitsyn was more or less out of the running at the 1613 Assembly of the Land. It is also said that Boyar F. I. Sheremetev wrote to him: "Let us have Misha Romanov, for he is young and not yet wise, and will be agreeable to us, the boyars." Following the Truce of Deulino, Golitsyn was on his way to be repatriated, but he died at Grodno, and on the orders of King

Sigismund was buried in the Brethren church of the Holy Spirit at Wilno on January 27, 1619. The Orthodox Brethren consisted of groups of pious laymen formed to counteract the vigorous officially backed proselytization by the Latin and Uniate churches. They endowed many churches and schools. His body later was returned to Muscovy. See entry on him in MERSH, Vol. 48, pp. 166-167. For details of his death and burial, see Volume 16, Chapter II of this series.

17. Mikhail Glebovich Saltykov had been employed on a number of diplomatic missions on behalf of Boris Godunov and False Dmitry. Saltykov was later to throw in his lot with the second pretender, and later with the Poles, playing a prominent part in the collaborationist regime in Moscow in 1610-1611. Thereafter he left Russia for permanent exile in Poland, where he died in 1621. See entry in MERSH, Vol. 33, pp. 45-49.

18. Prince Vasily Rubets-Mosalsky, as Soloviev relates, was one of those who remained loyal to False Dmitry, whom Shuisky very imprudently sent to governorships on the borderlands, in Mosalsky's case to Korela. He later was killed while fighting for Bolotnikov, trying to interdict the Muscovite force advancing to the relief of Kaluga.

19. Afanasy Vlasiev was employed on a number of diplomatic missions along with Mikhail Glebovich Saltykov, was Dmitry's proxy at the ceremony of betrothal to Marina, and was virtually in sole charge of routine government business at the time of the wedding celebrations. See Volume 14 of this series, pp. 27-28, 110-112 and passim. Sent by Shuisky into semi-honorific exile as governor of Ufa, his house was requisitioned for the incarceration of the Mniszech family. He is last attested when in 1610 he petitioned King Sigismund III for restoration of his confiscated estates. See entry in MERSH, Vol. 42, pp. 186-188.

20. Bogdan Belsky (d. 1611) was Ivan IV's last principal favorite and after–wards a partisan of Tsarevich Dmitry Ivanovich. He was also a nephew of Maliuta Skuratov, and hence a kinsman to Boris Godunov. Despite this, he was exiled during the reign of Fedor, being appointed governor of Nizhny Novgorod. In 1598 he led a conspiracy once again, this time against Boris Godunov, and was appointed to the command of the frontier town of Tsarevo-Borisov. Here his injudicious behavior caused him to be recalled to the capital, where he was degraded and sent into confinement. Restored to favor under False Dmitry I, he was raised to the rank of boyar in 1605, but after the fall of the pretender again was sent into exile, this time as governor of Kazan, where he was murdered in 1611. See the entry by Hugh F. Graham, MERSH, Vol. 4, pp. 1-2; also below, Chapter V, pp. 199-200.

21. Namely Ileika Muromets, who claimed to be Tsarevich Peter, a long-lost son of Tsar Fedor Ivanovich. He was on his way to Moscow in the spring of 1606 when he heard of the death of his "uncle" Dmitry. He later took part in the Bolotnikov rebellion, and was executed outside Moscow during the spring of 1608. See Volume 14 of this series, pp. 124-125; also entry in MERSH, Vol. 14, p. 143.

22. Mikhail Molchanov, besides being one of the murderers of Tsar Fedor Borisovich and his mother, was one of the constant boon companions of False Dmitry. After the murder of his patron he escaped from Moscow and spread the rumor that Dmitry was still alive. For a while he contemplated assuming the role of Dmitry himself, and to this end made himself at home at the Mniszech estate at Sandomir. It is likely that in this capacity it was he who commissioned Bolotnikov as High Commander of the forces acting in the name of Tsar Dmitry, and sent him on to Shakhovskoy at Putivl. Later, while the forces of Bolotnikov and the bogus Tsarevich Peter were being besieged in Tula, Shakhovskoy sent him a message, begging him to appear as Tsar Dmitry, but Molchanov refused. He later attached himself to the Tushino court, and was one of the Tushino Russians who presented themselves to King Sigismund III at his encampment before Smolensk on January 31, 1610. Under the collaborationist regime of Saltykov and Andronov he was put in charge of a special chancellery dealing with the Polish nobility. In the Dormition cathedral on August 27, 1610 he approached Patriarch Hermogen for his blessing, but the benediction was refused and Molchanov was ejected from the cathedral. His eventual fate is unknown.

23. Briefly tsar after the death of his father Boris Godunov on April 13, 1605, but murdered along with his mother by the supporters of False Dmitry on June 10. See Volume 14, pp. 93-98.

24. However both Isaac Massa and Konrad Bussow are quite positive that the body on Red Square was that of False Dmitry. "I knew him very well while he was still alive, and I saw him after he was murdered. It was of course the same man who had sat upon the throne, had reigned, had celebrated his marriage, etc. He was killed, he was dead, and he was burned to ashes and dust, and he will be seen no more on this earth. And no matter how many Dmitrys might appear after him, they all will be impostors and deceivers, and will not reach that worthiness which the dead man attained." Konrad Bussow, *Moskovskaia khronika 1584-1613*, ed. I. I. Smirnov (Moscow, 1961), p. 258. An English translation (my own) is currently in preparation. "When I saw him stretched out on the ground I recognized him readily, even though he was battered and covered with dust and blood dried by the heat. I recognized him readily from his physiognomy, his broad shoulders and slender build. Thus I was certain that he was the same man who was called Tsar Dmitry in Moscow in the years 1605 and 1606 and reigned these two years." Isaac Massa, *A Short History of the Muscovite Wars*, translated with introduction by G. Edward Orchard (Toronto, 1982), p. 157.

25. Both foreign observers Konrad Bussow and Isaac Massa give an account of the translation of the remains of the true Tsarevich Dmitry from Uglich to Moscow, together with ironical comments about the alleged miracles occurring at the burial place of the new "saint." See Bussow, p. 264; Massa, pp. 159-161.

26. Prince Grigory Petrovich Shakhovskoy (?-1612) first is mentioned in 1587 as one of the Russian prisoners in Poland during the Livonian war. He served under Tsars Fedor Ivanovich and Boris Godunov. In 1596 he was governor of Tula

and commander of the rearguard regiment at Krapivna. In 1597 he commanded the garrison of the Novomonastyrsk fortress near Chernigov. In 1598 he served as an escort for the Danish ambassador to Moscow, and in 1601 was commander of the vanguard regiment at Novosil. In 1601 he was senior governor of Belgorod, and in 1605 was at Rylsk, where he sided with False Dmitry. He took part in battles against the Muscovite forces, entered Moscow with the pretender and played a prominent part at his court. After the overthrow of the pretender, Vasily Shuisky sent him to be governor of Putivl, which he turned into a rallying point for the forces supporting False Dmitry II. He rallied the townspeople of Putivl by telling them that if Shuisky were victorious the same fate would befall them as had happened to the citizens of Novgorod under Ivan the Terrible. He claimed to be Tsar Dmitry's plenipotentiary, and disaffected elements streamed to Putivl to put themselves under Shakhovskoy's orders, including the rebel leader Bolotnikov, whom he sent on to Moscow. Shakhovskoy seems to have spent most of the time of the Bolotnikov rebellion in Putivl, but when the forces of Tsarevich Peter arrived and Shakhovskoy had not been able to persuade Molchanov to impersonate Dmitry or to find anyone else to play the role, he changed his tactics and moved with Tsarevich Peter to the relief of Kaluga. After the capture of Tula, Shakhovskoy was imprisoned on an island in Lake Kubensk, but was liberated by one of the Polish detachments of False Dmitry II, and immediately became once again a prime mover of the opposition to Shuisky. He received the rank of court servitor and boyar from False Dmitry at Tushino. After the fall of Tushino and the death of the second pretender, Shakhovskoy again changed his tactics and joined Liapunov's militia. In 1612 he tried to act as a mediator between the forces of Pozharsky and Zarutsky's cossacks, but failed. His later fate is unknown.

27. Prince Andrei Andreevich Teliatevsky was descended from the former princely house of Tver. He is first mentioned in 1587, when he was in the suite which met the Polish ambassador, Sapieha, at the time when Tsar Fedor's candidacy for the Polish throne was being proposed. He became involved in a precedence dispute with Prince A. P. Kurakin in 1591. He was promoted to boyar rank under Boris Godunov. During the initial campaign of False Dmitry he led a strong loyalist detachment out of Briansk to assist the defenders of Novgorod Seversk. Near Trubchevsk he took part in a council of Russian borderland governors, who sent a message to Jerzy Mniszech, urging him to quit the Russian land before it was too late. Immediately afterwards he took part in a battle at Trubchevsk, which resulted in defeat for the invaders. In 1605 he was one of the few commanders remaining loyal to young Tsar Fedor Borisovich, and fled from Basmanov's encampment to Moscow. He was arrested when supporters of False Dmitry gained the upper hand in Moscow, but swore allegiance to Dmitry and was set free. He then was chosen one of the leaders of the deputation bearing the submission of the city to Dmitry at his headquarters in Tula. Teliatevsky was kept waiting for an audience, was treated with extreme discourtesy, and was even threatened with physical violence. During Dmitry's reign he was apparently in

disfavor and played no part in state affairs. When rumors spread of a new Dmitry in 1607 Teliatevsky, who was loyal to the memory of Boris, resented the allegations, repeated at the time of the transfer of the remains of the supposedly real Tsarevich Dmitry from Uglich, that Boris had murdered the child. Paradoxically, he gravitated towards the second Dmitry since one of the rebels acting in his name was Bolotnikov, who formerly was one of Teliatevsky's military servitors. Teliatevsky became one of the chief commanders under False Peter. Defeating the tsar's commander Vorotynsky, he captured Tula and Dedilov. On May 2, 1607 Teliatevsky defeated a strong loyalist contingent under Prince Boris Petrovich Tatev, Prince Ivan Borisovich Cherkassky, and Prince Ivan Mikhailovich Vorotynsky, fifteen thousand of whose soldiers went over to Bolotnikov. After the battle on the Pchelna, Teliatevsky joined up with Bolotnikov and advanced on Kashira, but the rebels were defeated on the Vosma river. Did Teliatevsky desert at this point or not? Soloviev is evidently unsure. All we know is that he was not among those punished after the capitulation of Tula, and he died in 1612, still retaining his boyar rank.

28. Fedor Ivanovich Mstislavsky (?-1622) was the son of a prominent political and military figure during the reign of Ivan IV. Ivan Fedorovich was one of the more prominent advisors of the tsar during the 1550s and then, together with Prince I. D. Belsky, was joint head of the lands not absorbed into Ivan's crown domains (zemshchina). He was named to the council of regency on the death of Ivan the Terrible but in 1585 fell from power and entered a monastery. Fedor Ivanovich first is mentioned in court service in 1575 and became a boyar in 1576. With his father's banishment to a monastery in 1586 he became the ranking boyar in the council. In 1598 he was put forward by some as a candidate for the throne, but he himself refused to be considered. He was loyal to Boris Godunov and even on one occasion was offered the hand of the tsar's daughter, since apparently he had been a widower since 1586. When he refused, the tsar refused him permission to marry at all. This prohibition was lifted by False Dmitry in 1606, but there is no evidence that he took advantage of this dispensation. His military record was not very distinguished, though when he was reputedly wounded fifteen times at Novgorod Seversk in December 1604 he was given a hero's welcome in Moscow. On the other hand, he was defeated soundly by Bolotnikov on the Serpukhov highway in October 1606, and was forced to lift the siege of Kaluga when the relieving column under the bogus Tsarevich Peter arrived. Both in 1606 and in 1610 he refused to be considered as a candidate for the throne, but he was one of the "seven boyars" who formed the interim government after the deposition of Vasily Shuisky in July 1610. After the liberation of Moscow by Minin and Pozharsky he temporarily went into seclusion at Yaroslavl, but was present at the final session of the Assembly of the Land which elected Michael Romanov. It is estimated that as of 1613 he was the wealthiest private landowner in Muscovy, but since his two sons had predeceased him the line became extinct with his death on February 12, 1622. See entry by Emily V. Leonard, MERSH, Vol. 23, p. 160.

29. Peter Nikitich Sheremetev (?-1609) was orphaned at an early age when his father was executed by Ivan IV in 1564. He is first mentioned in 1577 as a landowner in the Kolomna district, and in 1580 he was one of the tsar's groomsmen at his marriage to Maria Nagaia. In 1581 he attended the reception for the papal legate, Antonio Possevino, and in 1585 similarly attended the reception for the Lithuanian ambassador, Luke Sapieha. Later in the same year he was appointed governor of Dedilov and took part in the Crimean campaign. In 1586 he was one of the delegation which received Alexander, tsar of Kakhetia, and in 1589 he took part in the Swedish campaign. He was particularly intimate with Boris Godunov, who is even said to have built a church in commemoration of a visit Sheremetev paid to one of his country estates, and certainly Sheremetev was entrusted with many important responsibilities during the reign of Boris. Despite all this, he seems to have regarded the appearance and triumph of False Dmitry with equanimity. He joined the delegation to Tula, married into the Nagoy family, and was named to Dmitry's Polish-style Senate. He was not happy with the enthronement of Shuisky, and conspired against him, but he was let off lightly and sent as governor to Pskov. He spent almost two years there, before being captured by the partisans of False Dmitry II, by whom he was imprisoned in a nearby fort. He was offered freedom if he would swear allegiance to the pretender, but he refused, and was murdered in 1609.

30. A full account of Bolotnikov's life and wanderings is contained in Konrad Bussow's chronicle, pp. 268-269.

31. *Prezhdepogibshaia Ukraina* is a term difficult to translate, but which Soloviev repeatedly uses. For Ukrainian historians "the ruin" refers to the period of the Thirteen Years' War (1654-1667), during which that territory was the main bone of contention between Russia and Poland.

32. The lands of Severia, in ancient times the homeland of the protoslavic Severiane tribe, had been very restive during the reign of Boris Godunov, and had provided a strong base of support for False Dmitry I during his initial invasion of Russia. Its principal towns Moravsk, Chernigov and Putivl were quick to surrender to him, though Novgorod Seversk held out for some time under Peter Basmanov. Similarly the province of Severia was to be a stronghold for the forces of False Dmitry II and his supporters, and Putivl in particular was to be the organizing centre for the Bolotnikov rebellion. See the entry by Chester Dunning in MERSH, Vol. 34, pp. 117-121.

33. Mikhail Nagoy (?-1618) took part in the Livonian campaign of Ivan IV in 1577. He was present at the marriage of the tsar in 1581 as one of the relatives of the bride. In 1584 he was appointed deputy governor of Kazan, and in 1585 occupied a similar position at Novotsarevo. In 1586 he was once again deputy governor of Kazan, and from 1600 to 1602 was principal governor of Ufa. He was promoted boyar in 1606, and was one of the party sent to the border to greet Marina on her way to Moscow. In 1608 he fought against the second False Dmitry at Bolkhov.

34. The fortress of Elets was of particular importance since False Dmitry I had stored there a considerable cache of arms for his projected campaign against the Turks and Crimeans.

35. Prince Ivan Mikhailovich Vorotynsky (dates of birth and death unknown) first comes to notice when his father was tortured to death by Ivan the Terrible in 1573, while he himself was imprisoned at Beloozero. Later he was restored to favor and served Boris Godunov, False Dmitry and Vasily Shuisky. He was a prominent opponent of the pro-Polish clique of Muscovite boyars who supported the candidature of Prince Wladyslaw. Although at one stage he was proposed by the Assembly of 1613 as candidate for the throne, in the end he loyally supported Michael Romanov, by whom he was rewarded lavishly.

36. Prince Yury Nikitich Trubetskoy (dates of birth and death unknown), cousin of the more famous Prince Dmitry Timofeevich, was originally loyal to Shuisky but changed sides after being accused of treasonous relations during the campaign against Bolotnikov. Unlike Prince Dmitry, who eventually sided with the national liberation forces, he remained loyal to False Dmitry. In fact, after False Dmitry had abandoned Tushino for Kaluga it was Prince Yury who came to Kaluga to urge the inhabitants to swear allegiance to Prince Wladyslaw, while it was his cousin Prince Dmitry who successfully urged them to refuse.

37. "*Shubnik*", an alliterative pun on the Tsar's surname.

38. Filipp Ivanovich Pashkov, generally known as Istoma, was a lieutenant of the gentry contingent of the Tula and Elets regions in 1606 which cast its lot with the opposition to Vasily Shuisky, and joined the forces of Bolotnikov either, according to some historians, at Kolomna or, according to others, directly outside Moscow. Either late in November or at the decisive battle of December 2, 1606 this force went over to the Muscovite side, and took part in subsequent operations against the Bolotnikov rebels. Nothing is known about Pashkov's later activities.

39. Grigory Fedorovich Sunbulov (also rendered Sumbulov) came from an ancient family of Riazan boyars. At the end of the summer of 1606 he was in command of a detachment in the army led by Prince N. M. Vorotynsky to combat the Bolotnikov rebels in the neighborhood of Elets. After the government forces were defeated Sunbulov changed sides, but later deserted Bolotnikov outside Moscow on November 15, 1606. During the winter of 1606-1607 he served as governor of Pereiaslavl, and took part in the siege of Tula. After an unsuccessful attempt to overthrow Vasily Shuisky in February 1609, he fled to the Tushino encampment. It is said that Shuisky offered Sunbulov a full pardon if he would return, but this offer was rejected. After the fall of Tushino and the departure of Zarutsky, Sunbulov returned to Moscow, consented to serve the "seven boyars" government and swore allegiance to Wladyslaw. No further information about him is available.

40. Prokopy Fedorovich Liapunov (?-1611) came from an important landed family in the Riazan region, and was one of five brothers, of whom Zakhar is the most famous after Prokopy himself. The Riazan gentry as a whole was hostile to

the regency and rule of Boris Godunov, for reasons which Soloviev probably attributes to them with some justification. There is no indication what, if any, reward the Liapunovs received for their support of the first False Dmitry, but they were certainly very active in opposition to his successor, Vasily Shuisky. Prokopy and another prominent Riazan landowner, Grigory Sunbulov (see preceding note), led a contingent of insurgent Riazan gentry to join the Bolotnikov rebellion but when the main force of Bolotnikov's army arrived before Moscow, composed of rebellious peasants and runaway serfs, conflict arose as to the goals of the rebellion. Prokopy then brought at least some of the Riazan gentry contingent over to the side of Vasily Shuisky on November 15, 1606. He received conciliar rank from the tsar, and also the post of governor of Riazan, which apparently he held for the remainder of his life. Prokopy and his brother Zakhar played a prominent part in the defeat of the rebel forces at the Vosma river, June 5-7, 1607, and was present at the siege of Tula. Apparently he was wounded in 1608 while fighting to clear his native Riazan region of supporters of False Dmitry II, and was forced for a while to retire from active service. Despite the fact that they were praised for their loyalty to the tsar and were held in high honor, the Liapunov brothers tried to get the popular hero, the tsar's kinsman Prince M. V. Skopin-Shuisky, to consent to a conspiracy to seize the throne. Although Skopin refused to have anything to do with the plot, he soon afterwards died, according to the Liapunovs and many others poisoned by his jealous kinsmen. When the tsar's untalented and unpopular brothers Dmitry and Ivan suffered the disastrous defeat at Klushino on June 24, 1610, the Liapunov brothers played a leading part in the deposition of Vasily Shuisky. Although Zakhar was induced to take part in the grand embassy to promote the candidacy of Wladyslaw, Prokopy tended to support the second pretender. After the death of False Dmitry II at the hands of his Tatar bodyguards on December 10, 1610 Prokopy was responsive to the appeals of Patriarch Hermogen to unite all Russians in defense of the land and of the Orthodox faith. The part Prokopy played in this movement is well known, and is described in great detail later in this volume. He led the first defense force for the liberation of Moscow, but because of cossack intrigues and Polish disinformation he was murdered on July 22, 1611. See entry by John Wiita, MERSH, Vol. 19, pp. 238-241.

41. Zakhary, or Zakhar Petrovich Liapunov, as related here, first came to the notice of the Muscovite government in 1603 for sending contraband materials to the Don Cossacks. In 1607-1608 he led a detachment of gentry from Riazan against rebellious peasants and supporters of False Dmitry II. In July 1610, as will be related later in this volume, he took the initiative in the movement which led to the dethronement of Vasily Shuisky. Then he was a member of the embassy sent to conclude an agreement with Sigismund III in his encampment outside Smolensk with regard to the accession of Wladyslaw to the throne of Muscovy. Before negotiations turned really sour, Zakhar Liapunov returned to Moscow, where his brother had been murdered and the first militia had collapsed, and fought in the ranks of the second militia and witnessed the liberation of Moscow.

42. A government (province) was an administrative subdivision of Soloviev's day. The nearest equivalent administrative unit today is an *oblast*, or region or province.

43. The Mordvins are people of Finnic stock, presently the indigenous inhabitants of the Mordvin ASSR, located along the right bank of the middle of the Volga basin. According to recent census figures, there are about one and a quarter million Mordvins, about 29 per cent of them actually living within the autonomous republic.

44. Prince Ivan Dmitrevich Khvorostinin (?-1614) was appointed table attendant some time before 1598, then served in a junior capacity in command of cossacks in various Tatar campaigns. He was assigned to escort duty for foreign emissaries between 1598 and 1602. Later in 1602 he was appointed governor of Borisov, but was recalled to Moscow the following year. He was appointed to the boyar council at the Easter festivities of 1604, and on March 3, 1605 was among the delegation attending the English ambassador. Under False Dmitry he was named to the tsar's inner council. In 1607 he was appointed by Shuisky to be governor of Astrakhan. There, apparently crediting rumors of Dmitry's survival, he roused the city against Shuisky, and resisted all attempts of the expeditionary force under F. I. Sheremetev to recapture the city for Moscow. Ivan Zarutsky, when he broke with the second national army eventually made Astrakhan his base. He was at first made welcome, but on becoming aware of the real nature of Zarutsky's regime and the probable permanence of Romanov rule, Khvorostinin began to send secret messages to Shah Abbas and the commander of the Terek Cossacks, discouraging them from any further support for Zarutsky. The rebel leader seized Khvorostinin and executed him on September 16, 1614, along with five hundred of the more prosperous citizens of Astrakhan.

45. A verst (Russian *versta*) is an old Russian linear measure equivalent to about one kilometer or two-thirds of a statute mile. For a table of weights and measures, see the beginning of this volume.

46. Kolomenskoe was a village to the southeast of Moscow, on a bluff overlooking the Moscow river. It was first mentioned in the will of Grand Prince Ivan I Kalita about 1339 and, as we read here, it was Bolotnikov's main headquarters during his siege of Moscow. The Ascension church, erected in 1532, is still preserved, and from the 1660s Kolomenskoe was one of the favorite country residences of the Muscovite tsars, with a wooden palace remarkable for its architecture. After the transfer of the capital to St. Petersburg, the palace fell into decay, and was demolished by order of Catherine II. The site is now a museum park, complete with historical structures moved from other locations, and served by a metro station. The village of Kolomenskoe was annexed to the city of Moscow in 1960.

47. The following is an extract from the report *The State of the Empire of Russia Since the Death of the Late Pretended Demetrie*, attributed to the English agent John Merrick: "Notwithstanding they continued the siege and writ letters

to the slaves within the town, to take arms against their masters and to possess themselves of their goods and substance, the fear of whom was almost as great, as it was of the enemy abroad and the rather in regard of the common sort of people who lately infected with robbing and spoiling of the Poles were very unconstant and ready to mutiny upon every report, as hoping to share with the rebels in the spoil of the city." (Spelling modernized)

48. The Danilov monastery was founded in 1282 by Prince Daniel, son of Alexander Nevsky and ancestor of the line of Moscow princes. Prince Daniel himself became a monk there before his death in 1303, and was buried On the grounds. The monastery repeatedly had served as a strongpoint for the defense of Moscow against Tatar incursions, most recently in 1591. It recently has been refurbished to become the official residence of the patriarch of Moscow.

49. *New Chronicler* (p. 74): "Many of these rebels were killed, and many taken alive, so that there was not enough room for all of them in the prisons and fortresses of Moscow. The brigand Ivashko Bolotnikov retreated with many of his followers, while others occupied the hamlet of Zaborie. These rebels, seeing their impossible situation, all surrendered. Tsar Vasily ordered them all brought to Moscow and distributed among the houses. It was ordered that they be given food, nor was anybody to molest them; but those who had been captured in battle were ordered to be drowned."

50. Prince Ivan Ivanovich Shuisky (?-1638) began his career in the household of Tsar Fedor Ivanovich. Although the date of his birth is unknown, he was probably much younger than his brothers Vasily and Dmitry, since he outlived them both by twenty-six years. He was named boyar in 1596, but there is no record that he saw any active service during the reign of Boris. After his brother's accession, as narrated here, he was sent to the relief of Kaluga, but without success. He was similarly unsuccessful in his mission to interdict the progress of Sapieha towards the siege of the Trinity monastery, being defeated at the battle of Rakhmantsevo. After this poor record he does not seem to have been called to active service again, but he became jealous of his successful kinsman, Skopin, whom he slandered to the tsar. The chief blame for the poisoning of the popular hero fell upon his brother Dmitry, but the hatred Ivan felt for Skopin was also well-known, and so Ivan shared the fate of his two brothers in being handed over to the Poles. Vasily and Dmitry died in Polish captivity in 1612. Ivan was allowed rather more freedom, but had to fend for himself in dire poverty, at times being placed under guard by a troop of hussars. When the Truce of Deulino was concluded he refused to return to Muscovy until Wladyslaw released him from his oath of allegiance. He finally appeared at Michael's court in 1630, thereafter taking part in diplomatic receptions as well as presiding over the Judicial Chancellery of Moscow and, after 1634, heading the Chancellery of Investigations. He died without heirs, and with him the Muscovite branch of the Shuisky family became extinct.

51. Prince Boris Petrovich Tatev (?-1607) is first mentioned in 1578. In 1600 he was governor of Orel, and played a leading part in repelling the Tatar attack

of that year by intercepting the raiders on the road between Belgorod and Kursk. In 1605 he was governor of Chernigov. Despite the fact that he remained loyal to Boris when the forces of False Dmitry appeared, there is suspicion that his appointment to Chernigov was an honorific exile, as he is mentioned as one of those who had been in disfavor with Boris, who were restored to favor under the pretender. He assisted at the marriage between Dmitry and Marina, was named to the boyar council and also to the Polish-style Senate proposed by Dmitry. He was also put in charge of the Chancellery of Crown Revenues. Towards the end of 1606 he was ordered to accompany Skopin and Prince Andrei Golitsyn to relieve Bolotnikov's siege of Kaluga. He was killed at the battle on the Pchelna river, May 1-3, 1607.

52. Ivan Nikitich Romanov (?-1640) is first mentioned in 1591, when he was summoned to Serpukhov to participate in the campaign against the Tatars. He returned with land grants, gifts and expressions of the tsar's goodwill. In 1597 he was present at the reception of the Imperial ambassador, Abraham Donau, and in 1599 was ceremonial cupbearer for Tsar Boris at the reception for Prince Gustav of Sweden. When the Romanov family fell into disgrace in 1601 Ivan Nikitich was sent to Pelym, where he was joined for a while by his brother Vasily, who died February 15, 1602. The following month the terms of his exile were alleviated, he was escorted to Ufa, and later was employed in some administrative capacity at Nizhny Novgorod. He was permitted to return to Moscow briefly, but spent the rest of Boris's reign under house arrest on his estate at Klin. In 1605 he was bidden to attend the coronation of False Dmitry, and thereafter was promoted boyar and named to Dmitry's Polish-style Senate. During the reign of Shuisky he was ordered together with a number of other boyars and commanders to Kozelsk. He was one of the groomsmen at the tsar's marriage on January 17, 1608. He served as second-in-command at different times to Prince Ivan Ivanovich Shuisky and Prince Mikhail Vasilievich Skopin-Shuisky. In 1610 Ivan Nikitich was responsible for persuading Patriarch Hermogen to withdraw his initial objection to the candidacy of Prince Wladyslaw, and his signature is prominent on the letter of the boyars to the inhabitants of Kostroma and Yaroslavl, urging them to discountenance the first militia commanded by Trubetskoy and Zarutsky. Yet when the second national army liberated Moscow he signed the confirmatory charter proclaiming the election of his nephew Michael. He was part of a family regency council consisting of himself, Prince Ivan Borisovich Cherkassky and Boyar Fedor Ivanovich Sheremetev. The senior boyar, Prince Fedor Ivanovich Mstislavsky, also made Ivan Nikitich his executor shortly before his death without heirs in 1622, and Ivan Nikitich on his behalf distributed his fabulous wealth among various religious foundations. He was mixed up in a series of precedence disputes, in which it was ruled generally that although the plaintiff came from a more illustrious family, Ivan Nikitich, as uncle of the tsar, must undoubtedly take precedence. In order to avoid more such unseemly incidents Ivan Nikitich seems to have made himself scarce at court. In any case he was fabulously rich, though it is not known

whether the estates confiscated by Boris in 1601 were restored to him. For ceremonial receptions of ambassadors he provided large contingents of mounted and armed men from his estates; for example, in 1626 forty out of the 177 members of the guard of honor were provided by Ivan Nikitich at his own expense. During the Russian-Polish war of 1632-1634 he contributed large amounts of provisions for the troops besieging Smolensk, also at his own cost. Ivan Nikitich died July 18, 1640. His widow Uliana Fedorovna attended the first marriage of Tsar Alexis on January 16, 1648, but she died on October 23, 1649. Both were buried in the New Savior monastery, and their funerals were attended by the tsar and the court. Ivan Nikitich had eight children, four sons and four daughters, but only two, Nikita and Martha, survived him. Martha married Prince Alexis Ivanovich Vorotynsky. Nikita was a life-long bachelor, and with his death in 1654 his estates escheated to the crown.

53. See below, Chapter V, Note 57.

54. Xenia was the daughter of Boris Godunov, who had been spared for the pleasure of False Dmitry I, and then forced to take the veil under the name Olga. The body of Boris Godunov, after being buried in the Archangel cathedral in the Kremlin, later was disinterred and reburied along with the corpses of his wife and son in the humble Barsonuphius monastery on Presentation street. As described here, the bodies of the Godunov family were given a more honorable burial in the forecourt of the Trinity monastery, where the stone sarcophagus still can be seen. Xenia was buried there after her death in 1622.

55. Job was the first patriarch of the Russian church, elected in 1588 largely through the support of Boris Godunov, then regent. However distinterested his actions at the Assembly of the Land in 1598, Job was perceived as returning a favor in securing the election of Boris Godunov as tsar. Seized by the partisans of False Dmitry while performing the sacred liturgy in the Dormition cathedral in June 1605, he was deposed and exiled to his former monastery at Staritsa. He was, as is related here, briefly recalled during the reign of Vasily Shuisky to reinforce the proclamations of Patriarch Hermogen against the supporters of the second Pretender. He died in 1607 and was canonized in 1652 at the instigation of Patriarch Nikon. See the entry by Nicholas Lupinin, MERSH, Vol. 15, pp. 136-138.

56. After the establishment of the patriarchate of Moscow, the suburban village of Krutitsa became the titular metropolitan see of the patriarch's chief suffragan. Paphnutius was abbot of the Miracles monastery at the time when Grigory Otrepiev was there prior to his adventures as Tsarevich Dmitry. He was present at the assembly which elected Boris Godunov, and later was appointed titular metropolitan of Sarai and the Don. He was one of the officiants at the marriage between Dmitry and Marina on May 8, 1606, and in June he assisted at the coronation of Vasily Shuisky. It is not known when he was consecrated metropolitan of Krutitsa, but in that capacity he travelled to Staritsa to escort ex-Patriarch Job back to Moscow. It is also not known when he died, but a chapter was held on July 29, 1612 to elect a successor.

57. The Trinity monastery, situated near present-day Zagorsk, had a hospice in the city of Moscow to lodge the archimandrite and other monastic officials who had occasion to travel to the capital. Thus Cellarer Avraamy Palitsyn, who was the business manager of the community and who later wrote a graphic account of the siege of the monastery by the Tushinites, was not actually present at the siege, since when it began he happened to be in Moscow on business.

58. An interesting twist, which does not escape Soloviev's attention, namely that in 1591 both Shuisky and Job had vouched for the official version that Dmitry had met his death by accident, but now he was "done to death innocently at the hands of those who betrayed him."

59. Boris's son, the young Tsar Fedor Borisovich Godunov, and his mother, Maria Grigorievna, were murdered on the orders of False Dmitry by Princes V. V. Golitsyn, V. M. Mosalsky and an official named Andrei Sherefidinov (in some sources Shelefidinov), aided also by three musketeers. Officially it was announced that they had committed suicide, but now it was acknowledged publicly that they were murdered.

60. Marina was of course a Catholic, not a Lutheran.

61. The Land Chancellery (zemskii dvor, zemskii prikaz) was the chief police and judicial office for the city of Moscow, which also collected taxes from the Moscow townsmen.

62. The "hundred" (sto or sotnia) was an administrative division of the urban population, comprising, as the name suggests, approximately one hundred households, and headed by an elected "hundredman" (sotskii).

63. This document, for which Soloviev does not give any citation, seems to be extremely garbled. It starts out as a petition by the people to Patriarch Job, and then begins to address the tsar, who in turn concludes the document in the first person!

64. This story is appended to the *Tale Concerning a Vision to a Certain Clergyman* (RIB, XIII, cols. 184-186), probably recorded by Archpriest Terenty of the Annunciation cathedral.

65. The Fiedler story is lifted rather haphazardly from the memoirs of Konrad Bussow (pp. 272-273).

66. The Zaporozhian Host (voisko zaporozhskoe) was the official title of the Ukrainian cossack army, encompassing all Ukrainian cossacks, not to be confused with the Zaporozhian Sech, a geographical location. The Sech was a cossack stronghold, situated on islands in the Dnieper river below the present-day town of Zaporozhie. The cossacks of the Sech clung fiercely to their independence and democratic traditions; as a significant factor in Moscow's fight against the Poles and Turks they were treated circumspectly by the Muscovite government. Under the Truce of Andrusovo (1667) the Sech came under Muscovite protectorship. The Sech was abolished by Catherine II in 1775.

67. There is apparently some confusion here, which Soloviev himself was unable to resolve. If indeed Teliatevsky, as stated in the preceding paragraph,

deserted Bolotnikov's forces at the battle on the Vosma river, he could scarcely have been with the besieged in Tula. The fact that he is not mentioned among those punished after the suppression of the rebellion seems to indicate that the former version is correct.

68. Prince Andrei Mikhailovich Kurbsky (1528-1583), a trusted military commander of Ivan IV, deserted to Lithuania in 1563, in the early stages of the Livonian war, and is best known for the acrimonious epistolary exchange which he then carried on with his former sovereign, though the authenticity of this correspondence was challenged in 1971 by Professor Edward L. Keenan, arousing an understandable furore in the scholarly world. See the entry on Kurbsky by Karl W. Schweitzer, MERSH, Vol. 18, pp. 171-174, and on the Kurbsky-Groznyi controversy by Robert O. Crummey, ibid., pp. 174-177.

69. The Belorussian chronicle in question is identified by Soloviev's Soviet editor as the Barkulabovsk Chronicle, preserved in the manuscript section of the State Historical Museum, Moscow. It has been more thoroughly studied in recent times by S. Maltsev. See Skrynnikov, *Time of Troubles*, pp. 309-310.

70. Shklov (in Polish Szklow) was situated on the Dnieper river in the neighborhood of Mogilev. In the seventeenth and eighteenth centuries it belonged successively to the Chodkiewicz, Sieniawski and Czartoryski familes. It was destroyed by fire in 1769 and was never properly rebuilt.

71. The identity of False Dmitry II never has been determined satisfactorily. See Skrynnikov, *Time of Troubles*, pp. 62-63.

72. Although he is mentioned in a number of sources, Miechowicki's origins are very obscure. Before his association with False Dmitry II he served in the military retinue of the Polish crown marshal Z. Myszkowski. He also took part in negotiations between the king of Poland and Janusz and Christoph Radziwill. The circumstances of his first connection with the Dmitry camp are unknown. According to Samuel Maskiewicz, he had some dealings with False Dmitry I and "knew the secrets of the deceased." After the death of the first pretender he took an interest in the affairs of Marina, and again according to Maskiewicz, was the chief initiator of the second pretender's appearance, the "author of the resurrection of *that* Dmitry." He also attracted support from Russians who were disaffected with the Shuisky regime. He wrote letters in Dmitry's name to the Polish senators, and attracted recruits by promising high rates of pay. In Poland he disseminated propaganda calling for vengeance for the deaths of the Poles killed in the Moscow uprising of May 17, 1606. In his initial campaign he won a victory at Karachev and relieved Kozelsk, which had been besieged by Muscovite forces under Mosalsky (October 18-20, 1607). But he did not enjoy the pretender's full confidence. Miechowicki was a political refugee who staked his fortune on Dmitry's venture, and tried to hold the "tsar" in dependence on him. His position grew untenable when Rozynski appeared, and eventually he was expelled from the camp on pain of death. Some of his supporters urged him to return, probably to facilitate negotiations between the Pretender and his putative wife Marina. However, a

brawl broke out in the "tsar's" tent in Rozynski's presence on October 7, 1608, and Miechowicki was killed. Samuel Maskiewicz (1580-1640) served in the Swedish campaign of 1601, and sided with the king during the rebellion (rokosz). In 1609 he participated in the Moscow expedition and fought at Klushino. After returning to Poland he took service with the Wisniowiecki family, later with the Radziwills. His memoirs, published in 1838, embrace the years 1594-1621, including sketches of the customs of the Russians and scenes of the Moscow expedition. His son Boguslaw (1625-1683) added a chronicle of the years 1643-1649, and a diary of the Moscow campaign of 1660.

73. Author of *Historya Dmitra falszywego*, RIB, Vol. 1 (St. Petersburg, 1872), pp. 81-364. Budzilo was a native of the Kiev region, near the Russian borderlands. Joining the forces of False Dmitry II on September 2, 1607, he drove the Muscovite governor from Briansk, but in October he quarrelled with Miechowicki at Kozelsk. In 1610 he commanded a special force which amounted to four hundred cossacks, six hundred light cavalry and two hundred hussars. When Sigismund advanced on Smolensk and Zolkiewski on Moscow, part of Dmitry's forces deserted to the king, but Budzilo remained with the pretender until his murder in December 1610. Budzilo then adhered to Sapieha, and on his behalf held Peremyshl and Likhvin. In 1611 he took part in Sapieha's campaigns in the vicinity of Moscow. Early in 1612 he helped Struys convey supplies from Rostov to the Polish garrison besieged in the Moscow Kremlin, and from January 31 until the surrender of the garrison in October he was among the besieged. After the capitulation he first was entertained by Pozharsky, and then kept in honorable captivity at Nizhny Novgorod until exchanged as a prisoner of war in 1619. Nothing is known about his subsequent career.

74. Bussow, p. 277. A more accurate rendering would read: "I have held true to my oath which I gave in Poland to him who called himself Dmitry. Whether he is so or not, that I cannot know, since I had never seen him before. I have served him faithfully, but he has abandoned me. Now I am in your power. If you wish to kill me, here is my sabre at the ready for it, but if, on the other hand, you will have mercy upon me according to your promise and your kissing of the cross, I will serve you as truly as hitherto I have served him by whom I am abandoned."

75. The *New Chronicler*, p. 77.

76. Information concerning these events is not entirely clear. The Russian chronicler makes no mention of any promise of pardon given to Bolotnikov, Ileika, Shakhovskoy and Teliatevsky. Bussow tells of a promise given to Bolotnikov and Ileika. According to the same source, Shakhovskoy was not a party to these negotiations, since he had been placed under guard by the besieged, who were angry at him because of his treachery. Shuisky, having taken the town, ordered all the prisoners to be released, including Shakhovskoy, who assured the tsar that the people had been angry with him because of his intention to submit to him, Shuisky. The secret execution of Bolotnikov is an indication that a promise existed, and confirms Bussow's testimony. But if we accept the reliability of Bussow's

testimony with regard to Bolotnikov, we must accept also the reliability of his testimony with regard to Ileika, namely that a promise of pardon was given him also. As far as Teliatevsky is concerned, there is general silence. Karamzin states: "Prince Teliatevsky, the most noble, and therefore the most guilty, of the traitors, out of respect to his illustrious ancestry forfeited neither his freedom nor his boyar rank, which was a slur on the aristocracy and a temptation to treason." Karamzin further cites a list of boyars where it is stated that Teliatevsky died with the rank of boyar in 1612. But Teliatevsky's death in 1612, while in the ranks of the boyars, does not exclude the possibility that he fell into disfavor during Shuisky's reign, and was restored to his former rank after the latter's deposition. On the other hand, we cannot ignore the testimony of Bussow to the effect that Teliatevsky had gone over to Shuisky at the time of the battle on the Vosma. (Soloviev's note)

77. The common expression "winter road" refers to the time when the frosts enable travel to resume on roads made impassable by the autumn rains.

78. Prince Roman Rozynski (1575-1610) was originally an officer with the regular Polish army, but joined the forces of the first False Dmitry and stayed on to serve the second pretender, ousting Mikolaj Miechowicki. He resisted the overtures of King Sigismund to bring over the Poles serving in the Tushino camp to the royal army. Deserted by most of his followers, he shortly thereafter died at Osipov on April 8, 1610.

79. Samuel Tyszkiewicz, a Polish-Ukrainian adventurer, was one of False Dmitry II's first supporters. When the pretender was fleeing Russia after the fall of Tula, Tyszkiewicz brought eighteen hundred cavalry and infantry to reinforce his supporters in the Komaritsk district late in 1607. He was originally a supporter of Miechowicki, but stayed on after Rozynski seized the hetmanship. When the Tushino camp collapsed Tyszkiewicz accused Rozynski of killing or concealing the tsar. His followers looted and set fire to Rozynski's tents before fleeing amid a volley of musketry.

80. According to most accounts Wisniowiecki was the first patron of the original False Dmitry. See Volume 14, pp. 75-76.

81. Alexander Jozef Lisowski (1575-1616) was a colonel of the Polish royal army and the organizer of irregular military bands known long after his death as *lisowczyki*. He joined the forces of False Dmitry II at Starodub, and the rest of his life was spent campaigning in Russia, either in the service of the pretender or of King Sigismund. See entry in MERSH, Vol. 20, pp. 60-62.

82. The Zebrzydowski rebellion (rokosz) was the culmination of the tension between King Sigismund III and the Polish nobility, who accused the king of intending to violate constitutional liberties and make Poland an absolute monarchy. Chancellor Jan Zamoyski led a determined opposition in the Sejm (parliament) of 1605 to the king's absolutist tendencies, but his opposition remained within legal limits. With his death later that year the mantle of the leadership of the opposition devolved upon Nicholas Zebrzydowski. Although a devout Catholic, he joined with leaders of the Protestant nobility, who were eager to oppose

the friend of the Jesuits and ally of Austria. The ensuing war against the king was the first general confederation of the nobility against the crown. The royalist cause found an able champion in Stanislaw Zolkiewski, at that time deputy hetman of Poland. Sigismund's preoccupation with the rokosz prevented him from taking advantage of the Troubles within Muscovy. Indeed, it was rather Sigismund's defeated domestic opponents who tended to seek their fortunes in Russia. See O. Halecki, *A History of Poland*, revised edition (London, 1983), pp. 140-147; Norman Davies, *God's Playground* (Oxford, 1981), I, pp. 341-343; id., *Heart of Europe* (Oxford, 1984), pp. 302-303.

83. Ivan Martynovich Zarutsky (?-1614) took part in the Bolotnikov rebellion and then joined forces with False Dmitry II, on whose behalf he commanded a band of Don Cossacks, and was named boyar by the pretender. After collapse of the Tushino camp he first went to King Sigismund at Smolensk, but then returned to Dmitry in Kaluga. After the murder of the pretender he took up the cause of Marina and her infant son. In January 1611 he joined the first national army and after the murder of Liapunov assumed the leading role. In 1612 he attempted to organize the assassination of Pozharsky; when this failed he fled to Astrakhan. With the approach of Tsar Michael's troops and a popular uprising within the city, Zarutsky fled to the Ural steppes but was handed over to the Muscovite government by his own cossacks, and was impaled outside the Serpukhov gates of Moscow. See entry in MERSH, Vol. 45, pp. 176-182.

84. Anna Koltovskaia, Ivan IV's fourth wife. She and Tsar Ivan were married in 1572 and divorced in 1575. There was no issue from this marriage. See R.G. Skrynnikov, *Ivan the Terrible* (Gulf Breeze: Academic International Press, 1981), p. 174.

85. Yurts were Tatar encampments and the lands pertaining to them.

86. The account of this vision is incorporated into the *So-called Other Tale* (RIB, XIII, cols. 101-105), and is printed separately under the title *Povest' o videnii nekoemu muzhu dukhovnomu* (Tale Concerning a Vision to a Certain Clergyman), ibid., cols. 177-184. See Note 64, above.

87. Following his pardon after his near-execution Shuisky was granted permission to marry, and was engaged to Princess Maria Petrovna Buinosova-Rostovskaia, but as we see here the marriage took place only in January 1608. This lends credence to persistent hints and, in the case of Ivan Timofeev, outright allegations, that Vasily Shuisky was homosexual. From this marriage there were one or two daughters, who did not survive infancy.

88. Bussow, pp. 252-256.

89. Alexander Gasiewski (?-1636), ambassador to the reigning False Dmitry, for a while imprisoned by Shuisky. After the departure of Zolkiewski from Moscow he was Polish commander in the Kremlin until its capitulation in 1612. He later played a part in the negotiations leading to the Truce of Deulino in 1618, and was appointed palatine of Smolensk.

90. In Muscovite custom, the offering of bread and salt is a token of welcome. In fact, *khleb-sol* is even in modern Russian an idiomatic expression for hospitality.

91. Mikhail Ignatievich Tatishchev was particularly acrimonious in exchanges with Polish diplomats during the reigns of Boris Godunov and False Dmitry. See Volume 14, pp. 18-25, 127, 131. He was the assassin of the first False Dmitry's closest companion, Peter Basmanov. Under Shuisky he was appointed governor of Novgorod. Early in 1609 Skopin placed him in command of the Muscovite column sent to interdict Kernozicki's advance on the city, but soon afterwards he was denounced for treason, summoned to Skopin's encampment and there was lynched without the formality of a trial. See below, Chapter II.

92. The sejm was the Polish parliament or diet, which developed in the fifteenth century and took final shape in 1493. The constitution *Nihil novi* ("Nothing new") of 1505 stated that the king could not introduce any innovations without the consent of the *sejm*. The *sejm* was composed of three estates: king, senate and deputies, elected by the gentry and to a limited degree by some towns. It had legislative powers, voted taxes, controlled state expenditure and decided upon war and peace. Ordinarily it was convoked every two years, normally in Warsaw, but every third sejm was held in Lithuania, normally at Grodno. A special session after the coronation of each king was held at Cracow. Decisions of the *sejm* generally had to be unanimous.

93. Prince Gustav of Sweden originally came to Russia in 1600 as a prospective bridegroom for Xenia, the daughter of Boris Godunov, but proved manifestly unsuitable. Since then he had been kept in semi-captivity in Russia.

94. Stanislaw Stadnicki (1551-1616), a personal enemy of Chancellor Jan Zamoyski, following the death of King Stefan Bathory supported the candidacy of Archduke Maximilian, on whose behalf he had fought at the battle of Byczyna in 1588. Initially one of the leaders of the rebellion in 1606, he soon quarrelled with the principal leader, Zebrzydowski, and made his submission to the king. He withdrew to his estate at Lancuc, from which he was driven by his personal enemy Lukasz Opalinski. He was slain in a vain attempt to regain his patrimony. See Norman Davies, *God's Playground*, Vol. 1, pp. 353-355.

95. Prince Ivan Mikhailovich Katyrev-Rostovsky (?-1640) was the last of the line of princes descended from the formerly independent rulers of Rostov, absorbed by Muscovy in 1474. His father, Prince Mikhail Petrovich, was one of the most noted military commanders during the latter part of the reign of Ivan IV. He also distinguished himself in 1605 as one of the few Muscovite commanders to remain loyal to Tsar Fedor Borisovich. Prince Ivan was awarded the rank of table attendant by Boris, and apparently remained at court during the reign of False Dmitry, whose marriage he attended in May 1606. He remained in favor with the new tsar, Vasily Shuisky, and his postion was for a time enhanced by the tsar's marriage to his kinswoman, Princess Maria Buinosova-Rostovskaia. Yet as a result of the engagement described here by Soloviev, Katyrev-Rostovsky was under a cloud, and from 1608 to 1612 was sent to be governor of Tobolsk. His first wife, Tatiana Romanova, died in 1611, but he continued to enjoy the favor of Tsar Michael through his kinship by marriage. From 1613 he appears again in the court

rolls, but he was never to attain the rank of boyar. In 1614 he was sent to Tula to counter a threatened Tatar invasion, and in 1615 he was placed in charge of the Trans River District of Moscow during another Tatar invasion. Later in the same year he accompanied the tsar on pilgrimage to the Trinity monastery, and in 1616-1617, according to the English agent John Merrick, was "in charge of the high table at court." In 1618 he was recalled to military duties, defending the Trans River District against the advancing Poles, and in 1619 to oppose the Crimean Tatars. In 1622 he was recognized as the most senior of the Moscow court gentry and in this capacity frequently is mentioned in the muster rolls. Between 1622 and 1629 he is cited frequently as having accompanied the tsar on pilgrimages and campaigns. He witnessed both of Michael's marriages, and in 1630 was placed in charge of the judicial office of Vladimir. From 1632 to 1636 he served as governor of Great Novgorod. He has been credited with authorship of the Muscovite *Book of Annals*, but recent scholarship seems to suggest that this work was in fact written by Prince S. I. Shakhovskoy. See entry in MERSH, Vol. 16, pp. 65-67 and G. E. Orchard, "Chronicle in Search of an Author. The Seventeenth-century Book of Annals," *Russian Review*, Vol. 37 (1978), pp. 197-203.

96. Tushino was formerly a village near Moscow, now well within the Moscow city limits. It is first mentioned as having belonged to Boyar Ivan Rodionovich Kvashin in the fourteenth century. Originally called Korobovskoe, it was renamed after the sobriquet of Kvashin's youngest son, Vasily Tusha. In 1570 it was given by the widow of Prince P. I. Teliatevsky to the Trinity monastery, in whose possession it remained until the 1760s. When it became the headquarters of False Dmitry II in 1608 it was fortified by earthen ramparts and wooden palisades. Within it were built a villa for the pretender, a residence for the so-called Patriarch Filaret, quarters for the Polish and Russian troops, and offices for the Tushino chancelleries. When it was abandoned in March 1610 Tushino was burned to the ground. Archeological excavations between 1898 and 1901 uncovered sabres, musket barrels, spearheads, axes, blacksmiths' implements and other artifacts, which are now preserved in the State Historical Museum, Moscow.

97. Jan-Piotr Sapieha (1569-1611), prefect of Uswiat, a military leader in the battle of Kirchholm against the Swedes in 1605, sided with the royalists in the Zebrzydowski rebellion in 1607. With the connivance of King Sigismund III he joined the forces of False Dmitry II at the head of a band of seventeen thousand men, and commanded the force besieging the Trinity monastery on behalf of the Tushino camp. Rather than obey the call to rally to the king's forces in 1609, he continued to operate independently, but later cooperated with Zolkiewski and the king. He died during the Kremlin siege in 1611, leaving behind a diary which is a valuable primary source for the Time of Troubles.

98. Mikhail Borisovich Shein (?-1634) is mentioned first in 1598, when he attested the confirmatory charter of Boris Godunov's election. In January 1605 he saved the life of the Muscovite commander, Prince F. I. Mstislavsky and was awarded the rank of lord-in-waiting. After taking part in the struggle against

Bolotnikov, in 1607 he was appointed boyar, and in April 1608 was appointed governor of Smolensk. He was still there when the fortress was besieged by the Poles in September 1609, and was taken prisoner after its capture on June 3, 1611. Ironically, he was appointed to command the force to retake Smolensk in 1632, but was executed in 1634 for his failure. See entry by Daniel B. Rowland in MERSH, Vol. 34, pp. 196-198; also entries by G. Edward Orchard, MERSH, Vol. 32, pp. 136-138 and Vol. 36, pp. 46-53.

99. This story is borrowed from Bussow, p. 284.

100. The first False Dmitry, following his conversion to Roman Catholicism in Poland, had carried on a very active correspondence successively with Popes Clement VIII and Paul V. Relations between the supporters of both pretenders and Rome are ably dealt with in the writings of the Russian-born Bavarian Jesuit historian Paul Pierling in his *La Russie et le Saint-Siege* (Vol. 3, Paris, 1901).

101. Strictly speaking, there is no "order" of St. Basil among the communities of Eastern Orthodoxy. Monasticism came to Russia from Byzantium, where it had a dual tradition. The eremetical life, begun by St. Anthony of Egypt (?-356), continued to exist throughout the Byzantine period and had many imitators within Russia. Coenobitic monasticism, founded by St. Pachomius (?-346), was regulated by St. Basil the Great (?-379) and received its definitive form early in the ninth century by St. Theodore the Studite. Monasticism in Russia assumed many forms, but all communities subscribed to the rule of St. Basil, though each monastery was independent. See entry by Martin Dimnik, "Monasticism in Russia," MERSH, Vol. 23, pp. 29-34.

102. The Uniates are Christians who acknowledge the pope as the head of the church while retaining the Orthodox liturgy and canon law. Sigismund III, an ardent champion of the Counter-reformation, by the Union of Brest (1596) imposed the Union upon the West Russian population of Poland-Lithuania. This move encountered strong opposition among members of the West Russian aristocracy and especially the cossack population, and the king was compelled in 1620 to sanction, in the Ukraine, the re-establishment of the Orthodox hierarchy, which was given legal recognition in 1633. The Brest Union was finally abrogated by a synod held at Lvov in 1946, though the Uniate church still does exist in emigration. See entry "Uniates" by Mark Elliott, MERSH, Vol. 40, pp. 210-219.

103. Soloviev acknowledges his debt to Prince Mikhail Andreevich Obolensky for information concerning the following document, but neither he nor his Soviet editor gives us any clue as to its present whereabouts.

104. The use of the imperial title (as opposed to the title of grand prince or tsar) had been a major bone of contention between the first False Dmitry and foreign diplomats. For full details, see Volume 14, pp. 113-114, 119-122.

105. This is clearly a reference to the so-called *translatio imperii* from the Romans to the Germans, as accomplished by the coronation of Charlemagne by Pope Leo III on Christmas Day, 800. It is difficult to understand how this argument could carry much weight in Moscow, which was in any case the "Third Rome"!

CHAPTER II

1. While still under a cloud in the aftermath of the dynastic crisis of 1497-1502, Prince Vasily Ivanovich was appointed prince of Pskov by his father Ivan III, but the inhabitants were reluctant to accept him. Succeeding as grand prince of Moscow in 1505, he annexed Pskov in 1510 and treated the city much as his father had treated Novgorod in 1478. The assembly bell was removed and Pskov boyars were deported to other Muscovite territories, their lands being distributed as service holdings.

2. The chronicler to which Soloviev is referring is the author of the Second Pskov Chronicle, who reflects an independent attitude in relation to the official version of events, and shows a marked sympathy toward the "lesser people." The chronicle in question is reprinted in PSRL, Volume 4, and also in *Pskovskie letopisi* (Pskov Chronicles), vyp. 2, Moscow, 1955.

3. Concerning Peter Fedorovich Sheremetev, see above, Chapter I, Note 29.

4. There were a number of secondary settlements, or bytowns, subject to Pskov. The principal of these were Izborsk, Gdov, Ostrov, Opochka and Pechory.

5. The term *nemtsy* (singular *nemets*), which ordinarily means "Germans", commonly was applied to all westerners of Teutonic race or speech. Hence "Swedish Germans", "Scottish Germans", etc.

6. Ivan Tarasievich Gramotin (?-1638) first appears at the court of the first False Dmitry, but was also party to the coup which overthrew him. Instead of being granted high office by Shuisky, he was appointed town secretary to Pskov, where he distinguished himself by his rapacity, which played no small part in provoking the disorders here described by Soloviev. He fled Pskov to Tushino after the revolt of September 1608. In 1609 he and M. G. Saltykov were sent to the Trinity monastery where Gramotin made a speech to the defenders, falsely asserting that the war was over and that Shuisky had made submission to Tsar Dmitry. After the fall of the Tushino encampment Gramotin was one of the deputation which visited to Sigismund III, urging him to become the protector of Muscovy. He became the king's trusted advisor on Russian affairs, and after the deposition and forcible tonsure of Shuisky was appointed keeper of the seal and conciliar secretary, and in January 1611 was named as assistant to the chancellor of foreign affairs. He served with the high embassy led by Filaret and Golitsyn, but when this failed and Moscow was relieved by Minin and Pozharsky he travelled with King Sigismund back to Warsaw. He managed to ingratiate himself with the newly installed Romanov regime. Returning to Moscow in 1618, he was reappointed conciliar secretary. He was to enjoy a distinguished career under Tsar Michael, although from 1626 to 1632 he was exiled to Alatyr, evidently having incurred the patriarch's disfavor. Restored to favor in 1634, he received the privilege of attaching the -*vich* suffix to his patronymic. See entry in MERSH, Vol. 13, pp. 92-94.

7. Fedor Kirillovich Pleshcheev (?-1633) was sent to Pskov in 1607 by the Tushino authorities to administer the oath of allegiance to Dmitry. The local

inhabitants asked the Muscovite governor, Sheremetev and the crown secretary, Gramotin, to protect them against Pleshcheev but instead they plundered the inhabitants and the people of the surrounding countryside. When rumors spread that the Swedes were approaching, the people rose up on September 1, 1608 in favor of Dmitry, and accepted Pleshcheev as governor. Soon thereafter he was transferred to Suzdal, where he remained for two years, conducting a lively correspondence with Sapieha. He accompanied Lisowski to many surrounding towns such as Shuia, Kineshma, Lukh and Vladimir, which had gone over to Dmitry. When it was proposed that Pleshcheev return to active service, the inhabitants of Suzdal petitioned that he remain rather than have Andrei Prosovetsky and Nekhoroshy Babkin as governors. Pleshcheev remained, with Prosovetsky as his deputy. After the fall of the Tushino encampment Pleshcheev declared for Wladyslaw and came to Zolkiewski, offering his submission, provided that he and other Tushino followers retain the same rank they had enjoyed at Tushino. When the boyars refused to agree to this condition Pleshcheev returned to the pretender and was appointed governor of Serpukhov. In 1611 he joined the first militia force under Prokopy Liapunov, and thenceforth supported the national liberation movement. In 1613 he was sent by Tsar Michael at the head of a detachment to relieve the Swedish siege of Tikhvin, but at Ustiuzhna he learned that the inhabitants had repelled the Swedes. In 1616 he was given command of a sector of the Moscow defenses, from the Neglinnaia river to the Frolov gates, alongside Prince F. I. Lykov. He was governor of Belgorod 1618-1619, and in 1623 was sent to Kashira to fortify it against the Nogay Tatars. He was deputy governor of Tobolsk 1623-1625. Between 1625 and 1628 he is mentioned five times as a table guest of the tsar, and was one of the groomsmen at Tsar Michael's second marriage. He served in the 1632 campaign at Sevsk, and was governor of Novgorod Seversk at the time of his death on December 28, 1633.

8.   The hearth tax (podymnoe) was the basic unit of taxation in Russia until the fourteenth or fifteenth century, but with the introduction of other taxes and dues its significance diminished, though it was not formally discontinued.

9.   Isidore, metropolitan of Novgorod (?-1619), first took vows at the Solovetsk monastery, of which he became abbot in 1597. In 1604 he was elected metropolitan of Novgorod. In 1605, on the death of Tsar Boris, he was one of the commissioners sent along with Peter Fedorovich Basmanov to administer the oath of allegiance in favor of the new tsar, Fedor Borisovich, to the army encamped outside Kromy. He had barely returned to Moscow after fulfilling this commission when he heard the news of Basmanov's treason. On June 1, 1606 he presided over the coronation of Vasily Shuisky. In 1608 Skopin was in Novgorod to negotiate the Swedish alliance, at which time Isidore and the citizens of Novgorod, seeing that Shuisky's enemies were multiplying, wrote to the tsar offering him safe refuge in Novgorod. When the Swedes forced their way into the city in 1611 Isidore conducted services by the walls, encouraging from afar the courageous resistance of Archpriest Amos. Yet after the city had been captured

Isidore and the governor, Prince I. N. Odoevsky, concluded an agreement with De la Gardie recognizing Prince Karl Philipp as suzerain of Novgorod, and undertaking to bring the rest of Muscovy into alignment with this agreement. After the election of Michael Romanov the Swedes still held on to Novgorod, which they evacuated only after the Peace of Stolbovo in 1617. Tsar Michael sent a letter to the metropolitan and the people of Novgorod promising full amnesty for their temporary lapse of allegiance, for they had been in no position to resist Swedish might. After the liberation of Novgorod Isidore asked for permission to resign his office and retire to the Solovetsk monastery, but by the time this permission arrived he had died. He is buried in the Holy Wisdom cathedral in Novgorod.

10. *Efimok* (plural efimki) is the Russian term for Joachimsthalers, large silver coins minted in the Joachimthal in Bohemia and frequently used in other foreign countries. In the absence of Russian silver coins of large denomination, efimoks were used in Muscovy in the sixteenth and seventeenth centuries. In 1655 for a short time they became an official monetary unity called *efimki s priznakami* (meaning, with marks), as they bore the Russian crown emblem. Efimoks were received in foreign trade transactions, and then either altered into small Moscow *dengi* or used intact. In the mid-seventeenth century the tsar's treasury accepted one efimok as equal to 50 copecks; and issued marked efimoks with a value of 64 copecks. S. G. Pushkarev, *Dictionary of Russian Historical Terms, from the Eleventh Century to 1917* (New Haven, 1970), p. 18.

11. Prince Dmitry Timofeevich Trubetskoy (?-1625) is first mentioned as being among the defenders of Novgorod Seversk against the forces of False Dmitry I in 1604. In 1608 he deserted the cause of Tsar Vasily Shuisky and was appointed table attendant and later boyar at the Tushino court of False Dmitry II. There he was joined by his cousin Yury Nikitich Trubetskoy, who had been exiled by Shuisky for alleged treason during the Bolotnikov rebellion. Prince Dmitry's uncle, Andrei Vasilievich Trubetskoy, remained in Moscow and after the overthrow of Shuisky became one of the "seven boyars" in charge of Moscow during the ensuing interregnum. At the same time Prince Dmitry obtained command of a band of cossacks and was among the besiegers of the city in the forces of the first militia force. After the murder of Liapunov he remained with his cossacks in the vicinity of Moscow while the second militia force was forming under Minin and Pozharsky. Unlike his colleague Zarutsky, he made his peace with the second militia force and with them participated in the liberation of Moscow. It appears that he was considered for the vacant Muscovite throne, but was bought off with lavish land grants in the Vaga region formerly belonging to the Godunov and Shuisky families, and which more latterly King Sigismund III had granted to Mikhail Glebovich Saltykov. Under the new reign he took part in the liberation of Novgorod from the Swedes, but later became involved in an embarrassing precedence dispute with V. P. Morozov, in which his compromising relations with the Poles were dragged up. He was among the delegation sent to greet Metropolitan Filaret on his return

from Polish captivity in 1619. Some time later he was appointed governor of Tobolsk, where he died in 1625. See entry by Daniel B. Rowland, MERSH, Vol. 39, pp. 241-244.

12. Prince Dmitry Mamstriukovich Cherkassky could claim kinship, through the marriage of his aunt Maria Temriukovna, to Ivan IV, to the ruling house. Temriuk was a ruler of Kabardia, and is reputed to have been fabulously wealthy. His second son, Mikhail, accompanied his sister to Moscow, and served in the Ivan IV's personal corps until he fell into disgrace and was executed in 1571. Temriuk's eldest son Mamstriuk remained in Kabardia, where he inherited much of his father's wealth, and appears to have been on good terms with Moscow. By 1601, however, Mamstriuk had been murdered and his son Dmitry fled to Russia, where he was taken into Muscovite service. After Shuisky's defeat on the Khodynka river (July 25, 1608) he deserted to Tushino, where he was awarded the title of boyar, and he and Trubetskoy were the last two Tushino boyars to remain with the second pretender at Kaluga. After the murder of the pretender he swore allegiance to Wladyslaw along with the other inhabitants of Kaluga, and on January 24, 1611 arrived at Sapieha's encampment. Forsaking the Poles, he joined the first militia force, and was dispatched against Chodkiewicz in 1612. He established his base at the Antonov monastery, from whence he cleared Uglich of roving cossack bands. For these deeds he was given a hero's welcome in Yaroslavl. He remained with the second militia force and was with it at the liberation of Moscow. His name appears on the charter granting the Vaga lands to Trubetskoy, and he took part in the early deliberations of the Assembly of the Land of 1613. After the initial rejection of Trubetskoy and Michael Romanov, the cossacks convolved a "circle" and proposed Cherkassky as a compromise candidate. Cherkassky, although a foreigner, was in Muscovite service, and he had exalted connections in Muscovy. His most recent feats had raised his stock with the second militia force, and he was indeed to have an illustrious career under Michael Romanov, becoming a table attendant in 1613, and then being given in 1619 a boyar rank more legitimate than his Tushino title. He served as head of the Chancellery for Kazan from 1624 to 1636. He died in 1651.

13. There were actually four Zasekin princes flourishing about this time. Prince Alexander Petrovich (?-1611) occupied a number of important military commands in the 1580s and 1590s, and was involved in a number of precedence disputes. He commanded the great regiment in the Muscovite stand against the Tatars on the Pakhra river just outside Moscow in 1591. In 1600 he received the Persian ambassador and was sent with the return embassy, arriving back in Moscow in 1603. In 1605, at the request of False Dmitry, he escorted Simeon Bekbulatovich to Moscow, and later that year was appointed governor of Toropets. In 1609 he was commander of the troops in Pskov for False Dmitry II, and sent a request to the Polish governor of Dorpat for auxiliaries for the upcoming campaign against Great Novgorod. In 1610 he was a supporter of Wladyslaw's candidacy, but later he aligned himself with the cossack commander Zarutsky.

In 1611 he was one of the members of the boyar council who voiced their sympathy for Patriarch Hermogen's call for national resistance, and as a result perished at the hands of the Poles occupying the Kremlin. Prince Ivan Andreevich (dates of birth and death unknown) was a veteran of the Livonian and Swedish wars of the last quarter of the sixteenth century. He too was involved in a long series of precedence disputes, the last noted being against Prince I. F. Basmanov. The dispute was resolved when Basmanov was slain in the Khlopko rebellion of 1603. Prince I. A. Zasekin is last mentioned as head of the Chancellery for Slavery in 1609. Prince Ivan Fedorovich (dates of birth and death unknown) attended Ivan IV and Tsarevich Ivan in 1570, and was among the groomsmen at the marriage of the tsar to Martha Sobakina in 1572. He occupied the governorships of Karachev (1581), Mikhailov (1584 and 1591), Roslavl (1598) and Oskol (1599-1600). He was also permanent commander of the rearguard regiment both in peacetime and in war. In 1604 he was at Mtsensk as second-in-command of the great regiment, under Prince M. B. Shein. He later occupied the governorships of Briansk (1605), Pereiaslavl-in-Riazan (also 1605), Surgut (1607) and Oskol (1608). Prince Fedor Mikhailovich (dates of birth and death unknown) is first mentioned in 1584 as governor of Kineshma. In 1610 he was one of the group led by Zakhar Liapunov, who declared to the deposed Vasily Shuisky that for the peace of the realm he must become a monk. He then moved to the pretender's camp, but later declared for Wladyslaw. He is mentioned in a letter to Siberia by the ranking boyar, Prince F. I. Mstislavsky, as being one the Pretender's leading supporters who had made submission to the Moscow authorities.

14. Prince Grigory Borisovich Dolgorukov-Roshcha (?-1613) first served under Ivan IV, and subsequently under Fedor Ivanovich and Boris Godunov. He apparently made no secret of his hostility towards the boyars and foreigners and so, despite his undisputed ability and bravery as a commander, was passed over for promotion. In 1608 he was appointed chief commander of the garrison of the Trinity monastery. The siege of the monastery was expected in August, but did not in fact commence until late September. Dolgorukov-Roshcha spent the intervening time putting the defenses in good order and stocking food and ammunition. After the siege was lifted he received a fur robe sewn in gold thread and a golden goblet from the hands of Tsar Vasily. In 1611 he was appointed commander of the troops in the Dvina lands, but was killed September 22, 1613 in riots which unexpectedly broke out in Vologda.

15. Archimandrite Joseph (?-1610), the third of that name to rule the Trinity monastery, was transferred there from among the brethren of the St. Paphnutius monastery of Borovsk. Having endured the siege of the monastery, he suddenly abandoned his charge and returned to his former monastery. He was slain when Polish marauders under Sapieha captured and sacked the St. Paphnutius monastery on July 5, 1610.

16. Soloviev's source for much of what follows is Avraamy Palitsyn's own account of the siege of the Trinity monastery, which includes much commentary

on contemporary political events. He was not himself present at the siege, but was able to draw on much first-hand evidence. *Skazanie Avraamiia Palitsyna* (Tale of Avraamy Palitsyn), ed. L. V. Cherepnin (Moscow and Leningrad, 1955), p. 208. See also MERSH, Vol. 26, pp. 195-197.

17. St. Sergius of Radonezh (1321-1392) was the original founder of the hermitage which eventually became the Trinity-St. Sergius monastery, the richest religious foundation in Russia. See entry by Faith Wigzell, MERSH, Vol. 34, pp. 77-80.

18. As previously related by Soloviev, Xenia-Olga had accompanied the remains of her parents and brother to the Trinity monastery to be reinterred in the stone sarcophagus in the forecourt. Evidently she had tarried there after the formal obsequies, and was caught in the siege.

19. Maria Vladimirovna, widow of Magnus, Ivan IV's vassal king of Livonia and daughter of Prince Vladimir of Staritsa. Concerning her, Giles Fletcher wrote: "Besides these of the male kind, there is a widow that hath right in the succession, sister to the old emperor and aunt to this man [Tsar Fedor Ivanovich], sometime wife to Magnus Duke of Holstein, brother to the King of Denmark, by whom she had one daughter. This woman since the death of her husband hath been allured again into Russia by some that love the succession better than herself, which appeareth by the sequel. For herself with her daughter so soon as they were returned into Russia were thrust into a nunnery where her daughter died this last year, while I was in the country [1588 or 1589], of no natural disease as was supposed. The mother remaineth still in the nunnery, where (as I have heard) she bewaileth herself and curseth the time when she returned into Russia, enticed with the hope of marriage and other fair promises in the emperor's name." *Of the Russe Commonwealth*, reprinted in *Rude and Barbarous Kingdom. Russia in the Accounts of Sixteenth-century English Voyagers*, ed. Lloyd E. Berry and Robert O. Crummey (Madison, 1968), p. 129. See also ibid., pp. 315-317 for Jerome Horsey's interesting version of the story. Soloviev does not offer any explanation as to why Maria Vladimirovna happened to be at the Trinity monastery during the siege.

20. Fedor Nikitich Romanov had been tonsured forcibly during the purge of the Romanov family by Boris Godunov in 1600, and had taken the religious name of Filaret. Released from monastic confinement by the triumph of False Dmitry, he was appointed metropolitan of Rostov. Some historians consider that he felt slighted by Shuisky at being passed over when the new patriarch, Hermogen, was chosen, and inclined to the Tushino camp. The indications are that he did not recognize the validity of the title bestowed upon him by Tushino, and that Hermogen was fully cognizant of this.

21. *Chronicle of Many Rebellions*, pp. 135-142.

22. The Stroganov family was descended from peasants in the northern maritime region. Fedor Lukich Stroganov became firmly established in the region of Solvychegodsk. There his son Anika (1497-1570) acquired a saltworks in 1515,

and from there expanded the industrial properties of the family considerably. In 1558 Ivan IV gave Anika and his descendants extensive territories along the Kama and Chusovaia rivers, and in 1566 the Stroganov lands were taken into Ivan IV's crown domains at their own request. The two Stroganovs mentioned here are Anika's grandsons, who had taken part in Yermak's original expedition for the conquest of Siberia, and for their pains were given additional landholdings. During the Time of Troubles they gave considerable material assistance to the Muscovite government, their cash contributions alone amounting to 842,000 rubles. In 1610 they were given the title of "distinguished people;" nor under the Romanov regime were their past services forgotten. See entry by V. I. Buganov, MERSH, Vol. 37, pp. 224-226.

23. Ustiuzhna Zhelezopolskaia is first mentioned in 1252 in a survey of the settlements pertaining to the principality of Uglich. Also occasionally called Zhelezny Ustiug, it was a major center for iron smelting from the fifteenth century. After the heroic resistance described here by Soloviev, it was properly fortified in 1609. In 1712 it was assigned to the Admiralty for the production of naval craft and fittings. After the development of the Ural iron deposits, Ustiuzhna declined in importance.

24. Probably a reference to the *pravezh*, whereby unsatisfied public or private debts were exacted by force, usually by beating the debtor across the shins in the market place until he revealed any hidden money in order to discharge the debt.

25. Evidently a namesake of the cossack bandit leader executed in Warsaw in 1597.

26. Fedor Ivanovich Sheremetev (1576-1650) was orphaned at an early age. His father was killed in the Livonian war in 1577, and his mother died in 1583. During his minority his estate was administered by his sister Elena Ivanovna, widow of Tsarevich Ivan Ivanovich. His earliest recorded service was in 1591, when the Tatars were threatening Moscow. In 1592 he was at the christening feast of Tsarevna Feodosia, and in 1597 was at the reception of the Imperial ambassador at the Palace of Facets. He was briefly governor of Chernigov in 1598, but was back in Moscow in time to witness the confirmatory charter concerning the election of Boris Godunov. Sheremetev seems to have shared in the fate of the Romanov clan in 1600, since he was in semi-honorific exile as governor of Tobolsk from 1601 to 1603, and then there is a gap in his service record until 1605, when he was sent with a large army to the relief of Kromy. From his petition to Prince Wladyslaw in 1610 it is apparent that Boris confiscated some of his estates in the Riazan region. With the advance of False Dmitry, Sheremetev found himself at Orel, where he greeted the Pretender on his arrival with bread and salt, crosses, icons and pealing of bells. When Dmitry restored to favor those who had been in bad odor during the reign of Boris, Sheremetev was not forgotten, and was appointed to the boyar council, which Dmitry renamed the Senate. He was put in charge of a levy of eighteen thousand men from the regions of Novgorod and Pskov, intended for Dmitry's proposed Crimean campaign. Probably the troops

which infiltrated the capital on the night of Dmitry's murder were commanded by Sheremetev. When Astrakhan under its governor Prince I. D. Khvorostinin declared for False Dmitry II, Sheremetev was ordered to recover the city. Despite the help of the Nogay khan, Ishterek, he was unable to do so, but instead set up his camp on the island of Balchik, about three versts upriver in the Volga delta. Many merchants from Astrakhan and the Caspian littoral sought refuge at Balchik. Although he was never able to recapture Astrakhan, he did pacify many of the towns of the lower Volga, and recruited levies from the various native peoples, including Cheremiss, Mordvin and Chuvash. He then sent aid to the governors of Nizhny Novgorod, A. A. Repnin and A. S. Aliabiev, thus enabling them to repel the rebels, not only from the city itself, but also from Balakhna, Vorsma and the village of Pavlovo. On the way Sheremetev defeated rebel detachments at Cheboksary and Sviyazhsk, and remained at Nizhny Novgorod until the dry season. Murom swore allegiance to Tsar Vasily even before Sheremetev arrived there, but Kasimov surrendered only after a prolonged resistance. Vladimir also surrendered without a struggle, and there Sheremetev made his headquarters. Despite the tsar's urging that Sheremetev proceed immediately to the relief of the Trinity monastery, he felt unable to advance further while leaving Suzdal untaken in his rear. An attempt to capture Suzdal was defeated by the pretender's governors, Pleshcheev and Prosovetsky, reinforced by a detachment led by Lisowski from the forces besieging the Trinity monastery. Retreating to Vladimir, Sheremetev corresponded with the other towns loyal to Moscow, principally Yaroslavl. Informed of Skopin's movements, he eventually managed to link up with the Russo-Swedish expeditionary force at Aleksandrovskaia Sloboda on November 11, 1609. Thereafter Skopin assumed command of the combined forces, and Sheremetev faded into the background. After the deposition of Vasily Shuisky, Sheremetev loyally supported the candidacy of Prince Wladyslaw. He was one of the boyars virtually held prisoner in the Kremlin from February 1611 to October 1612, but after a brief absence from Moscow played a leading part in the Assembly of the Land in 1613, and was one of the deputation sent to bring the newly elected Tsar Michael to the capital. From then on until his retirement in 1646 he played a leading part in the government. Before the return of Filaret and after his death he was virtual head of the chancellery network and the factual leader of the boyar council, though in the earlier period he was theoretically outranked by the easy-going Prince F. I. Mstislavsky. He accumulated fabulous wealth, as his will and the enormous endowments made to leading monasteries attest. He finally took monastic vows under the name Feodosy at the St. Cyril monastery near Beloozero in September 1649, and died there February 17, 1650.

27. Andrei Semeonovich Aliabiev (dates of birth and death unknown) as governor of Nizhny Novgorod, despite the promises of the Tushino brigand, was loyal to Tsar Vasily Shuisky. On December 2, 1608 rebel groups approached from the neighboring town of Balakhna. Aliabiev twice repulsed them, compelled Balakhna to kiss the cross to Tsar Vasily and hanged the rebel leader Timokha

Taskaev in Nizhny Novgorod. Three days later he destroyed another rebel group and pacified the towns of Vorsma and Pavlov. Later, when the Suzdal junior boyar Stepan Survotsky incited the peasants of villages around Starodub against the tsar, Aliabiev imprisoned him and persuaded the peasants to submit or suffer the fate of the people of Balakhna and Vorsma. On January 7, 1609 once again he repelled the Tushinites from Nizhny Novgorod and took their leader Timofey Lazarev prisoner, forcing the remainder under Prince Semeon Viazemsky to flee. He then moved against the rebels in Murom and Vladimir. Murom surrendered peacefully, but Aliabiev was compelled to send musketeer detachments to capture Vladimir. On May 27, 1609 the tsar sent him a letter of commendation. On August 30, 1611 he sent the inhabitants of Kazan a letter urging them not to recognize the son of Marina as tsar. His further service is unknown.

28.   Andrei Zakharovich Prosovetsky (?-1640) was the leader of a band of renegade cossacks which rallied to False Dmitry II. At Tushino Prosovetsky was given the rank of table attendant, and in March 1609 was appointed governor of Lukh. In April it was proposed to appoint him as senior governor of Suzdal, replacing F. N. Pleshcheev, but the citizens protested, so Prosovetsky was appointed deputy governor, with Pleshcheev remaining as senior governor. Pleshcheev and Prosovetsky tried to bring the city of Vladimir into submission to the pretender, but with the success of Skopin's relief expedition they were forced back onto the defensive. When Pleshcheev declared for Wladyslaw, Prosovetsky joined forces with Lisowski (see Chapter I, Note 81, above) and in the spring of 1610 moved off in the direction of Pskov, besieging and plundering the Kaliazin monastery on the way. When Shuisky was overthrown, Lisowski and Prosovetsky decided to fight against the Swedes, with whom they fought an unsuccessful engagement outside Yama. Thereafter Lisowski and Prosovetsky parted company, the latter setting up his camp at Ostrov, twenty versts outside Pskov on the Novgorod highway. The two former allies fought each other and Prosovetsky, being defeated, fled to False Dmitry's headquarters at Kaluga. After the pretender's death Prosovetsky returned to Suzdal, where he ruled as self-appointed governor, even sending help to the inhabitants of Vladimir to defeat Prince I. S. Kurakin, who was coming to administer the oath of allegiance to Wladyslaw. Prosovetsky then wrote to the other towns, urging them to adhere to the national liberation movement which was forming around Prokopy Liapunov. On behalf of the first militia force he held Pereiaslavl against Sapieha, but when the town was besieged and burned to the ground he was forced to flee. Although he had co-operated with Liapunov, he could find no common ground with Pozharsky, and therefore played no role in the final stages of the national liberation movement. He reappeared in the 1630s and 1640s as a "Moscow noble" and served as governor of Charonda (1635) and Kozmodemiansk (1639-1640).

29.   The Polish term, which Soloviev uses untranslated, is *pacholiki*, literally "youths", but which also denoted members of the lesser gentry who did not enjoy noble status.

30. Prince Roman Ivanovich Gagarin (?-1631) was governor of Putivl in 1601, and in 1605 commanded a section of garrison of Smolensk. In 1606 he was sent as second in command of the rearguard regiment in the expedition sent to pacify Severia. In September 1607 he was with the forces sent against the bogus Tsarevich Peter. As related here, he took part in the attempt to dethrone Shuisky, but his attempt was frustrated by Patriarch Hermogen. He fled to Tushino, but reappeared in Moscow May 28, 1608 with news that the so-called Dmitry was an impostor, and also that it was known in Tushino that Skopin and his Swedish auxiliaries were on their way to the relief of Moscow. He also asserted that the Troubles had been fomented by King Sigismund in order to destroy the Orthodox faith. In March 1612 he was appointed governor of Kostroma by Pozharsky, to replace I. P. Sheremetev, who had declared for Prince Wladyslaw. In 1616 he is reported as having a land and salary entitlement of seven hundred chetverts and fifty rubles. From 1618 to 1621 he was in charge of fire precautions for the greater area of the Moscow Kremlin, and in 1626 he was one of the attendants at Tsar Michael's second marriage. He also served in the Vladimir Judicial Chancellery, first alongside Prince I. V. Golitsyn and subsequently with Prince I. N. Odoevsky. He also took part in receptions for the Persian and Turkish ambassadors. From 1629 to 1631 he was governor of Rostov, and is last attested receiving an audience with the tsar on his return from this assignment.

31. Ivan Fedorovich Kriuk-Kolychev (?-1608) is first mentioned in 1580 as governor of Staraia Rusa. In 1585 he received the rank of lord-in-waiting. He was implicated in the Shuisky conspiracy of 1587, and was imprisoned for a while in Nizhny Novgorod. He does not appear to have been employed in any capacity during the reign of Boris. He was recalled to Moscow by False Dmitry I, and was later given a military command by Shuisky, subordinate to Skopin, in the operations against the Bolotnikov rebels. In 1606 he was appointed boyar and major-domo, but during the following year, as related here, he was implicated in a plot to assassinate Shuisky. He was tortured and executed on Red Square, although the existence of the alleged plot was never established.

32. Prince Boris Mikhailovich Lykov-Obolensky (?-1646) took part in various diplomatic receptions between 1593 and 1597. He was a signatory to Boris Godunov's confirmatory charter in 1598, and accompanied him on the Serpukhov campaign in the summer of that year. He was in the reception party for both of Tsarevna Xenia's suitors, Prince Gustav of Sweden and Prince Johann of Denmark. Late in 1602 he was appointed governor of Belgorod, where he remained for the rest of Boris's reign. Absence from court for several years was the result of the unsatisfactory outcome of several precedence disputes and apparent dissatisfaction with Tsar Boris. He became one of the closest followers of False Dmitry I, who sent him to the borderland towns to administer the oath of allegiance. He was appointed boyar April 13, 1606 and later married Anastasia Nikitichna Romanova, sister to Metropolitan Filaret. As related by Soloviev, under Vasily Shuisky he took a leading part in the struggle with the Bolotnikov rebels. In 1608

he was sent to the relief of Briansk, and then operated against the second pretender from his headquarters at Orel. Although he did not desert to Tushino, he was suspected of sympathies in this direction, especially since an expeditionary force under his command failed to engage Lisowski by reason of yet another precedence dispute. After Shuisky's deposition he was one of the commission of "seven boyars" which acted as an interim government pending the arrival of the newly elected Prince Wladyslaw. He presented a petition to Wladyslaw, from whom he received two small villages in the Riazan region; the only trouble was that King Sigismund simultaneously had granted the same villages to Ivan Mikhailovich Saltykov! Lykov was one of the signatories on letters to Shein demanding the immediate capitulation of Smolensk, and on another letter asking the ambassadors to urge the immediate dispatch of Prince Wladyslaw to Moscow. Like the other boyars held captive in the Kremlin, Lykov was absent during the initial deliberations of the Assembly of the Land of 1613, but was one of the signatories of Tsar Michael's confirmatory charter. After the coronation he brought a precedence dispute against Ivan Nikitich Romanov, but eventually consented to take his place at the tsar's table below the Romanovs. In May 1614, when Moscow was threatened with a Tatar attack, Lykov was put in charge of the defenses along the Yauza river. In September of the same year he was given the task of pacifying the southern borderlands, and defeated Zarutsky's marauding cossacks near Balakhna. He also acted against renegade cossacks and foreign mercenaries around Vologda and Beloozero in 1615. He rounded up three thousand cossacks and brought them to Moscow, where they swore allegiance to Tsar Michael. In September 1617 he was sent to Nizhny Novgorod to recruit forces in anticipation of Prince Wladyslaw's advance on Moscow, and in June 1618 he took part in the relief of Mozhaisk. In 1619 he was head of the Chancellery for Criminal Affairs, and was sent to Nizhny Novgorod to muster service cavalrymen. Between 1620 and 1622 he was senior governor of Kazan. In 1623 he headed the Chancellery of Investigations. He attended both marriages of Tsar Michael, in 1624 and 1626, and in the latter year superintended the refortification of Mozhaisk. He was head of the Monastery Chancellery 1628-1629, and from 1629 to 1635 headed the Postal Chancellery. In 1632 he became involved in a mestnichestvo dispute with Prince D. M. Cherkassky. He lost, had to pay damages in the amout of twelve hundred rubles, and both litigants were removed from command of the Smolensk expedition. In view of what happened to Shein, this was perhaps a blessing in disguise! In 1634 he was in charge of the extraordinary tax levies to defray the expenses of the Smolensk War, and from 1635 to 1642 he headed the Chancellery for Kazan and Siberia. When in January 1639 two of Tsar Michael's sons Ivan and Vasily died, Lykov kept vigil over the bodies day and night. In 1640 he was one of the commission of seven boyars left in charge of state affairs while Tsar Michael was absent on pilgrimage. Lykov died June 2, 1646, and was buried in a stone chapel adjoining the St. Paphnutius monastery of Borovsk.

33. Prince Dmitry Mikhailovich Pozharsky (1578-1642), who plays such an illustrious role in the succeeding chapters, makes his first appearance here. He had been appointed table attendant by Boris Godunov in 1602, and majordomo under the first False Dmitry. He served the government of Vasily Shuisky with outstanding loyalty, so much so, that the town of Zaraisk, of which he was governor, became a particular focus for pro-Shuisky forces. See entry by Daniel B. Rowland, MERSH, Vol. 29, pp. 151-156, and Ruslan G. Skrynnikov, *The Time of Troubles. Russia in Crisis, 1604-1618* (Gulf Breeze, Fla: Academic International Press, 1988).

34. Mikolaj Marchocki (1570-1636), author of *Historya wojny moskiewskiy* (Poznan, 1841). In 1607 he became a captain in the forces of Roman Rozynski. About New Year 1608 he was sent from Kromy to False Dmitry II at Orlov. In January 1609 he appeared before the Sejm urging Polish support for the pretender. He was unhappy at the king's invasion of Muscovy and siege of Smolensk, and in November of that year sent an embassy to the king's encampment. He fought at the battle of Osipov and remained with Rozynski until the latter's death on April 8, 1610. Thereafter he made contact with the royal army, and fought with Zolkiewski's forces at Klushino under the command of Alexander Zborowski. As related here, he quarrelled with Zolkiewski over the allocation of positions in occupied Moscow. At the time of the first skirmishes in Moscow between the Russians and Poles, he commanded one of the Kremlin bastions. In the autumn of 1611 he was sent once again to the Sejm to request pay for the soldiers in Moscow, but to no avail. On his way back from Warsaw to Moscow in January 1612 he was waylaid by a band of confederate detachments returning to Poland. Marchocki was barely able to fight them off, and took no part in further action in the Muscovite war. In 1613, as a captain of the royal army he received rich rewards from Sigismund III from the confiscated estates of Jan Wolski. Apart from his history of the Muscovite war, written between 1607 and 1612, he also wrote narratives of the Cecora campaign of 1620, and the campaign of Jan Karol Chodkiewicz against Turkey in 1621. He served in the capacity of provincial governor and Sejm deputy until his death.

35. I have used this term to translate *guliai-gorod*, a mobile siege tower which provided cover for an assault, or from which a drawbridge might be lowered onto opposing fortifications.

36. *New Chronicler*, p. 88.

37. Founded in 1295, this town was repeatedly a bone of contention between Sweden and Russia. It had been in Swedish hands from 1581 to 1595, but had been won back in Boris Godunov's Swedish war. It was captured by the Swedes in 1611, but retaken by Peter the Great in 1710. When the Swedes took the town it was renamed Kexholm, and this name was retained until 1948, when the town was renamed Priozersk.

38. The Karelians are a people of Finnic stock who inhabit the borderlands between Russia and Finland.

39. The Solovetsk monastery was founded about 1430 as a daughter house of the St. Cyril monastery of Beloozero. It was situated on Solovetsk Island in the White Sea. It soon developed extensive landholdings along the shores of the White Sea and in the basins of the rivers which flow into it. It was a major center of salt manufacture, as well as deriving much of its revenue from fishing, trapping and production of mica, iron and pearls. It was fortified extensively between 1584 and 1594, and between 1668 and 1676 offered stiff armed resistance to the Nikonian reforms. It successfully repelled foreign invaders in 1571, 1582, 1611 and 1854. See entry by V. I. Buganov, MERSH, Vol. 36, pp. 140-141.

40. Jacob Pontus de la Gardie (1583-1652) was the son of Pontus de la Gardie, a French nobleman who entered the service of the Swedish king, commanded Swedish armies against Russia, and was drowned at Narva in 1585. Jacob thus was orphaned at an early age and brought up at the Swedish court. He served his military apprenticeship in the Livonian war, was captured at Wolmar in 1601 and spent four years in Polish captivity. After a spell in Western Europe in the service of Prince Maurice of Orange, he re-entered Swedish service in both diplomatic and military capacities, leading a force of Swedish and foreign auxiliaries to aid Skopin's relieving force. The expedition was a triumph, but Skopin died and the Swedes' paymaster Shuisky was deposed, leaving the Swedes to fend for themselves. After the battle of Klushino some of the foreign auxiliaries under De la Gardie's command entered the service of the Polish victors, others chose to go home, while the main force moved off into northern Russia to await reinforcements. The latter, with the complicity of the Russian military governor, occupied Novgorod in the summer of 1611. De la Gardie was very active in negotiations with the national armies, first Prokopy Liapunov and then Minin and Pozharsky, with a view to placing the Swedish prince Karl Philipp on the Russian throne, and it is just possible that had the prince been less dilatory in making his journey to the Muscovite frontier his candidature would have succeeded. After the election of Michael Romanov the Swedes, frustrated in their attempts to place one of their princes upon the Russian throne, continued their occupation of Novgorod and the Baltic littoral, although they were less successful at seizing strongholds in the far north such as Kola, the Suma fort and the Solovetsk monastery. Further south the Swedes gained control of Koporie, Yama, Ivangorod, Oreshek, Gdov, Porkhov, Staraia Rusa, Ladoga and Tikhvin, and in 1615 an attempt, commanded by King Gustavus Adolphus in person, was made to take Pskov by siege. During this time the troops were commanded by De la Gardie, who was military governor of Novgorod. After the failure of the Swedes to take Pskov peace negotiations began in earnest, culminating in the Peace of Stolbovo, which was signed in February 1617. Sweden returned Novgorod to Muscovy, but retained the provinces of Karelia and Ingria. De la Gardie was awarded the title of count in 1615, and played a major role during Swedish participation in the Thirty Years' War. In 1619 he was appointed governor of Reval, and in 1622 governor-general of Swedish-held Livonia. After the death of Gustavus Adolphus in 1632 he was appointed to the

Council of Regency during the early part of the reign of Queen Christina. His son Magnus (1622-1686) was one of the organizers of the Swedish invasion of Poland in 1655. Jacob also wrote memoirs of the Muscovite campaigns, *Thet svenska i Ryssland Tijo ahrs krijgs-historie* (History of the War Between Sweden and Russia) (Stockholm, 1671). See entry in MERSH, Vol. 48, pp. 5-6.

41. See above, Chapter I, Note 91.

42. Veal was apparently a forbidden dish among the Muscovites. The fact that the pretender ate veal in Lent was therefore doubly reprehensible. It is notable that Vasily Shuisky's detractors also accused him of eating veal. On the altercation between Tatishchev and False Dmitry, see Volume 14, p. 127.

43. The *veche* was the town assembly of medieval Russia, normally summoned by the ringing of a bell, which thus became a symbol of ancient civic freedom. When Ivan III annexed Novgorod, or Vasily III Pskov, the *veche* bell pointedly was removed.

44. *Pskov Chronicles*, vyp. 2, p. 272.

45. The town of Torzhok, situated about a hundred versts from Novgorod, was repeatedly disputed between Novgorod and the princes of Vladimir-Suzdal. It was also the point where the Mongol armies advancing on Novgorod in 1238 turned back.

46. The patronymic with the *-vich* suffix was an indicator of superior social status. As we have seen (see above, Note 6), Ivan Gramotin was accorded this privilege only after many years of distinguished service.

47. Pereiaslavl-Zalessky, "beyond the forest", to distinguish it from Pereiaslavl-in-Riazan or the Pereiaslavl in Kievan Rus, now Pereiaslav-Khmelnitsky.

CHAPTER III

1. Karl IX (1550-1611) was the youngest son of King Gustav Vasa and in 1560 was invested as duke of Sudermania. When his cousin Sigismund III of Poland (reigned 1587-1632) also became king of Sweden in 1592 Karl led the movement against the new ruler's attempts to reintroduce Catholicism. At the Riksdag (Parliament) held at Söderköping he was appointed regent, and in 1598 thwarted Sigismund's armed attempt to regain effective rule. The following year Sigismund was declared deposed. Karl continued as regent until officially proclaimed king in 1604. Neither Sigismund nor his two sons and successors Wladyslaw IV (1632-1648) and Jan Kazimierz (1648-1676) ever renounced their rights to the Swedish throne. Sigismund fought three unsuccessful wars (1600-1611, 1617-1620 and 1621-1629) to regain his Swedish crown.

2. Jagiello (1350-1434) was the son of Olgerd and grandson of Gedimin, the founder of the Lithuanian ruling dynasty. Jagiello's mother was Olgerd's second wife, Princess Juliana of Tver. Jagiello was grand prince of Lithuania from

1377 to 1392, when he relinquished the rulership to his cousin Vytautas. Meanwhile he had become king of Poland through his marriage in 1386 to Jadwiga, the eleven-year-old heiress of the ruling Piast dynasty. By the Union of Krewo Catholicism became the official religion of Lithuania, in place of the traditional paganism, while Jagiello ruled Poland as King Wladyslaw II, thus becoming the progenitor of the Jagiellonian dynasty, which came to an end in the male line with the death of Sigismund II Augustus in 1572. Jagiello's second wife, Anna, may have been a Russian princess.

3. Ivan IV had advanced his own candidacy for the Polish throne on the death of Sigismund Augustus in 1572, and the candidacy of Tsar Fedor Ivanovich was advanced in 1586. There had been suggestions that King Sigismund III should marry Fedor's widow Irina, the sister of Boris Godunov!

4. Stanislaw Zolkiewski (1547-1620), who plays a prominent part in the succeeding narrative, was appointed crown hetman in 1588, and in 1594-1595 took a leading part in suppressing the Nalivaiko rebellion in the Ukraine. In 1608 he was named governor of Kiev. He was prominent in the Polish intervention during the Time of Troubles, and after Shuisky's deposition was instrumental in coming to an agreement with the interim boyar administration to admit a Polish garrison and to elect Prince Wladyslaw as tsar. When it became apparent that King Sigismund was attempting to advance his own claims to the Muscovite throne, Zolkiewski no longer wished to take part in the enterprise and abandoned the royal camp. He nevertheless retained the confidence of the king, who appointed him high crown hetman in 1613 and chancellor in 1617. He was killed while fighting the Turks at the battle of Cecora in 1620. He has left a valuable account of his Muscovite campaign, translated into English as *Expedition to Moscow* (London, 1959).

5. Smolensk is one of the earliest Russian cities, and since the middle of the twelfth century the center of an independent principality. It was annexed to the Polish-Lithuanian state in 1404, but was captured for Muscovy by Grand Prince Vasily III in 1514. Between 1596 and 1602 it was refortified extensively by the renowned military engineer Fedor Savelev Kon at the order of Boris Godunov. As described in this volume, Smolensk withstood the Polish siege from September 1609 to June 1611, when it was retaken by the Poles. Smolensk was also the main objective of the unsuccessful "Smolensk war" of 1632-1634, but was returned to Russia in 1654, this time definitively, in the opening stages of the Thirteen Years' War. On the siege of Smolensk see entry in MERSH, Vol. 36, pp. 46-53.

6. The burning of suburbs and other buildings which might afford cover to the besiegers was standard practice at the commencement of a siege.

7. Alexandrovskaia Sloboda, on the approaches to the Trinity monastery, is infamous as the headquarters of the crown domains of Ivan IV, who doubtless chose it because of its strategic location. It was occupied by Skopin's force on October 9, 1609.

8. Probably another Stanislaw Stadnicki, not "the devil of Lancuc," who was a bitter adversary of the Vasa king (see Chapter I, Note 94).

9. Note that Sigismund pointedly does not accord his cousin and arch-enemy Karl the royal title, since of course he considered himself to be the rightful king of Sweden.

10. For information on Tyszkiewicz, see Chapter I, Note 79.

11. "So-called" Patriarch Filaret, since his patriarchal title was conferred by the Tushino authorities. As Soloviev points out elsewhere, not even Filaret recognized the validity of the title, which the incumbent patriarch, Hermogen, charitably assumed that Filaret accepted under constraint.

12. In 1446 two Tatar princes, Kasim and Yakub, fled to Moscow and were accepted into Russian service. In 1452 Grand Prince Vasily II rewarded Kasim and his followers with the town and district of Gorodets Meshchersky, largely inhabited by Meshcherei and Mordvin, tribes of Finnish stock. In 1471, two years after Kasim's death, the town and district were renamed Kasimov in his honor. The tributary principality was always under a Muslim ruler and was internally autonomous, although a governor appointed by the Chancellery of Foreign Affairs kept a watching brief. The principality was dissolved in 1681 after the death of the last native ruler, Fatima Sultan. See entry by Edward D. Sokol, MERSH, Vol. 16, pp. 54-56.

13. Fedor (Fedka) Andronov was a merchant who attached himself to the court of the second pretender at Tushino, then joined the armies of Sigismund III at Smolensk. The king appointed him to the boyar council in Moscow, where he served as treasurer. He became the foremost collaborationist, and was seized on the orders of Pozharsky before he could escape Moscow. He was hanged at Moscow in October 1612. See entry in MERSH, Vol. 1, pp. 225-226 and below, pp. 268-269.

14. On the Union of Brest, see above, Chapter I, Note 102.

15. Bussow (p. 238): "The third captain was a Scot called Albert Wandmann [? Lambton], but he was called Pan Skotnicki, because he had served for a long time in Poland."

16. The monastery of St. Joseph is situated about 20 kilometers from the present-day town of Volokolamsk in Moscow oblast. It was founded in 1479 by Joseph Sanin, and in the sixteenth century became the center for the struggle against the non-possessors and heretics. In 1594-95 the estates of the monastery was the scene of a formidable peasant rebellion. During the Bolotnikov uprising the monastery mobilized its considerable financial resources in support of the government of Tsar Vasily Shuisky. The community suffered financial ruin when the monastery was occupied and plundered by Polish invaders in 1610, but its fortunes were restored during the reign of Tsar Alexis.

17. *Chronicle of Many Rebellions*, p. 177; *New Chronicler*, p. 96.

18. It is not indicated either in the chronicles or in offical acts when Sergius became archbishop. When Sigismund called for surrender Sergius is said to have replied: "In the shrine of the Virgin we have vowed not to betray our sovereign Vasily Ivanovich, or be enslaved forever by you, the Lithuanian king and your

lords." The archbishop inspired the defenders of the city, shared the hardships and dangers with them. When the city fell, Sergius was wounded and taken prisoner. He died in captivity, but it is not known exactly when. He was still alive in 1617, since Prince Wladyslaw wrote that both he and Patriarch Ignaty would accompany him to Moscow.

19. Grigory Lukianovich Belsky, better known as Maliuta Skuratov, was Ivan IV's favorite during the years of the crown domain. One of his daughters, Maria, married Boris Godunov while another, Catherine, married Prince Dmitry Ivanovich Shuisky.

20. *New Chronicler*, pp. 96-97.

21. Palitsyn, p. 206.

22. Zolkiewski (pp. 65-66): "Moreover it happened that, when his support was most needed, Skopin died poisoned (as was at once suggested) with Shuisky's complicity, on account of the rivalry that was between them. Nevertheless, in answer to the question what had happened, it is said that he died of fever."

23. Bussow (p. 185): "The unfortunate, courageous hero Skopin, who had been in the Swedish realm, and for the benefit of the tsar and his country had brought with him foreign troops, and even remained with them for a whole year, never complaining about his lot, and had fought valiantly against the foe, was graciously rewarded for his pains, in that Shuisky ordered that he be given venom and be poisoned to death. The reason for this was that the Germans and other nationalities, and even many of the Muscovites themselves, esteemed him for his prudence and bravery more highly than Shuisky. All of Moscow mourned at his death."

24. *Pskovskie letopisi* (The Pskov Chronicles), vyp. 1 (Moscow, 1941), p. 125.

25. *Chronicle of Many Rebellions*, p. 179; *New Chronicler*, p. 97.

26. *Chronograph of 1617*, RIB 13, col. 1304. See also A. N. Popov, *Izbornik slavianskikh i russkikh sochinenii i statei vnessennykh v khronografy russkoi redaktsii* (Selection of Slavic and Russian Works and Entries Inserted into the Chronographs of the Russian Redaction), (Moscow, 1869), p. 198.

27. Originally dedicated to the Nativity, the monastery was founded in 1444 by a baptized Tatar, St. Paphnutius (1394-1477), to whom the monastery later was rededicated. Joseph Sanin, the founder of the celebrated monastery near Volokolamsk, was originally a member of this community.

28. Zolkiewiski, p. 86.

29. The forbidden years, introduced during the last years of Ivan IV's reign, became general during the last decade of the sixteenth century, but were suspended temporarily by Boris Godunov during the "hungry years" of 1601-1603. The five-year recovery period relating to fugitive peasants, similarly suspended by Boris, was reinforced by False Dmitry I's decree of February 1, 1606. Shuisky's decree of March 1607 also reaffirmed the forbidden years and extended the period for recovery to fifteen years.

30. The "free years" (urochnye leta), as opposed to the forbidden years (zapovednye leta).

31. *Okhochie liudi*, usually native people enrolled as auxiliary troops.

32. *The Common Readings*, in Russian *Obshchaia Mineia*, was an anthology of edifying works.

CHAPTER IV

1. A reference to the sack of Rome by the Imperial troops of Charles V in 1527.

2. *Skazanie Avraamiia Palitsyna* (Tale of Avraamy Palitsyn), ed. L.V. Cherepnin (Moscow, 1955), p. 208.

3. The text of the treaty between Zolkiewski and the Moscow boyars, together with pertinent documents, is reprinted in *Sbornik imperatorskogo russkogo istoricheskogo obshchestva* (Collection of the Imperial Russian Historical Society), 142, (Moscow, 1913), No. 9. The petition of the ex-Tushinites to King Sigismund is reprinted in *Akty istoricheskie, sobrannye i izdannye Arkheograficheskoiu Kommissieiu* (Historical acts collected and edited by the Archeographic Commission), 2, (St. Petersburg, 1841), No. 311. Hereafter AI. The list of King Sigismund's appointments to the Moscow chancelleries is reprinted in AI, 2, No. 374.

4. For information concerning Fedor Andronov, see above, Chapter III, Note 13, and below, pp. 191–199.

5. The monastery of St. Nicholas on the Ugresha river, situated about 15 kilometers. from Moscow, was founded in 1380 by Dmitry Donskoy on his return from his victorious encounter with the Tatars on Kulikovo Field.

6. For information concerning Golitsyn, see above, Chapter I, Note 16.

7. For information concerning the Solovetsk monastery, see above, Chapter II, Note 39.

8. According to legend the Intercession (Pokrovsky) convent at Suzdal was founded by Alexander Nevsky in the earlier part of the thirteenth century, but officially it was founded in 1364. It became the place of banishment for unwanted females of the ruling house, including the first wife of Vasily III, Solomonia Saburova, who resided there from 1526 to 1542, Ivan IV's fourth wife Anna Koltovskaia (1576-1626), Evdokia Saburova and Praskovia Solovaia, the first two wives of Tsarevich Ivan Ivanovich, Xenia Godunova (1605-1622) and Peter I's first wife Evdokia Lupokhina (1698-1718).

9. Soloviev in the following pages is drawing extensively on the materials relating to the Smolensk embassy, later reprinted in *Sbornik imperatorskogo russkogo istoricheskogo obshchestva*, Vol. 142, No. 11, pp. 126-263.

10. On Pleshcheev, see Chapter II, Note 7.

11. See above, Chapter II, Note 34.

12. On Gramotin, see above, Chapter II, Note 6.

13. As far as can be determined, Ivan IV died of natural causes, although there were persistent rumors of foul play, as in the case of the death of his son Fedor.

14. Fedor Borisovich Godunov was deposed and murdered by supporters of the first False Dmitry only a few weeks after his accession. See Vol. 14, pp. 93-98.

15. The Sapieha family were among the West Russian nobility who changed from the Orthodox to the Uniate faith after the Union of Brest in 1596.

16. The Cherkassians were a Caucasian tribe who frequently served as auxiliaries in the Russian and Polish armies. Soloviev tends to apply the term to cossacks in Polish service. On the Cherkassians, see Volume 14, Chapter I, Note 30.

17. Probably Grigory Shorin, the father of the "merchant extraordinary" Vasily Shorin (?-1678). On the latter, see the entry by Samuel H. Baron, MERSH, Vol. 35, pp. 28-31, and his article in *Canadian-American Slavic Studies*, Vol. VI, No. 4 (1972), pp. 503-548.

18. The title master of the horse (*starokoniushii*) was one of the most important of the honorary offices of the royal household, and was held by Boris Godunov while regent. Since Boris's accession to the throne the office had been left vacant.

19. On Fedor Ivanovich Sheremetev, see above, Chapter II, Note 26.

20. The Vaga lands were awarded at the 1613 Assembly of the Land to Prince D. T. Trubetskoy either in recognition of his services during the liberation of Moscow or as a sort of compensation prize for his unsuccessful candidature to the throne.

21. Vasily Yakovlevich Shchelkalov was the younger of two brothers who were prominent administrators in the last quarter of the sixteenth century. Vasily was head of the Chancellery of Crown Service and Appointments (Razriadnyi prikaz) from 1577 to 1594 and of the Chancellery of Foreign Affairs from 1594 to 1601, as well as keeper of the seal from 1595 or 1596. He was disgraced and removed from office by Boris Godunov, possibly in connection with the Romanov affair. He was restored partially to favor before the death of Boris in 1605, and was given the rank of lord-in-waiting by False Dmitry, although his former estates were not fully restored, which probably accounts for the petition to King Sigismund herein mentioned. He appears to have enjoyed conciliar rank throughout the reign of Shuisky, although he did not enjoy his former eminent position in state affairs. He died some time during the winter of 1610-1611. See entries "Shchelkalov Brothers" by Hugh F. Graham and the separate entry on Vasily by Daniel B. Rowland, MERSH, Vol. 34, pp. 176-182.

22. For information concerning Vlasiev, see above, Chapter I, Note 19.

23. Archpriest Terenty was possibly the author of the *Chronograph of 1617* and the *Tale of the Year 1606*. See N. K. Gudzy, *History of Early Russian Literature* (New York, 1970), p. 372. Some of the larger churches were served by a group of priests of whom the senior member was designated archpriest (protopop). See Chapter I, Note 64.

24. Ivan Mikhailovich Saltykov later deserted the Polish camp and captured Ladoga from the Swedes. Nevertheless he was arrested by the inhabitants of Novgorod and despite protestations of loyalty to the Muscovite cause was cruelly put to death.

25. On Bogdan Belsky, see Chapter I, Note 20.

CHAPTER V

1. Given the unsatisfactory nature of Soloviev's annotation to this chapter, I have given rather fuller annotation than in previous chapters, particularly in relation to direct quotations from primary sources, of which there are many. *Akty sobrannye i izdannye v bibliotekakh i arkhivakh Arkheograficheskoi Ekspeditsii Akademii Nauk* (AAE), Vol. 2 (St. Petersburg, 1836), No. 176/II.

2. *Sobranie gosudarstvennykh gramot i dogovorov* (Collection of state documents and treaties), Vol. 2 (St. Petersburg, 1819), No. 223. Hereafter SGGD.

3. AAE, Vol. 2, No. 176/II.

4. SGGD, Vol. 2, No. 226.

5. AAE, Vol. 2, No. 176/II; SGGD, Vol. 2, No. 226.

6. The icon of Our Lady of Vladimir, the most revered in Russia, popularly was believed to have been painted by St. Luke, although it is in fact of eleventh-century Byzantine workmanship. It was originally a gift from Constantinople to Kiev, but from 1155 was kept in Vladimir. It was transferred to Moscow in 1395, during the reign of Grand Prince Vasily I, and was displayed in the Dormition cathedral. It is now in the Tretiakov Gallery. See David B. Miller, "Legends of the Icon of Our Lady of Vladimir. A Study of the Development of Muscovite National Consciousness," *Speculum*, . 43 (1968), pp. 657-670.

7. Peter, Alexis and Jonas were metropolitans of Moscow and were the first of the "Moscow miracle-workers." Peter (1308-26) was the first metroplitan to reside in Moscow. Alexis (1354-78) officially transferred the seat of the metro-politanate to Moscow, and was regent during the minority of Dmitry Donskoy. Jonas (1448-61) was nominated by Grand Prince Vasily II to replace Isidore, who had supported the resolutions on church union adopted at the Council of Florence-Ferrara. Jonas, moreover, was confirmed by a synod of Russian bishops without reference to Constantinople. As a token of this independence the same synod canonized Peter and Alexis.

8. AAE, Vol. 2, No. 176/I.

9. SGGD, Vol. 2, No. 241.

10. The Suma fortress (ostrog) was founded on the southern shore of the White Sea between 1584 and 1586, and became a dependency of the Solovetsk mon-astery.

11. AAE, Vol. 2, No. 180.

12. AAE, Vol. 2, No. 181.

13. For information concerning Isidore, see above, Chapter II, Note 9.

14. AAE, Vol. 2, No. 183.

15. AI, Vol. 2, No. 318.

16. AI, Vol. 2, No. 327.

17. *Chronicle of Many Rebellions*, pp. 204-206.

18. Before the elevation, in 1589, of the Moscow eparchy to patriarchal rank, the highest ecclesiatical dignity in Russia was that of metropolitan. After the creation of the patriarchate a number of Russian archbishoprics were elevated to metropolitan status, and the new see of Krutitsa, a village near Moscow, was created, the incumbent being the chief suffragan and coadjutor of the patriarch.

19. Wilno (Polish), Vilnius (Lithuanian) or Vilna (Russian) was the historic capital of Lithuania and is presently the capital of the Lithuanian SSR.

20. AI, Vol. 2, No. 324.

21. *New Chronicler*, p. 107.

22. The original Annunciation cathedral (Blagoveshchenskii Sobor) in the Moscow Kremlin was built between 1397 and 1416, and for a time housed the treasury of the grand princes. In 1405 it was decorated by Theophanes the Greek, Andrei Rublev and Prokhor of Gorodets. The present building (and the one referred to by Soloviev) was built at the order of Ivan III between 1484 and 1489 by stonemasons from Pskov. Side chapels were added in 1562-64 at the order of Ivan IV.

23. Traditionally on Palm Sunday there was a procession in Moscow where the patriarch went in procession seated on a donkey which the tsar led by the bridle.

24. The Trans River quarter, or Zamoskvorechie, was the commercial suburb on the south bank of the bend in the Moscow river, immediately facing the Kremlin and The Kitai quarter.

25. Nicholas Struys was a Dutch mercenary officer and brother-in-law of Jakub Potocki (see Note 27, below) in Polish service, who played a prominent part in the final phase of the Time of Troubles. After the capitulation of the Polish garrison in the Kremlin he was kept captive in Muscovy until the exchange of prisoners which took place in 1618 (see Volume 16, Chapter II). Thereafter he returned to Holland.

26. *Book of Annals*, RIB, Vol. 13, col. 609.

27. Jakub Potocki (1554-1613) succeeded his brother Andrzej in 1609 as castellan of Kamieniec. He served in the Livonian War under King Stefan Bathory between 1579 and 1582, and was a veteran of many campaigns against the Tatars, as well as the Moldavian campaign of 1595-1596. In 1601-1602 he served again in Livonia, being appointed governor of Weissenstein. He was loyal to the king during the Zebrzydowski rebellion. As related here, he led the storming of Smolensk in June 1611, and received the capitulation of the Muscovite forces. As a reward he was appointed governor of Braclaw by the king. When the king departed for Warsaw, Potocki was appointed commander-in-chief of the forces remaining in Smolensk. In the spring of 1612 he sent one thousand infantry and three thousand cavalry under his brother-in-law Struys to the relief of Moscow. Potocki died in Smolensk on January 26, 1613.

28. See Chapter II, Note 47.

29. The Russians doubtless also were making a pun on the name of Koniecpolski (*konets pol'skii*, or "end of the Poles.")

30. Jan Karol Chodkiewicz (1560-1621) studied in the Jesuit college at Wilno, then between 1586 and 1589 at the Jesuit academy in Ingolstadt, Bavaria, where he read philosophy and law. He was appointed to his first military command in 1595, when under the command of Zolkiewski he helped put down the cossack revolt led by Nalivaiko. In 1599 he was appointed elder of Zmud, in 1600 deputy hetman of Lithuania, and in 1603 administrator of the occupied territories in Livonia. He took part together with Zamoyski and Zolkiewski in the Wallachian campaign of 1600 and the Livonian war of 1601. He was first commandant of Kokenhausen, conquered Dorpat in 1603, Weissenstein in 1604 and Riga in 1605. His Livonian campaign was crowned with a brilliant victory over the Swedes at the battle of Kirchholm on November 2, 1605. In the Zebrzydowski rebellion he won a signal victory over the insurgents at Guzow (July 5-6, 1607). Returning to the Swedish front in 1609, he captured Pernau and defeated the Swedish fleet at Salis. Appointed against his better judgement to command the relieving force sent against Moscow, he was hindered greatly by mutiny amongst his troops, whose pay was in arrears. He was a personal enemy of Leo Sapieha and the Potocki brothers. He fought unsuccessfully against the Muscovite militia force from October 10, 1611 to September 7, 1612. He returned to Smolensk, where he succeeded Jakub Potocki as commandant of the royal garrison. In 1617-1618 he took part in Prince Wladyslaw's expedition to Moscow, capturing Dorogobuzh and Viazma, but failed in his attempt to capture Mozhaisk (see Volume 16 of this series). He took part in the Turkish campaign of 1620-1621, and after Zolkiewski fell in the battle of Cecora assumed command of the royal forces, but died before the end of the campaign.

31. This information is false, since Patriarch Hermogen was confined in the Miracles monastery, where he was starved to death. The St. Cyril monastery refers to the famous monastery near Beloozero.

32. Detailed documentation of the Smolensk embassy also is contained in SRIO, Vol. 142, pp. 126-263.

33. In 219 B.C. Hannibal laid siege to Saguntum, which had entered into relations with Rome. The Romans alleged that this attack constituted a breach of the treaty concluded between Rome and Carthage in 241. The siege lasted eight months, and the defenders put up a desperate resistance, in which there were even incidents of cannibalism. The Romans sent envoys to Carthage to protest, but did not send an army to Saguntum. This event marked the opening of the Second Punic War (218-183).

34. Piotr Skarga (1536-1612), King Sigismund's Jesuit confessor, and a popular preacher. See Norman Davies, *God's Playground*, Vol. I, pp. 357-360.

35. SGGD, Vol. 2, No. 263.

36. *Chronicle of Many Rebellions*, p. 222.

37. "Black" lands were those cultivated by independent peasants who owed no dues or labor services to landlords, but only taxes to the crown.

38. See above, Chapter I, Note 61.

39. The *Razriad*, or central service record, maintained in a special chancellery set up for the purpose, namely the *Razriadnyi Prikaz*, or Chancellery of Crown Service and Appointments.

40. *Chronicle of Many Rebellions*, p. 223; *New Chronicler*, p. 112.

41. *Chronicle of Many Rebellions*, p. 222.

42. *Chronicle of Many Rebellions*, p. 224.

43. On the monastery of St. Nicholas on the Ugresha, see Chapter IV, Note 5.

44. The Simonov monastery, also dedicated to the Feast of the Intercession, was founded in 1379, and was one of the main fortresses guarding the approaches to Moscow. It particularly enjoyed the favor of Dmitry Donskoy, and was one of the main promoters of northern colonization since both the St. Cyril and Ferapontov monasteries near Beloozero were its daughterhouses. Between the fifteenth and seventeenth centuries it was one of the richest ecclesiastical landowners. Both Vassian Patrikeev and Maxim the Greek, celebrated sixteenth century publicists, lived and wrote in the Simonov monastery. The outer walls and towers, built in the sixteenth century and refortified in the seventeenth, still remain, as does the refectory, built in the 1680s.

45. *Chronicle of Many Rebellions*, p. 225.

46. Concerning De la Gardie, see Chapter II, Note 40.

47. When two persons having the same name and patronymic, as well as surname, were simultaneously on active service, the muster rolls often distinguished between them by appending the additional sobriquet *Bol' shoi* (Greater, Elder) or *Men' shoi* (Younger or Lesser).

48. The Holy Wisdom cathedral (Sofiiskii Sobor) is the most ancient historical monument in Novgorod. It was built on the orders of Prince Vladimir Yaroslavich between 1045 and 1050 to replace the wooden cathedral which had been destroyed by fire. A second storey was added in the twelfth century and between 1108 and 1144 the cathedral was adorned with frescoes, fragments of which still remain. The western facade boasts the Korsun gates, fashioned at Magdeburg in the mid-twelfth century. From the early twelfth century it became the cathedral church of the archbishops and later metropolitans, and also for a time housed the city treasury.

49. The foregoing is largely a paraphrase of the *Third Novgorod Chronicle*, PSRL, Vol. 3 (St. Petersburg, 1841), pp. 264-267.

50. The Treaty of Teusen (or Tiazvin) was concluded between Russia and Sweden in 1595.

51. On the previous disorders in Pskov, see Chapter II, pp. 58–62. Much of the source material on which Soloviev draws is to be found in the *Pskov Chronicles*, II, pp. 275-278. Timofey Kudekusha-Strepets is singled out by the chronicler (p. 272) as the most violent of the popular leaders.

52. Zapskovie, or the district beyond the Pskov river (see Zamoskvorechie, above, Note 24).

53. Many churches in Russia were dedicated to SS. Cosmas and Damian, most commonly those founded by guilds of metal workers, of whom they were the patron saints.

54. Pechory was one of the bytowns of Pskov, and the site of the famous Caves monastery. See below, Note 70.

55. Sidorka first declared himself in Ivangorod in March 1611, and was supported by cossacks and musketeers from Novgorod and Pskov. In July he laid siege to Pskov where the "lesser" people held power, but in August was threatened by Swedish detachments, and fled back to Ivangorod. In December 1611 Pskov swore allegiance to the pretender, who proceeded to release from prison some of the "better" people, and opened negotiations with the first national militia force encamped outside Moscow. In March 1612 the cossack units around Moscow declared for Sidorka, but the hostility of the second militia force led by Pozharsky led them to renounce this allegiance. Ivan Pleshcheev was sent to Pskov with the demand that the pretender be surrendered. Sidorka attempted to escape, but was apprehended and sent on to Moscow. According to some accounts he was murdered by his own cossacks while on his way to Moscow, but there is no firm evidence for this assertion. See entry by V. D. Nazarov, MERSH, Vol. 35, p. 120.

56. The "New Style" was the Gregorian calendar at that time in use in Poland and most Roman Catholic countries, as opposed to the "Old Style" or Julian calendar, still in use in Russia. In the sixteenth and seventeenth centuries the new style was ten days ahead of the old.

57. "Adam Zolkiewski, who chanced to behold the royal treasure, could not contain his admiration for one rhinoceros horn. In medieval Europe such horns were considered a great rarity and only eminent persons were privileged to possess them. The hetman's nephew said he had once held a single horn worth 200,000 Hungarian gold pieces in his hands. The rarity he had beheld was badly damaged at one end. The untarnished horn discovered in the Moscow treasury was worth much more." Skrynnikov, *Time of Troubles*, p. 222.

58. Ignaty was a Greek, originally archbishop of Cyprus. After the Turkish conquest of that island he fled, and lived for a while at Rome. During the reign of Fedor Ivanovich he appeared in Russia, and under Boris was appointed administrator of the Riazan archbishopric. When False Dmitry was advancing on Moscow Ignaty solemnly greeted him at Tula, which lay within his eparchy. He accompanied the pretender, who four days after the surrender of Moscow appointed him patriarch in place of the deposed Job. In this capacity he officiated at Dmitry's coronation and his marriage to Marina. Immediately after the death of the pretender he was deposed from patriarchal and even from episcopal rank, and was imprisoned in the Miracles monastery as an ordinary monk. When Patriarch Hermogen was deposed and imprisoned, just before Easter 1611, Ignaty was released and proclaimed patriarch in concert with the boyars who supported

Prince Wladyslaw. Fearing dire consequences for himself after the liberation of Moscow, he fled to Poland, where King Sigismund granted him permission to live in the Uniate monastery in Wilno. When in 1616 Wladyslaw set off to conquer Moscow it was announced that Ignaty would accompany him, although it is not actually known whether he participated in the campaign. In any case the Muscovites were not informed that he had joined the Uniate church. Details of the latter part of his life are lacking; it may be assumed that he lived out the remaining years of his life in retirement. He died at Wilno in 1640. A letter from Leo Sapieha to the Uniate Archbishop Grolnitsky contains information that King Sigismund had granted Ignaty some estates in the Vitebsk region. See *Akty otnisiashchiesia k istorii Zapadnoi Rossii, sobrannye i izdannye Arkheograficheskoiu Kommissieiu* (Acts Relating to the History of Western Russia, Collected and Edited by the Archeographic Commission), Vol. 4 (St. Petersburg, 1851), No. 150.

59. Arsenius of Elasson (1548-1626) was a native of Trikka in Thessaly, an area of mixed Greek and Slav population, which probably accounts for his knowledge of Old Church Slavonic. Born and educated in a priestly milieu, he attracted the attention of Archbishop Jeremiah of Larissa, who later became patriarch of Constantinople. Some time in the early 1580s Arsenius was appointed suffragan archbishop of Elasson and Dimonikos. He was sent by Patriarch Theolyptus II in 1586 as part of a delegation to Moscow but on the return journey he was persuaded to stay on in the Polish-held city of Lwow as rector of the Brotherhood School. In 1588 he published a Greek-Slavonic grammar, the first of its kind. When Patriarch Jeremiah travelled in person to Moscow to solicit funds for the rebuilding of the patriarchal church in Constantinople, he passed through Lwow and included Arsenius in his delegation. Arsenius participated in the installation of Job as the first patriarch of Moscow, and remained in Moscow where he petitioned Tsar Fedor for a grant of estates and an archiepiscopal see. The former request was granted, and Arsenius occupied a prominent place at court, at first at the church of Dmitry Solunsky, immediately adjoining the tsar's palace, and then as honorary archpriest of the Archangel cathedral, the burial place of the Muscovite rulers. He seems to have been able to adapt himself to a bewildering succession of regimes, and with the death of Hermogen and the flight of Ignaty he became the ranking Orthodox cleric within the Kremlin. Because of hunger and privations he became gravely ill, but was healed reputedly by a vision of St. Sergius of Radonezh, who prophesied the imminent liberation of Moscow. On November 27, 1612 he was chief celebrant at the solemn service of thanksgiving in the Kremlin. Not only was he exonerated from all collaboration with the enemy, he was compensated for all damages suffered. He was one of the delegation sent to greet Michael on his arrival in Moscow on May 2, 1613, and his signature is sixth in order of precedence on the new tsar's confirmatory charter. In May 1613 Arsenius was named to the archbishopric of Tver, vacant since the murder of Archbishop Feoktist in 1608. Arsenius, however, remained in the Kremlin and continued to style himself "Arkiepiskop Arkhangel'skii". In 1615 he was appointed

archbishop of Suzdal, although he did not take up residence there until 1621. See entry in MERSH, Vol. 46, pp. 20-25. Arsenius's vision of St. Sergius on the eve of the liberation of Moscow is recounted by Palitsyn, pp. 227-228.

60. AAE, Vol. 2, No. 197.

61. On Avraamy Palitsyn, see above, Chapter II, pp. 85-86. The material on Dionysius which follows is largely extracted from the contemporary *Zhitie i podvigi prepodobnogo ottsa nashego arkhimandrita Dionisiia* (Life and Deeds of Our Most Worthy father, Archimandrite Dionysius), State Historical Museum, Synodal Collection, No. 416. A printed version was published at *Zhitie prepodobnogo ottsa nashego, arkhimandrita Sergievoi Lavry* (Life of our most worthy father Dionysius, archimandrite of the St. Sergius Abbey), Sergiev-Posad, 1908. Dionysius (1570-1633), in secular life David Fedorovich Zobnikovsky, was schooled in the Dormition monastery of Staritsa. He was delicate and meek, and frequently was tormented by his fellow pupils. When he grew to manhood he expressed the wish to become a monk, but this was opposed by his parents. Instead he married a girl called Vassia and in 1595 became a parish priest at the village of Ilyinskoe, near Staritsa. Within six years his wife and two sons died, and he became a monk at the Dormition monastery. Within three years he had risen to become archimandrite. When ex-Patriarch Job was sent to the Dormition monastery by False Dmitry, despite instructions to the contrary Dionysius treated him honorably as one unjustly persecuted. During the reign of Vasily Shuisky Dionysius attracted the attention of Patriarch Hermogen, whom he ardently supported by eloquent speeches in favor of proper order. Under these turbulent circumstances Dionysius frequently was absent from his monastery, spending most of the time in Moscow until on February 10, 1610 he was appointed archimandrite of the Trinity-St. Sergius monastery. Five months after Dionysius was appointed, Shuisky was deposed. When Moscow was destroyed by fire Dionysius sent help with Avraamy Palitsyn, and organized relief for refugees from the capital. He aided the second militia force by sending repeated appeals for the deliverance of Moscow. In April 1613 he greeted the newly-elected Tsar Michael on his way to Moscow. He took part in the early Assemblies of the Land of Michael's reign, but his political role was not as significant. On November 18, 1616 he was entrusted with correction of the typikon and other service books, with the assistance of Ivan Nasedka and the Greek Arseny Glukhoy, but became suspected of heresy and was excommunicated by a synod in 1618. He was consigned to the St. Cyril monastery near Beloozero, but it proved impossible to make the journey. Instead he was confined to the New Savior monastery where he was compelled to undergo humiliating penance. He was reinstated by Filaret, who in 1619 convoked a synod which reversed the convictions against Dionysius and his associates. Dionysius was honorably reinstated at the Trinity monastery where he received Patriarch Theophanes of Jerusalem, who had spoken in his favor at the synod. The rest of his life was devoted to the reconstruction of his monastic patrimony. He died May 10, 1633 and was canonized in the later part of the seventeenth century.

62. The "lower towns" refers to the settlements of the lower Volga, downstream from Nizhny Novgorod.

63. AAE, Vol. 2, No. 190.

64. Krasnoe Selo was a village to the north of Moscow where many rich merchants had their residences.

65. AAE, Vol. 2, No. 199.

66. Prince Vasily Andreevich Zvenigorodsky (dates of birth and death unknown) served in 1576 in the rearguard regiment under Prince G. A. Kurakin. In 1579-1581 he was governor at Rovno and Tula, in 1583 at Mtsensk and Novosil, 1584 deputy governor at Tula and from 1585 to 1587 governor of the Dvina lands, where he made the first comprehensive land survey. In 1591 he was deputy commander of the artillery in the army sent to stem the threatened Crimean invasion. Later that year he was appointed to a command in Novgorod for a projected Swedish campaign, but it is uncertain whether that campaign took place. At the end of 1592 he was again in Novgorod, and was commanded to advance against Vyborg. In 1595 he was commissioned to supervise the fortification of Smolensk. There is then a nine-year gap in his service record until 1606 when he was sent again to Smolensk as second in command to Prince Ivan Semonovich Kurakin, replacing Ivan Petrovich Romodanovsky. Both he and his brother were apparently out of favor with False Dmitry and Shuisky, and were kept posted away from the capital. In 1610, at the request of Leo Sapieha, Zvenigorodsky was appointed lord-in-waiting. In 1612 he was governor of Nizhny Novgorod, in 1615-1616 of Kolomna. Some time thereafter he took monastic vows at the Solovetsk monastery under the name Varlaam and died there. He was buried alongside the miracleworkers Savvaty and Zosima, according to the Dvina chronicle "in a church in the northern lands."

67. For information on Aliabiev, see Chapter II, Note 27.

68. Ivan Ivanovich Birkin was a member of the Riazan gentry who at one time went over to Tushino, whereupon Tsar Vasily confiscated his estates and awarded them to Zakhar Liapunov; but when Birkin returned and made his submission his lands were restored. In 1611 Birkin, at the behest of Prokopy Liapunov, proceeded to Nizhny Novgorod to incite the inhabitants against the Poles, and he remained there. The uprising started independently of him. Initially he was hostile to Minin, but joined the militia force and was chosen by Pozharsky as a fellow commander. In December 1611 he was sent to Kazan to recruit forces and confer with the Kazan governor, Shulgin, who was suspected of treason (see Volume 16 of this series). There were rumors that Birkin wanted to join Shulgin's conspiracy, but in 1612 he rejoined the militia force in Yaroslavl, bringing with him a detachment from Kazan and the Tatar captain, Miasnoy. But on the way Birkin quarrelled with Miasnoy about who was to assume the chief command, and plundered the places where he passed. The quarrel broke out afresh in Yaroslavl and when the council of the militia force found in favor of Miasnoy, Birkin left with his contingent. He played no further part in the liberation struggle. From 1615 to 1618 he served as governor of Mangazeia. His eventual fate is unknown.

69. Kuzma Minin (?-1616) was described as a *miasnik* (butcher), but to judge from the extent of his personal fortune he must have been quite a successful retailer rather than a simple butcher. On September 1, 1611 he was elected territorial elder (zemskii starosta) and thereafter took charge of the national movement to raise forces and collect money for the liberation of Moscow. Together with Prince Dmitry Pozharsky he led the militia force and was a prominent member of the Council of the Whole Land created at Yaroslavl to discharge the functions normally exercised by the central government. In 1613 he was promoted to the rank of conciliar noble, and many state documents of the early years of Michael's reign include his signature.

70. The Caves monastery in the town of Pechory arose in the fifteenth century when a number of monks began living as hermits in the caves of the local hills. In 1413 the Dormition church was founded on the site of one of these caves. The monastery was destroyed by invading Livonian forces early in the sixteenth century, but was restored by M. G. Munekhin, crown secretary of Pskov, in 1519. Between 1553 and 1565 the monastery was enclosed with walls and towers made of local limestone. It was besieged by Stefan Bathory in the winter of 1581-82, and during the Time of Troubles by the Polish forces of Chodkiewicz and Lisowski (1611-12), as well as by Swedish forces personally led by King Gustavus Adolphus (1615-16).

71. AAE, Vol. 2, No. 201.

72. *New Chronicler*, p. 117.

73. SGGD, Vol. 2, No. 276-277.

74. Ivan Petrovich Sheremetev (1586-1647) first is mentioned as a table attendant in 1606 at the court of False Dmitry. In 1611 he swore allegiance to Prince Wladyslaw but then appeared in the encampment of the militia force, though perhaps he was implicated in the murder of Prokopy Liapunov on July 25. He and his brother Vasily made themselves scarce for a while, but in September reappeared in Trubetskoy's army outside Moscow. He urged the cossacks to kill Pozharsky and prevent the second militia force from reaching Moscow. In the late autumn of 1611 he was sent by the boyar council to be governor of Kostroma. In March 1612, when Kuzma Minin advanced from Kineshma to Kostroma, he was met on the Ples river by some of the inhabitants, who warned him that Sheremetev did not wish him to enter the town. Pozharsky ordered the militia to halt in the nearby suburb. The inhabitants of Kostroma were divided, though eventually those who supported Pozharsky gained the upper hand, and would have killed Sheremetev, had not Pozharsky intervened personally to save him. Pozharsky then appointed Sheremetev governor of Yaroslavl and in this capacity Sheremetev greeted the newly-elected Tsar Michael and his mother on March 21, 1613 as they passed through the town on their way to Moscow. Sheremetev accompanied them as far as the Trinity monastery, and on April 23 was sent ahead to announce to Moscow the tsar's impending arrival. At the Trinity monastery Michael declared that he would proceed no further because of the disordered state

of the land. It was Sheremetev whom the Moscow commanders sent to the tsar urging him to continue his journey. Between 1613 and 1618 he played an important part in court ceremonial functions, and in September 1614 he was sent briefly to Mtsensk to command the vanguard regiment to counter a threatened Tatar invasion. He does not appear to have been in service between 1618 and 1622 but in June 1622 he was sent to Riazan, again to command forces on the Tatar frontier. From 1625 he was at court functions, assisted at the birth and christening of the tsar's children Irina, Pelagia and Alexis, and accompanied the tsar on pilgrimages. He disappears from court records between 1630 and 1633. In 1634 he was appointed boyar with a salary entitlement of four hundred rubles and was appointed governor of Kazan, where he stayed until 1636. On March 8, 1638 he escorted the remains of Prince Johann (died 1602) to the city gates of Moscow, on their way back to Denmark at the request of King Christian IV. Between April and September 1638 he was at Krapivna guarding the frontier against the Crimeans and Nogai. In 1639 he was appointed head of the Chancellery for Military Recruitment (Prikaz sbora ratnykh liudei). In April 1640 he was entrusted to conduct negotiations with the Polish envoys, and was given the title of lord lieutenant of Rostov. Between 1640 and 1647 he was in charge of the Vladimir Judicial Office. In 1642 he engaged in a precedence dispute with Prince Andrei Vasilievich Khilkov, head of the Moscow Judicial Office, which he considered inferior to the Vladimir post. Sheremetev won, and Khilkov was imprisoned. On January 28, 1644 Sheremetev met with Prince Waldemar. At the end of 1644 he negotiated with the Turkish ambassador, and in January 1645 with the Polish ambassador, Stempkowski. The he entered a precedence dispute with Prince Nikita Ivanovich Odoevsky, and as a result spent a while in prison. On September 28, 1645 he held the sceptre at the coronation of Alexis at the time of the tsar's anointing. He continued to head the Vladimir Judicial Office until his death on July 8, 1647. Prior to his death he took the monastic tonsure under the name of Jonas (Iona).

75. See above, Chapter II, Note 30.

76. AAE, Vol. 2, No. 202.

77. *New Chronicler*, p. 117.

78. Murzas were members of the Tatar nobility.

79. AAE, Vol. 2, No. 203.

80. *New Chronicler*, p. 119.

81. De la Gardie's reply to Prince Pozharsky is contained in SGGD, Vol.2, No. 280.

82. SGGD, Vol. 2, No. 281. Soloviev gives a somewhat abridged version of this document.

83. SGGD, Vol. 2, No. 282.

84. Cyril Zavidov (?-1619) was abbot of the St. Anthony monastery in Novgorod from 1580 to 1594. He was appointed archimandrite of the Trinity-St. Sergius monastery on July 31, 1594, and on March 18, 1605 was elevated to the metropolitanate of Rostov, and was present at the deathbed of Boris Godunov.

In April 1606 False Dmitry dismissed Cyril from the Rostov metropolitanate, appointing Filaret Romanov in his place. Cyril returned to the Trinity monastery, but when Filaret was imprisoned in Poland the militia force in Yaroslavl recalled Cyril and placed him in charge of the Rostov eparchy early in 1612. He is mentioned first in precedence in the list of hierarchs following the death of Hermogen. He summoned Michael to assume the tsardom and headed the reception, accompanied the new tsar everywhere in Moscow, and officiated at the coronation. He founded the St. Athanasius monastery in Yaroslavl, and founded many churches in his eparchy.

85. *Pamiatniki diplomaticheskikh snoshenii drevnei Rusi s derzhavami innostrannymi* (Memorials of diplomatic relations of Ancient Russia with foreign powers), Vol. 2 (St. Petersburg, 1852), cols. 1403-1432.

86. AAE, Vol. 2, No. 210.

87. Prince Fedor Rostislavich "the Black" (1240-1299) was the third son of Prince Rostislav of Smolensk. He was appointed prince of Mozhaisk, and occupied Smolensk from 1279 to 1281, but thereafter was active in the Suzdal region. He succeeded to the throne of Yaroslavl in 1294. His half-brother Michael mysteriously disappeared from historical records. Fedor Rostislavich's son David died in 1321. Apparently David and Constantine were sons of the prince's second marriage. See A.V. Ekzempliarskii, *Velikie i udel'nye kniazia* (Grand and Appanage Princes), Vol. 2 (St. Petersburg, 1891), pp. 73-84.

88. The Savior-Evfimy (Spaso-Evfimiev) monastery in Suzdal was founded in 1352 by Prince Boris Konstantinovich of Suzdal and Nizhny Novgorod, and by the monk Evfimy of the Caves monastery of Nizhny Novgorod. At first it was known as the monastery of the Transfiguration of Our Savior, but was rededicated when the remains of Evfimy were rediscovered in 1507. In 1766 it became a place of detention for those suspected of heretical views. Prince Dmitry Pozharsky was buried there in 1642, his final resting place only recently having been positively identified.

89. Ephraim succeeded Hermogen as metropolitan of Kazan, and died December 26, 1613. "Too many hierarchs had made common cause with hierarchs in the enemy camp. Patriarch Hermogen had died in captivity still hostile to the original militia. Isidor, metropolitan of Novgorod, who ranked next to the patriarch in the church, had entered into treasonous dealings with the Swedes. The metropolitan of Kazan had expressed sympathy with the national movement; the national council was disposed to acknowledge him as chief prince of the church, but the militia leaders never sought to bring him to Yaroslavl. The eparchy of Rostov and Yaroslavl had no incumbent since Filaret Romanov was a prisoner in Lithuania. False Dmitrii had deposed Kirill Zavidov, Filaret's predecessor in Rostov. Minin and Pozharskii summoned Zavidov from the monastery where he was staying, and restored him to the rank of metropolitan." However, when Pozharsky requested him to consecrate Isaiah, abbot of the Savva-Storozhevsky monastery of Zvenigorod, to replace the recently deceased Paphnutius, Ephraim declined. Skrynnikov, *Time of Troubles*, pp. 232-233.

90. Evidently Pahpnutius (see above, Chapter I, Note 56) had died. For further information on the see of Krutitsa, see above, Note 18.

91. Jacques Margeret (?-1619) was a French Huguenot soldier of fortune whose *Estat de l'Empire de Russie* (Paris, 1607) was dedicated to Henri IV after Margeret's first sojourn in Russia as a mercenary soldier, successively, of Boris Godunov, False Dmitry and Vasily Shuisky. He later returned to Russia, this time in the service of the second pretender, and was among the mercenaries in Polish service who occupied the Kremlin in 1610-1612. His memoirs are available in English translation by Chester P. Dunning, *The Russian Empire and Grand Duchy of Muscovy* (Pittsburgh, 1985). Unfortunately Margeret left no memoir of his second period in Moscow. As related here, Margeret and his companions, now out of work, requested work of Pozharsky, who could hardly be blamed for thinking that Margeret has collossal nerve! Pozharsky declined his application and sent troops to Archangel to prevent his re-entry into Russia. See Dunning's entry in MERSH, Vol. 21, pp. 96-99.

92. SGGD, Vol. 2, No. 285.

93. Palitsyn, pp. 224-225.

94. *New Chronicler*, p. 126.

95. See Note 7, above.

96. Palitsyn, pp. 226-227.

97. The Neglinnaia is a stream which flows into the Moscow river, but which since the fifteenth century has been channelled through a wooden pipe, and a street built over it, similar to what happened to the Fleet river in London. Intersecting the Neglinnaia is the Kuznetsky Most (Blacksmiths' bridge), nowadays a Mecca for searchers after antiquarian books.

98. See above, Note 47.

99 Haiduks were Hungarian mercenary foot soldiers in Polish service.

100. The Kamenny Most, or Stone bridge, a succession of which have been built across the Moscow slightly to the south and west of the Kremlin. The first clear evidence I have been able to find of a *stone* bridge across the Moscow river is the one erected in the 1680s, during the regency of Sophia, although there was certainly a bridge on that spot. Could Soloviev have been using a nineteenth-century designation?

101. See Note 59, above. The title Arsenius assumed pertained to the Archangel *cathedral* in the Kremlin, not the town of Archangel.

102. See Note 6, above.

103. *New Chronicler*, p. 127.

104. *New Chronicler*, p. 128.

105. See Chapter II, Note 42.

106. The source in question is the so-called Obolensky Chronograph, to which I have not been able to obtain direct access, but which is discussed in S. F. Platonov, *Drevnerusskie skazaniia i povesti o smutnom vremeni XVII veka* (Ancient

Russian Accounts and Narratives Concerning the Time of Troubles of the Seventeenth Century), 2nd edition (St. Petersburg, 1913), pp. 408-412, and described by I. E. Zabelin, "Vazhnyi khronograf osobogo sostava" (Important Chronograph with Special Contents), *Arkhiv istoriko-iuridicheskikh svedenii* (Kachalov), Vol. 1, otd. 6 (1850), pp. 31-38.

107. The choice of Michael Romanov was not as unanimous as the official record and the consensus of Russian and Soviet historians tends to suggest. If Karl Philipp, favored by Pozharsky, had put in a timely appearance, in all likelihood he would have been elected. See my article "The Election of Michael Romanov," *Slavonic and East European Review*, Vol. 67, No. 3 (July 1989).

INDEX

Abbas, Persian shah, 300.

Admiralty, 318.

Aksenov, Mikhail, 146.

Alatyr, 312.

Aleksin, 218.

Alexander, John T., historian, xv.

Alexander, Kakhetian khan, 297.

Alexander Nevsky, Grand Prince, vi, 1, 3, 20, 290, 301, 329.

Alexandrovskaia Sloboda, 117-118, 131-132, 134, 319, 326.

Alexis, Metropolitan, Muscovite miracle-worker, 20, 204, 280, 331.

Alexis Mikhailovich, Tsar, 303, 327, 340.

Aliabiev, Andrei Semeonovich, governor of Nizhny Novgorod, 86-87, 251, 319-320, 338.

Amos, Archpriest of Holy Wisdom cathedral, Novgorod, 238, 313.

Andronov, Fedor (Fedka), former tanner, Moscow merchant. Arrives in Moscow from Smolensk, 158; previous history, 192-196; promotes King Sigismund's cause in Moscow, 191-199; appointed conciliar noble and treasurer by King Sigismund,193; alleged sorcery and heresy, 192-193, 196; writes to Leo Sapieha excusing Hetman Zolkiewski for having concluded treaty, 193; proposes purge of former Shuisky supporters, 194; resented by boyar government, 194-195; petitions Leo Sapieha for grant of estates, 195; occupies house of archpriest of Annunciation cathedral, 219; denounced by Archimandrite Dionysius, 249; interrogated under torture after liberation of Moscow, 284; also mentioned xi, 122, 124, 202, 282, 294, 327, 329.

Andrusovo, truce of, 304.

Anna, second wife of Jagiello, possibly Russian princess, 326.

Anna Koltovskaia, tsaritsa, fourth wife of Ivan IV, 31, 308, 329.

Anthony, abbot of Solovetsk monastery, 206.

Anthony of Egypt, St., monastic founder, 311.

Apostolic See, 47.

Apraxin, Tushino crown secretary, 122.

Archangel, 89, 180, 200, 273.

Archival and Documentary sources. *Acts Collected in Libraries and Archives of the Russian Empire by the Imperial Archeographical Commission*, xii, 331-332, 336, 338, 339, 340-341; *Acts Pertaining to the History of Western Russia, Collected and Edited by the Archeographical Commission*, 336; *Collection of State Documents and Treaties*, xii, 291, 331, 333, 339-340, 342; *Collection of the Imperial Russian Historical Society*, vol. 142. 329, 333; *Historical Acts Collected and Edited by the Archeographical Commission*, xii, 329, 332; *Memorials of Diplomatic Relations of Ancient Russia with Foreign Powers*, 341.

Arsenius of Elasson, 245, 284, 336-337, 342.

Arzamas, 18, 86, 254-255.

Assembly (veche), 100, 312, 325.

Assembly of the Land (zemsky sobor), xi, 2, 6, 22, 162, 288-289, 291-292, 296, 303, 319, 322, 330, 337.

Astrakhan, 15, 31-32, 91, 258, 300, 308, 319.

Augustus, bogus tsarevich, 31.

Austria, 51, 265, 308.

Avrich, Paul, historian, xvi.

Babkin, Nekhoroshy, 88-89, 313.

Bakhterianov-Rostovsky, Prince, 23.

Balakhna, 76-77, 82, 86, 204, 259, 319, 322.

Balchik, island in Volga delta, 319.

Baltic Sea, 324.

Basil the Great, St., monastic founder, 53, 311.

Ephraim, Metropolitan of Kazan, 18, 246, 271, 341.

Evfimy, Archimandrite of Savoir monastery, 161, 188.

Evfimy, founder of Transfiguration monastery, Suzdal, 341.

False Dmitry I, vi, ix, 2-4, 7, 9-10, 18-19, 25, 34-36, 39-40, 46, 73, 99, 109-110, 116, 119, 124, 127, 147, 150, 156, 166, 171, 227, 245, 291, 293-299, 302-304, 307-309, 311-312, 314-315, 317-318, 321, 323, 328, 330, 335, 337-339, 341-342.

False Dmitry II. Appearance, 24-26; possible identity, 24-26; declares himself to inhabitants of Starodub, 25; composition of forces, 28; snubs Rozynski, 29-30; advance on Moscow, 32-33; victory at Bolkhov, 32; encourages social strife within Moscow, 33; promises rich rewards to Poles, 33; negotiations with Marina and her father, 45-46; secret marriage, 46; northern towns revolt against, 83; orders abandonment of siege of Trinity monastery, 107; escape from Tushino, 120-121; flees to Kaluga, 118-121; at Kaluga, 128-129; Tushino Poles correspond with, 137; advances on Moscow, 143-145; negotiations with Sapieha, 155; Sapieha detached from, 158-159; refuses Zolkiewski's conditions, 159; repulsed from Moscow, 158-160; fortifies himself in Kaluga, 163-165; support within Moscow, 198; Kazan swears allegiance to, 198; murder of, x, 200-201; also mentioned vii, ix-x, 7-9, 10, 14-16, 26, 40-43, 52, 54, 60-61, 63, 66, 74-76, 79, 82, 88, 93, 111, 117, 120, 130-131, 133, 138, 146, 152-154, 157, 167, 176, 178-180, 206, 228, 273, 293-295, 297, 299, 305-308, 310, 314-316, 319-320, 323, 326-327, 342. See also Tushino Brigand, Kaluga Brigand.

False Dmitry III, see Sidorka.

False Peter (Ileika Muromets). Joins with Bolotnikov in Tula, 23; besieged in Tula, 24; executed, 27; also mentioned ix, 9, 26, 31, 39-40, 47, 293-296, 306, 321.

Fatima Sultan, last native ruler of Kasimov, 327.

Fedor, bogus tsarevich, 32.

Fedor Borisovich Godunov, tsar, 9, 19-20, 173-174, 294-295, 304, 309, 313, 330; reported still to be alive, 111.

Fedor Ivanovich, tsar, viii, 10, 19, 31-32, 64, 111, 115, 139, 148, 151, 173, 291, 293, 295, 301, 316, 330, 335-336.

Fedor Rostislavich "the Black", Prince, Yaroslavl miracle-worker, 270, 341.

Feodorit, Archbishop of Riazan, 289.

Feodosia Borisovna, tsarevna, 318.

Feodosy, Archimandrite of Pskov Caves monastery, 252.

Feodosy, monastic name of Boyar F. I. Sheremetev, 319.

Feoktist, Archbishop of Tver, 16, 336.

Fiedler, Kaspar, German hired assassin, 22, 304.

Filaret (Fedor Nikitich Romanov), Metropolitan of Rostov, later Patriarch. Passed over for patriarchate in favor of Hermogen, 317; appointed Metropolitan of Rostov, 317; conveyed to Tushino and given patriarchal title by False Dmitry II, 73, 317, 327; palace built for him at Tushino, 310; letter to King Sigismund, 120-122; moves from St. Joseph monastery to Moscow, 137; appointed to Smolensk embassy, 160, 312; at king's encampment outside Smolensk, 169-191; conversation with Leo Sapieha, 178-179; remonstrates with Zolkiewski, 185-186; urges embassy to refuse to cede Smolensk, 187; reproaches Sydavnoy Vasiliev and Archbishop Evfimy for abandoning embassy, 190; urged by boyar government to submit to king, 209; refuses to comply with boyars' letter, 210; speech to final session of embassy, 213; rejects accusations of falsehood, 215; repudiates I. M. Saltykov's intervention, 215; told by Sapieha of burning of Moscow, 223; also mentioned x, 73, 93, 122, 125, 131, 153, 155, 161, 176, 189, 217, 225, 285, 312, 314-315, 319, 321, 337, 341.

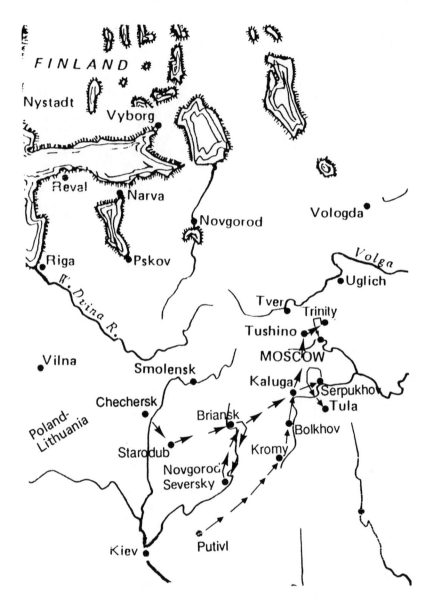

Bolotnikov and False Dmitry II

Bolotnikov's March in 1606 ——▶
False Dmitrii II's Operations in 1608 ——▶

Marches of Muscovy and Zolkiewski

Muscovite Counterattack in 1609 ->
Zolkiewski's March in 1610 →

Military Movements in 1612 and Swedish Invasion

Liapunov's Route in 1612 ✦
The Forces of Zarutskii and Trubetskoi in 1612 →
Swedish Invasion ➡

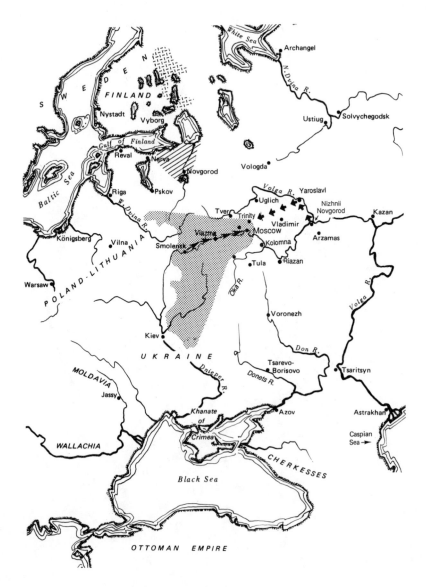

Minin and Pozharsky, Annexations

Area under Polish control, 1612-1613 ⠿
Chodkiewicz's March in 1612 →
Minin and Pozharsky in 1612 ✦
Area under Swedish control, 1613 //
Annexed by Sweden, 1617 ᐟᐠᐟ

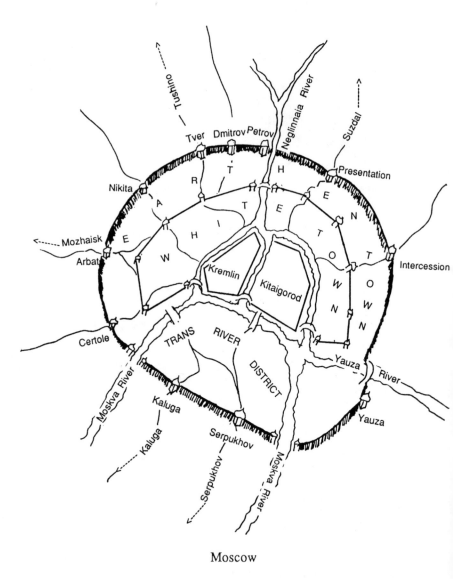

Moscow

Plan of Moscow attributed to Fedor Borisovich Godunov (1589-1605). K.V. Bazilevich et al., *Atlas istorii SSSR*, Vol.1, Moscow, 1950. Adapted by Sandra L. Carlson.

THE EDITOR AND TRANSLATOR

George Edward Orchard was born at London, England in 1935 and grew up in Hampshire, where he received his primary and secondary education. At the age of eighteen he was conscripted into the British armed forces, where he learned Russian at the Joint Services's School for Linguists, Bodmin, Cornwall, and then served with the 755 Signal Unit of the British Army of the Rhine. Having completed his military service he read Modern History at St. John's College, Oxford, receiving his Bachelor of Arts degree in 1959. After a year of teaching at Bemrose School, Derby, he studied at St. Mary's College, Strawberry Hill, for the Postgraduate Certificate in Education as an external student of the University of London. The subsequent two years were spent teaching at Owerri Grammar School, Imerienwe, Nigeria. Having migrated to Canada in 1963, he studied at McGill University, Montreal, from 1964 to 1966, receiving his Ph.D. in history in 1967. Since 1966 he has taught at the University of Lethbridge, as well as the occasional summer course at Nipissing University College, North Bay, Ontario. He has visited the Soviet Union three times, and was one of the first participants in the Canada-USSR Academic Exchange. During the academic year 1984-1985 he was a Visiting Fellow at the University of London School of Slavonic and East European Studies, and was the keynote speaker at the Annual Conference on Russian Studies at the University of Wales. His publications include a scholarly translation of Isaac Massa's *Short History of the Muscovite Wars* (Toronto, 1982), and he has contributed numerous entries to the *Modern Encyclopedia of Russian and Soviet History*, as well as articles and reviews on early Russian themes to numerous learned journals. He has recently completed a scholarly translation and edition of the memoirs of the early seventeenth-century soldier of fortune Konrad Bussow. Professor Orchard lives with his wife Ellen Claire and his daughter Catherine Jane in Lethbridge, Alberta.

FROM ACADEMIC INTERNATIONAL PRESS*

*Request catalogs **OP–out of print